Presidents, Politics, and Policy

Presidents, Politics, and Policy

Erwin C. Hargrove
Michael Nelson

The Johns Hopkins University Press

Baltimore and London

Hardcover edition published by
The Johns Hopkins University Press
Baltimore, Maryland 21218

The Johns Hopkins Press Ltd, London

Cover design: Mary Chris Welch
Cover photo: Afton Olson/Photo Researchers

Library of Congress Cataloging in Publication Data

Hargrove, Erwin C.
  Presidents, politics, and policy.

  Includes index.
  1. Presidents — United States. I. Nelson, Michael.
II. Title.
JK516.H285 1984   321.8'042   84–47959
ISBN 0–8018–3243–8

To our families

Preface

We have witnessed in recent decades a profusion of splendid studies of the American presidency by political scientists, historians, journalists, and other presidential scholars. Using a variety of approaches and methods, these students of the presidency have drawn attention to the importance of public opinion, personality, executive institutions, the Constitution, leadership style, and several other aspects of presidential power. With such a strong scholarly foundation to build on, we decided that the time was right to try to offer a new way of understanding the presidency. Presidential power, we argue, is a mixture of constitutional, cultural and political, and individual elements that manifest themselves in recurring historical cycles of politics and policy.

Although our main purpose in writing this book has been to present and develop this argument, we have tried to do other things as well. Readers will find an extended account of the politics of the Constitutional Convention in Chapter 2, especially timely in view of the bicentennial of that event in 1987; a short history of the presidency spread across Chapters 2 and 3; extensive profiles of the modern presidents in Chapter 4; and full discussions of the presidential selection process and presidential leadership of Congress in Chapters 5 and 7, respectively. We treat the presidency's relationship to the White House staff and the bureaucracy with special attention paid both to policy formation (Chapter 6) and policy implementation (Chapter 8).

Authors frequently are admonished to keep a particular audience in mind as they write, be it scholars, undergraduate students, the general public, or whomever. Perhaps we violated that admonition. We wrote this book for people who are interested in understanding the American presidency. It was — and is — our feeling that a book that really engages scholars who have this interest also will engage students and general readers who share it.

In writing this book, Erwin C. Hargrove took main responsibility for drafting Chapters 4, 6, 8, and 9; Michael Nelson for Chapters 1, 2, 5, and 7 and for polishing the final draft of the entire manuscript; and both authors for drafting Chapter 3. That division of labor aside, *Presidents, Politics, and Policy* is a joint intellectual endeavor, informed throughout by the authors' friendship and colleagueship.

We have many people to thank for the advice and encouragement they gave us during the writing of this book. Useful criticisms were offered by Fred

Greenstein, Francis Rourke, Arthur Schlesinger, and James Sundquist, who read the entire manuscript, and by Robert Birkby, Alexander Heard, Hugh Heclo, and, especially, James Fesler and Theodore Lowi, who read parts of it. Bertrand Lummus, David Rothberg, and Carol Flechner of Alfred A. Knopf provided valuable editorial assistance, as did Henry Tom of the Johns Hopkins University Press. Various drafts of the book were ably and cheerfully typed by Libby Boone, Elizabeth McKee, and Mildred Tyler. And our deepest thanks go to those to whom this book is dedicated — our families.

Erwin C. Hargrove
Michael Nelson

Contents

TABLES

FIGURES

PART ONE

Presidents and Politics

The presidency has been one thing at one time, another at another, varying with the man who occupied the office and with the circumstances that surrounded him.

—Woodrow Wilson, *Constitutional Government in the United States*

CHAPTER 1

Changing Views
of the Presidency

Henry Jones Ford, in his 1898 work *The Rise and Growth of American Government*, quotes Alexander Hamilton's prediction to a friend that the time would "assuredly come when every vital question of the state will be merged in the question, 'who shall be the next president?'" Ford cites this remark to support his argument that the "greatness of the presidency is the work of the people, breaking through the constitutional form. The truth is that in the presidential office, as it has been constituted since Jackson's time, American democracy has revived the oldest political institution of the race, the elective kingship."[1]

Although there is much truth in Ford's observations on the presidency, there also is a certain measure of confusion on two fundamental analytic issues. First, it is not clear whether Ford regards the presidency as primarily a person ("who shall be the next president?") or an institution (an "elective kingship"). Second, Ford blurs together empirical and normative analysis. Both are valid, but if accurate understanding of the presidency is the goal, empirical analysis matters more. Yet in the span of a few words Ford not only offers answers to the empirical question of what the presidency is but applauds its "greatness" as well.

Ford's was among the first modern works on the presidency (modern in the sense that it goes beyond constitutional exegesis), so it is not surprising to find that his theory is less than perfect. What is surprising, though, is that many years later, scholars still have not broken free of his twin confusions. We—and as notes 7 and 18 show, the accusatory finger points inward as well as outward—have continued to blur the analytic line between person and institution, constructing models of the presidency largely in response to our observations of individual presidents. In addition, we all too often have allowed our understanding of the presidency to be colored by our opinions about what ends it should serve.

This lack of clarity on basic theoretical issues has left presidential scholars ill prepared to explain the extraordinary shifts and turns that have taken place in presidential politics during the last quarter century, events that have included an assassination, a voluntary withdrawal from office, a forced resignation, the electoral defeat of two consecutive incumbents, legislative stalemate, legislative triumph, and so on. As a result, no fewer than four distinct scholarly models of the presidency have flourished and in most cases faded during this

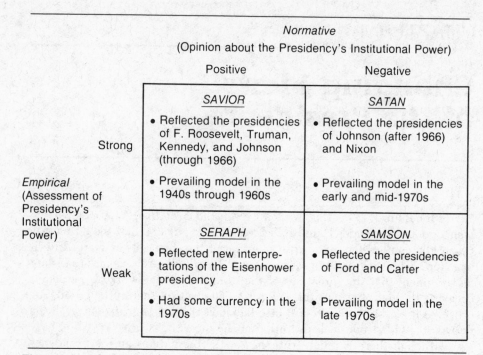

Figure 1.1   Scholarly Models of the Presidency

relatively brief period. Each of these models represents the unhappy combination of the answer to an empirical question (Is the presidency strong or weak?) and a normative question (Is this condition of presidential strength — or weakness — good or bad for the American political system?). Each is further flawed because it was created too much in the image of the incumbent who had served most recently at the time of its creation. We call the four models "Savior" (the presidency is strong, which is good); "Satan" (it is strong, which is bad); "Samson" (weak, which is bad); and "Seraph" (weak, which is good). They are presented in Figure 1.1.[2]

FOUR MODELS OF THE PRESIDENCY

Savior

The Savior model of the presidency portrays the office both as powerful and as a force for good in American society. It was shaped by scholars' reactions to the experience of Franklin Roosevelt, took form under the influence of Harry Truman, was sharpened by criticism of the presidency of Dwight Eisenhower, and lasted through John Kennedy's administration and part of Lyndon Johnson's. Nothing demonstrates the continuity and endurance of the Savior model better than Thomas Cronin's study of some three dozen political textbooks that were written in the 1950s and 1960s.[3] Cronin found that throughout this period political scientists characterized the presidency in their writings as both "omnipotent" and "benevolent." The idea that strength and goodness go hand in hand shone through, for example, in James MacGregor Burns's statement that "the stronger we make the Presidency, the more we strengthen democratic procedures"[4] and in this assessment by Grant McConnell: "To ask what is to become of the presidency is to ask what is to become of the entire American political order."[5] The omnipotence-benevolence nexus also underlay the most influential book on the presidency of this period, *Presidential Power.*[6] "A president's success" in maximizing power, wrote Richard Neustadt, "serves objectives far beyond his own and his party's. . . . [P]residential influence contributes to the energy of the government and to the viability of public policy. . . . [W]hat is good for the country is good for the president, and *vice versa.*"[7]

Underlying this model is a quasi-religious awe of the presidency that makes the term "Savior" less than facetious. Clinton Rossiter began his book *The American Presidency* by confessing his "feeling of veneration, if not exactly reverence, for the authority and dignity of the presidency," and went on to describe Abraham Lincoln as "the martyred Christ of democracy's passion play."[8] Herman Finer was equally reverent, though in a polytheistic way. Finer characterized the presidency not only as "the incarnation of the American people in a sacrament resembling that in which the wafer and the wine are seen to be the body and blood of Christ," but also as "belong[ing] rightfully to the offspring of a titan and Minerva husbanded by Mars."[9]

Thus, strength and the desire to be strong, power and virtue, omnipotence and benevolence — all were tied in with each other and with prevailing notions of presidential greatness in the Savior model. The reasoning of the Savior school was as follows: The president is the chief guardian of the national public interest. This is not only necessarily true in foreign policy, since no one else can speak and act for the nation, but also in domestic affairs because of the pluralistic structure of government and society. Congress overrepresents wealthy and influential special interests because members of Congress are most likely to be responsive to the organized groups within their constituencies. The president, on the other hand, can mobilize the unorganized and inarticulate and speak for national majorities against such groups.

Scholars' normative preference for presidential strength in this period had more to it than their value judgments about the proper distribution of power among the branches of government. William Andrews observed a partisan and ideological bias among his fellow political scientists, many of whom had worked in Democratic administrations that had stretched the powers of the presidency in the service of liberal causes. He concluded that when it comes to the presidency, "the constitutional theory follows the party flag."[10]

Satan[11]

The late 1960s and early 1970s witnessed the presidencies of Lyndon Johnson and Richard Nixon, two men who embodied those presidential qualities — strength and the desire to be strong — that scholars of the Savior school had been saying would benefit the nation. Yet the results of presidential strength in these two cases were not as desirable as had been predicted. The power of the presidency in foreign affairs was such that the nation was led into a large-scale war in Vietnam without serious public debate and remained there long after public opinion had turned against the war. The power of the presidency as "Chief Legislator," in Rossiter's phrase, prompted such rapid passage of a host of Great Society social welfare programs that their flaws, which might have been discovered in bargaining between the president and Congress, were not found until later. Finally, in 1972 and 1973 there came the many abuses of power that have been grouped under the umbrella term "Watergate" and that forced Nixon's resignation in August 1974.

These experiences not only convinced scholars that presidential strength and the general welfare were not synonymous; they caused some to argue that power and virtue were more likely to appear as opposites. Arthur Schlesinger, Jr. had helped create the Savior model with his glowing biographies of Jackson, Roosevelt, and Kennedy and in passages like this one from *A Thousands Days:* "Thinking of the young Roosevelts, lost suddenly in middle age, and of the young Kennedys, so sure and purposeful, one perceived an historic contrast, a dynastic change, like the Plantagenets giving way to the Yorks." In 1973, he came back with a book berating *The Imperial Presidency.*[12] Marcus Cunliffe called the office a "Frankenstein monster."[13]

The new task for scholars was to explain why presidential strength was likely to be harmful to the nation rather than helpful, as previously had been thought. Their search carried them into two primary areas: the person and the office. The expedition into personality as a source of presidential pathology was led by James David Barber. Barber's 1972 book *The Presidential Character* identified a presidential personality type, the "active-negative," whose efforts to maximize his power in office are born of a deep-seated and psychologically unhealthy need to dominate others.[14] When active-negatives encounter serious challenges to their power while in office, as all presidents do, they react with rigid and aggressive behavior. Such was the case with Johnson and Nixon. The nation survived their presidencies, but given the nature of modern weaponry, Barber argued, even one more active-negative could be too many.

Other scholars looked to the institution to explain why presidential strength was likely to be a force for bad. Cronin argued that the "swelling of the presidency"—the sheer growth in the size of the White House staff—had turned it into "a powerful inner sanctum of government isolated from the traditional constitutional checks and balances."[15] George Reedy suggested in his book *The Twilight of the Presidency* that "the life of the White House is the life of a [royal] court" in which the president "is treated with all the reverence due a monarch" and isolated "from all of the forces which require most men to rub up against the hard facts of life on a daily basis."[16]

Samson

When Samson, that strong and good judge from Biblical times, transgressed, his powers were stripped away from him. The response of the people of Israel to Samson's plight was not unlike that of presidential scholars toward the presidency after the administrations of Gerald Ford and Jimmy Carter, two weak presidents, in the middle and late 1970s: they beheld its weakness and were saddened.

The Samson model of the presidency — others have called it the "imperiled" or "tethered" presidency — came in startling contrast to those that preceded it.[17] It ruefully portrayed a large and growing gap between what presidents can do and what they are expected to do that is a prescription for weakness.[18] The model traced the president's incapacity to deliver to two sources: its constitutional dependence on other political institutions for support, and the recent decline in the ability or willingness of those institutions to provide it. According to Samson theorists, parties had grown too weak to help, Congress too decentralized to bargain with, the bureaucracy too fragmented and powerful to lead, and the media too adversarial to make its spotlight an asset for the president. Yet, the argument went, even as the president's ability to meet demands for action declined, the volume, intensity, and complexity of those demands — the other side of the equation — were rising. The American people expect too much of their president, argued Godfrey Hodgson.

> He must simultaneously conduct the diplomacy of a superpower, put together separate coalitions to enact every piece of legislation required by a vast and complex society, manage the economy, command the armed forces, serve as a spiritual example and inspiration, respond to every emergency.[19]

With demands on the presidency so high, Samson theorists argued, no individual president could be expected to meet them. That Ronald Reagan's inauguration on January 20, 1981, made him the sixth president to be sworn into office in just twenty years was put forward as sufficient evidence for the proposition that the presidency was weak. That this was a bad situation for the country seemed obvious when one considered that only two other twenty-year periods in American history are comparable. The first period was 1841–1861, when eight presidents failed to head off the approach of the Civil War. The second was 1877–1897, when the United States saw seven presidents, none of them sufficiently effective in office to mitigate the bad side-effects of rapid industrialization.

Seraph

The last of the four models of the presidency that have appeared in recent years is also the least, if scholarly currency is the standard of measurement. The presidency of the Seraph model is close kin to the angels whom Isaiah saw surrounding the throne of God — weak, to be sure, but good in their weakness. The idea that the presidency is weak and should be so was in part a response to new interpretations of the Eisenhower administration. In a 1978 essay, Fred Greenstein quoted from a letter Eisenhower sent to publisher Henry Luce — "The government of the United States has become too big, too complex, and too pervasive in its influence on all our lives for one individual to pretend to direct the details of its important and critical programming" — and concluded by agreeing with Eisenhower: "The buck—a term that presumably refers to all major policy making—neither stops nor starts only in the Oval Office. It circulates among many political actors."[20] Similarly, Peter Woll and Rochelle Jones argued that in his relations with the bureaucracy as in those with Congress or the Supreme Court, the president neither can nor should dominate—his very weakness is a virtue.[21] And in *The American Presidency*, an influential book of 1979, Richard Pious approvingly rolled back presidential power to its constitutional bare bones. "Presidents must rely on their constitutional prerogatives," he wrote, "because they cannot obtain an electoral mandate, do not gain control of party machinery, fail to lead their legislative parties, and cannot obtain the expertise from the advisory systems that would permit them to lead Congress and the nation by force of argument."[22]

IS THEORY POSSIBLE?

A summer 1981 political cartoon shows an angry professor storming out of a door marked "Political Science Department." Papers fly around the office in his wake, one a title page marked "The Limits of Power," another a newspaper with the headline "Stunning Tax, Budget Wins for Reagan." In the foreground, a secretary explains to a startled student: "He just completed the definitive, 600-page work on why special-interest groups, weak parties, and a fragmented Congress make presidential leadership impossible." In just a few months, President Ronald Reagan had given refutation to the weak presidency models just as the Johnson and Nixon administrations had to the Savior model and the Ford and Carter administrations had to the Satan model. Nor did the early Reagan administration necessarily augur a return to the Savior, for Reagan was conservative, not liberal, and easy-going rather than hard-working.

Savior, Satan, Samson, Seraph—the sheer velocity of the turnover in scholarly views of the presidency in recent years raises the question of whether one can hope to comprehend the office and its role in American politics and government. As noted earlier, it often is argued that the presidency is more person than institution. By this line of reasoning, generalizations—that is, characterizations of the presidency that are true at all times—are impossible.

That is so, but it is not the point. The larger and more difficult question is whether one can understand the conditions under which the presidency is relatively powerful or weak. A contextual understanding of the presidency would permit us to view a particular president in a larger framework, not the other way around. To develop such an understanding would require the identification of the important elements of Constitution, culture, and politics that empower the presidency, and the consequences for governance of the patterns in and among these empowering elements over time. This in turn would help us to assess the likely effectiveness of specific skills and strategies of presidential leadership, according to political conditions.

Such intimidating obstacles notwithstanding, Part I of this book—"Presidents and Politics"—is our attempt to suggest a way of understanding presidential power that meets these requirements. The structure of our idea is not unlike that of most common-sense theories of human behavior in the broadest sense: it recognizes the importance not only of individual choice but of hereditary and environmental influences as well.

Chapter 2 looks at the constitutional presidency, the office's legacy from birth. The basic contours of presidential power were defined at the Constitutional Convention of 1787, where delegates decided to make the presidency a unitary office with its own national constituency and a fixed term, operating in a government of "separated institutions sharing powers." Taken together, these decisions assured that to the extent the federal government became the main object of public demands for political action, the presidency would be the center — but not necessarily the master — of the American political system.

In the twentieth century, national — and thus presidency-centered — politics has been the rule. In Chapter 3, the empowering effects of culture and politics, which are the main elements of the political environment of the presidency, are assessed. American political culture limits the ideological bounds in which policy change occurs. It also assures that competition within those bounds will be intense and that change will be spasmodic. Indeed, we argue, the history of twentieth-century American politics and public policy is one of the recurring cycles of electoral politics and governmental policy making whose focus has been the presidency. Such cycles consist of a *presidency of preparation*, in which proposals for change are brought to the top of the nation's political agenda; a *presidency of achievement*, in which the reforms are enacted; and a *presidency of consolidation*, in which the reforms are rationalized.

Each stage of the cycle calls for the adroit exercise of leadership skill on the part of the president — the subject of Chapter 4. All presidents need some combination of a strategic sense of the "grain of history," an ability to present themselves and their policies to the general public through rhetoric and symbolic action, tactical skills suitable for Washington politics, and a capacity for the "management of authority" in both policy formation and policy implementation. But, we argue, presidents of preparation, achievement, and consolidation need these skills in different combinations.

Finally, Chapter 5 treats the matter of presidential selection in terms of our model — that is, given the requisites of leadership skill that the office's constitutional heredity and cultural and political environment require from presidents, does the present selection system help to foster the choice of candidates who have those qualities?

Part II, "Presidents and the Policy Process," is an effort to apply our understanding of the presidency to presidential policy making. In Chapter 6 we discuss the White House and the bureaucracy as institutions for *policy formation* in the domestic, economic, and foreign spheres. Chapter 7 contains our discussion of the president's relationship with Congress in the realm of *policy enactment*. Finally, in Chapter 8 we look at presidential influence over *policy implementation* by the bureaucracy.

In each of the chapters that make up Part II, we have tried to treat the general subject comprehensively, then apply the understandings that were developed in Part I in order to test how well they stand up and to see what new light they shed. In Chapters 6 and 8, which deal almost entirely with intra-executive branch politics, the Constitution figures little, but our theory of cycles and presidential skill turns out to be illuminating. In Chapter 7, which analyzes the relationship between president and Congress, all of the elements — constitutional, cultural and political, and individual — are seen to matter.

Few books on the presidency conclude without offering an agenda for reforming the presidency. Ours is among the few. In Chapter 9, we assess the leading schools of reformist thought and judge them to be limited in the same way the Savior, Satan, Samson, and Seraph schools of analytic thought are limited: each represents an overreaction to a particular type of presidential experience. The truth is that given our Constitution and culture, the presidency works well. Most current quarrels with the presidency really are quarrels with those deeper forces in the political system.

NOTES

1. Henry Jones Ford, *The Rise and Growth of American Government* (New York: Macmillan, 1898), pp. 196, 293.
2. Two caveats should be stated. First, this typology, like all typologies, is at best a strategic oversimplification. Its purpose is to provide a useful shorthand guide to reality. In the process many of the subtleties and refinements in the arguments of the scholarly works in each category are lost. Second, though one would not wish to underestimate the influence of scholarship on political life (citizens, after all, study the textbooks scholars write while growing up — even citizens who someday will be presidents, members of Congress, justices, and pundits), neither should that influence be overestimated. The justification for emphasizing the views of scholars who study the presidency is as much that they reflect the political culture as that they shape it.
3. Thomas Cronin, "Superman — Our Textbook President," *The Washington Monthly* (October 1970), pp. 47–54.
4. James MacGregor Burns, *Presidential Government: The Crucible of Leadership* (Boston: Houghton Mifflin, 1965), p. 330.
5. Grant McConnell, *The Modern Presidency* (New York: St. Martin's Press, 1967), p. 87.
6. Richard Neustadt, *Presidential Power* (New York: Wiley, 1960). The theme of Neustadt's book is that although presidents can do little by direct command, they can and should wield great power through skillful bargaining and persuasion.
7. *Ibid.*, pp. 183, 185. In the heyday of Lyndon Johnson, author Hargrove took Neustadt's argument to an extreme by asking what kinds of personalities had such political skills and concluding that they were people with deep-seated needs for attention and power. Presidents lacking such needs were portrayed as also lacking in ability — as with Eisenhower, they were almost too healthy to be good leaders. This thesis implicitly assumed that presidents were guided by moral purpose, and it was frankly biased in the direction of liberal presidents. *Presidential Leadership, Personality and Political Style* (New York: Macmillan, 1966).
8. Clinton Rossiter, *The American Presidency* (New York: Harcourt, Brace & World, 1960), pp. 15–16, 108.
9. Herman Finer, *The Presidency* (Chicago: University of Chicago Press, 1960), pp. 111, 119.
10. William Andrews, "The Presidency, Congress and Constitutional Theory," in Aaron Wildavsky, ed., *Perspectives on the Presidency* (Boston: Little, Brown, 1975), p. 38.

11. At one time, this model generally was referred to as the "revisionist" school. But further revisions (see Figure 1.1) have forced us to name each one separately. None, it should be noted, was entirely new — as Peri Arnold and L. John Roos show, each has its antecedents. Interesting early statements of the Satan, Samson, and Seraph models can be found in, respectively, Alfred de Grazia, *Republic in Crisis* (New York: Federal Legal Publications, 1965), James MacGregor Burns, *The Deadlock of Democracy* (Englewood Cliffs, N.J.: Prentice-Hall, 1963), and Willmoore Kendall, "The Two Majorities," *Midwest Journal of Political Science* (November 1960), pp. 317–45. Arnold and Roos, "Toward a Theory of Congressional-Executive Relations," *Review of Politics* (July 1974), pp. 410–29.

12. Arthur Schlesinger, Jr., *A Thousand Days* (Boston: Houghton Mifflin, 1965), p. 677, and *The Imperial Presidency* (Boston: Houghton Mifflin, 1973).

13. Marcus Cunliffe, "A Defective Institution?" *Commentary* (February 1968), p. 28.

14. James David Barber, *The Presidential Character* (Englewood Cliffs, N.J.: Prentice-Hall, 1972).

15. Thomas Cronin, *The State of the Presidency* (Boston: Little, Brown, 1975), p. 138.

16. George Reedy, *The Twilight of the Presidency* (New York: New American Library, 1970), ch. 1. See also Bruce Buchanan, *The Presidential Experience* (Englewood Cliffs, N.J.: Prentice-Hall, 1978), and Irving Janis, *Victims of GroupThink* (Boston: Houghton Mifflin, 1972).

17. Gerald Ford, "Imperiled, Not Imperial," *Time* (November 10, 1980), and Thomas Franck, ed., *The Tethered Presidency* (New York: New York University Press, 1981).

18. Author Nelson confidently articulated this view in several articles written in 1980.

19. Godfrey Hodgson, *All Things to All Men* (New York: Simon & Schuster, 1980), p. 239.

20. Fred Greenstein, "Change and Continuity in the Modern Presidency," in Anthony King, ed., *The New American Political System* (Washington: American Enterprise Institute, 1978), pp. 84, 85.

21. Peter Woll and Rochelle Jones, "The Bureaucracy as a Check upon the President," *The Bureaucrat* (April 1974), pp. 8–20.

22. Richard Pious, *The American Presidency* (New York: Basic Books, 1979), p. 17.

CHAPTER 2

The Presidency and the Constitution

The Constitution is the presidency's genetic code. Because of it the presidency is, by nature, a single-person office, chosen for a fixed term by a uniquely national constituency, sharing virtually all the powers of the federal government with an equally distinct and independent Congress. The constitutional presidency contains, as does an individual's configuration of DNA molecules, some ingredients whose meaning has been clear and unchanging from the moment of conception (eye color in a baby, the thirty-five-year minimum age requirement for presidents).[1] The Constitution also contains sentences and phrases that are the legal equivalent of genetically rooted baldness: their meaning, though determined at the very start, could be discovered only later. "[H]e shall take Care that the Laws be faithfully executed" first appeared as a passing constitutional reference—the fifth of six clauses in the single sentence that constitutes Article II, Section 3—but in subsequent years it came to be the presidency's strongest legal claim to such varied powers as acting against secession and directing the activities of an extensive federal bureaucracy. Finally, there are those attributes whose meaning can be found only in the vagaries of individual choice and environmental circumstance. Just as the importance of physical strength to well-being varies by individual and from situation to situation within an individual's life, so, for example, has the presidency's constitutional power to "recommend to [Congress's] Consideration such Measures as he shall judge necessary and expedient" varied in importance.

Two centuries of hindsight make clear that the latter two types of genetic message—the constitutional equivalents of baldness and strength—have had the most significance for presidential power. In some instances, the framers and, later, those who amended the Constitution anticipated the consequences of the decisions they were making when they created the presidency; in other cases they did not. But intended or unintended, consequences there have been.

This chapter is not about constitutional law but about constitutional politics: the politics of the Constitutional Convention itself, and the effects of its decisions on the politics of the living presidency. After briefly describing the setting in which the Convention met, we examine the Constitution makers' decisions and their effects in three clusters: *number and selection*, the series of choices that made the presidency a single-person office whose incumbent is selected by his own national constituency; *term and removal*, the former fixed in length, the latter difficult to achieve; and *powers and institutional separation*, which made the presidency one of three "separated institutions sharing power."[2] These decisions define the contours of presidential power, within which the varying effects of culture and politics (discussed in Chapter 3) and individual leadership skill (Chapter 4) are felt.

THE CONSTITUTIONAL CONVENTION

As John Roche has suggested, the Constitutional Convention that assembled in late May 1787 can usefully be described as a "nationalist reform caucus," a meeting of relatively like-minded politicians whose goals were to develop a plan of government that "would both bolster the 'National interest'" by being strong but not oppressive, "and be acceptable to the people," who would have to ratify and live under it.[3] Most of the great battles among the delegates who assembled in Philadelphia were not about the power of the new government — that was largely settled in the first week when they accepted James Madison's highly nationalistic Virginia Plan as their working draft — but rather about how power within that government should be allocated. More often than not, the issues in dispute lent themselves to compromise solutions: small states split the difference with larger states and provided for a bicameral legislature; North and South worked out the three-fifths rule for counting the slave population; and so on.

But when it came to the issue of the nature and powers of the executive, delegates labored in a realm of such intellectual and political uncertainty that the politics of compromise was largely irrelevant.[4] It was unclear to all groups of delegates how either of their primary goals could be met. An executive that would be strong but not oppressive? They had several models of what they did not want but few that they found attractive. The British king and his colonial governors, whom Americans had lived under until 1776, had been, in the delegates' eyes, tramplers of liberty. The state constitutions that were written after independence provided for nonoppressive governors but also rendered them weak to the point of impotence. The national government of the Articles of Confederation, such as it was, had no chief executive at all. And although the New York governorship seemed to offer a model of strong but safe executive power, its influence was slow to take hold at the Convention, in part because, for various reasons, all three New York delegates went home early.

Nor was it clear what the public would accept. The ambivalence toward political leadership that students of modern public opinion have detected in Americans seems to have been evident two centuries ago as well.[5] Hatred for monarchy existed side by side with a longing to make George Washington king. As Seymour Martin Lipset has shown, Washington was a classic example of Max Weber's charismatic leader, a man "treated [by the people] as endowed with supernatural, superhuman, or at least specifically exceptional powers or qualities."[6] Marcus Cunliffe notes:

Babies were being christened after him as early as 1775, and while he was still President, his countrymen paid to see him in waxwork effigy. To his admirers he was "godlike Washington," and his detractors complained to one another that he was looked upon as a "demigod" whom it was treasonous to criticize. "Oh Washington!" declared Ezra Stiles of Yale (in a sermon of 1783). "How I do love thy name! How have I often adored and blessed thy God, for creating and forming thee the great ornament of human kind!"[7]

But the longing for Washington, who was appalled by such antirepublican adulation, was just that: a longing for Washington, not for a hereditary monarchy.

The lessons the framers drew from these observations and experiences were widely varied. To Roger Sherman of Connecticut, history taught that the best executive for the new national government would be "nothing more than an institution for carrying [out] the will of the legislature . . . which was the depositary of the supreme will of the society."[8] Alexander Hamilton of New York wanted a powerful "Governour" selected for life by "electors chosen by the people."[9] Other delegates had ideas of their own or no firm ideas at all. But as their ready acceptance of the Virginia Plan shows, with its provision for a one-term executive chosen by the legislature, a plurality of delegates began the Convention as congressionalists. They were ready for strong national government (the Virginia Plan even allowed for federal veto of state laws) but not for a strong executive within that government.

As the Convention proceeded, the delegates' minds slowly changed, influenced by the powerful arguments and political shrewdness of executive power advocates such as Pennsylvanians James Wilson and Gouverneur Morris, and, in private lobbying, George Washington. Tentative decisions made in the early summer months of the Convention concerning number and selection, term and removal, and powers were revised in August and September in ways that made the presidency ever stronger. But as the constitutional power of the presidency grew, so did its responsibility and visibility. Both stories — how the powers of the presidency grew in the Convention and the amendment process, and how the burdens on the presidency have grown ever since — are told in the remaining sections of this chapter.

NUMBER

Charles Pinckney rose . . . to urge "a vigorous executive.". . . James Wilson followed Pinckney by moving that the executive consist of a single person; Pinckney seconded him.

A sudden silence followed. "A considerable pause," Madison wrote . . . A *single executive!* There was menace in the words, some saw monarchy in them. . . . [A] single executive for the national government conjured up visions from the past — royal governors who could not be restrained, a crown, ermine, a scepter!

—from Catherine Drinker Bowen, *Miracle at Philadelphia*[10]

Catherine Drinker Bowen's style of breathless prose may not suit all occasions, but it conjures well the significance of the Convention's decision to create a single rather than a plural, or committee-style, executive. So controversial a question was number that Madison's Virginia Plan had left it blank. (See Table 2.1 and the "Guide to the Tables in This Chapter.") The practical wisdom of his decision became clear after the Convention reconstituted itself on May 30 as a Committee of the Whole House to tinker with the plan and Wilson made his motion. Edmund Randolph instantly rose to argue for a three-person executive on the grounds that a single executive would constitute "the foetus of monarchy."[11] (As governor of Virginia, Randolph had considered himself only "a member of the executive.") Others offered equally dire predictions. But on June 2 the delegates accepted Wilson's defense of "a single magistrate, as giving most energy, dispatch, and responsibility to the office."[12] They stopped short only at the point at which Wilson urged them to append to his single executive the Virginia Plan's Council of Revision, a committee of judges with which the executive would share his decisions to veto legislation and which consequently would help to legitimate such decisions and buttress his power.

Wilson's list of purported single-executive virtues — "energy, dispatch, and responsibility" — demonstrates the political shrewdness that he, Morris, and their allies displayed all through the Convention. Their own desire was for as powerful an executive as possible. But realizing that they held a minority position in the Convention, the proexecutive forces advanced their ideas on number (as well as on selection, removal, powers, and so on) in terms that their reluctant colleagues could accept. Responsibility could be fixed with a single executive, Wilson argued; he could be checked when his actions were corrupt or incompetent. That would be impossible with a troika. As for energy and dispatch, Wilson's arguments spoke here to the widespread concern of the delegates, most of them personally prosperous, that the new government should be able to protect their property in the event of an insurrection. Shays's Rebellion of 1786 and the federal government's inability to help end it promptly had frightened them. A single executive, it was argued, could act quickly and decisively to protect property in such situations; a committee could not.

SELECTION

The Convention's decisions concerning selection also were influenced by the political shrewdness of the presidentialists. In June, July, and again in August the delegates reaffirmed Madison's initial proposal for selection of the executive by the legislature.[13] Wilson and Morris saw this as a serious problem: a president who owed his job to the legislature, they felt, would be subordinate to it. Their efforts for direct "election by the people at large" were unavailing. To the framers "democracy" was a synonym for mob rule; George Mason of Virginia said that allowing the public to choose would be like "refer[ring] a trial of colors to a blind man."[14] Failing that, the proexecutive forces still wanted to secure a provision for selection that would give the president an independent national constituency. This would make him the only person in government who could offer any claim at all to a mandate from the nation as a whole.

Table 2.1 The Development of the Constitutional Presidency: Number and Selection

	Virginia Plan	Committee of the Whole House	Committee of Detail	Committee on Postponed Matters	Committee of Style— Final Draft	Constitutional Amendments (1789–)
			Constitutional Convention (1787)			
NUMBER	Unspecified	*Single*[1]				
SELECTION	By legislature	By legislature[2]	• By legislature, joint ballot of all members[3] • Succession by president of Senate if presidency becomes vacant	• *By electoral college; runner-up is vice president (House of Representatives chooses if no candidate gets a majority of electoral votes)*[4] • *Succession by vice president if presidency becomes vacant* • *Selection limited to natural-born citizens thirty-five years or older and fourteen years a U.S. resident*		• *Twelfth (1804) – separate balloting for president and vice president* • *Twentieth (1933) – vice president-elect becomes president if president-elect dies; Congress must choose an acting president if no president or vice president has been chosen by Inauguration Day* • *Twenty-fifth (1967) – vacant vice presidency shall be filled by the president with the consent of Congress*

[1]Italicized type indicates that the final decision on the issue was made at this point.
[2]An electoral-college-style method was voted in on July 19 and then repealed on July 24.
[3]The joint-ballot provision was added on the floor on August 24.
[4]In the committee version, the Senate was to break electoral college deadlocks. The committee changed this to the House on September 6.

16

Guide to the Tables in This Chapter

Tables 2.1, 2.3, and 2.4 provide six "snapshots" of the constitutional presidency as it developed during the Constitutional Convention of 1787 and has continued to develop by amendment. The first five columns in the tables show how the presidency looked at five important stages of the Convention.

1. The *Virginia Plan* was introduced to the Convention and approved as a working draft on May 29.

2. The Convention met as a *Committee of the Whole House* from May 30 until June 13 to consider the Virginia Plan in detail and revise it.

3. A five-member *Committee of Detail* was appointed on July 26 to write a draft of the Constitution on the basis of resolutions already passed on the floor. It reported back to the Convention on August 6.

4. A *Committee on Postponed Matters,* consisting of eleven delegates, was appointed on August 31 to propose solutions to several unresolved issues. It reported to the Convention from September 1 through 4.

5. A five-member *Committee of Style* labored from September 8 through 12 in response to the Convention's injunction to produce a smooth, faithful, and final draft of the Constitution. The only noteworthy changes in the committee's report made on the floor were to reduce the margin needed in Congress to override a veto from three-fourths back to two-thirds and to clarify the president's appointment power.

The appendix at the end of the book quotes in full the parts of the Constitution that pertain to the presidency.

As it happened, two other developments at the Convention — one political, one philosophical — furthered their cause. The political event came on August 24, when the delegates defined legislative selection to mean that the House of Representatives and the Senate would vote jointly, each member having one vote. This convinced the small-state representatives that their people would be overwhelmed and effectively disfranchised. (Their own plan for a concurrent vote of the two houses, of course, would have alienated the large-state delegates if it had passed.)

The philosophical change was more gradual. Every summer vote in favor of legislative selection of the president had been accompanied by a vote to limit him to a single term. The delegates' fear was that a president eligible for reelection would spend his time trading favors for votes in Congress. But, some delegates began to argue, presidents would have little incentive for excellence in office if they could not be rewarded with reelection. Their reasoning, in combination with the small states' defection, carried the Convention. The task then became to develop a nonlegislative method of selection that would neither invite corruption nor alienate any part of the country. The people, the state governors or legislatures, and, among diehards, the national legislature all had their champions, but the decision of the Convention on August 31 (delegates were desperate to adjourn) to refer the whole issue to a Committee on Post-poned Matters is evidence enough that most delegates were looking for some new and creative proposal.

The Electoral College

The electoral college was the committee's "jerry-rigged" compromise solution to the selection stalemate.[15] An early version had been proposed by Oliver Ells-worth of Connecticut and briefly approved by the Convention in July, so the committee knew that the principle was acceptable if the politics were. To as-sure this result, the new version contained something for all factions. The elec-toral-college method entrusted the selection of presidents to a group of men chosen from their states by whatever methods the states provided. Each state received a total electoral vote equal to the number of its senators (two) and rep-resentatives (varied according to population) in Congress. The presumption was that most states would turn the choice of their electors over to the voters.[16] After months of struggle, the proexecutive forces had won all that they wanted short of direct popular election. The president would have a popular electoral base of his own, the only national constituency in government.

Interestingly, many delegates who still favored legislative election went along with the electoral-college idea. One reason was that the committee had spun off supplementary proposals to prevent voters from selecting as president anyone younger than thirty-five, fewer than "fourteen Years a Resident within the United States," or not a "natural born Citizen." The age requirement, it was felt, would limit the choice to men old enough to have revealed proven character and ability, not just "those brilliant appearances of genius and pa-triotism which, like transient meteors, sometimes mislead as well as dazzle" the public.[17] The apparent xenophobia of the citizenship and residency require-ments also was meant to prevent rash popular choices — namely, of foreign princes in general and the German Baron von Steuben, a revolutionary war hero but a sympathizer with Shays's Rebellion, in particular.[18]

A more important reason that legislative-selection proponents suffered de-feat gladly on the electoral-college issue was that many thought they actually had won a victory. Their assurance was based on the committee proposal's pro-vision that if no candidate received a majority of electoral votes, Congress would pick the president, choosing among the highest vote-getters. To attract small-state support, the committee proposal had the Senate doing the choosing; the Convention, while changing it to the presumably less aristocratic House, kept that support by restricting each state delegation to one vote. Mason guessed that Congress would choose some nineteen times in twenty, reducing the elec-toral college to a sort of nominating convention.

Mason's prediction has not stood up too well: as of 1984, the House had chosen the president in two out of forty-nine elections, the most recent in 1824. The early organization of American electoral politics into a two-party system, which the framers had not anticipated, helped to assure that in almost every election a major party candidate would win a majority of electoral votes. So did the Twelfth Amendment, ratified in 1804 after Thomas Jefferson and his party's vice-presidential nominee, Aaron Burr, ended up tied for first in the presidential election of 1800. This necessitated a long and dangerous contest between Jefferson and Burr in the House that was all the more distressing because, aside from some Federalist mischief-makers, it had been no one's intention, including Burr's. The reason for the mix-up was that the electoral college as constituted in the original Constitution called upon each elector to cast two votes for two different candidates from two states for president. (The framers assumed that if an elector had only one vote, he would cast it for a citizen of his own state.) The candidate with the greatest number of votes, assuming it was a majority, would be president; to assure that electors would not throw away their second vote (again, in the interest of helping local favorites), the Convention had provided that the runner-up would be vice president.[19] But when parties formed and began to nominate tickets, as the Democratic-Republicans did when they put forth Jefferson for president and Burr for vice president, there was no way for the electors to reflect this distinction in their two votes. The Twelfth Amendment cleared all this up expeditiously: "The Electors . . . shall name in their ballots the person voted for as President, and in distinct ballots the person voted for as Vice-President."

Selection by Vice-Presidential Succession

The vice presidency came into being at the Convention as a constitutional residue. As delegate Hugh Williamson of North Carolina, a member of the committee that drafted the electoral college, told the Convention, "Such an office as vice-President was not wanted. It was introduced only for the sake of a valuable mode of election which required two to be chosen at the same time."[20] The constitutional task assigned to the office was trivial—to preside over the Senate—and the reason for allowing it even that power seems to have been the one offered by Roger Sherman: without it "he would be without employment."[21]

A good side-effect of bringing the person whom electors presumably had judged second most qualified to be president into the government was that it solved the succession problem. Presidential selection in normal times might be by the electoral college, but the framers now decided that in the event of presidential death, resignation, or impeachment, selection would be by fiat: the vice president automatically would become president for the rest of the ex-president's term. (The vice president-elect also would serve the president's full term if the president-elect died, by virtue of the Twentieth Amendment, which was added to the Constitution in 1933.) If the president were judged disabled (an issue to be treated in the next section), the vice president would serve as "acting" president until the president's disability was ended. This means that the vice president would assume all the powers and duties of the presidency but not the office itself. Similarly, should the Senate succeed, in the event of electoral-college deadlock, in choosing a vice president (a likely outcome because the Constitution confined the choice to the top two vote-getters) while the House was failing to select a president, the vice president also would act temporarily but indefinitely as president.

NUMBER AND SELECTION: CONSEQUENCES

The most important decisions of the Convention with regard to number and selection, unaltered by subsequent amendment, were those that made the executive a unitary office whose occupant is chosen by its own national constituency. The consequences of those decisions have not always been those foreseen by the framers, but they are real and enduring nonetheless. The number and selection provisions combined the roles of *chief of government and chief of state* into one office. They assured that to the extent that *prerogative* power would be lodged anywhere in government, it would be in the presidency. Finally, they injected a powerful element of *psychological character* into an otherwise mechanistic plan of government. From the standpoint of modern presidential power, these decisions have had varied effects. They have made the presidency a more powerful office, but they also have made it a more vulnerable one.

Chief of Government, Chief of State

The framers realized that the executive function included not just a political role (chief of government) but a symbolic one (chief of state). But to them, the decision to have a single or a plural executive was a decision either to invest both these roles in an individual or to invest them in a committee. The idea that one could entrust political leadership to one office and the symbolic function to another did not occur to the delegates, even though that was exactly the separation that was taking place in Great Britain at the time they labored. Although the king remained the anthropomorphic symbol of the nation to the British people and the object of their patriotic love of country, William Pitt had transferred irrevocably the role of political leadership to the prime ministership.[22]

The significance of the chief-of-state role for the presidency lies not in the insignificant formal powers that accompany it or the activities it requires: to "make proclamations of thanksgiving and commemoration, bestow medals on flustered pilots, hold state dinners for the diplomatic corps and the Supreme Court, light the nation's Christmas tree," and so on.[23] Rather it is the emotions the role arouses in citizens. Long before they have any real knowledge of what the president actually does, children already think of him in terms of almost limitless power and benevolence. The president, as seen by grade-school children, "gives us freedom . . . worries about all the problems of all the states . . . is in charge of the United States and has many wise men to tell him what is best . . . makes peace with every country but bad."[24] The death of a president causes adults to react in an equally emotional way. Surveys taken shortly after the Kennedy assassination found that Americans displayed symptoms of grief that otherwise appear only at the death of close friends or relatives. They "didn't feel like eating" (43 percent); "cried" (53 percent); "felt very nervous and tense" (68 percent); and "felt sort of dazed and numb" (57 percent), among other things.[25] They also feared, for a short time at least, that the republic was in danger.[26] Similar emotional outpourings seem to have accompanied the deaths in office, whether by assassination or natural causes, of all presidents, whether popular or not. The assassination of William McKinley prompted a "universal spasm of grief . . . from end to end of the land"; after Warren Harding died in his bed, "Jewish leaders compared Harding with Moses dying before he reached the Promised Land."[27] In Great Britain, it is the monarch's death that occasions such deep emotions, not the prime minister's.[28] It is the chief of state whom children conceive of as powerful and good: 62 percent offer images of the queen that suggest she "rules, governs, commands"; only 24 percent volunteer similar images of the chief of government.[29]

Traditional views of the presidency hold that a president's chief-of-state role buttresses his more important function as political leader. "[N]o president," writes Clinton Rossiter,

> can fail to realize that all his powers are invigorated, indeed are given a new dimension of authority, because he is the symbol of our sovereignty, continuity, and grandeur. When he asks a senator to lunch in order to enlist support for a pet project, when he thumps his desk and reminds the antagonists in a labor dispute of the larger interests of the American people, when he orders a general to cease caviling or else be removed from his command, the senator and the disputants and the general are well aware — especially if the scene is laid in the White House — that they are dealing with no ordinary head of government.[30]

There is much evidence to support this view. The "honeymoon" that the new president enjoys with the people at the start of his term is, in a sense, an affirmation of faith in the office. As Table 2.2 shows, new presidents invariably receive the initial approval of millions of citizens who voted against them; vice presidents who succeed to the office, for whom no one voted, actually fare better. Even after experiencing two highly unpopular presidencies in a row, the second culminating in the near-impeachment and resignation of President Nixon, citizens rallied to the support of President Ford by a margin of 71 percent to 3 percent.

Some political scientists have tried to show that certain groups of citizens are disposed to support the president even after the honeymoon, regardless of who he is or what he does. Unfortunately, present research has left these scholars divided on the question of which groups these are. Samuel Kernell and his colleagues, for example, conclude that "presidential support is disproportionately located among citizens who are older, of fundamentalist religious persuasion, have fewer years of formal schooling, and may be described as psychologically inflexible."[31] Another study, by John Mueller, discovered that presidential "followers" — that is, people who see the presidency as the living embodiment of the nation and thus "are inclined to rally to the support of the president no matter what" — tend to be citizens who are younger and have more years of formal schooling than "nonfollowers."[32] Mueller was studying the public's record of support for presidents during recent wars and Kernell their disposition to support the presidency in an abstract sense, but the differences in their findings suggest a need for further study.

What does seem clear is that presidents usually can trade on their chief-of-state role with all population groups when they deal with foreign policy.

Table 2.2 The "Honeymoon" Effect

	A Popular Vote Margin in Election (percent)	B "Approval" Margin After Inauguration[1] (percent)	"Honeymoon" Effect (B − A)
Elected Presidents			
Franklin Roosevelt (1940)[2]	10	42	+ 32
Harry Truman (1948)	4	52	+ 48
Dwight Eisenhower (1952)	11	61	+ 50
Dwight Eisenhower (1956)	13	60	+ 47
John Kennedy (1960)	0	66	+ 66
Lyndon Johnson (1964)	23	51	+ 28
Richard Nixon (1968)	1	54	+ 53
Richard Nixon (1972)	24	34	+ 10
Jimmy Carter (1976)	2	58	+ 56
Ronald Reagan (1980)	10	38	+ 28
Vice Presidents Who Succeeded to the Presidency			
Harry Truman (1945)		84	
Lyndon Johnson (1963)		76	
Gerald Ford (1974)		68	

[1] The "approval margin" is the difference between the percentage of people who say "approve" from the percentage of people who say "disapprove" in response to the question "Do you approve or disapprove of the way [name of incumbent] is handling his job as president?" as administered in the Gallup poll.
[2] The approval question was not asked in 1944 or early 1945.

Source: *The Gallup Opinion Index* (October–November 1980), pp. 13–40; *The Gallup Report* (March 1981), p. 3.

Citizens will "rally round the flag" by supporting the president in all sorts of international circumstances. According to a study by Jong Lee, wars and military crises head the list of support-inspiring events, followed by new foreign-policy initiatives, peace efforts, and summit conferences.[33] In May 1943 a Gallup survey found that while only 31 percent said they would vote for Roosevelt in 1944 "if the war is over," 56 percent said they would "if the war is still going on."[34] Support for Nixon's Vietnam policies jumped in twelve days from 58 percent to 77 percent among those who heard his November 1969 "Vietnamization" speech.[35] His overall approval rating leaped twelve percentage points, a showing surpassed four years later when the Vietnam peace settlement brought him a 17-percent rise. Ford's approval rating was eleven points higher after he "rescued" the *Mayaguez*; Carter added twelve points to his rating as a result of the Camp David summit that brought Israel and Egypt together; and so on.

Lee also finds that foreign-policy setbacks usually hurt the president, but even here there are spectacular exceptions. Although John Kennedy publicly labeled the aborted Bay of Pigs invasion a failure and took responsibility for it, his approval rating went from 72 percent before the invasion to 83 percent afterward.[36] It also is unclear how presidents will be affected by new-style issues of international economics. One can speculate that in situations in which Americans perceive the president to be speaking for the nation to the world, as when Nixon altered U.S. international monetary policy in 1971, they will rally around him as chief of state in the familiar manner. But when it comes to trade or energy policies that, though rooted in international affairs, are seen to benefit some Americans more than others, they are likely to react to him more as a political leader, as they do on most domestic matters.

In a perverse way impeachment also highlights the political value to presidents of the public's emotional ties to the presidency. In late 1973 Nixon's approval rating dropped into the mid-twenties and stayed there for the rest of his term. Some 71 percent said in February 1974 that they thought he was guilty of either planning or covering up "the Watergate 'bugging.'" Yet only 38 percent thought he should be impeached.[37] Clearly, many citizens, perhaps as many as one-third, were looking upon impeachment not as a way of removing a president they disapproved of and felt to be criminally culpable, but as a blow to the nation they love in the person of the chief of state.

Nonetheless, Nixon ultimately was forced by public opinion to leave office. So, in less dramatic and thus more significant ways, have most recent presidents. The roster of failures in this regard is long — Truman, Johnson, Nixon, Ford, and Carter. The list of successes — Roosevelt, Eisenhower, and Kennedy (whose term was cut short) — is shorter. One reason is that in ways less obvious than those Rossiter described as helping presidents, the joining of the roles of chief of government and chief of state can hurt them.

Part of this has to do with the public expectations each role generates, expectations that the president is supposed to meet even though they seem contradictory. Thomas Cronin's ten "paradoxes" of presidential leadership are rooted in these expectations. Americans want the president to be, for example, "gentle and decent but forceful and decisive," "inspirational but 'don't promise more than you can deliver,'" a "national unifier-national divider."[38] At base, most of these paradoxes are one: citizens want the president to be a chief of state and represent the things that unite them, and a chief of government who will lead and thus divide them. James David Barber suggests that the public's needs for political leadership in pursuit of "progress and action" and for more symbolic leadership that offers "reassurance" and "legitimacy" fluctuate in relative importance and thus allow a president to emphasize one role or the other.[39] But the nexus remains vague at best.

A problem equal to but perhaps more avoidable than that of contradictory expectations is one of veneration. Each president inherits the public's adulation for the presidency as the nation's chieftainship of state. Bruce Buchanan argues that this exposes incumbents to excessive "deference" that "nurtur[es] systemic distortion in their perceptions of self and of external events," as well as to "dissonance," which "encourag[es] the use of secrecy, misrepresentation, and lying as weapons in the struggle for political success and survival."[40] Some handle this exposure very well, realizing that it is the office, not the incumbent, that the public reveres. (Truman, for example, wrote in his diary that when it came to "kudos and kowtows, . . . I knew always that the greatest office in the world was getting them and Harry S. Truman as an individual was not.")[41] But others fail to make this distinction.

Oddly enough, veneration-rooted failures seem most likely to occur when things are going well for a president. The consequences can be serious. It seems more than coincidental that each of the three twentieth-century presidents who won election victories of 60 percent or more of the popular vote (thus demonstrating their sensitivity to public opinion) instantly breached the bounds of permissible presidential power in a way that brought down the public's wrath: Roosevelt's court-packing proposal in 1937, Johnson's unilateral escalation of the war in Vietnam in 1965, and Nixon's coverup of the Watergate scandal in late 1972 and 1973. Ironically, the same veneration for the office that encourages such self-destructive acts then allows presidents who are temperamentally so disposed, as were Johnson and Nixon, to "circle up the wagons," all of them manned by deferential staffers, and seal the real political world out when things go badly. This isolation becomes yet another wellspring of the kind of politically foolish or dangerous action that eventually will bring a president down.

Prerogative

There is little doubt that most if not all of the delegates to the Constitutional Convention were influenced by John Locke's *Second Treatise of Government*. Locke argued for the general superiority of governments of laws and by legislatures, but in a chapter on prerogative he noted certain powerful exceptions to that rule. Legislatures are unable, Locke wrote, "to foresee, and so by laws to provide for, all accidents and necessities." They also are, by virtue of their size and unwieldiness, too slow to alter and adapt the law as circumstances may dictate in time of crisis. Thus, there may be occasions when existing, temporarily unsuitable laws should "give way to the executive power, or rather to this fundamental law of nature and government, viz., that, as much as may be, all the members of society are to be preserved." This is prerogative: "the people's permitting their rulers to do several things of their own free choice, where the law was silent, and sometimes, too, against the direct letter of the law, for the public good, and their acquiescing in it when so done."[42] The check on executive power in such an instance is not the law, but rather the elected legislature's subsequent decision to accept or reject the propriety of the "prerogatory" acts.

Madison probably was typical of most of the delegates in his response to Locke's argument. He agreed in *Federalist* No. 41 that "it is in vain to oppose constitutional barriers to the impulse of [national] self-preservation," but also realized that Americans would resist any proposed plan of government in which unbounded executive power, which they associated with monarchy, was thought to lurk.[43] For that reason, he told the delegates, it was politically necessary "to fix the extent of the Executive authority," to "confine and define" it in the Constitution.[44] In the end the definition the framers arrived at explicity contemplated only two mechanisms by which ordinary legal processes might be abridged: suspension of the writ of habeas corpus "when in Cases of Rebellion or Invasion the public Safety may require it," and the right "to grant reprieves and pardons." Of these two, only the latter was defined clearly as a power of the president, and it was accepted by the Convention mostly as a means of averting future Shays-style insurrections. As Hamilton wrote in *Federalist* No. 74, "In seasons of insurrection or rebellion there are critical moments when a well-timed offer of pardon to the insurgents or rebels may restore the tranquility of the commonwealth" and "the dilatory process of convening the legislature" may cause that moment to be lost.[45]

Whether and how much more than that the framers intended, up to and perhaps including Locke's definition of prerogative, is unclear. Does the constitutional oath sworn by new presidents to "preserve, protect, and defend the Constitution of the United States" include a Lockean responsibility to do whatever it takes—legal, extralegal, or illegal—to keep the nation independent and the Constitution supreme? Do the words "the executive Power" in the opening sentence of Article II imply the existence of powers beyond those enumerated afterward? Constitutional exegesis cannot answer these questions.

Be that as it may, emergencies unanticipated in the law have arisen, and presidents, inevitably, have responded in prerogatory style. For example, Jefferson spent unappropriated money for munitions after the British fleet attacked the *Chesapeake* in 1807. Lincoln, responding to the secession of some southern states, called forth volunteers, ordered southern ports to be blockaded, seized several newspapers, and spent unappropriated money, among other things. Long before any American declaration of war was made, and in all but direct contradiction of the law, Franklin Roosevelt effectively entered the United States into an alliance with Great Britain by transferring to it fifty destroyers.

In most cases, presidents have tried to link such actions to specific provisions of the Constitution. Lincoln, for example, found his justification in the habeas corpus clause, the commander-in-chief clause, the "take care" clause, and his oath.[46] In truth, though, it was the Convention's decision to make the presidency a unitary office selected by a national constituency that provides the real constitutional source of presidential prerogative. What other federal office but a unitary one could act with "most energy and dispatch"? What other than the only nationally elected one could do so with any claim to legitimacy?

Whether intentionally or not, then, the Constitution conferred prerogative power in time of emergency on the president. Efforts to define "emergency" by legislation and thus limit the president in such cases have run up against Locke's warning about the futility of trying to legislate for crises yet unknown. In truth, most emergency legislation has been perceived as expanding presidential power, which is why the mid-1970s attack on the "imperial presidency" included the stripping of most such laws from the books.[47]

Still, as Richard Pious argues, prerogative has been a mixed blessing for presidents.[48] To be sure, some prerogatory responses to crisis have had "frontlash" effects — that is, successful crisis management has been greeted by judicial and congressional acquiescence. Most frontlash effects have occurred in national security crises such as the Civil War. They leave a powerful precedent for similar presidential efforts in similar future circumstances. But other prerogative-style actions have produced "backlash" (the crisis was managed successfully, but the other branches challenged the president's authority) or even "overshoot and collapse" (the president's efforts were checked before they took effect, with severe political repercussions). These tend to follow actions in response to situations that are essentially domestic but that presidents perceive as having national security implications. Truman's seizure of the steel mills exemplifies the milder backlash effect: it got the mills going but was flatly undone by the Supreme Court in *Youngstown Sheet and Tube* v. *Sawyer*.[49] Overshoot and collapse followed Andrew Johnson's effort to reconstruct the South in ways contrary to congressional desires. Not only was Johnson impeached, but the presidency was weaker for his actions.

The problem for presidents is that although the constitutional system calls upon them to act in time of crisis, it does not define either what a crisis is or which responses are suitable. Success can make a president "great" in the eyes of historians and the presidency a more powerful office. But the desire to emulate such success can tempt presidents to behave rashly or even duplicitously, as Nixon did in claiming a special executive privilege to withhold Watergate-related evidence from the other branches as part of his cover-up.

Psychological Character

A basic tenet of the framers' political philosophy was that whatever its institutional form, the strong but nonoppressive government they were seeking would be a "government of laws and not of men." They associated liberty with law and tyranny with rulers who departed from law, as had George III and his colonial governors. Mason bespoke this sentiment when, after the Convention's decisions on presidential number and selection were made, he said: "We are not indeed constituting a British Government, but a more dangerous monarchy, an elective one."[50] All the more remarkable, then, that his fellow delegates did not listen.

Several reasons seem to explain the framers' decision to inject such a powerful dose of "character," both in the moral and psychological senses of the word, into their new plan of government. First was the assurance that Washington would be the nation's first president. Just as his charismatic "gift of grace" would legitimate the new government, so would his personal character assure its republican nature. The powers of the president in the Constitution "are full great," wrote South Carolina delegate Pierce Butler to a British kinsman,

> and greater than I was disposed to make them. Nor, entre nous, do I believe they would have been so great had not many of the delegates cast their eyes towards General Washington as President; and shaped their Ideas of the Powers to be given to a President, by their opinions of his Virtue.[51]

Things would be all right after Washington, it was felt, because the election of presidents, whether by electors or members of the House, would involve selection by peers, personal acquaintances of the candidates who could screen out those of defective character.

But even faith in Washington and in electors was faith in men. Could not someone of low character slip through the net and become president? If so, the framers felt that they had structured the office so as to keep the nation from harm. "The founders' deliberation over the provision for indefinite reeligibility," writes Jeffrey Tulis, "illustrates how they believed self-interest could sometimes be elevated."[52] Whether motivated by "avarice," "ambition," or "the love of fame," say *Federalist* Nos. 71 and 72, a president will do his best in order to secure reelection to the office that allows him to fulfill his desire.[53] Underlying all this was the assurance that in a relatively slow-paced world there was only so much damage a mad or wicked president could do before corrective action could remove him. "So far as the fear of punishment and disgrace can operate," states *Federalist* No. 64, "that motive to good behavior is amply afforded by the article on the subject of impeachment."

The framers' decision to inject character, then, was a conscious one. But it was made for reasons that no longer obtain. Washington is gone; "peer review" never really took hold in the electoral college. The destructive powers at a president's disposal are ultimate and swift in the atomic age; the removal processes now seem uncertain and slow. The rise of the national broadcast media make the president's personality all the more pervasive. In sum, the framers' carefully conceived defenses against a president of defective character are gone.

Unfortunately, present understandings of the nature of the relationship between character and performance in the White House are as uncertain as our sense of the relationship's significance is clear. Nothing demonstrates this better than the deficiencies of the boldest attempt to date to link personality theory to presidential performance in a systematic way, that of James David Barber.[54]

Barber holds that one can usefully "type" presidential character by answering two questions about a president: Is he active or passive ("how much energy does the man invest in his presidency")? Is he positive or negative ("relatively speaking, does he seem to experience political life as happy or sad, enjoyable or discouraging . . . in its main effect")? "Active-positives," argues Barber, are those who come to maturity with a deeply rooted sense of personal security that allows them to work hard at political life (active), enjoy what they do (positive), and, consequently, be productive and successful presidents. All other personality types make defective presidents because, according to Barber, they subconsciously use the office to serve personal rather than public purposes—that is, to compensate for a lack of an inner sense of worth. "Passive-positives" seek affection through compliant and agreeable behavior and "passive-negatives" the feeling of usefulness that comes from performing a widely respected duty. "Active-negatives" are truly threatening in Barber's view. The attraction of political office for them is dominance and control over other people. When they feel their power challenged, they react with rigid, defensive, even dangerous behavior.

Provocative though it may be, Barber's theory unravels even as he applies it. A "healthy" political personality turns out not to be the guarantor of presidential success he had predicted: Barber classed Ford and Carter early in their presidencies as active-positives, for example. Nor, as Figure 2.1 shows, does Barber's notion of character unsuitability seem to correspond to failure in office. The ranks of the most successful presidents in three recent surveys by historians include some who have been classified by Barber as active-positives (Jefferson, Truman, and Franklin Roosevelt) but also an equal number of active-negatives (Wilson, Lyndon Johnson, and John Adams) and others whom Barber labeled passive-negatives (Washington and Eisenhower). The most perverse result of classifying presidents by this standard involves Abraham Lincoln, whom Jeffrey Tulis, correctly applying Barber's theory, found to be an active-negative.[55]

One lesson of all this is that personality theory is still too murky to explain the very important matter of presidential character. As Alexander George points out, "The concept [of character] is not at all well defined within the realm of personality theory."[56] The other, more important lesson is that however much character may matter in the modern presidency, it is not everything. Tulis notes that Lincoln's behavior as president is explained much better by his

Figure 2.1 "Great" Presidents and Barber's Character Typology*

	Active	Passive
Positive	Jefferson F. Roosevelt Truman	
Negative	J. Adams Wilson L. Johnson (Lincoln)	Washington Eisenhower

*For the purposes of this figure, a "great" president is defined as one who ranked among the first ten in at least one of the three recent polls of historians: Steve Neal "Our Best and Worst Presidents," *Chicago Tribune Magazine* (January 10, 1982), pp. 9–18; David L. Porter, letter to author (January 15, 1982); and Robert K. Murray and Tim H. Blessing, "The Presidential Performance Study: A Progress Report," *Journal of American History* (December 1983), pp. 535–55. Four others who achieved this ranking (Jackson, Polk, T. Roosevelt, and McKinley) are not included because Barber did not classify them according to his typology.

political philosophy and skills than by his psychological constitution. Similarly, one need not resort to psychology to explain the failures of "active-negatives" Hoover and, in the latter years of his presidency, Lyndon Johnson. Hoover's unbending resistance to federal relief in the face of the depression may have stemmed from ideological beliefs rather than psychological rigidity. Johnson's refusal to change policy in Vietnam could be interpreted as the actions of a self-styled consensus leader trying to steer a moderate course between "hawks" who wanted full-scale military involvement and "doves" who wanted unilateral withdrawal.[57] That these actions were ineffective does not necessarily mean that they were irrational.

A Note on the Vice Presidency

"My country," wrote John Adams, the first vice president, to his wife Abigail, "has in its wisdom contrived for me the most insignificant office that ever the invention of man contrived or has imagination conceived."[58] Adams did not realize that the vice presidency actually was at a peak of influence during the period he served. Because the Senate was small and tie votes reasonably likely, Adams was able to cast a record twenty decisive votes.[59] More important, because in the pre-Twelfth Amendment electoral college the vice president was the recipient of the second highest number of votes for president, the office was occupied by a logical heir apparent. The nation's first and second vice presidents, Adams and Jefferson, became its second and third presidents.

When passing the Twelfth Amendment, members of Congress were unusually prescient in forecasting the bad side-effects it would have on the vice presidency. Because "the vice president will not stand on such high ground in the method proposed as he does in the present mode of a double ballot," predicted Samuel Taggert, the nation could expect that "great care will not be taken in the selection of a character to fill that office." William Plumer warned that such care as was taken would be "to procure votes for the president."[60] In practice, vice presidents after 1804 generally were chosen simply to provide regional or ideological balance to the party's ticket. For almost a century and a half vice presidents seemed to have had little more to do than reflect on their condition. John Nance Garner, the first of Franklin Roosevelt's three vice presidents, said the office "isn't worth a pitcher of warm s[p]it." Thomas Riley Marshall, vice president to Woodrow Wilson, compared himself to "a man in a cataleptic fit; he cannot speak; he cannot move; he suffers no pain; he is perfectly conscious of all that goes on, but has no part in it." (Marshall also told the story of the two brothers: "One ran away to sea; the other was elected vice president. And nothing was ever heard of either of them again.")[61]

Unlike George Clinton, who refused to attend President James Madison's inauguration; Richard Johnson, who spent most of his term running a tavern; Schuyler Colfax, who was nearly impeached for his financial dealings; or Chester Arthur, who denounced President James Garfield to a newspaper editor, Marshall was fairly typical of vice presidents in this period. At the 1912 Democratic convention, then-Governor Marshall of Indiana received his nomination from Wilson's supporters in exchange for his state's delegates. For the first several years of his term, his "only business as vice president," he said, was "to ring the White House bell every morning and ask what is the state of health of the president." When Wilson went to Europe to negotiate the Treaty of Versailles, Marshall presided over cabinet meetings — itself a precedent — but, he made clear at the outset, he was doing so "informally and personally." (Wilson invited him to only one more meeting after his return.) There was talk, but no serious action, directed at awarding Marshall his party's presidential nomination in 1920.[62] No vice president had received one since 1837; indeed, none of the four nineteenth-century vice presidents who had become president after a presidential death was nominated, much less elected, for another term.

A turning point in the history of the vice presidency came in 1945, when Truman became president after Roosevelt's death and discovered that he had been kept ignorant not only of the nation's plans for war and negotiations for peace, but of the very existence of the atomic bomb. The "cold war" between the United States and the Soviet Union and the proliferation of intercontinental nuclear missiles heightened the sense that the vice president should be not just willing, but ready and able to step into the presidency at a moment's notice.

The lessons of 1945 had little effect on Truman's relationship with his own vice president, Alben Barkley, whom he treated in much the same manner as earlier presidents had treated their vice presidents. But they had three significant consequences in the years that followed. The first was that all presidents from Eisenhower on not only have kept their vice presidents informed, but also have tried to keep them busy and in the public eye. In part, this has involved the conferring of high-sounding but relatively inconsequential titles: chairman of the Aeronautics and Space Council (Lyndon Johnson), vice chairman of the Urban Affairs Council (Agnew), and the like. In part, too, it has meant assigning the vice president the job of making speeches the president does not want to make — slashing attacks on the press or the other party, for example — and visiting countries that the president needs to but does not want to visit. "I go to funerals," said Nelson Rockefeller when he was asked what he did as vice president. "I go to earthquakes."[63]

A second consequence of the atomic age for the vice presidency was the Twenty-fifth Amendment. As thorough as the Constitution had been in providing for vice-presidential succession to fill a premature vacancy in the presidency, it said nothing about the situation in which there is no vice president at the time one is needed. The Convention left it to Congress to decide this by legislation. Congress did, but in an erratic way. A law passed in 1792 put the president pro tempore of the Senate first after the vice president in the line of succession to the presidency; he was replaced in an 1886 law by the secretary of state, who in turn was replaced in 1947 by the speaker of the House. In all cases political, not constitutional considerations, governed. The Eightieth Congress, for example, simply wanted a Republican speaker instead of a Democratic secretary of state to be president if Truman left office prematurely.[64] The single exception to this pattern of behavior was the Twentieth Amendment, added to the Constitution in 1933, which provided that should Congress fail to select, in the event of electoral-college deadlock, either a president or a vice president by Inauguration Day, it would be entitled to pick some other temporary stand-in.

By 1964, however, partisanship no longer seemed sufficient to the task of assuring selection by succession. John Kennedy's assassination and Vice President Lyndon Johnson's elevation to the presidency had left the vice presidency vacant once again, the sixteenth time this had happened in thirty-six presidencies: seven times by death (and once by resignation) of the vice president, eight times when the president died.[65] Speaker John McCormack, who would have succeeded Johnson, was seventy-two years old; President Pro Tempore James Eastland, next in line, was an unreconstructed Mississippi segregationist. A year later, Congress passed the Twenty-fifth Amendment, which provided that should the vice presidency ever become vacant again, the president was to nominate a new one, subject to confirmation by a majority of each house of Congress.

Congress seems to have assumed that death (either the president's or the vice president's) would produce the vice-presidential vacancies that activate the succession provisions of the Twenty-fifth Amendment, as it had in fifteen of sixteen previous cases. But in 1973, Vice President Spiro Agnew resigned as part of a deal that enabled him to avoid prosecution on political corruption charges, and President Nixon and a Democratic Congress used their new constitutional power to make House Republican leader Gerald Ford vice president. A year later Nixon resigned rather than undergo an impeachment trial. When Ford became president, the vice presidency was vacant once again. He nominated former New York governor Nelson Rockefeller, and Congress again approved. One consequence of all this was that the legitimacy of the new process of executive selection in unusual times passed an early test. In the year of their bicentennial, Americans accepted without protest the right to rule of a president and vice president who had been selected not in an election, but through a method that by involving Congress, is closer kin to the legislative selection provision of the Virginia Plan.

The third result of the 1945 experience, one that seems to have affected the power position of the vice presidency, has been a greater emphasis in the selection of vice-presidential nominees on experience, ability, and, reversing the pattern of the past, ideological harmony with the presidential candidate. Winning votes for the ticket still is the goal, but voters now care more about a vice-presidential candidate's ability to succeed a president ably and faithfully than they do about having all regions of the country or factions of the party represented in the White House. The 1976 Carter campaign, like others before it, responded to these concerns in its advertising. One television ad showed pictures of Robert Dole, the Republican vice-presidential nominee, and Carter's running mate Walter Mondale, and then asked: "When you know that four out of the last six vice presidents have wound up being president, who would you like to see a heartbeat away from the presidency? Hmmm?"[66]

These developments have created the conditions for a relatively stronger vice presidency. Constitutionally, the office is as weak as ever; vice-presidential power remains a function of the president's willingness to delegate. But presidents are most likely to assign responsibility to their vice presidents, writes Joel Goldstein, when the two are "personally congenial, " "personally compatible," and the president "believes the vice president has something to offer him" in the way of talent[67] — three conditions that are likely to be met (and were, most notably, in the Carter administration) as a consequence of the new selection criteria. The modern vice presidency is more in the Adams-Jefferson mold than it has been since the days of Adams and Jefferson.

TERM

Questions of term, reeligibility, and method of selection were interwoven in the minds of the delegates. One scholar has compared their efforts to sort out these issues to a game of "three-dimensional chess."[68] Underlying this complexity, however, was a basic choice: Which did the delegates care about more, legislative selection of the president or eligibility for reelection? As Max Farrand summed up the issue: "If the executive were to be chosen by the legislature, he must not be eligible for re-election lest he should court the favor of the legislature in order to secure for himself another term. Accordingly the single term of office should be long. But the possibility of re-election was regarded as the best incentive to faithful performance of duty, and if a short term and re-eligibility were accepted, the choice by the legislature was inadvisable."[69]

At the start of the Convention, legislative selection—and thus, a long, single term—was favored. (See Table 2.3.) Later, when the relative virtues of reeligibility rose in the delegates' esteem, they shortened the term and changed the mode of election to accommodate it. No science governed their choice of four years. At various times, proposals for terms of three, six, seven, eight, eleven, fifteen, and twenty years floated around, along with Hamilton's idea for tenure "during good behavior."[70]

After the Convention, indefinite reeligibility took on a specific meaning, first in practice, then in law. Washington and Jefferson each retired voluntarily after two terms, Jefferson explaining that to stand again for election would make the term "in fact for life" and the office only "nominally elective." (He had raised the same objection during the ratification debate.)[71] Few presidents (notably Ulysses S. Grant) seemed interested in challenging this precedent—the mid-nineteenth century custom actually was to promise to serve only one term[72]—and only Franklin Roosevelt, arguing that the conditions of wartime uncertainty that prevailed in 1940 and 1944 necessitated an exception to the general rule, succeeded. But his action brought down the wrath of the Republican Eightieth Congress, which in 1947 passed a constitutional amendment to limit the president to two terms. Although its purpose was blatantly partisan, Congress found ready acceptance for the Twenty-second Amendment in the states, forty-one of which ratified it, and among the public. Even in 1960, when the amendment denied citizens a chance to reelect to a third term the vastly popular Eisenhower, a poll found that they supported the two-term limit by a margin of 6 to 1.[73] In their eyes, reported Roberta Sigel, "it was seen as a time limit on otherwise almost unlimited presidential power and as an effective bar to dictatorship."[74]

A desire to strengthen, not weaken, the presidency lay behind the only other constitutional amendment bearing on term. The original Constitution had been silent on the question of precisely when the president's four years were to begin. Congress passed a law in 1792 setting the March 4 following the election as the start of the term, but as time went by, the hiatus between election and inauguration came to seem excessively long. For those four months, it was argued, the outgoing president was a "lame duck," presumably unable to do anything of consequence. The president-elect was forced to maintain a discreet silence at the very time when his mandate for action was most fresh. The Twentieth Amendment moved the March 4 date up six weeks, to January 20.

One idea that did not influence the delegates' discussion at Philadelphia and that has been raised only rarely since was for a term whose length was not fixed. At various times during the Convention, proposals were offered to make the president removable simply by petition of the state legislatures or Congress, but they did not attract much interest. Perhaps this was because an unspecified term was antithetical to the positions of both sides in the term-selection-reeligibility controversy. To those who favored legislative selection of the president, a term of fixed length was thought vital to the preservation of executive autonomy. As for electoral-college adherents, they would have found it difficult to conceive the logistics of irregular elections even if they had been so disposed.

REMOVAL

Although the framers fixed the length of the president's term, they provided methods for his premature removal under certain extraordinary circumstances. But they did so in ways guaranteed to assure that removal would be difficult to effect and thus rare to occur.

Impeachment

Provision for presidential impeachment was a part of the Constitution in all its working drafts. Although Morris initially argued that impeachment would open the door to legislative encroachment, most proexecutive advocates defended it on the grounds that unless the Constitution contained some means of removing presidents who behaved badly, they never would be able to convince their fellow delegates to accept a strong presidency.[75] Throughout the Convention, the delegates tinkered with both the mechanism and the grounds for impeachment. The mechanism grew ever more political, moving from the Supreme Court alone to the Court and the House of Representatives, then finally to the House and the Senate: the House to indict and the Senate to try, with a two-thirds vote needed to convict. Simultaneously, the grounds for impeachment grew less political. The Committee of the Whole had offered "malpractice or neglect of duty," a broad standard; the Committee of Detail narrowed this somewhat to "treason, bribery, or corruption"; then the Convention itself replaced "corruption" with "other High Crimes and Misdemeanors," a term borrowed from English law. "Corruption," it was felt, could be perverted to

Table 2.3 The Development of the Constitutional Presidency: Term and Removal

| | Virginia Plan | Constitutional Convention (1787) | | | | Constitutional Amendments (1789–) |
		Committee of the Whole House	Committee of Detail	Committee on Postponed Matters	Committee of Style—Final Draft	
TERM	Length unspecified; one-term limit	Seven years; one-term limit[1]	Seven years; one-term limit	Four years; no[2] limit on terms		Twentieth (1933)—term starts on January 20 following the election. Twenty-second (1951)—two-term limit
REMOVAL	Impeachment by "supreme [judicial] tribunal"	Impeachment and conviction by supreme tribunal on grounds of "malpractice, or neglect of duty"	•Impeachment by House and conviction by Supreme Court on grounds of "treason, bribery, or corruption" •In case of disability, president of Senate acts as president until disability ends. No definition of disability or how it is to be determined.	•Impeachment by House and conviction by Senate, with two-thirds vote needed to convict •In case of "inability," vice president acts as president	•Grounds of "treason, bribery, or Other High Crimes and Misdemeanors"	Twenty-fifth (1967)—presidential disability can be determined by the president, the vice president and a majority of the Cabinet, or, in case of dispute, by a two-thirds vote of each house of Congress

[1] On June 19, the Convention rejected for a time the one-term limit.

34

mean anything; "other High Crimes and Misdemeanors," although not confined to criminal offenses, clearly referred only to serious abuses of power.

No president was impeached until 1868, when Andrew Johnson was accused by the House of violating the year-old Tenure of Office Act by firing Secretary of War Edwin Stanton. Johnson's defense was that he had to violate the act in order to get a case before the Supreme Court that would test its constitutionality, which he challenged. Further, Johnson argued, the whole thing was a charade whose purpose was to get rid of a president whom Congress simply did not like. The Senate agreed (narrowly), as did history (emphatically), and impeachment in general received a bad name. James Bryce wrote in 1888 that "impeachment is the heaviest piece of machinery in the constitutional arsenal, but because it is so heavy, it is unfit for ordinary use." Not long after, Henry Jones Ford compared impeachment to a "rusted blunderbuss that will probably never be taken in hand again." Rossiter, writing in 1960, "predict[ed] confidently that the next president to be impeached will have asked for the firing squad by committing a low personal rather than a high political crime—by shooting a senator, for example."[76]

Gun imagery of this kind is a leitmotif in discussions of impeachment, perhaps because the process is a legal form of regicide. In this regard, the Nixon case offers an ironic exception. By early 1974, most members of Congress seem to have been convinced that Nixon had abused the powers of his office so severely that he should be removed. But not until the heralded "smoking pistol" was found, a tape recording that seemed to prove that Nixon's involvement in the Watergate cover-up was criminal in nature, did it become clear that the Senate would vote to convict, forcing his resignation.

Disability

The original Constitution, although it provided for presidential impeachment in a way that has made it almost impossible to achieve, at least spelled out a basis and a process for it. But when it came to the question of removal on grounds of disability, the language of the document, introduced by the Committee of Detail on August 6, was so vague as to be meaningless. "In case of the . . . inability [of the president] to discharge the Powers and Duties of the said Office," reads Article II, Section 1, "the Same shall devolve on the Vice President . . . until the Disability be removed, or a President shall be elected." "What is the extent of the term 'disability'?" John Dickinson asked the Convention on August 20, "and who is to be the judge of it?" No one answered him.

Lack of a definition or procedure for removal effectively left the nation without a leader for parts of eleven presidencies prior to 1967. James Garfield, who hovered near death for eighty days after he was shot (fatally, it turned out) in 1881, and Woodrow Wilson, an apparent invalid for the final seventeen months of his term, offered the most notorious examples.[77] In both instances, nearly everyone in Washington recognized that the president was disabled, but no one could find a way to transfer his authority to the vice president without appearing to be a usurper.

President Eisenhower's ailments—a heart attack in 1955, an ileitis attack and operation in 1956, and a stroke in 1957—finally brought matters to a head. In an age of nuclear confrontation, it was felt, the country could not run the risk of being leaderless even for an hour. His short-term solution was to write then-Vice President Nixon a public letter stating that if Eisenhower ever were disabled again, he would instruct the vice president to serve as acting president until the disability passed. If Eisenhower were unable to communicate for some reason, Nixon could make the decision himself. In either event, Eisenhower would decide when it was time to resume his powers.

Presidents Kennedy and Johnson endorsed this arrangement when they took office, but it hardly solved the problem. For one thing, a letter, even a presidential letter, lacks the force of law. Equally important, no provision was made to relieve a president who was disabled, perhaps mentally, but refused to admit it. Congress passed the Twenty-fifth Amendment in 1965 (hastened in its labors by the Kennedy assassination), and the necessary number of states ratified it by 1967.

Three very different situations are covered by the disability provisions of the Twenty-fifth Amendment. In the first the president is temporarily "unable to discharge the powers and duties of his office" and recognizes it. Such a situation could arise if the president's doctors advised him to rest during recovery from a stroke or similar malady, or if he were going to be anesthetized during surgery for a few hours. (It was just such an instance that prompted Eisenhower to comment, after he was under anesthesia for two hours, that "the country was without a Chief Executive, the armed forces without a Commander-in-Chief.")[78] In either case, the president would sign a letter to the president pro tempore of the Senate and the speaker of the House telling them he would be disabled. The vice president would then become acting president, assuming the full powers and duties of the presidency but not the office itself, until such time as the president signed another letter saying that he was restored.

The second situation that is anticipated by the Twenty-fifth Amendment is one in which the president is disabled but unable to say so, perhaps because he has gone suddenly unconscious. In this case the vice president or any head of an executive department could call a cabinet meeting to discuss the situation. If a majority of the heads of the executive departments declared that the president was disabled and the vice president agreed, the vice president would become acting president. When the president was once again able, he would write a letter to the congressional leaders and, within four days, resume office.

The amendment's provisions in these first two situations essentially ratified the Eisenhower letter. But what happens if the disability is in doubt, if the vice president and the cabinet say the president is disabled and the president says he is able? In many such instances (sudden blindness, suspected mental illness, or paralysis) there would be room for honest disagreement about whether a severe disability existed.

The Twenty-fifth Amendment deliberately gives no definition at all to the word "inability." It is clear from the congressional debates what inability is not—namely, unpopularity, incompetence, impeachable conduct, or laziness.

But as to what it is, it was thought best to leave that undefined so that those actually confronted with such a situation would not be bound by an incomplete or outdated definition written in 1965.[79] Thus, any decision regarding presidential disability is by its nature a subjective one.

Assuming then, that the vice president and a majority of the cabinet declared the president disabled and the president disagreed, Congress would decide who it thought was right, taking no longer than three weeks to do so. It may request that the president undergo tests or make himself available for questioning. If, within that three-week period, two-thirds of both the House and the Senate, voting separately, decided against the president, the vice president would continue to serve as acting president.

But even that would not necessarily be the end of it. For after Congress made its decision against him, the president could, in a day or a week or whenever, start the whole process over again by declaring that he was once again able. As many times as he did so, Congress would have to decide the issue again. The possibility of a half-crazed Lear stalking Washington and the nation, howling for vindication and tying up Congress for the rest of his term, is a real one. More dangerous, perhaps, would be the president whose mental disability, though known to his associates, could be disguised in carefully managed public appearances. The prospect of such a president rousing the public could prevent the cabinet from acting in the first place.

Similarly, if one-third plus one of either house of Congress sided with the president, there would be nothing to stop the vice president and cabinet from again declaring him disabled and throwing the issue back to Congress for another vote. The president could fire all the cabinet members and replace them with his supporters—Truman once said that if his cabinet removed him while he was flat on his back, his first act on rising would be to send them all packing.[80] But the Twenty-fifth Amendment leaves Congress an option. It is allowed, by simple majority vote of both houses, to create or designate a body to take the cabinet's place in making the decision. If this new body (which could be Congress itself or one of its committees) and the vice president agreed that the president should be removed, the issue would go back to Congress yet again.

It is one thing to be aware of all the things that could go wrong under the Twenty-fifth Amendment's disability provisions, should they ever be needed; it is something else to condemn it simply for not being absolutely air-tight. The assumption that underlies the amendment is the same assumption that underlies the entire Constitution: that people of reasonable good faith and judgment will be there to implement it. Like Gandhi, constitution makers realize the futility of trying to design "systems so perfect that men need not be good."

What is distressing, though, is that the amendment dismally failed its first real test, even though the test was a simple one. When Ronald Reagan was shot on March 30, 1981, it was clear to all, including himself, that he would be anesthetized in surgery for an indefinite period. International tensions were high. It seemed conceivable that Soviet troops might enter Poland at any time. Yet Reagan signed no letter that temporarily turned the powers and duties of the presidency over to Vice President George Bush.[81]

The first result was that once again "the country was without a Chief Executive; the armed forces without a Commander-in-Chief." The second was confusion at the White House over who really was in charge since Reagan was unconscious. After some angry squabbling in the cabinet, Secretary of State Alexander Haig appeared in public to say that he was "in control," at least until Bush's plane returned to Washington. But constitutionally, neither he nor anyone other than the incapacitated Reagan possessed the powers of the presidency during the hours of surgery and recuperation.

TERM AND REMOVAL: CONSEQUENCES

Removal of a president on grounds of disability is similar to removal by impeachment for reasons of "treason, bribery, or other High Crimes and Misdemeanors"; it is constitutionally possible but politically near-impossible. The Constitution's provisions for term and removal make it all but certain that a president who stays alive and willing can almost count on at least four years in office.

One traditional advantage of the four-year, "no cut" contract for presidents has been that they could take time to learn their job. As Richard Neustadt, among others, has argued, the first two years of a president's term is "a learning time for the new president who has to learn — or unlearn — many things about the job."[82] A second advantage has been that presidents could risk short-term unpopularity for the sake of pursuing sound but initially unpopular policies. Presidents would less likely be able to do this if they lived in fear that they would not be around to see the long run, because a vote of no confidence by the state legislatures, as was proposed at the Convention, or by the national legislature, as in parliamentary systems, would render them instantly unemployed.[83]

But the value of these advantages for presidents is waning. The "short" in short term is growing ever more brief. Election-year politics has always forced presidents to try to get their popularity up in the last six months of the fourth year of their term, but for reasons explained in Chapter 5 the modern president who wishes to be renominated by his party, much less reelected, needs to have his approval ratings in good shape by not much later than halfway through the third year of his term. If he cares about his party's fortunes in the midterm congressional elections, as most presidents do, he probably will not want to chance letting the risk-taking period in his administration run very much past the middle of the second year. Edward Tufte reports that almost as much economic "pump-priming" (the very opposite of long-term planning) goes on in the second as in the fourth year of a president's term.[84]

That leaves the first year or so as the only time left for real accomplishment. As Lyndon Johnson told his special counsel Harry McPherson:

> You've got to give it all you can that first year. Doesn't matter what kind of majority you come in with. You've got just one year when they treat you right, and before

they start worrying about themselves. The third year, you lose votes. . . . The fourth year's all politics.[85]

Johnson seems to have spoken for all recent presidents. In his study of presidential policy choice from Kennedy to Carter, Paul C. Light found that in every case presidents made more new legislative requests to Congress in their first year than in any other year. Further, a majority of each president's first-year requests came during his first five months in office.[86]

Aggravating the problem is the Twentieth Amendment, whose shortening of the transition period between election and inauguration by six weeks encourages haste as well as dispatch. New presidents are anxious to "hit the deck running," to move policies and personnel into position quickly while their honeymoon with Congress and the voters still is new. But speed of action in what Neustadt calls "the eleven-week scramble" may mean sloppily designed policies and the appointment of people who are not well known to the president.[87] The general dissatisfaction recent presidents have expressed with the loyalty and competence of their first-term cabinet and subcabinet appointees reflects in part the haste with which they made their appointments. As for policy, Alfred de Grazia has argued, often "'time saved' is time wasted: important decisions are badly made, consequences are not foreseen, opposing views are not taken into account, and remedial measures are sooner called for."[88]

In sum, the only time in his first administration that a president can afford to pursue wise but initially unpopular courses of action is the time when he is least likely to know which courses of action are wise. The first and second years of the second term are better suited to providing the traditional advantages of the fixed term (assuming the president achieves a second term), but the two-term limit usually makes his final two years a period of political weakness.

The tenure of most modern presidents seems relatively short in other ways. The Constitutional Convention envisioned a House of Representatives whose members would serve a term of two years, half that of the president. The idea was that the president would provide stability in contrast to the expected turbulence in the House. In truth, presidents tend to stay in office for much briefer times than House members. Even Eisenhower, the most recent two-term president, found in his eighth year that he still faced a House in which 62 percent of the members had served as long or longer than he had. A new president may find, as Nixon did in 1969, that all but 8 percent of the House membership already has been there for at least two years. Further, the gap between House and presidential tenure is growing. Presidents in the first part of the century tended to stay in office slightly longer than members of the House. But between 1961 and 1981 the average president served four years, the average House member ten to twelve, and the average senator almost that long. Because legislators stay on so much longer than presidents, their policy perspectives may be longer, less amenable to the sense of urgency that calendar-watching presidents seem so anxious to create.

Of the constitutionally prescribed methods for removing a president prematurely, impeachment and disability have accounted for the removal of none, resignation (by letter to the secretary of state) for one, and death by natural causes for four. A final method of premature presidential removal needs to be mentioned. Assassination not only has been the most frequent cause of presidential removal before the expiration of the term, it has accounted for almost as many removals — four — as all the constitutional methods combined.[89]

POWERS

The power of the presidency consists of a great deal more than the sum of the enumerated powers — "Commander in Chief of the Army and Navy," "receive[r of] Ambassadors," and so on — that are listed in the Constitution. Number and selection, term and removal — these structural characteristics of the office carry with them important implications for presidential power.

The framers, or at least the presidentialists among them, seem to have understood this well. This can be seen in the early history of the Convention. Shortly after Madison's Virginia Plan was offered, Wilson made a countermotion pertaining to the executive.[90] Madison's proposal was regarded as a plan for an executive weaker than the legislature, Wilson's as one that would make the executive the legislature's equal or superior. In truth the two plans differed greatly in their notions of how the executive should be structured. The Madisonian executive would have been chosen by the legislature for a single term and perhaps would have been plural in number; Wilson's unitary executive was to be eligible for continuing reelection by the people. But when it came to the stated powers of the executive, Wilson virtually copied the provisions of the Virginia Plan: "a general authority to execute the National laws"; a veto, to be shared with a council of judges; and "the Executive rights vested in Congress by the [Articles of] Confederation," which Madison defined as the "power . . . to appoint to offices in cases not otherwise provided for."[91] (See Table 2.4 on pages 42–43.) Clearly Wilson felt that presidential power would flow from constitutional provisions other than those pertaining to "powers."

But this position of Wilson's rested on his assumption that the powers of the legislature also would be loosely defined, thus creating a constitutional "free-fire zone" in which the two branches would contend for dominance in policy making, both foreign and domestic. The Committee of Detail, of which Wilson was a member, invalidated this assumption. Against Wilson's wishes, the committee decided to enumerate the powers of the legislature, which it christened "Congress."[92] This decision altered the presidentialists' strategy: if powers were to be enumerated after all, the presidency (which also got its name from the committee) would suffer if it did not get its share.

It would be wrong, of course, to suggest that the Convention enumerated powers for purely expeditious reasons. As Jeffrey Tulis argues, a political theory underlay the delegates' actions. They felt that the goals of "ensuring the protection of liberty or individual rights, . . . ensuring the security of the nation, and crafting policies that reflected popular will" could be served best by making each of the three branches "superior (though not the sole power) in its own sphere, and in its own way." The Court was to have primary responsibility for protecting rights, Congress for representing public opinion, and the president for national security. But Congress was to assume partial responsibility for national security, the president for reflecting the popular will, and both for safeguarding liberty.[93]

In the end the draft document produced by the Committee of Detail went far toward giving the presidency its "share" of the enumerated powers in both senses of the word. If Congress was empowered to "make all laws," the president still could report to it on "the state of the Union," recommend "such measures as he shall judge necessary and proper," convene it on "extraordinary occasions," and veto the laws it passed, subject to override by a two-thirds vote of each house. If Congress was charged "to make war" (later changed to "declare") and "subdue a rebellion in any State," the president nonetheless was to be commander in chief of the army, navy, and militia that actually would do the warmaking and subduing. Congress was to create the departments and appropriate their funds, but the president had the power to appoint their officers. And both branches could point to identical vesting clauses that were clear as to the constitutional basis of their powers:

> The legislative power shall be vested in a Congress.
> The Executive Power of the United States shall be vested in a single person . . . 'The President of the United States of America.'

The presidentialists' general satisfaction with the report of the Committee of Detail was tempered by their dislike of the preeminent role that the Senate was ordained to play both in foreign affairs (where it could "make treaties" and appoint ambassadors, leaving the president only to receive ambassadors from other nations), and in the courts, whose judges the Senate alone was to appoint. In this concern they found common cause with large-state delegates, who felt that the committee had gone too far in its effort to accommodate the small states by excessively empowering "their" part of the government. In floor action the proexecutive forces helped the large-state delegates to pry loose exclusive control of the treaty-making and appointment powers from the Senate. The large-staters returned the favor by helping to turn initiative in the exercise of these powers over to the president (leaving the Senate to accept or reject executive proposals).[94] The committee also authorized the president to "require the Opinion, in writing" of the heads of the executive departments. This was not all the presidentialists had wanted — Morris and Charles Pinckney had proposed a complete constitutional organization of national administration on the basis of clear control by the president — but it added some weight to the presidency's claim to superintendence of administration.[95]

Morris tossed another "joker," as historian Charles Thach called it, into the Constitution in his capacity as chief draftsman for the Committee of Style, whose charge was to put the Constitution into smooth language. "Positively with respect to the executive article," notes Thach, Morris "could do nothing." All eyes were on him, aware of his personal biases. So Morris left the vesting clause of Article II intact and quietly altered the corresponding clause of Article I to read: "All legislative powers *herein granted* shall be vested in a Congress of the United States." (Emphasis added.) Thach suspects that Morris did his

Table 2.4 The Development of the Constitutional Presidency: Powers and Institutional Separation

	Virginia Plan	Constitutional Convention (1787)			Committee of Style – Final Draft
		Committee of the Whole House	Committee of Detail	Committee on Postponed Matters	
POWERS	• Veto[1] by a "council of revision" consisting of "the executive and a convenient number of judges." Legislature could override by repassing the bill • Execute the national laws • "The Executive rights vested in Congress by the Confederation"	• Veto by the executive alone. Legislature could override by repassing the bill with a two-thirds vote in each house[2] • "Appoint to Offices in cases not otherwise provided for"	• "The executive Power . . . shall be vested in a [President of the United States of America]" • "Appoint officers in all cases not otherwise provided for by this Constitution" • "From time to time" give "information" to Congress on "the State of the Union" • "Recommend" to Congress "such Measures as he shall judge necessary and expedient" • "Convene" Congress on "extraordinary occasions" and adjourn it when its houses cannot adjourn themselves	• Appoint officers in all cases not otherwise provided for by this Constitution" • "Make treaties," subject to ratification of two-thirds of Senate • Nominate Supreme Court justices and ambassadors, subject to Senate approval • "Require the Opinion in writing" of department heads • "Preserve, protect, and defend the Constitution," by oath	• Appoint all officers except those which Congress "may by Law vest . . . in the courts of Law, or in the Heads of Departments"

INSTITUTIONAL SEPARATION			
•No member of the legislature shall hold another office during his term or for an unspecified number of years after *•The legislature cannot alter an incumbent executive's salary*	•No member of the legislature shall hold another office during his term or, in the case of national office, for a year after	*•"Receive Ambassadors" and "correspond with the supreme Executives of the several states"* *•"Grant reprieves and pardons"* *•"Commander-in-Chief of the Army and Navy" and "state militia"* •No member of the legislature shall hold another office during his term or, in the case of senators, for a year after	•No member of the legislature shall hold another office during his term

¹Italic type indicates that the final decision on the issue was made at this point.
²The legislative vote needed to override was raised to three-fourths on August 23, then reduced back to two-thirds on September 12.

43

tinkering "with full realization of the possibilities" — namely, that presidents later could claim that the different phrasing of the branches' vesting clauses implies that there is an executive power beyond that "herein granted," else why would the Constitution not apply those restricting words to the president? "At any rate," Thach concludes, "whether intentional or not, it admitted an interpretation of executive power which would give to the president a field of action wider than that outlined by the enumerated powers."[96]

The history of the Convention's decisions concerning powers usually is recounted as a march of executive progress from few powers to many. Certainly more executive activities are referred to in the Constitution than in the Virginia Plan. But there also are more references to legislative powers. In truth, as Wilson seems to have realized, the primary consequence of the decision to enumerate the powers of the two branches was that the presidentialists had to fight continuously to get back to where they had been in the Virginia Plan, in which powers had been referred to in very general language. With powers unspecified it was assumed that they were shared, the nature of the sharing to be revealed only by experience. After the process of enumeration was over, it was known that they were shared; but the nature of the sharing still was not known. Whatever the framers' intentions about the primary responsibility of the two political branches, the free-fire zone between president and Congress remained unoccupied.

INSTITUTIONAL SEPARATION

The various decisions that blurred the responsibilities of president and Congress were accompanied by related decisions, made at the start of the Convention and substantially unaltered, to keep the institutional line between the two branches clear and absolute. The main constitutional provision was clear: no member of one branch could simultaneously hold an office in the other.[97] (In the same spirit, Congress could not alter an incumbent president's salary.) So was the reason behind the provision: fear of corruption such as that the delegates had seen in Great Britain, which drew no such boundary. Butler, for example, "appealed to the example of G. B. where men got into Parlt. that they might get offices for themselves or their friends" and where George III, to further his goals, "put some of [his opponents] out of the house of commons [and] made [them] lords."[98]

To presidentialists, the risk of corruption was worth taking in order to give the president some leverage in Congress. John Mercer of Maryland warned hyperbolically that to "deprive him of influence by rendering the members of the Legislature ineligible to Executive offices" would reduce the president to "a mere phantom of authority."[99] But their frequent efforts to reverse the Convention's initial decision were unavailing. The most important enduring effect of their failure has been to foreclose the possibility for ministerial government in which the president, if so disposed, could forge a link with the legislative branch by choosing his cabinet from the sitting membership of Congress.

POWERS AND INSTITUTIONAL
SEPARATION: CONSEQUENCES

The framers, then, designed a system that amounted not to separation of powers, but "separated institutions sharing powers." The phrase is Neustadt's, as is the understanding it represents — namely, that because powers are shared by an institutionally distinct president and Congress, there are powerful limits to what a president can do to exercise his constitutionally enumerated powers without the acquiescence of the other branch that shares those powers with him. Such acquiescence, Neustadt argues, usually will come only through bargaining. For a president to move members of Congress in support of his policies, he must "induce them to believe that what he wants of them is what their own appraisal of their own responsibilities requires them to do in their interest, not his."[100]

As this discussion has shown, Neustadt is right in his characterization of the American constitutional system and in his emphasis on devices that promote interbranch cooperation, including presidential bargaining. But the history of the national government shows that there is more to it than that. The boundaries of presidential power have not shifted back and forth purely according to the bargaining skills of incumbents or other presidential leadership skills. Nor have they remained constant, fixed eternally by the constitutional design of government as a building is fixed by the architect's design. Indeed, a few years after the framers' plan moved from parchment to practice, the presidency found itself an extremely weak office.

It took the first 125 years of American political history under the Constitution for all the enumerated powers of the presidency even to be enlivened. The history of how this happened, important in its own right, also illustrates the theme of this book: that although both the Constitution and individual leadership skills are by themselves important, it is only by understanding the dynamic interplay between them and a third force, culture and politics, that we can comprehend presidential power in the American political system. In Chapters 3 and 4 we will explore a different kind of interplay between these forces in the modern presidency. First, however, we need to see how, through the invigoration of its constitutionally enumerated powers, the modern presidency came to be.

FROM PARCHMENT TO PRACTICE, 1789–1913

"The Constitution," writes James Sundquist, "put two combatants in the ring and sounded the bell that sent them into endless battle."[101] Certainly the presidency was not a very powerful combatant during the third of a century that followed George Washington's tenure in the office.[102] Although the Constitution had given the president several toeholds in the legislative process (the veto, limited rights to adjourn and convene Congress, the obligation to report to Congress on the state of the union and to "recommend to their Consideration such Measures as he shall judge necessary and expedient"), Congress dominated the lawmaking process through most of this period, disdaining any real presidential involvement. James Sterling Young records the power of the "separated institutions" ethic:

> Etiquette forbade the Chief Executive to set foot inside the legislative compound for any purpose but inauguration, attending at a few other ceremonial functions, and to sign bills on the last day of the session, the last being an accommodation to Congress. . . . [C]onfinement in the White House was a rule never broken by any Jeffersonian President for missions of persuasion, political negotiation, or leadership to Capitol Hill.[103]

Even the veto power was rendered almost meaningless: presidents were enjoined to use it only if they felt a legislative act to be unconstitutional, not when they simply disagreed with it. Three of the first six presidents cast no vetoes at all.

Congress also vitiated the presidency's constitutional powers over administration. While exercising its own share of this shared power to the utmost, Congress not only defined the structure of the executive branch by statute, it itemized every office in each of the departments and agencies it created and fixed the salary of every employee. Thomas Jefferson found that only 600 of the federal government's 2,700 civilian positions were his alone to fill. Congress had entrusted the postmaster general with more appointments than the president. The best domestic jobs — department heads, United States attorneys, and territorial governors — required Senate confirmation, which meant realistically that most "presidential" appointments went to members of Congress, ex-members, and their friends. Even cabinet members (desirous of the nomination for president that a caucus of the congressional party alone gave at that time) resisted the president's leadership. When James Monroe invoked his constitutional power to "require the Opinion, in writing" of his department heads and asked the cabinet not to send departmental messages to Capitol Hill before clearing them with him, he was greeted with general silence, then told by a secretary that their practice had existed "ever since the establishment of Government" and presumably would continue.[104]

Only in foreign affairs did the president's constitutionally enumerated powers seem to have any life. The clause that empowered the president to "receive Ambassadors," for example, became in practice a right to decide which foreign governments the United States would recognize; the power to appoint ambassadors, unlike the other appointment powers, was real.[105] Nor was the president's leadership in the treaty-making process usually challenged. Congress readily confirmed the Jay Treaty, the treaty to purchase Louisiana, and several dozen others. It even assented to certain unilateral presidential assertions of foreign policy, such as the Monroe Doctrine.

Foreign affairs aside, the early history of the federal government was so much one of congressional domination that it seems almost misleading for historians to present it in terms of presidential administrations. The reason for executive weakness can be found in the cultural and political environment of the day. Americans wanted very little from their national government. The number and selection-based constitutional strengths of the presidency — its ability to act with energy and dispatch and claim the justification of a national constituency for doing so — were irrelevant because there was no popular desire for quick and decisive federal action. Foreign affairs was the exception because the political environment that surrounded that policy area was uniquely amenable to presidential power. The United States felt a real threat to its security from the European powers and thus a need to allow the president flexibility and license in acting.

Could skill — the leadership choices and abilities of individual presidents — make a difference in such an environment? Only temporarily. Washington's leadership in most matters of government was accepted by Congress, but his charismatic authority made him singular in that regard. Jefferson was a skillful leader. His skills, however, also were exceptional in ways that affirm the general rule. To the extent that Jefferson led Congress, he did so with such sleight of hand as to persuade legislators that they were not being led at all. He had agents on Capitol Hill who advanced his proposals, but their success depended on their association with Jefferson being kept confidential. (When they were found out, their colleagues branded them with such epithets as "toads that live upon the vapor of the palace.")[106] Further, Jefferson's legislative proposals generally involved the reduction of federal power — a smaller military, a decrease in the national debt, the abolition of direct taxation, and the like — which hardly challenged the thinking of the day. When Jefferson left office, the office he left was no stronger than when he had entered.

For the next president of strong will and ability, conditions were different. Andrew Jackson, like Jefferson, wanted to dominate the government. But changes in the political environment gave him advantages his predecessors had lacked. The popular base of American politics had broadened, both socially and geographically. By 1828, presidential electors commonly were chosen by vote of the people rather than by the state legislatures. The suffrage now belonged to virtually all white males, not just those who owned property. Many of them had moved into frontier states such as Jackson's Tennessee. They ignored the congressional caucus method of nominating presidential candidates in 1824 and soon replaced it with grass-roots party nominating conventions. The new electorate still did not look to Washington for much in the way of positive programs to better their lot, but they did begin turning to it for protection against eastern social and financial power.

Jackson rallied these new expectations in support of his efforts to revive some heretofore dormant constitutionally enumerated presidential powers. In his first annual message to Congress, Jackson attacked the "corruption," "perversion," and "indifference" of an administrative system dominated by eastern elites, then declared his fabled policy of rotation in office, or "spoils." His vigorous firing and hiring of federal civil servants both made the government more representative of the nation as a whole and involved more people in it, which further contributed to the establishing of a popular constituency for the presidency. Jackson replaced more presidential officers than his predecessors combined had in twenty years.[107]

Jackson also vetoed more bills than all the first six presidents, often because he simply disliked their content. Jackson's veto of the bill to recharter the Second Bank of the United States in 1832 offers the most dramatic example. "Though addressed to Congress," observes Wilfred Binkley, "the veto message was an appeal to the nation. Not a single opportunity to discredit the old ruling class was missed. . . . So adroitly was it phrased that the common man saw in it the apt expression of his own sentiments."[108] Equally significant is what happened some months after the veto. Jackson, interpreting his landslide victory in the 1832 election as an endorsement of his action and not content to wait the legally specified four years for the bank's original charter to expire, ordered the secretary of the treasury to withdraw all federal deposits from it immediately. This was as direct a challenge to Congress's control of administration as Jackson could have devised: it required the treasury secretary, whose department Congress traditionally had considered to be uniquely its domain, to defy a legislative act in obedience to an order by the president. Secretary W. J. Duane refused. Jackson fired him and appointed Roger Taney, who willingly obeyed.

Presidents prior to Jackson had realized that the result of behavior such as this would be congressional retaliation so debilitating as to render the initial victory pyrrhic at best. The Senate did, in fact, pass a stinging resolution that censured Jackson. But because of the changes that had taken place in the political environment and Jackson's skill at capitalizing on them, the result of this action was far different than it would have been in the past. Jackson and his partisans successfully pressured one state legislature after another to demand the resignation of senators who had voted for the censure resolution. Not long after, in an historic *mea culpa*, the Senate voted to literally "draw black lines round said resolves, and write across the face thereof in strong letters the following word: Expunged."[109]

Jefferson's skills had been tactical skills of bargaining with Congress; Jackson's were primarily rhetorical and aimed at the public. Jefferson's administration left no enduring mark on presidential power; Jackson's did. One indication of just how much things had changed for the presidency can be found in the fulminations of Jackson's opponents. "The American elective monarchy frightens me," wrote Chancellor Kent to Justice Story. "The experiment, with its foundations laid on universal suffrage . . . is of too violent a nature for our excitable people." "A Briareus sits in the centre of our system," lamented Daniel Webster, "and with his hundred hands touches everything, controls everything."[110] But the real test of the presidency's new power position came later, when John Tyler, a weak, unpopular president, exercised these same powers of veto, appointment, and removal and got away with it. If further indication of the enhanced importance of the presidency was needed, it came in 1860, when, in response to the mere election of a president who was only thought to be hostile to slavery, seven southern states seceded.

Lincoln's election did more than reflect presidential power; it set in motion events that would enhance that power. In prosecuting the war Lincoln exercised his constitutional power as commander in chief in an unprecedentedly direct and vigorous way; he was, in more than one historian's assessment, the Union's greatest general. Lincoln also exercised prerogative powers not specified in the Constitution. Among other things, he suspended the writ of habeas corpus, declared martial law, increased the size of the army and navy beyond the levels authorized by Congress, spent money that Congress had not appropriated, and freed the slaves by a simple unilateral proclamation of their emancipation. Congress, an essentially one-party Republican body after secession, acquiesced in all these decisions. Finding itself in agreement with Lincoln's ends, Congress conceded the presidency's institutional superiority in the matter of deciding and executing suitable means to achieve them.

Lincoln justified his extraordinary actions in a variety of ways, many of them rooted in specific reference to constitutional language. Tactical as well as rhetorical skills sustained his leadership; no president used spoils as a bargaining chip for congressional influence more than Lincoln. But his most forthright defense of what he had done on behalf of the Union was Lockean in sentiment, if not language. In a public letter to a Kentucky newspaper editor, he wrote:

> My oath to preserve the Constitution to the best of my ability imposed on me the duty of preserving, by every indispensable means, that government — that nation, of which that Constitution was the organic law. Was it possible to lose the nation and yet preserve the Constitution? By general law, life and limb must be protected, yet often a limb must be amputated to save a life; but a life is never wisely given to protect a limb. I felt that measures otherwise unconstitutional might become lawful by becoming indispensable to the preservation of the Constitution through the preservation of the nation. Right or wrong, I assume this ground, and now avow it.[111]

Lincoln's words suggested that there was, after all, inherent "executive power" to be found in the first sentence of Article II beyond those detailed in the Constitution. His actions meant that a precedent (and an expectation) had been set for strong and prompt presidential action not only in time of war, but in any nation-threatening emergency, in the broadest sense of the term.

As after the Jackson presidency, action brought reaction: a period of congressional ascendancy, albeit within the new bounds of expanded presidential power. After the Civil War, Congress developed and enacted a program of Reconstruction, a feat of comprehensive, sustained policy making unmatched in its history. Though never reaching this zenith of power again, Congress continued to dominate the presidency through the rest of the century, a period that was described in 1881 by Johns Hopkins political scientist Woodrow Wilson as one of "congressional government."[112] Congressional initiative prompted 78 percent of the major items of legislation enacted between 1870 and 1900, found Lawrence Chamberlain; presidential initiative underlay only 8 percent.[113] Much of this was due to the dramatically increased power of Congress's own leadership, especially the speaker of the House.

But even as Congress reigned, several developments were taking place in the late-nineteenth-century political environment that set the stage for the next quantum leap in the living powers of the presidency. One was the rise of corporate power in a newly national economy. This was to produce ever-growing popular demands on the federal government for positive programs of welfare and regulation that would protect workers and consumers from the bad side-effects of a corporate economy. A second was the simultaneous glorification in business and in society generally of executive leadership. The success of entrepreneurs such as Rockefeller, Carnegie, and Vanderbilt seemed to show that all great things began with executive power and initiative, and the developing "scientific management" school of business and public administration argued that success endured through such leadership too. There were, in addition, the rise of the Progressive movement in revulsion against corrupt politics, which it tended to associate with legislatures, and a series of Supreme Court decisions that took a very expansive view of presidential power.[114]

These developments taken together served to enhance the status of executives in comparison to legislators. In so doing they helped to pave the way for Theodore Roosevelt, the next strong-willed, politically skillful president, as did the fact that in 1901 both houses of Congress were controlled by the president's party, a rare occurrence in preceding decades. Roosevelt offered the most expansive view of presidential power in ordinary times yet heard. He viewed the president as

> a steward of the people bound actively and affirmatively to do all he could for the people, and not to content himself with keeping his talents undamaged in a napkin. . . . My belief was that it was not only his right but his duty to do anything that the needs of the nation demanded unless such action was forbidden by the Constitution or by the law.[115]

Roosevelt's bold actions matched his theory. He ordered the transformation of public lands into national forests, intensified antitrust prosecution efforts, "took the [Panama] Canal Zone and let Congress debate," ordered the naval fleet on an around-the-world sail, and dared Congress not to appropriate the money to finance its return home. But his major innovation as president was to enliven a long-dormant enumerated power of the presidency for which he did have "specific authorization to do it" from the Constitution: to recommend legislation to Congress. Roosevelt was alternately bold and modest in doing this. He was the first president to speak of "my policies," but his public advice to Congress usually was quite general and his modus operandi discreet: he and Speaker Joseph Cannon would confer privately, and if Cannon approved of some idea Roosevelt was proposing, it would be sent from the White House to Capitol Hill. But a way had been found around the barrier between president and Congress that had obstructed so long the legislative process in noncrisis times. And the public began to expect such presidential involvement. Analyzing the unsuccessful presidency of Roosevelt's successor, a newspaper editor wrote that "failure to dominate Congress was Mr. [William Howard] Taft's chief shortcoming in the public mind."[116]

Building on Roosevelt's precedent and the public's new expectations, and animated by a clear agenda of policy goals, Woodrow Wilson was able to transform presidential involvement in the legislative process into presidential leadership. As a scholar, Wilson had noted that although "the President is at liberty, both in law and conscience, to be as big a man as he can, . . . [he] has no means of compelling Congress except through public opinion."[117] But the public could not be rallied through quiet discussion with congressional leaders; besides, there no longer were any leaders of Cannon's influence. In 1913,

Wilson took his "New Freedom" legislative platform directly to Capitol Hill, where he appeared on the floor of the House (the first president in more than one hundred years to do so) to "give to the Congress information of the State of the Union" and urge that his bills be enacted. His real audience for these speeches was the electorate, which having chosen an overwhelmingly Democratic Congress in 1912, now was roused to pressure it to follow Wilson's lead. Congress did; rhetorical skill had enlivened another enumerated power. And when the United States entered World War I, Congress passed the Overman Act, whose effect was to give the president the kind of emergency powers that Lincoln previously had seized.

Wilson's success as "chief legislator" marked a milestone in the history of the presidency. After a century and a quarter of American political history under the Constitution there was not a single enumerated power of the office that had not been inaugurated successfully by some skilled and willful president and, because of changes in the cultural and political environment, accepted by Congress and the public. Practice at last conformed with theory. Nothing demonstrates this better than the events of the inevitable period of retrenchment — the "return to normalcy" — that followed the Roosevelt-Wilson–spawned burst of presidential power. Warren Harding, Calvin Coolidge, and Herbert Hoover all were weak presidents, to be sure, but new-style weak presidents now did things as a matter of course that once had been considered outrageously bold. Harding, for example, carried the day on a soldier's bonus bill by speaking to the Senate in its chamber; Coolidge recommended and vetoed bills freely; and Hoover's legislative initiatives took the presidency deeper into the nation's economic life than ever before, however modest those efforts may seem in retrospect.

SUMMARY AND CONCLUSION

The decisions of the Constitution's framers and, later, its amenders about the number and method of selecting the executive, its term and susceptibility to removal, and its powers and institutional distinctiveness have had important and enduring effects. One understanding that grows from close examination of these decisions and their practical consequences concerns presidential power: almost every such decision both raised high the power of the presidency and, simultaneously, made it more vulnerable. A second understanding has to do with the nature of presidential reform, which commonly has had consequences that were unintended as well as intended.

Power and Vulnerability

Each of the three clusters of decisions made by the framers turned out in practice to have "raised the stakes" for the presidency: more power, greater risks. Taken as a whole, the Constitution sets the bounds within which the varying effects of culture, politics, and skill are felt.

Number and Selection. By making the presidency a unitary, nationally elected office, the framers combined in it the roles of chief of government and chief of state. In doing so, they placed at the disposal of the nation's political leader its people's intense feeling of patriotism. But they also made him the object of the contradictory expectations that attend these two roles. Similarly, the number and selection decisions, while in effect empowering the president to exercise prerogative to meet unusual crises, also made him vulnerable to criticism if his actions were deemed unsuccessful or inappropriate.

Term and Removal.   The term and removal provisions of the Constitution all but guarantee the president a span of time in which he can try to succeed without fear of removal. Their definition of that time as four years, however, has come to seem ever more brief.

Separated Institutions Sharing Powers.   Presidents from 1789 to 1913 struggled long and hard to enliven the enumerated powers of their office. In all cases they succeeded, eventually to the point where the presidency gained the initiative, if not always the upper hand, over the institutionally distinct Congress. As a result, the public's expectations that presidents will exercise the powers of the federal government successfully have been raised. In 1820, a time of severe economic depression, President James Monroe realistically had no power to initiate measures to alleviate distress; in 1932, President Herbert Hoover did. But voters in 1820 did not expect the president to do anything; indeed, they reelected Monroe with the greatest electoral vote margin in history (231 to 1). Hoover, who faced a public whose expectations were much higher, lost by the greatest electoral vote margin of any president up to his time. Franklin Roosevelt, Hoover's successor, stretched the powers of the presidency and the federal government in ways that met voter expectations about the economy and was rewarded with reelection.

Limits of Institutional Reform

The framers designed an executive that, on the whole, has fulfilled their basic goals: it was politically acceptable to the state ratifying conventions and has been strong but not oppressive in practice. When one considers the atmosphere of philosophical and historical uncertainty about executive power in which they labored, this achievement seems all the more remarkable.

Reformers often point to the framers' success as evidence that institutional tinkering can bring about desired goals. Yet, curious as it may seem, it was the framers' efforts to engineer specific results through particular constitutional provisions that were least successful. Any number of devices were included in the Constitution for the purpose of keeping people of defective "character" out of the presidency, but to little avail. Within a few years of the Constitution's ratification, legislative selection through the congressional caucus, which the Convention had rejected so painstakingly, became the norm, only to be succeeded by mass selection, which also had been scorned. The framers' notion of

Congress as the primary vehicle for representing the popular will was dismissed out of hand by Jackson, who claimed the mantle of tribune of the people for himself and for all presidents who, like him, had been nationally elected.

Efforts to bring about specific changes through the amendment process also have been notably successful. The Twelfth Amendment cleared up the confusion about how to fill the vice presidency, but it also rendered incumbents of that office politically impotent by taking away their claim to an electoral base. The Twentieth Amendment, which advanced the inauguration date, was meant to strengthen the presidency by getting lame-duck incumbents out and newly elected presidents in more quickly. One effect, however, has been to rush presidents into early decisions that later return to haunt them.

Similarly, it is by no means self-evident that the two-term limit imposed by the Twenty-second Amendment has had the desired effect of limiting presidential power. For one thing, it never really needed limiting of a kind that a term restriction could give. Of the thirty pre-Roosevelt presidents, only one, Ulysses S. Grant, seemed anxious for a third elective term. (Twenty never even made it to a second.) There also is the testimony of recent ex-presidents such as Eisenhower, Johnson, and Carter, each of whom has spoken out for a constitutional amendment that would limit the president to a single term of six years. Their argument has been that lame-duck status would be a small price to pay for the added power they feel that freedom from reelection pressures would give them.

Efforts to alter the boundaries of presidential power by statute also have been notably unsuccessful. For example, attempts to revive the plural executive principle as a means of limiting the presidency have had exactly the opposite effect in practice. At the Convention, Wilson's proposal for the presidency included, as did the Virginia Plan, a Council of Revision or committee of judges with which the executive would share its decision to veto legislation. Wilson saw this gesture in the direction of a plural executive not as a mechanism to constrain the presidency, but as a source of power for it. The support of the judges, he reasoned, would help to legitimate veto decisions and thus buttress executive power.

Wilson probably was correct in his reasoning, and his fellow delegates eventually turned down his bogus plural executive as firmly as they turned down Randolph's real one. Latter-day congressionalists have not been as astute. The Eightieth Congress, for example, created a National Security Council and a Council of Economic Advisers in the expectation that they would force the president (especially Democratic President Truman) to share his power to make economic and security decisions with "experts." In practice, the influence of both councils has depended almost entirely on the president's willingness to consult them, which in turn has usually depended on their willingness to support him.[118] Ironically, the closest the presidency has come in practice to the original plural executive idea is the modern White House staff, a presidential creation that politically sensitive chief executives nonetheless find must include the requisite liaisons to labor, business, women, minorities, and other powerful interest groups.[119] Because the loyalty of the liaison staffer usually is as much to the interest group as to the president, the latter often feels hemmed in in a manner not unlike that desired by Randolph.

Two more recent efforts to confine by legislation the bounds of prerogative also may turn out to have the opposite effect. The War Powers Act of 1973, an attempt to restrain military actions by the executive, requires a president either to secure Congress's approval of his order to send American soldiers into combat within sixty days or to withdraw them. In so doing, however, the law actually recognizes for the first time a power of the presidency to make war unilaterally. As for the sixty-day review period, experience shows that to be the time when military actions are likely to be at the height of their popularity and thus most likely to secure congressional approbation.[120] In 1974, Congress passed the Budget and Impoundment Control Act, again for the purpose of preventing prerogatory acts. In this case, the target was presidential refusals to spend money that Congress had appropriated, and the remedy was a congressional budget process that would provide Congress for the first time with a mechanism to determine a spending level for the entire federal budget. (In the past, the overall figure simply was the sum of the dozen or more separate appropriations bills Congress passed each year.) Again, this has become an occasional new source of power for presidents, especially those whose goal is to reduce the budget. Under the new system, as Ronald Reagan showed in 1981, a president who can move Congress on a few important votes per year in effect can write the budget.

Presidential power is, to be sure, influenced by law and Constitution. Were it not, the temptation to reform — with a six-year term, an item veto, a quasi-parliamentary election system, or some other remedy — would not be so great. But the precise calculations that underlie institutional tinkering are seldom accurate. The problems of presidential power, like all aspects of presidential power, are rooted not just in the institution, but in the cultural and political environment and the skills of individual presidents that we discuss in the next two chapters.

NOTES

1. Even this stipulation is not wholly unambiguous. Does thirty-five refer to the time of election or of inauguration? Probably election, according to Edward S. Corwin, *The President: Office and Powers*, 4th ed. (New York: New York University Press, 1957), p. 32.
2. Richard E. Neustadt, *Presidential Power*, 3rd ed. (New York: Wiley, 1980), p. 26.
3. John P. Roche, "The Founding Fathers: A Reform Caucus in Action," *American Political Science Review* (December 1961), p. 799. Clinton Rossiter suggests one reason why the level of consensus was so high: "The largest factor in determining [the Convention's] make-up was, quite simply, free choice: those who were there wanted to be there, and, with [a] few glaring exceptions, . . . they wanted to be there to give a boost to the nation." *1787: The Grand Convention* (London: MacGibbon and Kee, 1968), p. 141.
4. So, to an extent not always recognized, was political theory. Louis Fisher, *President and Congress* (New York: Free Press, 1972), ch. 1.
5. William C. Mitchell, "The Ambivalent Social Status of the American Politician," *Western Political Quarterly* (September 1959), pp. 683–98; Roberta S. Sigel and David J. Butler, "The Public and the No Third Term Tradition: Inquiry into Atti-

tudes Toward Power," *Midwest Journal of Political Science* (February 1964), pp. 39–54.

6. Seymour Martin Lipset, *The First New Nation* (New York: Basic Books, 1963), ch. 1; Max Weber, *The Theory of Social and Economic Organization* (New York: Oxford University Press, 1947), p. 358.

7. Marcus Cunliffe, *George Washington: Man and Monument* (New York: New American Library, 1958), p. 15.

8. Max Farrand, *The Records of the Federal Convention of 1787* (New Haven: Yale University Press, 1966), Vol. I, p. 65.

9. *Ibid.*, p. 292.

10. Catherine Drinker Bowen, *Miracle at Philadelphia* (Boston: Little, Brown, 1966), p. 55.

11. Farrand, *Records*, Vol. I, p. 66.

12. *Ibid.*, p. 65.

13. An electoral-college–style method of presidential selection was approved on July 19, then rejected once again on July 24. Charles C. Thach, Jr., *The Creation of the Presidency, 1775–1789* (Baltimore: Johns Hopkins University Press, 1923), pp. 101–2.

14. Farrand, *Records*, Vol. II, p. 30.

15. John P. Roche, "The Electoral College: A Note on American Political Mythology," *Dissent* (Spring 1961), p. 198.

16. Clinton Rossiter, ed., *The Federalist Papers* (New York: New American Library, 1961), Nos. 64 and 68, pp. 390–96, 411–15.

17. *Ibid.*, p. 391.

18. Thach, *Creation*, p. 137.

19. Richard P. McCormick, *The Presidential Game: The Origins of American Presidential Politics* (New York: Oxford University Press, 1982), pp. 22–23.

20. Farrand, *Records*, Vol. II, p. 537.

21. *Ibid.*

22. Wilfred E. Binkley, *President and Congress*, 3rd ed. (New York: Vintage, 1962), ch. 1.

23. Clinton Rossiter, *The American Presidency*, rev. ed. (New York: New American Library, 1960), p. 15.

24. Fred Greenstein, "The Benevolent Leader: Children's Images of Political Authority," *American Political Science Review* (December 1960), pp. 934–44. Cf. Dean Jaros *et al.*, "The Malevolent Leader: Political Socialization in an American Subculture," *American Political Science Review* (June 1968), pp. 564–75, and F. Christoper Arterton, "The Impact of Watergate on Children's Attitudes Toward Political Authority," *Political Science Quarterly* (June 1979), pp. 269–88.

25. Paul B. Sheatsley and Jacob J. Feldman, "The Assassination of President Kennedy: Public Reactions," *Public Opinion Quarterly* (Summer 1964), pp. 197–202.

26. *Ibid.*, p. 197.

27. *Ibid.*, pp. 208–10.

28. Sebastian de Grazia, *The Political Community* (Chicago: University of Chicago Press, 1948), pp. 112–15.

29. Fred Greenstein, "The Benevolent Leader Revisited: Children's Images of Political Leaders in Three Democracies," *American Political Science Review* (December 1975), p. 1380.

30. Rossiter, *Presidency*, pp. 16–17.

31. Samuel Kernell *et al.*, "Public Support for Presidents," in Aaron Wildavsky, ed., *Perspectives on the Presidency* (Boston: Little, Brown, 1975), p. 178.

32. John Mueller, *War, Presidents and Public Opinion* (New York: Wiley, 1973), pp. 69–74, 122–40.

33. Jong R. Lee, "Rally Round the Flag: Foreign Policy Events and Presidential Popularity," *Presidential Studies Quarterly* (Fall 1977), p. 255.

34. George H. Gallup, *The Gallup Poll, 1935–1971* (New York: Random House, 1972), Vol. I, p. 388.

35. *Ibid.*, Vol. III, p. 2222.
36. Jimmy Carter's approval rating rose from 32 percent at the time of the Iranian hostage seizure to 61 percent a month later. *Gallup Opinion Index* (October–November 1980).
37. George H. Gallup, *The Gallup Poll, 1972–1977* (Wilmington: Scholarly Research, 1978), Vol. I, pp. 234–37.
38. Thomas Cronin, "The Presidency and Its Paradoxes," in Thomas Cronin and Rexford Tugwell, eds., *The Presidency Reappraised*, 2nd ed. (New York: Praeger, 1977), pp. 69–85.
39. James David Barber, "Man, Mood, and the Presidency," in Rexford G. Tugwell and Thomas E. Cronin, eds., *The Presidency Reappraised* (New York: Praeger, 1974), pp. 205–14. See also James David Barber, *The Pulse of Politics* (New York: Norton, 1980).
40. Bruce Buchanan, *The Presidential Experience* (Englewood Cliffs, N.J.: Prentice-Hall, 1978), pp. 7, 23.
41. Robert H. Ferrell, ed., *Off the Record: The Private Papers of Harry S. Truman* (New York: Harper & Row, 1980), p. 270.
42. John Locke, *The Second Treatise on Government* (Indianapolis: Bobbs-Merrill, 1952), pp. 91–96.
43. Rossiter, *Federalist*, No. 41, p. 257.
44. Farrand, *Records*, Vol. I, pp. 66, 70.
45. Rossiter, *Federalist*, No. 74, p. 449.
46. Joseph M. Bessette and Jeffrey Tulis, "The Constitution, Politics, and the Presidency," in Joseph M. Bessette and Jeffrey Tulis, eds., *The Presidency in the Constitutional Order* (Baton Rouge: Louisiana State University Press, 1981), p. 21.
47. A. S. Klieman, "Preparing for the Hour of Need: Emergency Powers in the United States," *Review of Politics* (April 1979), pp. 235–55.
48. Richard M. Pious, *The American Presidency* (New York: Basic Books, 1979), ch. 2.
49. 343 U.S. 579 (1952).
50. Farrand, *Records*, Vol. I, p. 101.
51. *Ibid.*, Vol. III, p. 302.
52. Jeffrey Tulis, "On Presidential Character," in Bessette and Tulis, *Presidency in the Constitutional Order*, p. 287.
53. Rossiter, *Federalist*, Nos. 71 and 72, pp. 431–40.
54. James David Barber, *The Presidential Character*, 2nd ed. (Englewood Cliffs, N.J.: Prentice-Hall, 1977), ch. 1.
55. Tulis, "Character," pp. 293–301; Barber, *Character*, pp. 13–14, 17–18, 146, chs. 7–10.
56. Alexander George, "Assessing Presidential Character," *World Politics* (January 1974), pp. 234–82.
57. Erwin C. Hargrove, "Presidential Personality and Revisionist Views of the Presidency," *Midwest Journal of Political Science* (November 1973), pp. 819–35; Michael Nelson, "The Psychological Presidency," in Michael Nelson, ed., *The Presidency and the Political System* (Washington: Congressional Quarterly Press, 1984), pp. 156–78.
58. Corwin, *The President*, p. 60.
59. *Ibid.*, p. 61.
60. Joel K. Goldstein, *The Modern American Vice Presidency* (Princeton, N.J.: Princeton University Press, 1982), p. 6.
61. Michael Dorman, *The Second Man* (New York: Dell, 1968), p. 6.
62. Goldstein, *Vice Presidency*, pp. 7–8, 80, 136–37, 139, 250.
63. Joseph E. Persico, *The Imperial Rockefeller* (New York: Simon & Schuster, 1982), p. 262.
64. Aaron Wildavsky, "Presidential Disability and Succession," in Aaron Wildavsky, ed., *The Presidency* (Boston: Little, Brown, 1969), pp. 779–80.
65. The seven vice presidents who died in office (all by natural causes) were George

Clinton (1812), Elbridge Gerry (1814), William R. King (1853), Henry Wilson (1875), Thomas A. Hendricks (1885), Garret A. Hobart (1899), and James Sherman (1912). John C. Calhoun resigned in 1832. The eight presidents who died in office are listed in note 89.

66. Goldstein, *Vice Presidency*, p. 120.
67. *Ibid.*, pp. 147–48.
68. Roche, "Founding," p. 810.
69. Max Farrand, *The Framing of the Constitution of the United States* (New Haven: Yale University Press, 1913), p. 78.
70. *Ibid.*, p. 117.
71. Corwin, *President*, p. 35; McCormick, *Game*, p. 20.
72. McCormick, *Game*, p. 245.
73. Sigel and Butler, "Public," pp. 39–54.
74. Roberta S. Sigel, "Image of the American Presidency: Part II of an Exploration into Popular Views of Presidential Power," *Midwest Journal of Political Science* (February 1966), p. 124.
75. Pious, *Presidency*, pp. 32–33.
76. The quotes are from Rossiter, *Presidency*, p. 49; and from James Bryce, *The American Commonwealth*, rev. ed. (New York: Macmillan, 1910), p. 212.
77. The others: Madison, William Henry Harrison, Arthur, Cleveland, McKinley, Harding, Franklin Roosevelt, Eisenhower, and Kennedy. John D. Feerick, *The Twenty-fifth Amendment* (New York: Fordham University Press, 1976), ch. 1.
78. Louis W. Koenig, *The Chief Executive*, 4th ed. (New York: Harcourt Brace Jovanovich, 1981), pp. 79–83.
79. Feerick, *Amendment*, pp. 200–2.
80. Koenig, *Chief*, p. 85.
81. A full account of the aftermath of the attempted assassination of President Reagan can be found in Lawrence I. Barrett, *Gambling with History: Reagan in the White House* (Garden City, N.Y.: Doubleday, 1983), ch. 7.
82. Neustadt, *Presidential Power*, p. 149.
83. James L. Sundquist, "Reflections on Watergate: Lessons for Political Accountability," *Public Administration Review* (September/October 1974), pp. 453–61; Lloyd Cutler, "To Form a Government," *Foreign Affairs* (Fall 1980), pp. 126–43.
84. Edward R. Tufte, *Political Control of the Economy* (Princeton, N.J.: Princeton University Press, 1978), p. 25. Ronald Reagan's 1982 economic policies were an exception; of course, his party suffered substantially in the midterm elections.
85. Harry McPherson, *A Political Education* (Boston: Little, Brown, 1972), p. 268.
86. Paul C. Light, *The President's Agenda* (Baltimore: Johns Hopkins University Press, 1982), pp. 41–45.
87. Neustadt, *Presidential Power*, p. 219.
88. Alfred de Grazia, *Republic in Crisis* (New York: Federal Legal Publications, 1965), p. 94.
89. Four presidents died in office of natural causes: William Henry Harrison, Zachary Taylor, Warren G. Harding, and Franklin Roosevelt. Nixon resigned. The four assassinated presidents were Lincoln, Garfield, McKinley, and Kennedy.
90. Thach, *Creation*, pp. 85–87.
91. Farrand, *Records*, Vol. I, pp. 20–21, 67.
92. Rossiter, *1787*, p. 208.
93. Tulis, "The Two Constitutional Presidencies," in Nelson, *Presidency and the Political System*, pp. 59–86.
94. Thach, *Creation*, pp. 127–35; Rossiter, *1787*, p. 220.
95. Thach, *Creation*, pp. 118–23.
96. *Ibid.*, pp. 138–39.
97. Members of the executive and judiciary were not forbidden to serve in each others' branches, and especially during the 1790s several did. Robert Scigliano, "The Presidency and the Judiciary," in Nelson, *Presidency and Political System*, pp. 392–418.

98. Farrand, *Records*, Vol. I, p. 376.
99. *Ibid.*, Vol. II, p. 284.
100. Neustadt, *Presidential Power*, p. 35.
101. James L. Sundquist, *The Decline and Resurgence of Congress* (Washington: Brookings Institution, 1981), p. 16.
102. James Sterling Young, *The Washington Community, 1800–1828* (New York: Harcourt, Brace & World, 1966).
103. *Ibid.*, pp. 158–59.
104. John Quincy Adams, *Memoirs*, ed. Charles F. Adams (Philadelphia: J. B. Lippincott, 1874–75), Vol. IV, pp. 217–18.
105. Arthur M. Schlesinger, Jr., *The Imperial Presidency* (Boston: Houghton Mifflin, 1973), p. 14.
106. Young, *Community*, p. 165.
107. David H. Rosenbloom, *Federal Service and the Constitution* (Ithaca, N.Y.: Cornell University Press, 1971), p. 65.
108. Binkley, *President and Congress*, p. 86.
109. *Ibid.*, p. 102.
110. Quoted in Corwin, *President*, pp. 21–22.
111. Abraham Lincoln, "The Prerogative Theory of the Presidency," in Harry A. Bailey, Jr., ed., *Classics of the American Presidency* (Oak Park, Ill.: Moore, 1980), p. 34.
112. Woodrow Wilson, *Congressional Government* (New York: Houghton Mifflin, 1885).
113. Lawrence H. Chamberlain, *The President, Congress, and Legislation* (New York: Columbia University Press, 1946).
114. C. Herman Pritchett, "The President's Constitutional Position," in Thomas E. Cronin, ed., *Rethinking the Presidency* (Boston: Little, Brown, 1982), pp. 117–38.
115. Theodore Roosevelt, "The Stewardship Doctrine," in Bailey, *Classics*, p. 45.
116. Quoted in Sundquist, *Decline and Resurgence*, p. 32.
117. Woodrow Wilson, *Constitutional Government in the United States* (New York: Columbia University Press, 1908), p. 70.
118. Edward S. Flash, Jr., *Economic Advice and Presidential Leadership* (New York: Columbia University Press, 1965), pp. 308–13; Anna Kasten Nelson, "National Security I: Inventing a Process (1945–1960)," and I. M. Destler, "National Security II: The Rise of the Assistant (1961–1981)," in Hugh Heclo and Lester M. Salamon, eds., *The Illusion of Presidential Government* (Boulder, Col.: Westview Press, 1981), pp. 229–85.
119. Martha Kumar and Michael Grossman, "The Presidency and Interest Groups," in Nelson, *Presidency and the Political System*, pp. 282–312.
120. Lee, "Rally," p. 255.

CHAPTER 3

Culture, Politics, and the Presidency

The constitutional nature of the presidency assures that to the extent the federal government is the object of public demands for political change, the presidency will be the center of the American political system. In the nineteenth century this condition was the exception. In the twentieth century it has been the rule. As much as the Constitution, the political environment empowers the presidency. The ways it does so, though not deterministic, are patterned according to enduring cultural values. American political culture limits the ideological bounds in which policy change occurs; it also assures that competition within those bounds will be intense and that change will be spasmodic. Indeed, the history of modern American politics is one of recurring cycles of electoral politics and governmental policy making whose focus has been the presidency. Culture and politics also have implications for foreign policy making and for presidential leadership skill, the third main element of presidential power.

AMERICAN POLITICAL CULTURE

Serious contests involving social and economic policy take place within fairly narrow ideological bounds in the American political system. These boundaries become apparent when one compares the political success of socialist parties of the left (and even, on occasion, fascist parties of the right) in Western Europe with similar movements in the United States. The high-water mark for any socialist candidate in an American presidential election was 1912, when Eugene V. Debs won 6.0 percent of the popular vote. (George Wallace's right-wing populist campaign in 1968 attracted 13.5 percent.) The depression of the 1930s, which threw European politics into ideological turmoil, witnessed little variation in the American tradition of two-party centrism. Survey data from this period indicate that even among the unemployed, only a small minority favored drastic changes in the economic system or any change at all in the Constitution. Majorities of the unemployed endorsed statements such as "the government should see that everyone is above subsistence" and "the government should provide relief for those in need." But so did majorities of every other group, including "upper white collar."[1]

Much of the explanation for the narrow ideological bounds of American political competition can be found in the nation's political culture and the historical forces that have sustained it. Political culture consists of deeply rooted values that can be grouped loosely into three interrelated categories: purpose values (the ends that government ought to serve), process values (how the government ought to work), and certain broader social values that have important political implications. In the United States the culture's most important purpose values are equality and liberty, which includes property rights as well as due process and freedoms of expression; its leading process values are "higher law" and popular sovereignty; and its most politically significant social values are idealism, including religion and nationalism, and pragmatism. What these values mean and how they apply has been the subject of continuing, sometimes intense, political disagreement. But they are so widely shared among the general population, particularly its most politically active members, that Gunnar Myrdal, Samuel Huntington, and others have labeled them collectively as the "American Creed."[2]

The source of some creedal values was inherent in the circumstances of the seventeenth-century founding. America was colonized by a middle-class Puritan "fragment" of English society that had failed in its opposition to the power of crown and church but that dominated the colonies. So, to an even greater extent, did Puritan values, including higher law, liberty, and idealistic religious "nationalism."[3] These political values were reinforced by American interpreters of John Locke and the eighteenth-century European Enlightenment. Thomas Jefferson, for example, wrote the Virginia Statute of Religious Liberty, appealed in the Declaration of Independence to the "Laws of Nature and of Nature's God," and proposed that the seal of the United States be a picture of "the children of Israel, led by a cloud by day and a pillar of fire by night."[4] Other political values, most of them latent in evolving Puritan thought, were added by these secular thinkers: equality, popular sovereignty, and Benjamin Franklin–style pragmatism.

Various theories — the absence of a feudal legacy, the abundance of free or cheap land, the shortage of labor — have been offered to explain why a creedal consensus on these purpose, process, and social values took such deep root in America. Other theories have ventured to explain why the consensus has endured: its "givenness" and the early extension of universal manhood suffrage at a historical moment when an industrial working class otherwise might have formed; sustained economic growth, resulting in vertical as well as horizontal mobility; and so on.[5] But whatever the explanation, the phenomenon of cultural endurance itself seldom is questioned. Foreign visitors from Alexis de Tocqueville (Americans "are unanimous upon the general principles that ought to rule human society") to Myrdal ("Americans of all national origins, classes, regions, creeds and colors have something in common: a social ethos, a political creed") have observed it.[6] Presidents since George Washington have enunciated it in their inaugural addresses.[7] Modern social scientists have documented it in several dozen studies.[8]

Widespread agreement on liberty and equality, higher law and popular sovereignty, idealism and pragmatism helps to explain why domestic policy conflict in the United States has been so ideologically narrow. But it also helps us to understand the intensity of the conflicts there have been and the leadership skills presidents are called upon to exercise in their service.

Purpose Values: Liberty and Equality

The tensions between the values of liberty and equality have been the stuff of political philosophy since classical times. But more important in the American experience have been the tensions within each value that different groups have tried to exploit in the service of their own causes.

Early American notions of liberty included property rights, due process of law, and freedoms of expression. In all cases, these involved restrictions on government, then regarded as liberty's main nemesis. The Bill of Rights, which reads like a list of instructions to government about what it cannot do, incorporated this view into the Constitution. But when the rise of a national industrial economy in the late nineteenth century brought concentrations of corporate power harmful to workers, farmers, and small businessmen, they cried out for government regulation to defend their liberties against private threats. In the 1930s the rhetoric of liberty was used to urge an even more vigorous role for government. Franklin Roosevelt defined economic security — "freedom from want" — as the precondition for all other liberties and defended Social Security and other New Deal welfare programs in libertarian terms. The best evidence of Roosevelt's success is that the word "liberalism" became associated with active government rather than passive.

Equality went through a similar transformation quite early, from equality before God and the law (its meaning in the statement "all men are created equal") to "equality of opportunity," that is, an equal chance to develop and pursue one's talents. The United States, which later would lag far behind Europe in welfare policy, began the development of its much more extensive system of public education in the early nineteenth century. This early transformation was an enduring one: equality of opportunity still was equated with a combination of public education and legal equality in 1922, when Herbert Hoover wrote that "we, through free and universal education, provide the training of the runners; we give to them an equal start; we provide in government the umpire of fairness in the race."[9]

If the battles of the 1910s and the 1930s were fought within the rhetorical bounds of liberty, the 1960s were marked by efforts to redefine equality. Liberal critics targeted not the opportunity ideal or even the footrace image, but rather the notion that, as Lyndon Johnson put it, the race could be fair for those who began it far behind the starting line: poor children who left unlivable homes with empty stomachs to go to inferior schools, or black adults who bore the legacy of more than three centuries of slavery and discrimination. Traditional equality-based arguments lent rhetorical heft to a host of Great Society programs.

New definitions or applications of liberty and equality have proliferated over the years, but the words have endured and by themselves constrain the range of political debate among politically active Americans. In addition, all the earlier meanings of liberty and equality remain in the culture and form the ideological basis for resistance when new ones are asserted. One result of this is widespread uncertainty among citizens. They tend to be "operational liberals" who endorse specific programs that expand the government's social and economic role, especially programs that are seen as serving their own interests. (In this sense the New Deal, which benefited many millions of people in ways they could see in their personal lives, had deeper popular support than the Great Society, so much of which was directed at racial and economic minorities.) But citizens also tend to be "ideological conservatives" who reject the philosophical basis for even a limited welfare state.[10]

Just as the Constitution implicitly stipulates that tactical bargaining skills are important to presidential leadership, so do the culture's purpose values suggest a need for skills of public rhetoric in the selling of programs and intraexecutive "management of authority" in developing them. (See Chapter 4.) Presidents who push for liberal causes face great public resistance if they fail either to develop programs that seem realistic or present their goals in the language of ideological conservatism. Conversely, conservative presidents may be elected by talking a good ideological game but will retain their public standing only if they choose "operational" program targets with great care. And all presidents are constrained within the policy bounds that liberty and equality can be stretched to cover.

Process Values: Higher Law and Popular Sovereignty

Deeply rooted in American political culture is the belief that government ought to work in accordance with "higher law," some ultimate standard of right. This certainly was true of the Puritans, who, for example, found in the New Testament Book of Acts the basis not only for congregationally controlled churches but the town-meeting form of government. Myrdal observes that "the concept of natural rights in the philosophy of the Enlightenment corresponded rather closely with the idea of moral law in the Christian faith," as did several centuries of experience with an English Parliament whose legitimacy rested on "the fiction that they only 'declared' or 'explained' . . . a 'higher law' existing independent of all formally fixed rules."[11] Higher-law philosophy certainly prevailed in the America of 1776, when, as Gordon Wood has shown, "the traditional covenant theology of Puritanism combined with the political science of the eighteenth century [Enlightenment] into an imperatively persuasive argument for revolution" ("We hold these *truths* to be *self-evident*").[12] It endures in the Americans' practice of "inscrib[ing] their ideals into law," ranging from moral codes that regulate personal behavior to legally meaningless statements of congressional good intention such as the Humphrey-Hawkins Act of 1978 and the proposed nuclear-freeze resolutions of the early 1980s.

Americans also believe in popular sovereignty, a value made up of the related ideas that the only basis of legitimate political authority is the consent of the governed (Abraham Lincoln's "government of the people") and that government is supposed to work in accordance with what the public wants ("by the people"). This belief not only infuses virtually every political writing of the revolutionary period, but forms the philosophical basis of the Constitution itself: "*We the people . . . do ordain and establish* this Constitution of the United States of America." Since 1787 it has manifested itself in an endless and, by the standards of other Western democracies, radical series of democratic political reforms: suffrage expansion; direct election of senators, presidential electors, and, in many states, judges, school boards, and executive department heads; initiatives, referendums, and recalls; even citizen participation in the workings of bureaucracy. Popular sovereignty underlies the public's widely shared expectation of elected legislators, whom it wants to vote as instructed "delegates" of constituency opinion, not independent-minded "trustees" of the public interest.[13]

The apparent contradiction in these cultural beliefs about the political process is obvious: How can Americans expect their government to work to fulfill some higher law if they also expect it to mirror the popular will? The cultural "resolution" to this contradiction was stated most explicitly by Andrew Jackson, but it predates him by at least a century:

> I believe that man can be elevated; man can become more and more endowed with divinity; and as he does he becomes more God-like in his character and capable of governing himself. Let us go on elevating our people, perfecting our institutions, until democracy shall reach such a point of perfection that we can acclaim with truth that the voice of the people is the voice of God.[14]

The endurance of the *vox* (American) *populi, vox Dei* doctrine is reflected in comparative studies of civic competence and social trust. To a far greater extent than Britons, Germans, Austrians, Netherlanders, Mexicans, Italians, or the French, Americans feel personally competent to participate intelligently in politics and trust each other to do the same.[15] In short, they see no contradiction between "government of the people, by the people" and government "for the people."

This solution to the higher-law–popular-sovereignty tension, however satisfactory it may be at the cultural level, is problematic in practice. Government does not always appear to citizens to be working well, especially when judged against such high standards. The result is a cultural by-product of ambivalence to authority that is no less present today than at the Constitutional Convention. (See Chapter 2.) On the supportive side, Americans not only trust themselves, they revere their form of government. When asked in 1960 what aspect of their country made them most proud, 85 percent of Americans mentioned their governmental and political institutions; Britons were scarcely half as likely to do so, Germans and Italians hardly at all.[16] In a 1972 survey 86 percent agreed with the statement "I am proud of many things about our form of government"; in 1976 only 25 percent said the political system needed major changes, which further questioning usually revealed to mean tinkering with the electoral process.[17] But, as Donald Devine concluded in 1972 after studying more than three decades of survey data, these "high amounts of community and regime trust [exist] together with limited amounts of authority trust."[18] Since then distrust of governmental authorities has grown even higher. Majorities of the public feel that the federal government is "run by a few big interests" and can be trusted "only some of the time." They also feel that the "people in government waste a lot of money" and "don't seem to know what they're doing."[19]

Ambivalence to political authority reinforces the cultural bias toward narrow but sometimes vigorous policy debate that we noted in connection with the purpose values of liberty and equality. Americans want government to embody their notions of what is right, but their suspicion of the motives and competence of their governors limits their willingness to entertain policy proposals that involve greater federal power. Cultural attitudes toward the presidency and Congress are described at length in Chapter 7, but clearly the president engages both the trust and distrust elements of this ambivalence in extreme form. As we saw in Chapter 2, he is regarded not just as a political chief of government, but also as chief of state, the anthropomorphic symbol of the polity. Americans applauded Franklin Roosevelt's extraordinary exercise of presidential power and reelected him three times. But after mourning his death, they almost instantly endorsed the Twenty-second Amendment, which denies any subsequent president the chance to serve more than two terms, the only such limit in all the federal government. Roberta Sigel, writing in 1966, summarized the presidential job description implicit in the political culture:

> Wanted is a man who is strong, who has ideas of his own on how to solve problems, and who will make his ideas prevail even if Congress or the public should oppose him. The personal qualities most desired in a president are those which would enhance his leadership potential rather than those which would make him a pleasant neighbor. Finally, this powerful man should exit from his office after eight years lest he become too powerful.[20]

A 1979 survey, taken near the end of the term of the fifth consecutive president "to exit from his office after" less than six years, found that the public's list of preferred presidential qualities still had not changed: "strong," "forceful," "decisive," and "ability to get things done."[21]

The central process values in American political culture also reinforce the purpose values in their implications for presidential skill, especially public rhetoric. Presidents who wish to promote policy change are enjoined by the political culture both to exalt popular sovereignty, as Jimmy Carter did so effectively in 1976 when he repeatedly promised a government "as good and honest and decent and truthful and competent and compassionate and as filled with love as the American people," and to invoke moral purpose in the manner of John Kennedy's 1961 inaugural address: "Let us go forth to lead the land we love, asking His blessing and His help, but knowing that here on earth, God's work must truly be our own." Unifying rhetoric can be a potent tool in the service of domestic policy change, but it is hard to sustain: the reallocation of resources is controversial almost by nature. The culturally induced temptation to presidents is to shroud their domestic policy proposals in the garb of bipartisanship, which further limits the range of policy debate.

Social Values: Idealism and Pragmatism

If the process value of higher law leads Americans to measure the merits and performance of their political institutions against some ultimate standard, the broader social value of idealism both defines that standard and assures Americans that they have a special Providence to meet it. "At the heart of our culture," writes William McLoughlin, "are the beliefs that Americans are a chosen people; that they have a manifest (or latent) destiny to lead the world to the millennium; that their democratic-republican institutions, their bountiful natural resources, and their concept of the free and morally responsible individual operates under a body of higher moral law."[22]

For Puritans the "new chosen people" or "American Israel" belief was an explicitly Christian one. "The Lord will be our God and delight to dwell among us as his owne people, and will command a blessing upon us in all our wayes," wrote John Winthrop on board the *Arbella* to America in 1630, self-consciously echoing the "exhortacion of Moses, that faithful servant of the Lord in his last farewell to Israell, Deut. 30." Tocqueville confirmed the continuing existence of this strain of idealism in the early nineteenth century ("There is no country in the world where the Christian religion retains a greater influence over the souls of men than in America"), as does modern survey research in the late twentieth century. More than twice as many Americans as in almost all other industrialized democracies (58 percent in 1975) say their religious beliefs are "very important" to them; the United States stands as the only exception to the rule that social and economic development reduces the importance of religion to a people.[23] "Great Awakenings" marked by widespread Christian conversions not only seem to have predated the American Revolution and the Jacksonian and Progressive reform eras, but helped to cause them as well. Unboundedly optimistic feelings of personal rebirth and renewal were directed into social and political channels in the hope that American "perfectionism" might hasten the millennial second coming of Christ.[24]

But although Christian millennial groups such as the Moral Majority provided much of the energy for Ronald Reagan's successful presidential candidacy in 1980, such explicitly religious political activity has become more controversial, and thus less influential, in recent years. It did not prompt much public complaint in 1899, when President William McKinley explained that he had decided to keep the Philippine Islands after he "went down on my knees and prayed Almighty God for light and guidance" and was told "to take them all, and to educate the Filipinos, and uplift and civilize and Christianize them."[25] But in March 1983 President Reagan was widely criticized for asserting that the Soviet Union is "the focus of evil in the modern world" and that "we are enjoined by Scripture and the Lord Jesus to oppose it with all our might."

What endures in the culture, however, is a value of idealistic nationalism that allows presidents to make only slightly less sweeping statements without drawing fire. "I have always believed," Reagan frequently affirms, "that this anointed land was set apart in an uncommon way, that a divine plan placed this great continent here between the oceans to be found by people from every corner of the Earth who had a special love of faith and freedom."[26] Such providential idealism has an enduring and generally uncontroversial existence of its own in American culture, apart from any explicitly Christian doctrine. Jefferson's proposal for the seal of the United States already has been mentioned; fellow Enlightenment deist Franklin offered a picture of Moses leading the Israelites across the Red Sea. The Continental Congress finally settled on an inscription that embodied the sentiments of both: *Anno Coeptis, Novus Ordo Seclorum* ("He favored this undertaking, the new order of the ages"). Presidents since Washington, notes Robert Bellah, have reiterated this providential "civil religion" theme in their public oratory, apart from any mention of Christ.[27] Yet most American Christians do not seem to mind. As Reinhold Niebuhr explains, although "the [early] New England theocrats . . . thought of our experiment as primarily the creation of a new and purer church" and "Jefferson and his coterie . . . thought primarily of a new political community," both strains believed that "we had been called out by God to create a new humanity" in conformance with the purpose and process values of the American Creed.[28]

This idealistic element in American culture is accompanied by pragmatism, which Louis Hartz and others have identified as America's distinctive contribution to philosophy. Pragmatism tests the worth of ideas and practices according to their workability. Yet far from existing in opposition to idealism in American culture, the two values are joined in a cultural synthesis: optimism. The political manifestation of this optimism is what Austin Ranney has called the "Divine Science" of "political engineering." "The main articles of that faith," writes Ranney, "hold that for every problem there is a solution. That it is better to do something about a problem than to do nothing, even though that something may be less than perfect." Political engineering has "animated our history's most powerful political movements."[29]

Broad social values of idealism, pragmatism, and optimism have political implications that are consequential for presidential leadership in particular and federal policy making in general. These social values reinforce the already noted presidential skill requirements of public rhetoric and management of authority. Idealism cries out for inspiration, pragmatism for a presidential capacity to develop practical ideas in the service of these ideals. And although cultural optimism about the pragmatic possibilities of effecting creedal values does nothing to alter the primacy of liberty, equality, higher laws, and popular sovereignty, its passionate tone of expansiveness can offset some of the internal tensions in these purpose and process values, at least for short periods of time.

CYCLES OF POLITICS AND POLICY, 1901–1976

Samuel Huntington observes that political cycles, which he defines as "regularly recurring patterns of interaction among variables," most frequently develop not in the "ideologically pluralistic, class-based politics of western Europe," but in nations where a "fundamental consensus" on political values exists. A consensual culture "defines the limits of change," writes Huntington, "and the search for change within those basic limits swings from one pole to the other."[30] Cer-

Cycle	Preparation	Achievement	Consolidation
1	Theodore Roosevelt	Woodrow Wilson	Warren Harding Calvin Coolidge Herbert Hoover
2		Franklin Roosevelt	Dwight Eisenhower
3	John Kennedy	Lyndon Johnson	Richard Nixon

Figure 3.1   Cycles of Politics and Policy, 1901–1976

tainly this has been true in the modern United States, where cultural tensions both within the widely shared purpose values of liberty and equality and between process values that exalt political authority and those that support it (all underlaid by optimistic social values about the attainability of goals through purposive action) make political debate as intense at times as it is narrow. The history of domestic political change during at least the first three quarters of this century can be understood in terms of recurring cycles of electoral political competition and public policy making within the bounds of American political culture. The focus of these cycles has been the presidency. (See Figure 3.1).

At the heart of each twentieth-century cycle has been a "presidency of achievement" — parts, but not all, of the administrations of Woodrow Wilson, Franklin Roosevelt, and Lyndon Johnson — in which great bursts of creative legislative activity occurred that altered the role of government in society in the service of some combination of purpose values of liberty and equality and process values of higher law and popular sovereignty. Such reform periods are made possible by overwhelming, if very general, popular mandates for change. They are brief, sometimes lasting only two years, and end when political fervor lapses; when older meanings of cultural purpose values are reasserted, along with the antipower strand in the cultural ambivalence to authority; and when administrative difficulties arise from attempting to achieve social change through government action so quickly.

Each presidency of achievement has been followed by a "presidency of consolidation" in which reform was not rejected but rationalized, slowed down, and in effect legitimized for earlier opponents. The 1920s presidencies of Warren Harding, Calvin Coolidge, and Herbert Hoover were of this kind, as were those of Dwight Eisenhower and Richard Nixon. Such presidencies end a cycle, but also overlap with the period in which the seeds of the next cycle are planted. New social discontents and policy ideas to meet them may emerge to which the president of consolidation, empowered only with a negative mandate and preoccupied with the agenda of his own cycle, is likely to be inattentive.

Eventually, the social discontents become strong enough to cast the consolidating regime from office, but the mandate of the next president, elected because of his ability to articulate the new problems and remedies, is incomplete. The most important contribution of a "president of preparation" such as Theodore Roosevelt or John Kennedy is to lay the political groundwork for the president of achievement who follows. To be sure, a president of preparation could move into the achievement phase with a large reelection majority, as Kennedy might have done had he lived.

Although the cycle of preparation, achievement, and consolidation is rooted in American political culture, we derive it more from historical observation than from any theory of historical determinism. It is recurring but not inevitable.

A system-threatening political crisis can break the cyclic flow: the abruptness of the depression catapulted Franklin Roosevelt's New Deal into existence without a preceding presidency of preparation. So can a mismatch between presidential purpose and public mood. The presidency of William Howard Taft foundered because Taft, who had been hand-picked by Theodore Roosevelt and elected by the people to carry on Roosevelt's agenda of reform, turned out to be philosophically and temperamentally unsuited to the task. Taft was interested in consolidating Roosevelt's relatively small gains and did: he doubled the number of antitrust prosecutions, for example. But the public was looking for achievement-style leadership of a kind that, after Taft's four-year interlude, Wilson provided. Taft's was a "presidency of stalemate," one in which the president's agenda bears little resemblance to what the public is willing to accept. The presidency of Harry Truman also fits into this category, although, unlike Taft, Truman was trying to set off a new round of achievement in the face of a strong public disposition for consolidation. Truman-style periods of stalemate also have occurred within each presidency of achievement. After a few years, older meanings of cultural purpose values reappear, along with resentment of what appears to be the excessive power of the presidency. For example, Franklin Roosevelt's period of domestic achievement came to a halt when, in 1937 and 1938, he tried to extend the power of the presidency over the other two branches by "packing" the Supreme Court and "purging" Congress of anti–New Deal Democrats.

The administration of Gerald Ford also fell outside the cycle, though not for reasons of stalemate. His was a time of drift rather than deadlock, a "presidency of stasis." In such a presidency, policy problems are new and unprecedented. There is great intellectual confusion about the nature of these problems and few ideas about solutions. Confusion at the governmental level is accompanied by comparable uncertainty among voters. It is not that the public and the president want different things, as in a presidency of stalemate, but rather that confusion about how government can accomplish even widely shared goals prevents their accomplishment.

Still, for the first three-quarters of this century, presidencies that did not fulfill a function in the policy cycle were rare. Presidential politics and domestic policy making flowed along a fairly regular course. That course is described below, cycle by cycle. Its dynamic is then examined, and its relation to American foreign policy is explored. In the conclusion to the chapter, we speculate about where the nation and the presidency are in the final quarter of the century.

From Theodore Roosevelt to Hoover

It is not surprising that the first domestic policy cycle overlapped with the last stage of the long process, described in Chapter 2, through which the enumerated powers of the presidency were invigorated. After all, the presidency was empowered for legislative leadership by Theodore Roosevelt and Wilson precisely because the rise of a national economy in the late nineteenth century meant that twentieth-century pressures for political reform would be directed more at the national than at the state or local governments. Elihu Root described the economic and political transformation in a 1912 speech:

> Instead of the give-and-take of free individual contract, the tremendous power of organization has combined with great aggregations of capital in enormous industrial establishments working through vast agencies of commerce, . . . so great in the mass that each individual concerned in them is quite helpless by himself. The relations between the employer and the employed, between the owners of aggregated capital and the units of organized labor, between the small producer, the small trader, the consumer, and the great transporting and manufacturing and distribution agencies all present new questions for the solution of which the old reliance upon the free action of individual wills appears quite inadequate. And in many directions the intervention of that organized control which we call government seems necessary to produce the same result of justice and right conduct which obtained through the attrition of individuals before the new conditions arose.[31]

The view of Theodore Roosevelt, who succeeded to the presidency after William McKinley's assassination in 1901 and was elected in his own right in 1904, was that the federal government's response to the transformation Root described should be to "recognize the inevitableness of combinations in business and meet it by a corresponding increase in governmental power over big business."[32] He drew his philosophy from the Herbert Croly wing of the urban middle-class progressives of the 1890s. The "Square Deal" was Roosevelt's legislative effort, first, to ease the task of breaking up those trusts, holding companies, and other "combinations" whose purpose was to stifle competition and keep prices high, and second, to empower the federal government to regulate the behavior of all corporations engaged in interstate commerce. Roosevelt achieved neither of these goals: his election victory in 1904, though substantial, was not sufficient to convince Congress that his platform had widespread public support. But his vigorous use of the White House as a "bully pulpit" placed progressivism at the top of the national political agenda and set the stage for its later success, albeit in slightly different form. Arthur Link's judgment that Roosevelt's "chief contribution to the reform cause was the publicity he gave it" may sound condescending, but it defines a successful president of preparation.[33]

Woodrow Wilson, whose bias was toward Louis Brandeis–style corporate smallness, nonetheless inherited and built upon Roosevelt's efforts. His election in 1912 was not only impressive in its own right, but was accompanied by the largest gain in history for a president's party in the House (sixty-three seats) and a ten-seat gain in the Senate that gave control to the Democrats for the first time in twenty years. Wilson used his mandate not only to advance the progressives' cause, but to reshape the relationship between presidents and their political parties. As James Ceaser has pointed out, previous presidents had been regarded as agents of their party. Wilson's view, novel at the time but accepted ever since, was that the purpose of the election process was "to elevate a dynamic leader above the political party and make the party serve his will."[34] This Wilson did, securing rapid passage of a host of "New Freedom" legislation, including: the Clayton Act, which strengthened the federal government's antitrust powers; the Federal Trade Commission Act, which gave it authority to punish unfair business competition; the Underwood-Simmons Tariff Act, lowering tariffs and providing for an income tax; and the Federal Reserve Act, giving a new Federal Reserve Board control over the nation's credit system.

The achievement of the first cycle was to inaugurate a role for the federal government as an "umpire" that would regulate the excesses of private economic power in defense of personal liberty. For all Harding's talk in the 1920 campaign about a return to the "normalcy" of the McKinley years, neither he, Coolidge, nor Hoover did much to roll back the Roosevelt-inspired, Wilson-enacted changes, which had the effect of consolidating the progressive agenda into the fabric of government. They did, however, try their best to keep Congress from extending the federal role to "player," or active promoter of the general welfare. Harding vetoed a soldier's bonus bill and Coolidge the McNary-Haugen Farm relief bill, and Hoover resisted for as long as possible various efforts to create public works projects for unemployed workers. Ideas such as these were the stuff of the next cycle.

From Franklin Roosevelt to Eisenhower

Because of the suddenness of the depression that followed the stock market crash of October 1929, the second policy cycle had no president of preparation. Hoover was, in every sense, part of the previous era. "Economic depression," he told Congress in 1930, "cannot be cured by legislative action or executive pronouncement," only by "self-reliance."[35] But neither was a preparation stage needed. Roosevelt's overwhelming victory in 1932 (the largest ever against an incumbent president until 1980) was accompanied by a ninety-seat gain for his party in the House (far exceeding Wilson's previous record) and a change in the Senate from a one-seat deficit to a twenty-five-seat majority. This was evidence enough that the public already was anxious for new and dramatic policies.

Roosevelt's inauguration on March 4 was followed by the celebrated "first hundred days." An emergency banking bill, completed by the president and his advisers at 2:00 A.M. on March 9, was passed unanimously by the House that same day after thirty-eight minutes of debate and became law within hours when the Senate followed suit. Other bills followed in rapid succession and were rushed through after testimonials such as House Democratic leader Joseph Byrns's ("This . . . is a time to get behind our great leader and follow him and be guided by his judgment, rather than our own") and this one from Bertrand Snell, the House Republican leader: "If you are going to accomplish this purpose you must put it up to the President of the United States and hold him responsible."[36] The Spring calendar of achievement included the following:

March 9:	Emergency Banking Act
March 26:	Economy Act
March 31:	Civilian Conservation Corps
April 19:	Gold standard abandoned (ratified June 5)
May 12:	Federal Emergency Relief Act, Agricultural Adjustment Act, Emergency Farm Mortgage Act
May 18:	Tennessee Valley Authority Act
May 27:	Truth-in-Securities Act
June 13:	Home Owner's Loan Act
June 16:	National Industrial Recovery Act, Glass-Steagall Banking Act, Farm Credit Act

A "second hundred days" followed the 1934 congressional elections, in which the president's party, contrary to precedent, gained seats: nine in the House, ten in the Senate. It included the National Labor Relations Act, the Social Security Act, acts to strengthen previous banking and Tennessee Valley Authority legislation, and a tax bill that increased the responsibility of the wealthy.

The legislation of the second hundred days was aimed more at restructuring the economy than was the legislation of the first hundred days, which had been preoccupied with the need to salvage it. But the "public philosophy" of the New Deal was fairly consistent throughout: within the bounds of capitalism and private ownership, the federal government is ultimately responsible for securing the foundations of the people's liberty: welfare, security, and employment. Its intellectual debt to ideas that had been propounded in the 1920s and before was varied. As James MacGregor Burns notes, Roosevelt "had grasped the standard of Wilsonian reform in his measures for federal supervision of securities, friendliness to labor, business regulation. He had trod Cousin Theodore's old path in conservation and in the elements of planning in the AAA. He had filched a plank from American socialism in the public ownership features of TVA," and later, in the social security and tax bills.[37]

Roosevelt was reelected in 1936 by the largest electoral-vote margin in history, which he took to be a mandate to continue the reform process to whatever ends and through whatever obstacles he wanted. But his party's gains in the 1936 congressional elections were relatively modest. As a result, legislators in 1937 were less likely than in the preceding four years to attribute their present or future success in holding office to obedience to Roosevelt. Congress resisted his "court packing" plan, and voters in 1938 refused Roosevelt's pleas to defeat anti–New Deal Democrats in primary elections. What one author calls "deadlock on the Potomac" ensued.[38] But America's intervention in World War II, discussed below, rendered domestic politics and policy less relevant.

Roosevelt died in April 1945. Truman succeeded to the presidency with domestic policy achievement high on his list of goals. (He was determined, he later wrote in his memoirs, not to allow "the progress of the New Deal to be halted in the aftermath of the war as decisively as the progress of Woodrow Wilson's New Freedom had been halted after the first World War.")[39] Before the year was out Truman had called on Congress to enact legislation for full employment, public housing, farm-price supports, government health insurance, and civil rights, among other new and dramatic causes. Congress's response was tepid; the reaction of voters in the 1946 midterm elections was to make Truman the first president — and the only Democrat — in this century to face a Congress in which both houses were controlled by the other party. With the notable exception of civil rights, Truman downplayed his reform agenda during the Eightieth Congress and won a surprising and substantial reelection victory in 1948. But when he revived it under the rubric "Fair Deal" during the second term, his popularity once again dwindled. Truman's domestic policy proposals were to make up much of the agenda of the next cycle, but it brought him only political stalemate during his own presidency.

Eisenhower, elected in 1952, was the quintessential president of consolidation. (See Chapter 4.) Ignoring pleas from the conservative wing of his party to abolish TVA, severely reduce federal spending, and generally undo "twenty years of treason," Eisenhower pursued a course that was responsive to the public desire for a slowdown but not a reversal of course. Eisenhower called his program "dynamic conservatism," but "passive liberalism" was more like it. Few steps were taken to roll back the New Deal. Indeed, coverage for social security and unemployment compensation was broadened, the minimum wage was raised, and a "soil bank" was begun that paid farmers to plant trees instead of cultivating marginal land. Eisenhower's conservatism was confined mostly to bringing fiscal and administrative order to the Roosevelt-induced changes.

From Kennedy to Nixon

The consolidating stage of one cycle is the "incubation" stage of the next. The Progressive movement developed as a force in national politics in the 1890s. Senator Robert La Follette, who ran for president in 1924 as the nominee of the Conference for Political Action, articulated some of the social discontent of his time. Much of what eventually became the New Deal was germinating among intellectuals and progressives in Congress during the 1920s.

In the late 1950s, some congressional Democrats, especially in the Senate, advanced a number of policy initiatives whose purpose was to extend the government's active concern to racial and economic minorities whom New Deal programs really had not helped and to "quality of life" issues: Medicare, civil rights, federal aid to education, and environmental protection among them. Their style of policy entrepreneurship embodied the nexus between advocacy groups, academic advisers, and legislators on the fringes of congressional power. For example, in 1958 the Joint Economic Committee of Congress held hearings organized by a temporary staff of Harvard economists that, in a 1959 report, called for a tax cut and deficit spending to stimulate economic growth and reduce unemployment.

Voters responded to these developments. The birth of sophisticated election surveys took place in the 1950s, and studies of voting behavior in the 1952 and 1956 elections revealed that the links between candidate choice and issue preference were tenuous at best. Some political scientists concluded that most voters did not, and probably could not, think about politics in "ideological" terms,[40] but they were ignoring the lack of clear issue differences between Eisenhower and Adlai Stevenson, his opponent in both elections. Starting with the 1958 congressional election, Democrats infused their campaigns with the new policies they had been developing. This worked to their benefit: James Sundquist has shown a strong relationship between voting for Democratic congressional candidates and dissatisfaction about economic conditions.[41] An era of issue politics and, consequently, issue voting began.

As a representative and senator in the 1950s, John Kennedy had not been a particularly liberal or crusading legislator. However, as a candidate first for the Democratic presidential nomination in 1960 and then for the presidency, he consciously adopted the increasingly popular issue positions that had been germinating among liberal legislators and intellectuals. Kennedy won against the Republican nominee, Richard Nixon, but only by three-tenths of a percentage point in the popular vote. His party actually lost twenty seats in the House. Most of these losses were in the North and West, which left the southern conservative wing more powerful. Even some liberal Democrats in Congress said at the time that they sensed neither a great public imperative that new programs be passed nor a willingness to pay for them with higher taxes. Public opinion, though supportive, was not solid.

The legislative measures that Kennedy flagged as most important during his brief presidency failed to pass: federal aid to education in 1961; medical care for the aged and a Department of Urban Affairs in 1962; and civil rights legislation, a tax cut, and, again, Medicare and education aid in 1963. These failures, however, were part of a coherent strategy, which was to submit controversial legislation to Congress with accompanying presidential messages as a form of public education. Kennedy's eyes were on 1964 and the creation of a large personal electoral majority that also would give him the increase in congressional support that he needed. In our terms, he saw his first-term presidency of preparation becoming a second-term presidency of achievement.

Ironically, it was Kennedy's death and the accompanying sense of crisis and catharsis that hastened public support for his programs the most. Johnson, who succeeded to the presidency, pleaded for passage of the civil rights bill and tax cut in the name of the fallen leader ("Let us continue") and in 1964 accomplished the victories. In the fall Johnson ran an essentially nonpartisan, "president of all the people" campaign against Barry Goldwater, an extreme conservative who violently opposed the new liberal platform. Johnson portrayed Kennedy's "New Frontier" and his own "Great Society" programs as moderate and acceptable to all Americans, in contrast to the alleged desire of Goldwater to dismantle social security and abolish TVA. His astonishing landslide victory, which brought thirty-seven new liberal Democrats into the House with him, triggered the next burst of presidential achievement. As Roger Davidson writes, "The legislative record of the 89th Congress (1965–66) reads like a roll call of contemporary government programs: Medicare-Medicaid, Voting Rights Act of 1965, Older Americans Act, Freedom of Information Act, National Foundation of the Arts and Humanities, highway beautification, urban mass transit, clean water, and the Departments of Transportation and Housing and Urban Development, among others."[42]

The New Deal had committed the federal government to the economic security of the vast majority of Americans; the Great Society added quality-of-life concerns to that commitment and extended its coverage to racially and economically deprived minorities in the name of equality. But the new center could not hold. Popular support for civil rights and antipoverty programs never had been as unambiguous as the 1964 election seemed to suggest. Voters were defending the New Deal against Goldwater as much as affirming the Great Society. Surveys did show overwhelming popular support for Johnson's social programs from 1964 to 1966, but a great majority of these "operational liberals" also felt that the poor were to blame for their condition. As long as three-fourths of the American public held to the "ideological conservative" belief that any able-bodied person could find a job and earn a living, there simply was no solid support for a "war on poverty."[43]

Political culture aside, even the achievements of the 1960s somehow went sour. Civil rights and antipoverty measures, though not radical, created such turmoil in their implementation that large numbers of Americans sought a period of respite. It was painfully clear, even to adherents of the Great Society, that many of its programs had been designed badly and were not meeting early hopes. Concentration on legislative enactment had meant a failure to see in advance the potential bureaucratic snarls of administration. For example, many educational and antipoverty policies had been formulated as categorical programs designed and funded for specific purposes but without regard to their relationship to similar programs. The result was a multitude of specific programs fragmented across a number of departments and agencies and bound to strict limits set by law.

These issues, in addition to the Vietnam War, broke the Johnson coalition wide open, dividing white southerners and blue-collar workers against blacks and professionals. Nixon's victory in 1968 over Vice President Hubert Humphrey, combined with the large vote for George Wallace's independent candidacy, affirmed increasing public distress about the war, social unrest, and racial conflict.

Presidents of consolidation seldom are elected on the basis of positive policy proposals. They can, however, play a constructive role in rationalizing and legitimizing the programs of achievement presidents. Nixon and a number of his appointees brought a managerial style to government. They did not formally reject the purpose of the Great Society — an ambivalent public could not be said to be any more squarely against these programs than for them, and program beneficiaries and administrators had come to constitute a powerful lobby in Congress on their behalf. But the Nixon administration did search for ways to change the way programs worked. This eventually resulted in plans for general and special revenue sharing with state and local governments, a "New Federalism." The idea was to consolidate similar categorical programs into block grants to lower levels of government, which would have discretion about how to spend the funds according to local needs. Nixon's New Federalism was too abstract a notion to serve as the basis for a new political majority, despite his hopes that it would. As unusual as his administration was in other ways, in the realm of domestic policy it served as a typical presidency of consolidation.

What was atypical about this period, however, was the nature of the intellectual ferment and social discontent that was occurring outside government. New-style policy problems seemed less tractable than older ones had been: in the economy, simultaneous high inflation and high unemployment; in social policy, worsening minority youth unemployment; in foreign policy, disorientation about the post-Vietnam American role in the world. Liberals seemed to have lost confidence in their ability to define the direction of change and to develop appropriate programs to achieve it. Some of them joined ranks with new-style, intellectually aggressive "neo"-conservatives. Meanwhile, voters became much more unpredictable in their electoral behavior and much less willing to identify themselves with either party or link their votes for senator and representative to their presidential vote.[44]

The presidency of Gerald Ford, nominally a continuation of the Nixon administration, inherited this intellectual and social confusion. Ford's administration was a presidency of stasis. Neither it nor its opponents had useful answers to the new-style policy problems or to the challenge of energy production and conservation presented by the Organization of Petroleum Exporting Countries. The depleted intellectual capital of the times was especially apparent in the ad hoc and contradictory twisting and turning of Ford's economic policy: "Whip Inflation Now" was followed by the largest public employment program and budget deficits in peacetime history. The cycle simply did not continue.

Whether this departure from the cyclic pattern was an aberration or an augury of things to come is an issue we return to at the end of this chapter. In order to do so, however, we need to examine more closely the nature of the cycle itself.

DYNAMICS OF THE CYCLE

The cycle of presidencies of preparation, achievement, and consolidation in domestic policy making can be thought of as a kind of machine. This image will be used to explain how the cycle works, but it also is meant to suggest how subject it is to breakdown if any of its components fails. The "engine" that drives the cycle from stage to stage is presidential elections; the "fuel" on which it runs is ideas; and presidential leadership skill is the "carburetor" that activates the fuel in response to the engine's requirements.

Elections

Many political scientists would argue that there is very little relationship between the distribution of citizen preferences on issues and the actions of government. This is certainly true if the test is how fully the government acts to mirror the issue positions of a majority of citizens on a wide range of policy questions. But one needs to supplement this test with a sense of a historical process in which changes in political attitudes across time by large groups of voters either make it politically possible for government to act in new ways or preclude such action. Not all issues are equally important. The concerns that social discontent and intellectual ferment have brought to the fore at any given time are the ones that presidential candidates must respond to and, if elected, deal with in some manner. Sometimes popular demands are reasonably clear. V. O. Key and other have shown that shifts on issue positions by substantial segments of voters can determine the results of presidential elections.[45] But this is not always the case. In 1932, for example, Americans were disenchanted with limited government and ready for new ideas, but it is unlikely that a majority would have endorsed the specifics of the New Deal if Roosevelt had described (or even had known) them in the campaign. What they offered Roosevelt was a "permissive consensus" to experiment and, if successful, be rewarded with their approval.[46]

Presidencies of achievement, which form the heart of each cycle, are the most direct products of the election process. They become possible only when three conditions are met: first, a candidate campaigns for the presidency with promises, however general, of significant reform; second, he is elected by a large majority; and third, his election is accompanied by large gains for his party in Congress. It is the size of the gains, more than the size of his party's contingent in Congress, that matters, because the gains invariably are attributed, accurately or not, to the president-elect's coattails or to a "mandate" that he and Congress share. Either way, the election creates a heightened disposition among legislators of both congressional parties to support the president's first-year legislative initiatives: co-partisans because they want to ride his bandwagon, members of the opposition who represent districts the president carried because they want to avoid being flattened by it. A president whose election is not accompanied by large gains is more likely to be seen by legislators as politically tangential to their own electoral fortunes. As we saw, Franklin Roosevelt had an easier time with the Congress that was elected in 1932, which contained many new Democratic faces, than with the Congress chosen in the 1936 election, in which the Democrats made only small gains. This was so even though the total Democratic membership in the later Congress was higher. More recently, Jimmy Carter had very little success with his first Congress, which Democrats controlled by 61 to 38 in the Senate and 292 to 143 in the House, partly because the 1976 election added only one member to the House Democratic ranks and no new senators. Reagan, who faced a narrowly Republican Senate (53 to 46) and a Democratic House (192 to 243), did very well because his election in 1980 was joined to a net gain of 12 Republican senators, enough to take control of the Senate, and 34 Republicans in the House. The governing coalitions that presidents of achievement construct are personal as much as party coalitions.

As Table 3.1 shows, presidents of preparation can be distinguished from presidents of achievement by the size of their electoral mandates, which are smaller. Presidents of consolidation, however, commonly are ushered in by enormous, achievement-style election victories. Such victories can be misinterpreted: Eisenhower, a landslide winner in 1952, frequently was criticized by both

Table 3.1   Initial Elections of Presidents of Preparation, Achievement, and
Consolidation, T. Roosevelt to Nixon

	Victory Margin over Nearest Opponent		Gains for President-Elect's Party in Congress	
	Popular Vote (%)	*Electoral Vote*	*House*	*Senate*
PREPARATION				
T. Roosevelt				
(1904)	18.8	196	43	0
Kennedy (1960)	0.3	84	−21	0
ACHIEVEMENT				
Wilson (1912)	14.4	347	62	9*
F. Roosevelt				
(1932)	17.7	413	97*	12*
Johnson (1964)	22.6	434	37	1
CONSOLIDATION				
Harding (1920)	26.4	277	63	11*
Coolidge (1924)	25.3	246	22	3
Hoover (1928)	17.4	357	30	8
Eisenhower				
(1952)	10.7	353	22*	1*
Nixon (1968)	0.7–14.2†	110–156†	5	6

*Asterisk indicates that the president's party won control of that house of Congress away from the other party.
†The larger number includes the vote for George Wallace, who shared Nixon's opposition to further Great Society-style domestic policy change.

liberals and conservatives for not using his popularity to move the government on behalf of their respective causes in the manner of a president of achievement. In truth, the mandate of the president of consolidation comes as a result of his promise *not* to push for substantial domestic policy changes. Presidents of consolidation are empowered by their elections, but only to consolidate.

Ideas

As we saw in Chapter 2, success for the delegates to the Constitutional Convention meant coming up with ideas for a new government that would be not just desirable (strong but not oppressive), but politically appealing to the American people. These are still the criteria for successful policy making. To be sure, expert knowledge is important. Theories based on evidence and analysis may permit the problems they address to be managed and alleviated, if not solved. Such theories also may supply a president with a confident sense of purpose and direction that can be communicated to others as the basis for political support.

Economic policy provides the clearest case in which formal theory is the source of policy ideas because the discipline is well developed and has a strong practical orientation. But even the recommendations of economists have been found wanting on occasion; besides, not every policy can pretend to draw on formal theory. What is the nature of poverty? Is it a simple lack of jobs for the poor that is rooted in the structure of the economy, or is it a cultural problem that reflects the inability of the poor to respond to the vocational requirements of a technological society? Experts are divided.

Even when accurate expert theories are available, they are insufficient. Successful ideas are syntheses of expert knowledge, political culture-based moral sentiment, and short-term political reality. They not only are accepted by policy experts and political elites as workable, but respond in culturally acceptable terms to the social discontent of the times.

A rigorous definition of ideas such as this may make the task of developing them seem difficult. It is, but, as we have seen, each cycle managed to generate the intellectual fuel on which it ran. The explanation is twofold: time and resources. Ideas go through long periods of incubation, and the task of developing them engages virtually everyone in or on the fringes of political power, from intellectuals and interest groups who have causes to advocate to bureaucrats and legislative staff members who want to enhance the status of their employers to electoral politicians looking for issues. But success is not guaranteed, and without success the cycle has no fuel to run on.

Skill

The presidency's constitutional nature and the cultural and political environment in which it functions do not predestine the performance of individual presidents, but they do set leadership skill requirements that are essential for presidential success. We already have noted the Constitution's requirement for tactical bargaining skills and the importance the political culture implicitly attaches to skills of public rhetoric and management of authority. As we will see in Chapter 4, which is devoted entirely to leadership, presidents at different stages of the cycle need certain of these skills more than they need others.

The skill that all modern presidents need most, however, is one that grows from the cycle itself: a strategic sense of the "grain of history." It is crucial to a president's success in office that he understand the possibilities for action permissible in the politics of his time. Not all presidents have the opportunity to be Franklin Roosevelts because not all historical situations allow heroic action. Kennedy understood himself to be a president of preparation who was laying the groundwork for social reforms that could come in his second term. Eisenhower understood his task as providing stability and predictability to government, and few presidents have been better matched to the popular expectations of their times. On the other hand, neither Taft nor Truman swam with the current in domestic policy: Truman swam against it, and Taft trod water.

FOREIGN POLICY

Most students of American politics draw fairly sharp distinctions between foreign policy making for national security and policy making in other areas. Such distinctions are obvious and important. Because security policy usually seems to citizens to be of less immediate consequence than domestic or economic policy, they are not nearly as informed, interested, or organized to influence government as on those issues. Also, because security policy involves politics among as well as within nations, the public is more likely to tolerate secrecy in government and defer willingly to presidential leadership. One of the ways that presidents try to resolve the public's Constitution and culture-rooted ambivalence to their authority is to turn their attention to foreign policy, where in speaking to the world they can claim more successfully to be speaking for the nation.

Yet there are striking similarities between twentieth-century American foreign policy and the domestic cycle of preparation, achievement, and consolidation. The most obvious is the coincidence of achievement presidencies and war: Wilson and World War I, Roosevelt and World War II, Johnson and Vietnam. The wars frequently were justified in terms of idealistic, even messianic, nationalism. Wilson pledged to "show the way to mankind in every part of the world to justice and freedom and liberty" and insisted that "America must be ready to exert her whole force, moral and physical, to the assertion of those rights throughout the round globe." Wilson's idealistic Fourteen Points ("open covenants openly arrived at," disarmament, etc.) may have "bored" Clemenceau of France ("Even God almighty only has ten!"), but they were very much in tune with the American people's sense of purpose.[47] A generation later, Roosevelt rallied the nation for World War II with similar language:

> The Japanese and the Fascists and the Nazis . . . know that victory for us means victory for freedom . . . [and] democracy. They know that victory for us means victory for religion. And they could not tolerate that. The world is too small to provide adequate "living room" for both Hitler and God. . . . There never has been — there never can be — successful compromise between good and evil. Only total victory can reward the champions of tolerance, and decency, and freedom, and faith.[48]

Johnson sometimes justified America's role in Vietnam in moralistic terms ("to abandon this small and brave nation to its enemy, and to the terror that must follow, would be an unforgivable wrong"),[49] but his failure to do so consistently left the public wondering why American forces were there. Truman failed to secure sustained support for his Korean War policies for the same reason his domestic agenda failed: he was acting like a president of achievement at a time when the public's desire was for consolidation.

Although there is nothing deterministic in the relationship between war and presidencies of achievement, what is common to both war and domestic achievement is a high tide of cultural optimism. In each case the belief is strong that the American people, through their government, have the power to remake the system, whether domestic or international, in conformance with their ideals.

Presidents of domestic policy preparation also seem to have played that role in foreign policy. Theodore Roosevelt, the American embodiment of the early twentieth-century "muscular Christianity" ideal, fufilled the second half of his "Speak softly, and carry a big stick" credo more faithfully than the first. His administration built up the navy and, though generally restrained in its policies, added a "Roosevelt Corollary" to the Monroe Doctrine by announcing:

> Chronic wrongdoing, or an impotence which results in a general loosening of the ties of civilized society . . . may force the United States, however reluctantly, in flagrant cases of such wrongdoing or impotence, to the exercise of an international police power.[50]

Kennedy, invoking in his inaugural address "the same beliefs for which our forebears fought . . . the belief that the rights of man come not from the generosity of the state but from the hand of God," promised that "we shall pay any price, bear any burden, meet any hardship, support any friend, oppose any foe to assure the survival and success of liberty" around the globe. The Peace Corps was a civilian manifestation of the idea that Americans should remake the world; the Green Berets and the 16,500 American troops Kennedy sent to Vietnam were their military counterpart.

In foreign policy Franklin Roosevelt acted as his own president of preparation. American public opinion in the 1920s was extremely isolationist and pacifist; the depression seems to have deepened these feelings. Interestingly, Roosevelt failed when he tried to change this mood by appealing to American self-interest, as he did after Japan "dissolved" China in 1937. His success came when, for example, he offered his "Four Freedoms" in defense of lend-lease, which he compared to lending a neighbor a hose when his house is on fire:

> [T]he democratic way of life is at this moment being directly assailed in every part of the world. . . . Let us say to the democracies: "We Americans are vitally concerned in your defense of freedom. We are putting forth our energies, our resources, and our organizing powers."[51]

The consolidation idea does not apply as well to security policy; how can one state consolidate change in a system that includes many other states? Still, each war had a reactive aftermath. If "messianism" describes American involvement in World War I, "monasticism" may be the word for the 1920s and 1930s. Harding articulated the national mood in 1920: he did not want to "menace the health of the republic in Old World contagion."[52] Reaction in the next two cycles was a mixture of moral and pragmatic strains. In the 1950s John Foster Dulles's speeches about the nation's international "mission . . . assigned us by Providence"[53] were juxtaposed with Eisenhower's foreign-policy restraint. (Eisenhower's usual response to guerrilla insurgency in Vietnam and elsewhere was to admit ruefully that American power was bound by a "tyranny of the weak" that, because it could not be controlled, should be ignored.) *Realpolitik* also was the basis of détente, Vietnamization, the opening to China, and most other aspects of Nixon's foreign policy. But in the 1970s the moral strain in

American culture surfaced outside government in the form of guilt, especially over Vietnam. At root, penance is a variation on the moralistic cultural theme. "Both the illusion and the disillusion seem to reflect a belief that the United States is unique," writes Anthony Lake. "If it is not the most generous and responsible nation in the world, then it is the worst."[54]

Penance, however, is the exception in American foreign policy, oscillation between messianism and monasticism the rule. The idealistic nationalism of the American Creed, with its sense of the United States as a nation ordained to inspire and uplift humankind, is the source of both. "An absolute national morality is inspired either to withdraw from 'alien' things or to transform them: it cannot live in comfort constantly by their side," Louis Hartz observes. "Its messianism is the polar counterpart of its isolationism, which is why Harding and Wilson are both 'Americanist' thinkers."[55]

CARTER, REAGAN, AND THE POLICY CYCLE, 1977-

By no later than the midterm congressional elections of 1982, a conventional understanding had congealed among academic and journalistic observers of Ronald Reagan's presidency, just as it had around Jimmy Carter a few years earlier. Reagan, like Carter, came to be seen as the latest, but probably not the last, in a series of stasis presidents that began with Nixon's resignation in August 1974. In part, the argument went, this was because of personal deficiencies in leadership skill, born of an absence of "peer review" in the modern presidential nominating process. (In Reagan's case these deficiencies were likely to be identified as laziness and lack of curiosity rather than excessive attention to detail at the expense of politics and vision, which were Carter's alleged flaws.)[56] More important to this theory, though, were the perceived weaknesses of government in general and the presidency in particular, which we described in Chapter 1 as the "Samson" model. The public, it was said, expects presidents to do more; social and governmental fragmentation enables them to do less; and Carter and Reagan were just the most recent victims of this structural mandate for failure.[57]

We reject this analysis. No lack of political skill or institutional responsiveness hamstrung Reagan; indeed, he has all of the hallmarks of a president of achievement. Articulating new ideas of economic, social, and foreign policy, writes Arthur Schlesinger, Jr., Reagan "redefined the terms of the national debate. In domestic affairs, he has placed a stigma on 'big government' and exalted the capacity of the unregulated marketplace to solve all our problems. In foreign affairs, he has placed a stigma on détente and has exalted large military budgets and an indefinitely escalating arms race."[58] Reagan's policy ideas, in addition to being dramatic, involve a sufficiently clear change in the direction of federal activity as to make them "heroically incremental" in the tradition of previous presidents of achievement. And though conservative in substance, they are imbued with familiar cultural optimism about the capacity of political engineering to bring about desired change: prosperity through tax cuts, the defeat of leftist revolutionaries abroad through American military aid and advice, and so on.

Like previous achievement presidents, Reagan drew his ideas from others. The ingredients of "Reaganomics," deregulation, "New Federalism" decentralization, a hawkish foreign policy, and moral conservatism were percolating during the 1970s in conservative "think tanks" such as the Heritage Foundation, Hoover Institute, and American Enterprise Institute; in journals of opinion (*The Public Interest* and *Commentary*, among them); and in groups of legislators led by Jack Kemp, David Stockman, and others. Further, for all the sound and fury of the 1980 campaign (reminiscent of the mutual disdain of Wilson and Theodore Roosevelt in 1912), Carter served as a president of preparation for Reagan and his policy ideas. Carter's major campaign themes in 1976, the most conservative of any Democrat since the 1920s, foreshadowed Reagan's: moral conservatism, by example if not by legislation; fiscal restraint; economic deregulation; and an antibureaucracy posture that more than anything else accounted for his rise from obscurity to the Democratic nomination.

Even in security policy Carter prepared the way for Reagan. Although he campaigned in 1976 with a call for defense spending reductions, Carter reversed course in office and ended up projecting increases very close to those Reagan later urged. The moralistic tone of Carter's foreign policy also anticipated Reagan's, even though for Reagan the "messianic" imperative was the spread of anticommunism rather than a Carter-style human rights campaign.

Carter's actions in office paralleled his rhetoric but did not fulfill it. Reagan's election and the first years of his presidency were clearly in the achievement mode. His electoral-vote margin against Carter surpassed Roosevelt's previous 1932 record for defeat of an incumbent; his party gained thirty-four seats in the House, the largest increase since 1964; and Republicans won control of the Senate for the first time since 1952. As had happened after previous achievement-inducing elections, Reagan's co-partisans in Congress lined up almost unanimously on behalf of his legislative initiatives, along with a substantial number of Democrats from states and districts, mostly southern, in which he was especially popular. A *New York Times* study of Reagan's first two years found that he won on 60 percent of his eighty-four efforts to reduce or eliminate domestic federal programs, including "85 to 90 percent of the dollar savings he wanted in 1981."[59] Most of these cuts came from programs that previously had been considered politically untouchable: housing, public service employment, food stamps, child nutrition, and aid to working welfare mothers. Reagan also won passage of a three-quarter trillion dollar "supply side" tax cut, with most of the money earmarked for businesses and high-income individuals on the theory that they would invest it and contribute to capital formation. At the same time, Congress approved his recommendations for a near-doubling of defense outlays from 1980 to 1984, increasing the Pentagon's share of total federal spending from less than one-fourth of the federal budget to more than one-third. Because of Reagan's budget cuts and hiring freeze, federal employment dropped more than 10 percent in the domestic bureaucracy after two years, while rising in the Defense Department. Reagan was less successful in having his way on social issues such as abortion, but by his own admission, they were lowest on his agenda.

In sum, Reagan did the things that presidents of achievement do and that the weak-presidency theorists had been saying were no longer possible because of institutional impediments. He articulated prevailing public discontents, mobilized them into a substantial election victory, drew ideas for suitable policy responses from the intellectual capital of the day, and secured their enactment over the opposition of liberals and a host of adversely affected bureaucrats, client groups, subcommittee chairs in Congress, and others.

Is Reagan, then, a president of achievement? Almost certainly.[60] The only event that would cause us to reject this understanding would be the election in 1984 or 1988 of a Democrat who campaigned on the promise that he would undo all that Reagan had achieved: restore the domestic budget cuts, slash defense spending, raise taxes, and so on. In truth, all of the main candidates for the 1984 Democratic nomination shied away from such a posture from the beginning. The election of any one of them would have resulted in a presidency of consolidation in which Reagan's achievements would have been modified but not repealed.

In addition to his policy successes Reagan has pointed the presidency in the right direction for the reinvigoration of the office. His efforts to construct a new, empowering electoral majority based on ideas and programs have been to good effect. Indeed, the popular and intellectual foundation for strong presidencies may be greater than ever. Even in the heyday of the "Savior" model of a powerful and virtuous presidency, conservatives were suspicious of executive power, which they identified with liberals such as Franklin Roosevelt. Now conservatives realize that a strong presidency can bring about their goals as well. Liberals, who generally have identified the fortunes of their causes with a strong presidency, have heeded Reagan's lesson about the necessity of ideas for leadership. Virtually all the Democrats who were considering a race for the 1984 presidential nomination made a very public point of identifying themselves with the search for new, workable policy ideas. It still is not clear that such ideas are available, but the odds of discovery certainly improve as the search intensifies.

NOTES

1. Sidney Verba and Kay Lehman Schlozman, "Unemployment, Class Consciousness, and Radical Politics: What Didn't Happen in the Thirties," *Journal of Politics* (May 1977), p. 302.
2. Gunnar Myrdal, *An American Dilemma*, 2 vols. (New York: Harper & Bros., 1944), ch. 1; Samuel P. Huntington, *American Politics: The Promise of Disharmony* (Cambridge, Mass.: Harvard University Press, 1981), ch. 2. Louis Hartz uses "liberalism" and "Americanism" in *The Liberal Tradition in America* (New York: Harcourt, Brace & World, 1955).
3. William L. McLoughlin, *Revivals, Awakenings, and Reform* (Chicago: University of Chicago Press, 1978); Conrad Cherry, ed., *God's New Israel* (Englewood Cliffs, N.J.: Prentice-Hall, 1971); Huntington, *American Politics*; Myrdal, *American Dilemma*.

4. Quoted in Reinhold Niebuhr, *The Irony of American History* (New York: Scribner's, 1952), p. 70.
5. Hartz, *Liberal Tradition*; Donald J. Devine, *The Political Culture of the United States* (Boston: Little, Brown, 1972); Daniel J. Boorstin, *The Genius of American Politics* (Chicago: University of Chicago Press, 1953); Ira Katznelson, *City Trenches* (New York: Pantheon, 1981); David M. Potter, *People of Plenty* (Chicago: University of Chicago Press, 1954).
6. Alexis de Tocqueville, *Democracy in America*, 2 vols. (New York: Vintage Books, 1954), vol. 1, p. 409; Myrdal, *American Dilemma*, vol. I, p. 3.
7. John McDiarmid, "Presidential Inaugural Addresses: A Study in Verbal Symbols," *Public Opinion Quarterly* (July 1937), pp. 79–82.
8. Devine, *Political Culture*, p. 185.
9. Herbert Hoover, *American Individualism* (Garden City, N.Y.: Doubleday, Page, 1922), p. 9.
10. Lloyd A. Free and Hadley Cantril, *The Political Beliefs of Americans* (New York: Simon & Schuster, 1968).
11. Myrdal, *American Dilemma*, vol. I, pp. 10, 15.
12. Gordon S. Wood, *The Creation of the American Republic, 1776–1787* (Chapel Hill, N.C.: University of North Carolina Press, 1969).
13. Almost twice as many voters in a 1978 survey said that when a congressman sees a conflict between "what the voters think best" and "what he thinks best," he should obey the voters. Morris P. Fiorina, "Congressmen and Their Constituents: 1958 and 1978," in Dennis Hale, ed., *The United States Congress* (Chestnut Hill, Mass.: Boston College, 1982), p. 39.
14. McLoughlin, *Revivals, Awakenings*, ch. 3.
15. Gabriel A. Almond and Sidney Verba, *The Civic Culture* (Princeton, N.J.: Princeton University Press, 1963), pp. 185, 367; Samuel H. Barnes and Max Kaase, *Political Action* (Beverly Hills, Calif.: Sage, 1979), pp. 541–42, 574.
16. Almond and Verba, *Civic Culture*, p. 102.
17. Jack Citrin, "The Changing American Electorate," in Arnold J. Meltsner, ed., *Politics and the Oval Office* (San Francisco: Institute for Contemporary Studies, 1981), p. 52; Jack Citrin, "The Political Relevance of Trust in Government," *American Political Science Review* (September 1974), p. 975.
18. Devine, *Political Culture*, p. 102.
19. James Q. Wilson, *American Government*, 2nd ed. (Lexington, Mass.: D. C. Heath, 1983), p. 82.
20. Roberta S. Sigel, "Image of the American Presidency," *Midwest Journal of Political Science* (February 1966), p. 125.
21. Stephen J. Wayne, "Great Expectations: What People Want from Their Presidents," in Thomas E. Cronin, ed., *Rethinking the Presidency* (Boston: Little, Brown, 1982), pp. 193–94.
22. McLoughlin, *Revivals, Awakenings*, p. xiii.
23. Tocqueville, *Democracy in America*, vol. 1, p. 314; *Public Opinion* (March 1979), pp. 38–39; Walter Dean Burnham, "The 1980 Earthquake," in Thomas Ferguson and Joel Rogers, eds., *The Hidden Election* (New York: Pantheon, 1981), pp. 132–35. Winthrop is quoted in Cherry, *God's New Israel*, p. 43.
24. McLoughlin, *Revivals, Awakenings*, passim.
25. C. S. Olcott, *The Life of William McKinley*, 2 vols. (Boston: Houghton Mifflin, 1916), vol. II, pp. 110–11.
26. This version was spoken on November 25, 1982, according to *Newsweek* (December 27, 1982), p. 44. On February 3, he said: "I've always believed that this blessed land was set apart in a special way, that some divine plan placed this great continent here between two oceans to be found by people from every corner of the earth—people who had a special love for freedom." *Christianity Today* (March 4, 1983), p. 47.
27. Robert Bellah, "Civil Religion in America," *Daedalus* (Winter 1967), pp. 1–21. (Jefferson and Franklin quotes on p. 20.)

28. Niebuhr, *Irony*, p. 24.
29. Austin Ranney, "The 'Divine Science': Political Engineering in American Culture," *American Political Science Review* (March 1976), p. 147.
30. Huntington, *American Politics*, p. 147.
31. Quoted in Samuel Eliot Morison, *The Oxford History of the American People* (New York: Oxford University Press, 1965), pp. 811–12.
32. *Ibid.*
33. Arthur S. Link, *Woodrow Wilson and the Progressive Era, 1900–1917* (New York: Harper & Row, 1954), p. 2.
34. James Ceaser, "Presidential Selection," in Joseph M. Bessette and Jeffrey Tulis, eds., *The Presidency in the Constitutional Order* (Baton Rouge: Louisiana State University Press, 1981), p. 236.
35. Quoted in James L. Sundquist, *The Decline and Resurgence of Congress* (Washington: Brookings Institution, 1981), p. 133.
36. *Ibid*, p. 135.
37. James MacGregor Burns, *Roosevelt: The Lion and the Fox* (New York: Harcourt, Brace, & World, Harvest ed., 1956), p. 179.
38. *Ibid.*, p. 337.
39. Sundquist, *Decline and Resurgence*, p. 72.
40. Angus Campbell *et al.*, *The American Voter* (New York: Wiley, 1960).
41. James L. Sundquist, *Politics and Policy: The Eisenhower, Kennedy, and Johnson Years* (Washington: Brookings Institution, 1969), pp. 456–70.
42. Roger Davidson, "The President and Congress," in Michael Nelson, ed., *The Presidency and the Political System* (Washington: Congressional Quarterly Press, 1984), p. 385.
43. Free and Cantril, *Political Beliefs*, pp. 5–40.
44. Norman H. Nie, Sidney Verba, and John Petrocik, *The Changing American Voter* (Cambridge, Mass.: Harvard University Press, 1976); Morris P. Fiorina, "The Presidency and the Contemporary Electoral System," in Nelson, *Presidency and Political System*, pp. 204–26.
45. V. O. Key, Jr., *The Responsible Electorate* (Cambridge, Mass.: Harvard University Press, 1966).
46. The term is V. O. Key's. *Public Opinion and American Democracy* (New York: Alfred A. Knopf, 1961).
47. Quoted in Morison, *Oxford History*, p. 861.
48. "Annual *Message to Congress*, January 6, 1942," in Cherry, *God's New Israel*, p. 297.
49. "Johnson's Speech on Vietnam, Johns Hopkins University, April 7, 1965," in Henry Steele Commager, ed., *Documents of American History*, vol. 2, 9th ed. (Englewood Cliffs, N.J.: Prentice-Hall, 1973), p. 699.
50. Quoted in Morison, *Oxford History*, p. 826.
51. "Roosevelt's 'Four Freedoms' Speech, January 6, 1941," in Commager, *Documents*, pp. 446, 448.
52. Quoted in Hartz, *Liberal Tradition*, p. 297.
53. "Freedom's New Task, February 26, 1956," in Cherry, *God's New Israel*, p. 327.
54. Anthony Lake, *The Vietnam Legacy* (New York: New York University Press, 1976), p. xxi. See also C. Vann Woodward, "The Fall of the American Adam," *The New Republic* (December 2, 1981), pp. 13–16.
55. Hartz, *Liberal Tradition*, p. 286.
56. See, for example, Nelson W. Polsby, *The Consequences of Party Reform* (New York: Oxford University Press, 1983).
57. See, for example, the books reviewed in Michael Nelson, "Sentimental Science: Recent Essays on the Politics of Presidential Selection," *Congress and the Presidency* (Autumn, 1982), pp. 100–106; and Elizabeth Drew, "A Reporter in Washington," *The New Yorker* (February 14, 1983), pp. 97–106.
58. Arthur M. Schlesinger, Jr., "The Democratic Party after Ted Kennedy," *The Wall Street Journal* (December 7, 1982).

59. Robert Pear, "The Reagan Revolution," *The New York Times* (January 31, 1983).
60. One could construct an argument that the presidency of Ronald Reagan is one of re-
    sumed consolidation of the Great Society reforms of the third cycle. In this view,
    Reagan is completing a process that was interrupted by Watergate and its after-
    shocks, which crippled the Ford and Carter administrations. Reagan's New
    Federalism is, after all, similar to Nixon's, and the federal "safety net" that he marked
    as immune to substantial change includes many of the essential New Deal and Great
    Society programs: Social Security, Medicare, and supplemental security income
    (SSI) for the handicapped and elderly poor, among them. One also could argue that
    Reagan will turn out a president of preparation. His rhetoric about social issues such
    as abortion, busing, and school prayer, and about shrinkng the federal
    government's share of the economy through a balanced-budget constitutional
    amendment may be setting the stage for a "New Right" triumph in the 1988 election
    that will secure the enactment of their agenda into law.

    Neither interpretation, though arguable, comports with the cycle theory. The
    consolidation interpretation's assumption is that unless a president seeks to change
    all or most of government, he cannot be classed in one of the change-oriented cate-
    gories: preparation, achievement, or even Truman-style stalemate. But none of the
    previous presidents of change, including Wilson, Franklin Roosevelt, and Johnson,
    sought to destroy or replace the government he inherited. Nor should we expect such
    presidents to do so, given the fairly narrow ideological bounds within which serious
    issues are fought in the United States. What marks a consolidation presidency is an
    absence of concern for changing or accelerating the *direction* of government in-
    volvement. By that definition, Reagan clearly is excluded. As for presidents of prep-
    aration, their chief characteristic is that they articulate ideas that not only lead, but
    reflect a broad change in the direction of public opinion. In Reagan's case, the ex-
    treme conservative issues that he has promoted but not enacted seem to be losing
    rather than gaining public support. In 1982 conservative political action committees
    were as unsuccessful in electing candidates who reflected their positions as they had
    been successful in 1980.

CHAPTER 4

Presidential Leadership

Presidents are not powerful by virtue of being president. Constitutional, cultural, and political forces empower a president at some times and on some issues, and, as the preceding chapter illustrates, presidents are, in varying degrees, able to influence the politics that cause the public at large and other leaders to follow them and support the policies they advocate. Political "skill" is crucial to leadership. Individual presidents can make a difference. Nonetheless, different kinds of presidencies face different strategic problems, and the political resources available to them vary. A president of preparation tries to create new political resources. A president of achievement invokes existing resources and directs them into channels of action. A president of consolidation must use existing political resources to rationalize reform.

SKILL

The dictionary gives three complementary definitions to the word *skill*: great ability or proficiency; an art, craft, or science; and knowledge, understanding, or judgment. It also adds an archaic definition, "to make a difference."[1] The study of skill in political leaders requires an understanding of these characteristics. Individuals possess a range of natural abilities to influence others. One can identify the cluster of abilities that is said to typify the art or craft of political leadership, just as one knows a skillful physician, sailor, or actor. Finally, skill consists of more than manipulative ability; it requires knowledge, understanding, and a capacity for judgment.

We regard four skills as central to the exercise of presidential leadership. Each type of president must create a different configuration of these skills because presidential tasks differ according to historical circumstances. All skills are not equally important to all presidents. The four capacities are *strategic skill*, which includes the ability to formulate coherent policy goals that match the historical situation and to develop strategies for their attainment that are based on the political resources that are available or can be developed; *skill at presenting oneself and one's ideas to the public* through rhetoric and drama; the *tactical capacity* to construct coalitions of power holders to secure agreement on particular questions; and *skill in managing authority* for policy formation and administration.

Strategic Understanding

The central task of political leadership is to articulate plausible and politically appealing remedies for public problems. Presidents borrow ideas from others and build on the political traditions from which they come. But every historical period is characterized by uncertainties and ambiguities. A president who can persuade people to accept his diagnosis of outstanding problems and the remedies he proposes has created a political base that is difficult to assail.

A leader has a better chance of attaining the ends he seeks if he has a strategic approach to achieving those goals. A strategic approach is one in which ends are joined to means within the context of what is, or can be made to be, politically possible. Goals must be ranked not only in order of importance, but also according to the feasibility of their attainment. Leaders must assess the effect of seeking one goal on the chances of obtaining another. The available political support for a range of goals must be calculated. Leaders will decide not to attempt some things at all because political soundings suggest that action would be not only fruitless, but would damage their political support. This is not as calculable as it sounds because one must take advantage of unexpected opportunities, and crises intervene to frustrate plans. But it is important to keep a strategic perspective so that resources are neither wasted nor squandered but brought into play at the best possible time.

Presidents are not the passive instruments of a historical dialectic. But neither are they the creators of the large patterns of social and political forces that they face in office. The central task of presidents is to be skillful in understanding and acting to fulfill the historical possibilities in their time.

Presentation of Self

The skillful leader must be able to dramatize himself and his ideas for public audiences. If a president lacks this ability to capture the attention and the adherence of millions of people, he is denied a crucial instrument of leadership. Public speaking is one way to win public support. But the presentation of self includes both other verbal public encounters, such as press conferences and interactions with crowds while campaigning, and symbolic actions, such as Jimmy Carter's return to the White House on foot after his inauguration.

Tactics

The actual achievement of goals requires the tactical ability to bring all the components of a situation together in a way that permits one to dominate events. Thus, a president who is trying to persuade a group of congressional leaders to do something may have paved the way with public statements, private bargains, and personal persuasion. He may have asked others whom they respect to talk to them. If he is shrewd, he will have calculated the messages necessary to meet their goals and political incentives, and this is all done through constructing a mosaic of appeals around them.

A skillful president must understand the motives of other political people not only as individuals, but as classes of actors. He must understand the ambitions and incentives that animate those whom he must persuade. For example, if he is trying to persuade a group of senators to support a bill, he must know what they think about their own electoral futures, the interest groups they must placate, their ambitions for higher office, and how these factors affect the way they treat him; some of them may want his job. Cold-eyed realism is crucial to both survival and success in the presidency. The motives of people are building blocks of policy.

A president must be personally sensitive to the dimension of power in institutional life. He must be aware that other people possess power that he does not control and that they may use it against him. He is naive if he assumes either that they will agree with him automatically or that they will not seek to use their power for their own purposes. On the other hand, he also has powers as president that give him strong bargaining chips against other power holders. Just as agreements are forged out of the appeal to political incentives, so do they come from bargains that embody a recognition of the consequences to one's power of failure to agree.

Management of Authority

There are two aspects to the management of authority. The first is the ability to establish a position of authority over presidential lieutenants in the White House and cabinet so that they will give a president respect and loyalty but also tell him the truth as they see it. This is a skill at guiding and supporting people. It derives from the personal attributes of a president. He must be respected by his colleagues for his competence as a leader of government; he must bring insights to problems of governing that embrace but go beyond their own specific expertise. He must be emotionally secure and intellectually open so that they can suggest new ideas to him and state unpleasant truths. In the absence of this skill, processes of policy formation are likely to founder for lack of respect, loyalty, and freedom of discussion.

The second aspect of this skill is managerial in the conventional sense: ability to organize government for orderly and efficient policy implementation. It is possible for presidents to be good at managing authority relationships with lieutenants and to be poor at administrative leadership. The capacity for administrative leadership requires experience and knowledge of how organizations work most effectively, of how best to combine staff advisers and operating administrators, of how to delegate authority for policy implementation and yet keep oversight and control.

These four skill requirements are not presented as a model for presidential "greatness." Not all presidents can be Lincolns or Roosevelts. Greatness in this sense is possible only at critical junctures in the nation's history when the very definition of the society is at stake, as with the Civil War and the depression of the 1930s. But no matter how modest their goals—and the problems and politics of the times may call for modesty—all presidents can be skillful in their leadership. The profiles that make up the body of this chapter illustrate the variety of leadership styles that are compatible with high levels of skill and also reveal the consequences of presidential skill, or its absence, for effectiveness.

Our definition of effectiveness is implicit in the idea of strategic skill. Effectiveness is making the most of what you have to work with. The public must be persuaded to accept goals and follow the president; coalitions for policy must be created; lieutenants must be directed toward constructive action; and scarce political resources must be deployed in behalf of goals in ways that are not wasteful. This is not to say that a great deal will be achieved by skillful leadership. But more will be achieved than would be the case if the president were not skillful.

Types of Presidents and Skill

The three types of presidents require different arrays of skills, whose composition can be derived deductively from the theory of political cycles. Each is an "ideal type" in its abstractness. No president will correspond fully to the type in which he is placed. Our central argument is that the purposes of each type of president will be served best by a configuration of skills that meets the requirements of leadership in its historical period. All presidents need highly developed strategic skills because providing historical direction and defining the strategic political situation are essential to the full use of political resources. But presidents of different types will have very different strategic objectives, which entail different companion skills.

Presidents of preparation should match presentational skills to their strategic sense. Their principal task is to prepare the way for presidents of achievement by placing issues on the public agenda. Skills of tactical leadership are less valuable because teaching is more important at this stage than legislative achievement. However, a few well-chosen victories can be important in giving a sense of momentum. A capacity to manage processes of policy formation within an administration is important, but management of the implementation of policy takes a back seat.

Presidents of achievement should combine a high order of strategic perception with rhetorical and tactical skills in order to build coalitions for dramatic action. They are favored by temporary ground swells of political support for legislative action. Their rhetorical ability may contribute to the strength of the ground swells, and the capacity to construct coalitions for legislative passage is necessary to channel diffuse political forces in specific directions. The management of processes of policy formation for presidents of achievement is even more important than for presidents of preparation, and it is difficult to distinguish this from tactical skill because the same ability to sort and sift ideas and interests is at work in both cases. The management of policy implementation does not figure large because so much energy goes into enactment.

As we saw in Chapter 3, although most presidents of achievement have been progressives, there is nothing in American life to preclude conservative ones. In such a case the style of presidential leadership is somewhat different than for a progressive president of achievement. The conservative is likely to carry over some of the values of consolidating presidents with regard to management and administration.

Presidents of consolidation should combine their strategic understanding with strong conceptions and practices of administrative management in which past policies are rationalized, made more efficient and economical, and retired from the list of partisan issues. They do not need strong tactical skills to do this. The capacity to foster a sense of confidence in the administrative capabilities of their government must be presented to the public, so some teaching skill is required. The president of consolidation needs a gift for affirming and unifying across coalitions.

These propositions about the skills required for each type of president are deductions from the central ideas of the cyclic theory of politics and policy. Empirical descriptions of presidents are necessary in order to establish the degree of correspondence of the "ideal types" to reality. They also are the basis on which evaluative judgments can be made about how well a given president matches the requirements of his time. The evaluation of presidents should take account of historical context, strategic possibilities, and the skills appropriate to that context.

Some presidents will have more skills than their times will permit them to exercise. Theodore Roosevelt would have been a marvelous president of achievement had he been elected in 1912, but he came into the presidency too early for the full exercise of his abilities and had to operate with great restraint as a president of preparation. Other presidents may have less than the full complement of skills necessary to play their role. Jimmy Carter was perhaps deficient in the rhetorical and teaching skills necessary for a president of preparation. Therefore, we are not arguing that the cycle automatically throws up the "man of the hour."

THREE SUCCESSFUL PRESIDENTS: ROOSEVELT, EISENHOWER, AND KENNEDY

Franklin D. Roosevelt, Dwight D. Eisenhower, and John F. Kennedy were "successful" presidents in that each fulfilled the requirements exacted of presidents of achievement, consolidation, and preparation, respectively.

Roosevelt transformed the policy commitments of the American national government at home and abroad. He also altered the presidency as an institution in terms of both the development of the White House and executive office staffs and of popular expectations of the presidency. As a president of achievement, Roosevelt evoked political and intellectual forces that were ripe for expression and gave them direction. He did not cause these forces to exist, but became their voice. The leadership of presidents of achievement is a happy combination of empowerment through the expression of popular tides of opinion and skillful direction of opinion on the part of the president. Successful presidents of achievement will recognize the limits for action. They never cease to be politicians, but they also must articulate a new direction.

Eisenhower achieved the consolidation and legitimation of the New Deal and stabilized the foreign policy of the cold war. He accepted the institutionalized presidency and improved it organizationally. As a president of consolidation he sought unity rather than conflict, did not innovate to any great extent, and emphasized administration over policy.

Kennedy began a new political cycle after the Eisenhower presidency as a president of preparation. He was elected in 1960 by a very thin plurality. A number of innovative policy ideas had been incubating during the 1950s, and Kennedy sought to be their voice. But it was part of his strategy to popularize such ideas in his first term and translate them into policy after a successful re-election in 1964. Lyndon Johnson was the beneficiary of these efforts. As a president of preparation, Kennedy sought to persuade the public and governmental leaders of the desirability of new ideas. He can be considered successful not only because most of his proposals eventually were enacted, but because his policy initiatives were grounded in a realistic understanding of popular politics.

Franklin D. Roosevelt

Strategy.   Roosevelt was guided by two general ideas about the depression and the war. He knew that American capitalism had failed to provide the economic security that the people of the country demanded and, therefore, must be reformed. He also recognized that once a European war began, the United States would have great difficulty staying out of it. The central themes of his presidency are to be found in his search for ways to implement these two insights. Roosevelt often shifted his ground as it became apparent that the direction he had chosen was not politic. Thus, the first New Deal, with its emphasis upon national planning, gave way to the second New Deal and increased attention to the reform of industry through regulation and greater competition. Initial attempts to warn the nation against the aggressive designs of Hitler and Mussolini were not heeded and gave way to carefully calculated efforts at public education in response to specific events such as the Battle of Britain. Roosevelt's tactics changed, but he generally understood that his political resources were limited and should not be squandered.

Roosevelt's understanding of policy problems often was confused, particularly when there was no consensus of opinion about what to do. Thus, the nation did not come out of the depression until wartime because he could not find an economic theory of recovery that satisfied his instincts. He might have applied the theories of Keynesian economics had he understood them, but he did not, nor did most of his contemporaries. So he improvised, with predictable results. New measures of social welfare, income security, and business regulation were passed to ensure that another depression would not occur so easily or be so severe. But the New Deal was a regulatory and welfare program that lacked an economic theory. Roosevelt could not supply a theory. Nor could any president. He did, however, understand the American people. He knew that they wanted reform without radicalism, and that is exactly what he gave them. He knew that they were fearful of foreign entanglements, so he very cautiously introduced the idea of an American role in the world. One of his White House aides remembered:

> He never tried to get too far ahead of the American people in his judgment. In 1937 he went to Chicago and made the quarantine speech about perhaps using the Navy to quarantine the Nazis' and fascists' shipping, and the reaction was so strong

against it he really just pulled back for a while. He was always trying to help the allies but he didn't know how far he could go. . . .I went in to talk to him about some minor point and he looked rather crestfallen. He said, "The Japanese are moving their troops south; they're moving them into Indonesia, maybe Singapore, certainly more into Manchuria, and there's nothing I can do about it. The American people will not let me use the Navy to stop them." He looked very discouraged. Of course, Pearl Harbor came along and solved most of that kind of problem, but he was always watching the American people, how far he could go, what the Congress was doing. . . . He was essentially a politician, practically all the time.[2]

One may criticize Roosevelt's cautious approach to the possibility of war, but he was able to secure help for Britain, to persuade Congress to pass a draft law, and to begin modest defense mobilization so that, when war came, the first steps had been taken.

Roosevelt created his own political resources out of the calamity of the depression. He forged an electoral coalition in the 1934 and 1936 elections that was to last until the 1970s. The New Deal programs served the needs of labor, farmers, the unemployed, the poor, and millions of people who were worried about their long-term security. But the coalition was forged out of Roosevelt's legislative program. It was not the basis for that program. The program came first, and then the coalition was created through the Democratic party. And once it was created, it became less useful to the president because its constituent groups became preoccupied with their own interests than with broad goals of social reform. By the time war came, farmers and labor were far more concerned about their share of the economic pie than they were about reform.[3]

Presentation of Self. When Roosevelt told the nation in his first inaugural address that "we have nothing to fear but fear itself," he struck a chord of hope in the optimistic American culture that was deeply rooted in his own buoyant personality. After Roosevelt died several people told the writer John Gunther, "I never met him, but I felt as if I had lost my greatest friend."[4] Arthur Schlesinger, Jr., describes Roosevelt's appeal:

It was the image of human warmth in a setting of dramatic national action which made people love him. . . . It was not any technical wizardry as a politician but rather his brilliant dramatization of politics as the medium for education and leadership which accounted for his successes. Beyond the backdrop of the depression and the deeds of the New Deal, Roosevelt gained his popular strength from that union of personality and public idealism which he joined so irresistibly to create so profoundly compelling a national image.[5]

Roosevelt used the radio to put himself in the living rooms of the nation. The color and warmth of his voice and his facility of expression were perfect for broadcasting. His "fireside chats" used direct, homey language and clear analogies. For example, he justified the program of military aid to Great Britain before the United States entered the war as similar to lending a neighbor a garden hose when his house is on fire. When his secretary of labor, Frances Perkins, sat with people as they listened to his radio talks, she noticed that they sensed that Roosevelt felt concern and affection for them and they responded in kind.[6]

Tactics.   Roosevelt had great tactical virtuosity. His strategic judgment was to delay Social Security legislation in 1933, although he wanted it, because he felt that public opinion was not ready for what would appear to be so "radical" a measure. By 1934 he judged the time to be right and moved with great tactical skill. Roosevelt first mentioned the idea at a press conference for business editors in 1934 at which he stressed the actuarial soundness of workers saving for their retirement through their own contributions, matched by employers, and emphasized the limited role of government in such a plan. From June 1934 until January 1935, when the bill was sent to Congress, he engaged in an educational campaign, subtly tied to the 1934 congressional election. He sent Congress a general message that discussed Social Security's objectives, set up a commission to study the issue, devoted two fireside chats to explaining that Social Security was simply people saving for themselves, and raised the issue in several speeches around the country.

In January 1935 Roosevelt discussed the bill in his State of the Union message. But he did not raise the matter again except briefly in an April fireside chat, to nudge Congress along. His only comments were in "background" statements in press conferences, for which he was not quoted directly. He did not want to appear to be pressuring Congress but kept the issue alive. The tactics worked.[7]

Roosevelt always tried to work very closely with legislative leaders, and his appeals to the public were couched in general terms, with little specific reference to particular measures. His successes with congressional leaders came through personal diplomacy. James MacGregor Burns records:

> Roosevelt's leadership talents lay in his ability to shift quickly and gracefully from persuasion to cajolery to flattery to intrigue to diplomacy to promises to horse trading—or to concoct just that formula which his superb instincts for personal relations told him would bring around the most reluctant congressman.[8]

Roosevelt boasted to aides about his handling of legislators, whether through charm or implied threat. However, he did not browbeat Congress publicly and seldom painted it as an obstacle to be overcome. His greatest resource with Congress was that he tied his tactical skills to great policy objectives for which he was able to win public support. He picked up the mantle of moral leadership and progressive reform in a time of crisis, and the nation responded.[9]

Authority.   The central principle of Roosevelt's management of men and women was the stimulation and management of centrifugal forces. He chose as lieutenants people of vision and liveliness and gave them opportunities to be creative. But knowing that such people are likely to break loose in all directions, Roosevelt also found ways to guide and control them. He did this through both loyalty and fear. An agency chief once said that "after spending an hour with the president, I could eat nails for lunch."[10] Perkins remembered that he administered "by the technique of friendship, encouragement and trust. The method of not giving direct and specific orders to his subordinates released the creative energy of many men." And, she added, "his capacity to inspire and encourage those who had to do tough, confused and practically impossible jobs was beyond dispute. I, and everyone else, came away from an interview with the President feeling better."[11]

Roosevelt also tested his aides by using a competitive approach to administration, giving two people the same assignment. This created insecurity, which forced them to drive even harder for achievement. People would be encouraged to proceed in opposite directions, in part because Roosevelt was an experimentalist and wanted to see how ideas worked in practice but also because he was tolerant of a high degree of variety and conflict among his policies and official family.[12]

There was never any doubt that Roosevelt was in control. He never completely gave himself or his ideas to anyone, and all of his associates feared that they were expendable. In his desire for competition and maximum pressure, he almost seemed to be manipulating them like marionettes.[13] But he also gave them freedom and encouragement and, most important, inspiration. They would go to see him on a matter and, although they might not get what they asked for, he would give them a sense of participating in a larger enterprise. They would learn that he was better informed, through sources unknown to them, on their problems than they were. They would be able to see how their piece of the puzzle fit a larger political strategy. Roosevelt's virtuosity in managing the strings of government was overwhelming, and this skill, when joined to a great cause in which they all believed, made up for the many frustrations they felt about his using them without fully disclosing his purposes.[14]

Roosevelt balanced his authority with his need for information through an elaborate system of intelligence gathering. He was very accessible for a president. Nearly one hundred government officials could reach him on a direct telephone line. He read widely — newspapers, mail from the public, the *Congressional Record*, government reports — but his antennae were best stimulated through conversation with the endless stream of visitors to his office, whom he questioned vigorously about conditions in the country. He also traveled a great deal and talked with people directly. He listened when he talked because he was an expert at gauging the effect of his words on others; thus, he was always trying ideas out on visitors to the White House, often to their confusion since they had come to see him about something else.[15] His possession of so much information prevented any of his subordinates from dominating channels of intelligence to him and kept them honest in what they told him for fear that he would know better if they did otherwise.

Roosevelt's skills at managing people were directed more at policy formation than implementation. In fact, the application of the same methods to policy implementation, particularly the competitive principle of giving two people the same assignment, made for less than orderly administration. But his goal was ferment rather than efficiency. He wanted to challenge established agencies, shake up routines, and inject new life into the federal government. If the price was a corresponding absence of administrative regularity, it was a price worth paying for a creative president of achievement.

Conclusion.   Roosevelt understood himself to be what we call a president of achievement and embodied the necessary skills in abundance. His greatest capacity was for moral leadership, and his greatest moments were in the crises of depression and war, when he could lead by inspiration. In periods of drift and uncertainty, when public opinion was at sea, he was a cautious president who attempted to go no further than people would be led.

Roosevelt's second term was characterized more by failure than success. His effort to increase the size of the Supreme Court in order to win Court support for New Deal programs failed in Congress. It did achieve increased support from the Court but also undermined his credibility with many Americans. The "conservative coalition" of southern Democrats and middle-western Republicans in Congress resisted additional New Deal reform measures. Isolationism in Congress and the nation frustrated his efforts to aid the Allies or increase U.S. defenses.

These defeats in the second term illustrate that great leadership skill by itself is an incomplete political resource. Skill is most effective when joined to empowerment through politics. Roosevelt patiently waited out the period of weakness and used the rising tide of war and his reelection in 1940 to become once again a moral leader of the nation in crisis. Without rising tides of political support his great skill appeared to be mere cleverness and manipulation, as in the Court fight, and was of little use to him.

Roosevelt's greatness was in his understanding of both the possibilities for and limits to achievement. His critics have taken him to task for not radicalizing the Democratic party and remaking America in a more progressive image.[16] But Roosevelt understood the possibilities for leadership in American democracy better than his critics.

Dwight D. Eisenhower

Strategy.   Eisenhower was a national hero even before he became president. He had been the supreme Allied commander in Europe during World War II and was seen as the architect of the victory over Germany. However, his popularity was based less on military skills than on the picture of "Ike" as a good manager of men who had brought together the talents of diverse generals from several armies and nationalities and established his authority over them. He presented a combination of relaxation and strength to the American people that made both political parties wish to nominate him for president in 1948.

When Eisenhower became president in 1953, the nation was bogged down in the bitterly divisive Korean conflict. This unresolved issue was stimulated by Republican charges that the Democratic Truman administration had "lost" China to the communists in 1949 and that there were many disloyal civil servants in the State Department and other high places. Although President Truman had been reelected in 1948, it was the last gasp of the New Deal coalition. The nation had had enough of domestic reform, and the Truman Fair Deal program, much of which was to emerge later in the Kennedy New Frontier and Johnson Great Society, was politically stillborn. Eisenhower was elected president because a majority of the people wanted a presidency of consolidation that would bring strength, order, and efficiency to government without repudiating the policies of New Deal reform.[17]

Eisenhower pretended not to be a politician and indeed did not like conventional party politics. But he fully understood what was required of him and the political resources that were available. He was his own chief political resource: the Republican party was a handicap not only because it was a minority party, but because its national congressional leaders were not accustomed to cooperating with the president. Eisenhower had to bring them toward the center in support of a domestic agenda that included acceptance of the New Deal reforms, fiscal restraint in government spending, and modest proposals for federal aid to education and civil rights. In due course, he was able to bring most Republican congressional leaders over to his view and to cooperate with the centrist Democratic leadership that controlled Congress for six of his eight years as president. He was, in fact, more conservative in his personal views about domestic policy than the programs he advocated would suggest. But he explicitly thought it necessary to pursue a middle path in order to marry his party to mainstream opinion.[18]

The central theme of Eisenhower's foreign and defense policies was the search for a stable, predictable, economically sound set of policies that would contain Soviet adventurism without causing the United States to embark on similar adventures. He negotiated a truce in Korea during his first year in office. Defense policy, which was geared to an expected long period of rivalry with the Soviets, was based on the idea that mutual nuclear deterrence would prevent general war. Weapons development, he felt, should balance strategic needs and economic capacities so that neither national security nor the health of the economy would be endangered. Eisenhower was very cautious about involving the nation in limited military engagements. He avoided possible U.S. military action to help the French in Southeast Asia by setting down conditions for American participation that could not be met. But the implicit threat of intervention was always present.[19] A Gallup poll that was released on January 18, 1961, two days before Eisenhower left office, asked a sample of the public what they considered his greatest single achievement. The majority reply was direct: "He kept the peace."[20]

One can infer that Eisenhower understood the historical context of his presidency from the balance and moderation of his actions. The 1950s were not going to be a period of either reform or reaction; instead they provided a perfect opportunity for a consolidating leader. Although Eisenhower was not a professional politician, he seems to have understood, as did Roosevelt, both the possibilities for and limits to action, and, also like Roosevelt, he knew that his standing with the public was his chief political resource. This credibility had to be used carefully and not squandered.

Presentation of Self.   No one ever claimed that Eisenhower was an accomplished orator. His delivery was not polished, and he avoided dramatic and arresting phrases, striving to use plain, homey language. His speeches were an extension of a public persona that had been created long before he was president, as supreme Allied commander in Europe in World War II. His open, boyish, middle-western personality had made him popular with soldiers and public alike as a "GI general," so that by the time he ran for the presidency he was a folk hero.[21] But this appeal did not include hero worship. Robert Devine, a historian, describes it:

> Eisenhower's optimism, his sense of proportion, above all his innate practicality, appealed enormously to the American people. Douglas MacArthur had been an equally successful war leader, but his evident ambition and his theatrical qualities made the voters suspicious. In Eisenhower, a nation beset with the problems of the nuclear arms race and the Red Scare had a man who promised calm leadership and the restoration of national confidence. In the course of the 1952 campaign, he would make the politician's usual promises, but his greatest appeal was his own appearance of serenity. Throughout the war, he had gotten talented men of conflicting views to pull together. He had the knack of delegating authority and yet never surrendering control. He had the ability to stand aloof from the passions of the moment and to assess the broader implications of the situation.[22]

In short, Eisenhower's greatest attribute as a public leader was the optimism and strength that he had taught himself to convey as a wartime leader. He believed that one must show optimism and deliberately hide concern or pessimism. In this way, one could appear to be in control of events.[23]

Authority.   Eisenhower was both experienced and clever in managing subordinates and creating efficient administrative mechanisms. He used the cabinet meeting not to make decisions, but to hold his administrative team together behind his objectives. Through an elaborate system of staffing, he developed an effective policy planning and implementation system. During Eisenhower's presidency it often was said that he was the prisoner of the staff bureaucracy that he had created, but he always drew a distinction between formal and informal structures and information. Eisenhower wanted every decision formally staffed for thoroughness but made decisions on the basis of continuous informal probings and discussions. Each framework complemented the other in his own mind so that errors that might be attributed to reliance solely on either method were avoided.[24]

Eisenhower's diaries, letters, and recorded remarks to others are filled with perceptive comments about the men with whom he worked, and he often made suggestions to associates about how to deal with certain individuals. These estimates of people, including his closest colleagues, Soviet and European leaders, and members of Congress, informed all his actions.[25]

Contrary to the impressions of the time, Eisenhower kept Secretary of State John Foster Dulles on a very tight leash.[26] He was virtually his own secretary of defense and worried that his successor would not be able to keep the armed services under control. This was one reason that he warned the nation of the dangers of a "military-industrial complex" in his farewell address.[27] He was not the inexperienced politician that many of his detractors thought him to be because he had worked intimately with political questions as Army chief of staff, as supreme Allied commander, and as a War Department congressional liaison officer in the interwar years. The chairman of his Council of Economic Advisers remembered that he never spent an hour with Eisenhower talking about economic trends that he did not learn something about government.[28]

Tactics.   As president, Eisenhower pursued the leadership strategy that he had developed as a general. He was a president above politics, who cultivated the chief-of-state image and disguised the politician part of the role, through what Fred Greenstein calls a "hidden hand" style of leadership. Political calculations and tactics were kept in the background or under cover. By appearing to rise above controversy, he maintained the highest level of consistent popular support of any president since World War II, a 64 percent average approval rate over his two terms.[29]

Eisenhower was much better at operating behind the scenes in both foreign and domestic policy than he was at leading an open charge. This was because his above-politics public stance was incompatible with leadership that might produce conflict.[30] The essence of the "hidden hand" style is that the leader's influence is kept secret. For example, Eisenhower might use one person to persuade another but ensure that the one to be persuaded knew nothing of his role. He made many suggestions to his aides about managing congressional relations without congressional leaders knowing about it. He felt that he had ended the Korean War by subtly threatening the Soviets and the Chinese that it might be necessary to use nuclear weapons, but the threat was sent through indirect channels so that U.S. allies and the American public did not know about it. He may have been bluffing, but the communist nations could not be sure.

The reverse side of the coin was that he was often awkward and inept when caught in an open conflict. Eisenhower was able to deal easily with his secretary of the treasury behind the scenes on most issues. But when the secretary criticized the administration budget for being too high, the president did not rebuke him but invited Congress to cut the budget if it could and thereby forfeited his authority.[31] He could defend his program against congressional assaults, as in the string of vetoes of big budgets in his last years. But he was not willing to use his resources and his popularity to lead charges. His nonpolitical approach to leadership did not permit it.

Eisenhower's sense of the power of the presidency was not as great as Roosevelt's in domestic politics and policy, probably because of his lack of experience. For example, he told a press conference that he could not conceive of a circumstance that could cause him to send troops to southern school districts to enforce court-ordered school desegregation. This was a clear signal to southern governors that he could be defied, and indeed Governor Orval

Faubus of Arkansas took the risk in Little Rock and eventually forced the president to recant his words and act.[32] But Eisenhower understood how to keep foreign adversaries guessing. For example, the Chinese never could be sure whether he would defend the offshore islands of Quemoy and Matsu because he said vaguely that the United States would fight if a Chinese invasion of the islands appeared to be a prelude to an invasion of nearby Formosa.[33] His foreign policy and military experience gave him the sure sense of the ambiguities of power relationships that his limited experience with domestic politics denied him.

Conclusion. It was understandable that, as a president of consolidation, Eisenhower would fail to see emerging problems and that the opposition would use this blind spot as a basis for criticism. There were two severe economic recessions during his second term. The civil rights movement was building strength. Opinion polls revealed growing public support for federal action to meet the medical needs of the elderly and to provide aid to schools that were overwhelmed with children from the postwar baby boom. The president also was criticized for his opposition to a contest of space exploration with the Soviet Union. This was sometimes confused with U.S. strategic inferiority, something John Kennedy made much of in the 1960 campaign. In fact, there was no "missile gap," and a race to the moon was thought wasteful by Eisenhower. The Democrats also criticized the Eisenhower administration for its seeming lack of sensitivity to the need to strengthen conventional armed forces in order to resist Soviet-inspired wars of "national liberation." The seeds of the later intervention in Vietnam might have been in such rhetoric. This is to suggest that while Eisenhower resisted additional domestic reform, he also held the line against excesses in foreign and military policy.[34] His desire to stay in the center of what he conceived to be not only sound policy but the mainstream of opinion is central to understanding his presidency.

John F. Kennedy

Strategy. Kennedy came into office in the strategic position of a president of preparation. His New Frontier legislative program was derived from the policy incubation that had been taking place in activist circles of the Democratic party in the 1950s. Public opinion, as measured in polls, was moving gradually in the direction of social reforms such as Medicare, federal aid to education, and, less strongly, civil rights. Kennedy was elected by a tiny plurality over Richard Nixon and with no clear "mandate." The greatest public discontent was with a faltering economy. The "conservative coalition" dominated Congress, as it had since 1938.

Kennedy and his advisers developed a strategy of legislative leadership that would dramatize issues for which he did not have the votes, such as Medicare and federal help for schools, in order to get them squarely on the policy agenda for future enactment when support developed. They also agreed to avoid divisive questions like civil rights that might break apart the fragile Democratic coalition. Kennedy's initial actions on civil rights were administrative, primarily taken in the enforcement of court-ordered integration of southern universities. He hoped that southern Democratic members of Congress would be so mollified by the absence of civil rights legislative proposals that they would give their votes to other administration measures. It was the president's judgment to seek legislative victories on a few important measures, both for their own sake and to enhance his professional reputation for future contests. The approach worked on less controversial bills such as economic development, work training, public housing, minimum wage increases, farm price supports, and a trade expansion act. But the centerpieces of the New Frontier—federal aid for schools and college building construction, medical care for the aged, and the creation of a Department of Urban Affairs—could not summon a majority.[35]

Another characteristic of Kennedy's strategy and style was to test altogether new initiatives cautiously before introducing them. The classic case was the proposal to apply Keynesian economic theory to the persistently sluggish economy in order to stimulate recovery. Kennedy had been elected in large part because of the two recessions in Eisenhower's second term. People were fed up with high unemployment. Industry was operating with slack capacity, and human and material resources were greatly underused. Kennedy had promised to get the economy moving again, but he was a fiscal conservative who also had pledged to balance the budget. His economic advisers tried to convince him that a large cut in taxes, with a consequent federal deficit, would stimulate recovery. Inflation would be avoided because of the idle capacity of labor and capital in the economy. Kennedy understood the argument but feared political criticism of deficits. Neither was he politically prepared to support a program of government spending as an alternative to a tax cut in order to put people to work. As he told Walter Heller, the chairman of the Council of Economic Advisers, "Nixon will slaughter us if we go the expenditure route."[36]

There was no support for a tax cut among Kennedy's cabinet members, who feared that such an action would deny them expenditures for their departments, or among the Democratic leadership of Congress, who, like Kennedy, were skeptical of an economic theory that called for large deficits.[37] It was too risky politically in the face of Republican charges of fiscal irresponsibility.[38] However, Kennedy was disappointed that economic recovery did not come, and in early 1962 he began to listen to Heller again about the need for a tax cut. Heller felt in retrospect that his tutelage had turned Kennedy into an economic liberal. But he also acknowledged that there were two other concerns on Kennedy's mind. The president feared a "Kennedy recession" in the election year of 1962.[39] He also began to realize that, if the economy did improve, it would be possible for government to pay for the proposed social programs of the New Frontier. The president told Heller, "Walter, first we're going to get your tax cut and then we're going to get my expenditure programs."[40] In a June 1962 speech at Yale, Kennedy called on the nation to face economic problems with pragmatism rather than ideology, and in a speech later that summer he spoke for a tax cut. The proposal was sent to Congress early in 1963. It passed in 1964, after Kennedy's assassination.

The tax cut illustrates more than Kennedy's political flexibility. It also presents a picture of widening strategic sensitivities. In late 1962 Kennedy read two articles in *The New Yorker* about poverty in America that stimulated him to ask Heller for more information and, eventually, for an economic analysis of the problem. Thus was the antipoverty program of the Johnson Great Society born.[41] This step followed logically from the decision to ask for tax reductions. Kennedy was reaching out to ask what government might do not only to stimulate the economy, but to eradicate its most persistent problem.

In June 1963 Kennedy made an uncharacteristically strong public commitment to the cause of civil rights. Police violence had erupted in Birmingham, Alabama, against peaceful protestors who were trying to register to vote. Kennedy addressed the nation on television and introduced the bill that was to become the Civil Rights Act of 1964. It is possible that in mid-1963 Kennedy already was thinking of a big electoral victory in 1964 that would empower him as a president of achievement for a second term. This could help to explain his increasing strategic boldness. Kennedy always grounded his initiatives in what he thought to be politically possible.

Until the traumatic shock to American liberalism of the Vietnam War, progressive presidents were activists in foreign policy. Kennedy campaigned in 1960 for a more vigorous foreign policy and a stronger national defense. He argued that there was a "missile gap" in favor of the USSR and that conventional arms should be stockpiled to permit United States involvement in limited wars. After complaining that the Eisenhower administration had failed to curb Cuban intervention in Latin America, Kennedy permitted the Bay of Pigs invasion of Cuba to occur. He also dramatized conflict with the Soviets over the status of West Berlin by calling Army reserve units to active duty, faced down the Soviets in the Cuban missile crisis, and increased the number of American military advisers in South Vietnam from 700 to 16,500 in less than three years. His actions in Vietnam were prompted in part by his conviction that the United States could show no signs of weakness anywhere in the world in the face of Soviet pressures.[42] In sum, Kennedy paved the way for activist foreign policies under Johnson just as he prepared the ground for the passage of the Great Society legislation.

Presentation of Self.   Kennedy was not a natural politician with an intuitive feel for the appeals that move others. His speaking style throughout his career had a forced, stacatto quality. But his public personality was magical. Kennedy was an expert in the presentation of self, especially through the mass media. He was at his best when he could reveal his intelligence. The first debate of the 1960 presidential campaign against Richard Nixon gave Kennedy, who was less well known than the vice president, an opportunity to portray himself as mature, responsible, and intelligent to voters who were skeptical about a forty-three-year-old candidate. He was especially good at press conferences, where his ability to think on his feet, knowledge of issues, and quick humor charmed reporters. A short speech in the White House Rose Garden to Peace Corps volunteers would be picked up by the evening news programs to illustrate the idealism and grace of the young president appealing to a new political generation in his call for excellence and intelligence in government.

Kennedy was less successful in leading public opinion on behalf of his policies. He did not like to use rhetoric for political effect. His wide popular appeal appears to have been based on his handsome physical appearance, his attractive family, his intelligence, and the general sense of vitality and activity he brought to government. After his death, studies revealed that citizens had read their diverse hopes into Kennedy and his promise for a better future. Minorities saw him as a civil rights leader; youth saw him as an idealist; the elderly saw him as concerned for their needs; and so on. However, his personal popularity was stronger than was support for his policies.[43]

Kennedy faced the dilemma of a president of preparation who wishes to teach the public but dares not get too far ahead of prevailing sentiment. Rather than be strident on issues, these presidents are inclined to pick carefully the questions they wish to dramatize.

Tactics.   Kennedy was not a skillful tactician. He had not been an active legislator as a member of Congress and was not particularly comfortable with legislative folkways. There is very little evidence of his devising clever tactics to pass legislation. His approach as president was primarily one of rational appeals, and he occasionally would tell members of Congress that he understood why their relations with their constituents kept them from supporting his proposals.[44] A Kennedy associate who worked closely with Congress remembered that its members looked on Kennedy "as a nice boy, but not a guy who could get what he wanted."[45]

A study of five major Kennedy legislative initiatives reveals that he was most effective with Congress when he either endorsed proposals that had great support, such as public housing, or worked cautiously with congressional leaders to prepare the ground for eventual future passage through an approach of delay and avoidance, as with Medicare and civil rights. He usually failed when he attempted to outmaneuver congressional groups and thereby achieved a reputation for uncertainty.[46] For example, Kennedy initially declared himself opposed to federal aid to parochial schools for fear that his Catholicism would tarnish a positive proposal. However, in response to pleas from the Catholic bishops, he shifted to a two-bill strategy so that the question of help for parochial schools could be considered separately from that of aid to public schools. Even so, Catholic legislators blocked passage of a general aid bill in the absence of a compromise that would assure something to parochial schools.[47] Kennedy also showed his lack of tactical skill in his approach to the creation of a Department of Urban Affairs. The only possible path to a majority on a matter on which congressional interest was so limited was bipartisan support. But Kennedy responded to a rejection of the measure by the House Rules Committee with a broadside attack on House Republicans, then attempted to have the bill released from an unfriendly Senate committee by a discharge petition in order to put pressure on the House to act. None of this legislative cleverness worked with Congress; as he later told Tom Wicker of the *New York Times:* "I played it too cute."[48] Kennedy provided the strongest leadership of his career in his advocacy of the civil rights law by building on bipartisan support in the House

House Judiciary Committee. This was in October 1963, and he was killed on November 22. Much more remained to be done by the president before the bill could pass, but he had seized the political initiative and acted to provide moral leadership. The prudence of his initial delay was consistent with what one would expect from a president of preparation, but so was the decision to act once politics seemed to support action. In this sense Kennedy's actions on the tax cut and civil rights were the same — first delay and then act in response to enhanced political possibilities.[49]

Authority. Kennedy commanded great personal loyalty from those who worked for him. Walter Heller remembered: "Working in the Kennedy Administration — with rare exceptions — was sheer joy. You always had the feeling that the most competent ideas would win out."[50] The basis of this belief was Kennedy's ability to get the best out of others. Wilbur Cohen, who developed much of the Kennedy-Johnson legislative program in health, education, and welfare, tells a story that any of Kennedy's aides could have told:

> I was one of those who met with President Kennedy . . . to deal with his message on civil rights. . . . He went around the table asking each person to state his views. . . . I said, "Mr. President, in addition to the political aspects of civil rights, you must include some things that improve education and work and training for black and minority people. . . . And you have to put some money into the program to do that." President Kennedy shot back at me and he said, "Wilbur, I don't have any money to do that now and you know it. . . . " He seemed quite irritated with my comments. Two weeks later on Saturday night at 11:30 p.m., I got a call from Mr. Sorensen [Theodore Sorensen, presidential assistant], who said, "The President has thought it over and he's approved your program. Get it in shape."[51]

Cohen tells how he spent the rest of the night in his office putting together a memorandum for the president, which was delivered to the White House at 3:30 A.M. The program later became law. He adds:

> the only point of the story here is, I felt that I had a relationship with Kennedy in which he could bawl me out or take me down or do whatever he wanted, but he knew that what I told him was something that I believed was the right thing. And in that case and in other cases, he would take my advice. So I felt I had a good relationship because I loved the man and I think he respected me and that was a good working relationship.[52]

Kennedy sought to be like Roosevelt in his disregard for administrative formality in favor of openness to fresh ideas. He accepted the advice of political scientist Richard Neustadt that, in contrast to the Eisenhower practice, there should be no chief of staff in the White House and the bureaucracy of the National Security Council should be dismantled. This approach worked well for the generation of ideas in domestic policy. It worked less well in foreign affairs. For example, the debacle at the Bay of Pigs occurred because Kennedy and his principal advisers failed to review skeptically a poorly conceived CIA plan for the invasion of Cuba by a refugee army. The dismantled NSC structure would have permitted careful examination of the plan.[53] The activism and self-confidence of the new president and his advisers had failed to protect them in a situation in which they were ignorant and in which the political constraints that induced caution in domestic affairs were weak.

Conclusion.   Kennedy was an effective president of preparation because his strategic sense of what was politically possible in domestic policy matched the reality of the times. He prepared the way for a subsequent president of achievement, which he might have been himself had he lived and been reelected. Johnson took Kennedy's initiatives as his point of departure. Kennedy did not attempt to do things that would have been expected of a president of achievement, although he edged in that direction in 1963 with his increasing boldness in economic and civil rights policies. Criticism of him for being too cautious or for not getting his major program ideas passed by Congress is unjustified. Kennedy understood what was possible. As a cold warrior, he reflected his times, expressed cultural idealism about the American role in the world, and, in this sense as well, prepared the way for his successor.

TWO FLAWED PRESIDENTS: JOHNSON AND NIXON

Lyndon Johnson and Richard Nixon each had the force and strength to push government through the remaining two phases of the cycle of politics and policy that began with Kennedy. But the shocks to popular confidence in government that took place during their administrations, largely as a result of their actions, created discontinuities and disorientations in American politics that lasted long after their presidencies.

Lyndon Johnson was a successful president of achievement in his leadership for the legislative enactment of the Great Society programs. Like Roosevelt, he creatively rode political tides not of his own making, which in Johnson's case were strengthened by Kennedy's death and the Republican mistake of nominating an extreme conservative in 1964. Also like Roosevelt, he ran out of political steam after the initial burst of achievement because public support was withdrawn.

Johnson's failure was an inability to know the limits of action and achievement. This may appear paradoxical because presidents of achievement are the "heroes" of American politics and in our political mythology all credit for achievement is given to the hero. Americans cite with approval Woodrow Wilson's axiom that the president is "at liberty to be as big a man as he can." In fact this mythology is inaccurate. A president only can reinforce and guide political tides. This was clearly illustrated in both the Roosevelt and Johnson presidencies. When support was withdrawn, skill was not sufficient to produce achievement. Johnson tried to impose both the Great Society and the Vietnam

War on American society without calculating whether the public would support such actions or whether the domestic conflict that ensued would overload democratic processes. He misread the historical possibilities.

Nixon was flawed in similar ways. To be sure, he was a successful president of consolidation in two respects. He presented a coherent domestic policy program for the rationalization and improved management of Great Society programs and he secured a détente with the Soviet Union and China that provided a framework for a temporarily stable international equilibrium. His failure, like Johnson's, was an inability to know the limits of action, though in a different sphere. Presidents of consolidation must manage authority skillfully. Nixon undermined his authority by abusing it through illegal actions.

Lyndon B. Johnson

Strategy. Johnson had a strong strategic vision of domestic policy and politics. He wanted to be a great reform leader like Woodrow Wilson and Franklin Roosevelt and understood greatness to mean success in passing legislative programs such as the New Freedom and the New Deal. The memory of the martyred president, John F. Kennedy, was a great political resource when Johnson wanted to transform the New Frontier into the Great Society. Johnson's smashing victory over Barry Goldwater in the 1964 election brought many additional Democratic members to Congress and with them the votes that Kennedy had lacked. But Johnson also knew that periods of legislative creativity are brief and that sooner or later both congressional and popular support would decline. He often explained this to his assistants with explicit reference to the experiences of Wilson and Roosevelt.[54]

It is likely that Medicare, Medicaid, federal aid for education and disadvantaged students, the Model Cities program, and numerous other items of health, education, and welfare legislation would have been enacted had Kennedy been president because the measures had been incubating for years and required only a landslide election victory for fulfillment. But it is not likely that most presidents would have tried to do so much or have been able to win support for such programs so easily. Not all of them were programs that were created by popular demand. Johnson's achievement was to sell actions for the disadvantaged to the middle classes by combining reform with a period of prosperity. No one was hurt, and the cultural ideals of the society were invoked. But eventually the Great Society, like the New Deal, mobilized greater expectations than it could meet, and the consequent unrest and dissatisfaction among the disadvantaged produced a backlash against both the programs and the Johnson administration. Great Society programs that met the needs of all classes, such as Medicare, were well accepted. But resentment developed among blue-collar and middle-class people against compensatory services for minorities because of competition for jobs. In addition, Johnson had pushed hard and fast for the enactment of so many programs with little attention to the administrative consequences. Among the results of the Great Society were implementation failures, political divisiveness, and alienation. Many problems were addressed, but new divisions in the society also were produced.[55] The political manifestation of this backlash was the rise of Governor George Wallace of Alabama as a presidential candidate in 1968 who spoke for resentful whites.

Johnson's strategic vision in foreign policy was that of his generation of political leaders and of the foreign-policy establishment. Ever since the appeasement of the dictators by the democracies in the 1930s, American leaders had believed that the proper response to aggression was to oppose it with force.[56] The Truman administration interpreted the invasion of South Korea by North Korea in 1950 as an act of Soviet-inspired aggression. International communism was seen to be monolithic in its designs on free nations. Johnson and his advisers interpreted the conflict between North and South Vietnam in the same terms. If South Vietnam were permitted to fall to a communist aggressor, they felt, the free world would be vulnerable to other aggressive actions, inspired by the Chinese and Soviets.

Johnson's perceptions and actions in foreign policy also were grounded in his understanding of domestic politics. He remembered two important facts of history. The first was that partisan charges in the 1950s that the Truman administration had "lost China" to the communists had poisoned domestic politics with unusual rancor and generated a search for traitors and spies in American government. The second was that the American intervention in Korea was so costly in money and lives that the program of domestic reform advanced by President Truman was forgotten.[57] Johnson may have remembered a third fact: the Korean War revealed that the American people would not support a limited conflict that dragged on for years. The lesson was that American troops should never be committed to a ground war in Asia. However, the lesson of the first fact was contradictory with the lesson of the next two, and this was Johnson's dilemma.

Johnson and his advisers knew that American efforts to save the regime of South Vietnam through military action would be costly and painful, but, given their world view, there was no alternative. If South Vietnam were to fall, they believed, so would the rest of Southeast Asia. Therefore, the United States had to make a stand. However, as in the Korean conflict, they chose a middle ground between withdrawal, with all the political costs that entailed, and total war. U.S. military actions were incremental, with escalation gradual and always limited in order not to produce war with China or the Soviet Union. As in Korea, it first was thought that U.S. airpower would be sufficient, but, as this proved to be mistaken, a decision was made in mid-1965 to commit ground troops.[58]

Johnson believed that he had to act as he did in Vietnam in order both to stop aggression and to prevent a recurrence of the poisonous politics that had followed the "loss" of China. But he was determined not to lose the Great Society.[59] Timing was crucial because it became apparent to the president and his advisers in 1965 that the escalation of the bombing of North Vietnam the previous winter had not checked the enemy sufficiently. Yet the Great Society programs were working their way through Congress that spring and summer. This may help to explain Johnson's furious push for passage. But it also explains the muted way he introduced American combat troops into South Vietnam in July 1965. The announcement was made by the president at a midday news briefing. There was no speech to the nation on the moral challenge at hand or the need for national support for a great endeavor. Johnson avoided every action that might suggest that the United States was committed to a major military effort. He hid the estimated cost of the war from his economic and budget advisers, although they knew that his figures were wrong and by the end of 1965 were advising him to raise taxes to pay for the war and avoid inflation. The president resisted any such action until 1967 with the argument that he could not get a tax increase from Congress when inflation was only latent and not a reality. In truth, Johnson might have won the increase had he gone to the people on the issue and been willing to scale back social-program proposals as congressional leaders suggested. His unwillingness to do this caused the disastrous inflation from which the nation subsequently suffered.[60]

Johnson had two alternatives to the course he took. He could have disengaged from Vietnam and pursued the Great Society. This would have taken great political skill and even more courage, but, given his world view, it was not a serious possibility. Or he could have satisfied himself with the legislative achievements of 1964 and early 1965, which were great, presented the war to the public and Congress as morally imperative and vital to the national interest, and thereby secured the resources to fight the war. But, as he later said, to do so would be like cutting off his right arm.

Johnson's deceptions of 1965 and his desire to have both the Great Society and the intervention in South Vietnam would not have been fatal to his presidency had his judgment been correct about the prospects for success in Vietnam. His analysis of the political feasibility of having both the Great Society and the military intervention caused him to minimize the short-term costs through deception, and to take a gamble on the long-term political possibilities, of which there were two. The first, which Johnson hoped for, was that U.S. military power could make the North Vietnamese back down and stabilize the situation in South Vietnam so that the government there might survive. The second was that the military effort would be inconclusive, the war would drag on, and the American people would lose confidence in their president. Johnson's failure and that of his advisers to estimate the difficulties in Vietnam realistically brought down that consequence on his presidency.[61]

This was not solely Johnson's failure, although personal insecurity and vainglory help explain his desire to have both the Great Society and the war. There were few experts on Southeast Asia in the American government. Johnson's advisers favored the war, and their views were supported by the national foreign-policy establishment and the major journals of opinion. But it is difficult to imagine other presidents attempting to do both. In contrast to Roosevelt, Johnson had too little feel for the limits of policy action.

The war brought Johnson down in 1968. The public had turned against him, doubting his ability either to win or to end the war diplomatically. The dramatic North Vietnamese Tet offensive in January 1968 produced the impression that the United States was losing. Senator Eugene McCarthy almost defeated Johnson in the New Hampshire presidential primary. The generals were asking for 200,000 more combat troops. Johnson became convinced that he had lost the support necessary to fight a limited war and that it was not politically possible or desirable to escalate the conflict.[62] He therefore decided that the best course was to try to end the war through negotiation and that his credibility, at home and abroad, would be greater if he took himself out of the presidential race. Political reality had intruded, and Johnson finally recognized it.

Tactics.   Johnson had great skill as a tactical leader in understanding the psychology of other individuals. He once told an aide that there were only two things he wanted to know about another man: Did his mother marry beneath her, and what were his father's greatest frustrations? Johnson believed that people define themselves out of such experiences and develop goals through which they can meet the expectations their mothers place on them and thereby overcome the failures of their fathers. He was, in fact, generalizing from his own experience with a mother who was disappointed with her husband and nurtured her son's ambition as a substitute.[63] Not every politician whom Johnson would seek to persuade would embody those particular characteristics. But he believed that everyone wanted something out of life as a result of such driving pressures and that if he could uncover the secret, he could influence that person. He dealt with individual associates in terms of such knowledge, both as Senate majority leader and as president.[64]

A second tactical skill was derived from the first. Johnson had the capacity to construct coalitions on specific issues without open debate by appealing to the sum of individual interests. As Senate leader, he knew how to win the votes of senators through individual bargains. This permitted him to be different things to different people.[65] He tried to lead Congress in this manner once he was president. One of his economic advisers recalled how Johnson "would play his own legislative aide" at White House meetings on congressional strategy, quoting the president:

> If you write the bill this way, it'll go to this committee; if you write it this way, you may be able to get it through the Commerce Committee instead of that other one and that chairman is going to like it better. Let's see, we have got this many votes I can count on and there are two more people who may be interested in that. When is that . . . appointment that this Senator's been trying to push on me? How bad would that be?[66]

When Johnson became president, he used his skills of persuasion with individual members of Congress to win support for the tax cut in 1964 and the Economic Opportunity Act, which inaugurated the war on poverty.[67] In 1965 and 1966, empowered by larger majorities, he pushed harder for action but did not forget the importance of coalition building. For example, he would not let the bill that was to become the Elementary and Secondary Education Act of 1965 go to Congress until the Catholic bishops and the National Education Association had agreed on a compromise regarding federal aid to parochial schools.[68]

Johnson also was a master at public appeals that commanded wide support without conflict. The most dramatic example was his speech to Congress in behalf of the Voting Rights Act of 1965. In March 1965 Alabama state police used clubs on black citizens who were marching to the courthouse in Selma, Alabama, to register to vote. The scene was captured on national television. Johnson seized the opportunity to speak to Congress at night and on national television to demand passage of the bill in terms of the basic American right to vote. Who could deny such a claim? This drive for a national consensus always characterized his leadership on civil rights legislation.[69]

These tactical skills, both for bargaining and for arguing a consensus, were not always sufficient to subdue opposition. When they failed, Johnson's response was often defensive. He derided his Senate critics when he was majority leader. In response to criticism of his sending marines to the Dominican Republic in 1965 to protect Americans caught in a domestic civil conflict, Johnson overreacted rhetorically by claiming beyond the evidence the threat of a communist coup and deriding public criticism of his actions.[70] This exemplified the dark side of Johnson's desire for consensus without debate and foreshadowed his responses to popular backlash from the Great Society and the Vietnam War.

Presentation of Self.   Johnson was not capable of taking a divisive issue to the American people and asking them to support one side or the other. He sought either private bargains or public unanimity. It often was noted that Johnson was less effective with large audiences than with individuals and small groups. His persuasive power depended upon his capacity to read the reactions of his audience as he spoke, which is more difficult with large groups and impossible with television. But his problems with the American people were not the result of faulty technique. He had succeeded in his early presidency in impressing Americans with his idealism and had created respect, perhaps even awe, for his formidable abilities. The speech after Selma is only one example. His ebullient campaigning in the 1964 election in response to enthusiastic crowds and his barnstorming in behalf of the Great Society in early 1965 are instances of Johnson's ability to strike fire with audiences and with the people at large.

Johnson's problem with the American public in his last year in office was that they no longer trusted him.[71] Large numbers of people did not believe that he was telling the truth about the conduct of the war in Vietnam. His skill at concealing issues through the manipulation of factions or through the invocation of consensus had so obscured the purposes of the war and the progress of the effort in the minds of Americans that he no longer had credibility. For example, in August 1964 Johnson had pushed the Senate to pass the Gulf of Tonkin resolution, which authorized the president to retaliate against attacks on American forces in Southeast Asia, by assuring that it would not be used to justify U.S. military intervention. Yet Johnson later invoked the resolution as a justification for all of his actions in Vietnam. His position was tarnished even more when evidence emerged that the supposed attacks on U.S. ships that inspired the resolution may never have taken place.[72] This is only one illustration of Johnson's declining credibility on Vietnam, which was not caused by failures of technique.

Authority. Johnson was a challenging leader who knew how to get the most and the best out of subordinates. The Great Society legislative programs were developed by task forces of talented academic people, White House aides, cabinet officers, and civil servants, all driven by Johnson's idealism and determination. His ability to join a sense of purpose to political realism was similar to Roosevelt's, and he presided over an administration of great variety and vitality. Johnson arbitrated the main policy questions himself, relying on experts to advise him about the proper course of action but always asking about political feasibility. His associates found the drive, the pressure, and the idealism to be exhilarating.[73]

This stimulating style of administrative leadership, however, was predicated upon general agreement about purposes. Johnson was open to new ideas and facts, but only if he was convinced that his advisers were on his side.[74] As the war in Vietnam pressed in on him, he became defensive and intolerant. If it became apparent that an adviser was weakening in his support for the president's policy, he was first isolated and eventually removed. Vice President Hubert Humphrey was excluded from presidential meetings for a time because Johnson believed him to be "soft" on the war. When Johnson discovered in late 1967 that Secretary of Defense Robert McNamara was increasingly skeptical about the chances of American success in Vietnam, he eased him out of the administration by making him president of the World Bank. His obsession with consensus increasingly caused him to narrow the circle of Vietnam advisers.[75] As one biographer notes, "For Johnson the exhilaration of power was nearly always accompanied by deep insecurity."[76]

Conclusion. Lyndon Johnson functioned well as a political leader when his authority to act was limited by other power holders and when his personal knowledge and experience permitted him to calculate realistically the prospects for achieving his goals. Both of these conditions were met when he was majority leader of the Senate. They also were met during his first year as president. Johnson worked skillfully with congressional leaders to secure passage of the unenacted Kennedy agenda and drew on his instinct for national consensus to reassure the nation of continuity and unity in the wake of the assassination.

It was in foreign policy, an area that he did not know well and in which fewer constraints operate on presidential action, that Johnson failed. His insights into the substance of policy choices were not guided by experience, and he did not confront his advisers with the same skepticism he showed in the formation of domestic programs. The decision to escalate the war cannot be blamed on Johnson alone. But his failure to choose between domestic reform and war, when combined with his mistakes in judgment about the war itself, give us a picture of a political leader who was so determined to be great that he overreached himself and brought about his own downfall.

Richard M. Nixon

Strategy. Nixon had a very strong strategic sense, which joined politics and policy. His foreign policy took advantage of historical opportunities to establish a *modus vivendi* with the Soviet Union and create an alliance of limited but mutual interest with the Republic of China, thus healing the breach caused by the Korean War. The overriding theme was stabilization of relations among the world powers.[77]

Nixon was able to accomplish the opening to China, the SALT I agreement on arms reduction with the USSR, and the conclusion to the Vietnam War through highly personal, secret diplomacy, using Henry Kissinger as his negotiating agent. Although historians will differ as to how much Nixon derived his strategic conceptions from Kissinger, there is considerable evidence to support the view that Nixon developed his own strategic sense of the historical possibilities and that Kissinger's theories provided intellectual coherence for the practices of the president.[78]

Foreign-policy achievements of this kind won the overwhelming approval of the American people. The promise of a period of stability and equilibrium in international relations was irresistible and contributed greatly to Nixon's strong reelection victory in 1972. A more difficult problem for him was the manner in which he terminated American involvement in the Vietnam War. Nixon's conception of the balance of power meant he could not accept a withdrawal of U.S. troops from South Vietnam in 1969 without attaining the original American objective of an independent South Vietnam. To settle for less, in his mind, would weaken international confidence in American resolve. However, Nixon did not think a military solution possible, and, after the intense public outcry against the U.S. military strike against North Vietnam strongholds in Cambodia in 1970, he became convinced that he no longer could hold out for the withdrawal of North Vietnamese troops from South Vietnam. Although more Americans approved the Cambodian action than opposed it, Nixon saw that the intensity of the opposition was such that he would have to settle for an imperfect agreement.[79] Eventually, negotiations were fruitful and the United States withdrew in 1973, but not before Nixon again incurred great popular opposition by bombing North Vietnam heavily at Christmas 1972 in order to force final agreement. He also had risked Soviet cancellation of a summit meeting when he mined the harbor of Haiphong, the main North Vietnamese port, earlier in 1972. Nixon took such risks not to be popular, but to achieve his objectives. But he was able to carry a majority of the American public with him throughout, despite the intense opposition of a very large minority. His strategic sense of how to combine policy and public support did not desert him.

Nixon had a less developed strategic sense for domestic policy. He did not invest time and energy in domestic questions, and his uncertainties about the proper direction of policy were great. But he had strategic impulses. His election coalition consisted, in part, of groups in the society that he envisioned as constituting a new Republican majority: white southerners, blue-collar workers, and ethnic Catholics, as well as the solid middle classes and upper-income groups that had supported Republicans regularly. Nixon's appeals were to patriotism, consolidation of social reform with greater attention to law and order, the scaling down of the federal role in social action programs, and economic stability that was achieved temporarily through his dramatic imposition of wage and price controls in 1971.[80]

In 1972 and again in 1973, buoyed by his reelection triumph, Nixon resolved to overcome his frustrations with Democratic opposition in Congress to the domestic-policy presidency of his first term by a series of dramatic moves. He issued a challenge to Congress on the budget by impounding certain appropriated funds with the argument that it was his constitutional responsibility to practice fiscal responsibility in the face of a Congress that created yearly deficits.[81] He appointed four cabinet officers as counsellors to the president with authority to oversee and coordinate the work of other cabinet officers. This informal two-tier cabinet was an effort to achieve, through administrative action, departmental reorganizations that had been denied him by Congress. He also ordered departments to begin to implement his unenacted special revenue-sharing proposals for domestic programs through administrative regulations, again bypassing a Congress that had resisted his legislative requests. Finally, a number of presidential loyalists were placed in the departments to facilitate the administering of government directly from the White House through the hierarchy of "super" cabinet officers. New appointments to the second tier of cabinet departments were given to people without standing or experience in government. These interrelated actions later were described as the "Administrative Presidency," which was appropriate because it was an effort to direct the executive branch from the top rather than through the diverse, fragmented, and decentralized departments.[82]

Nixon was headed for confrontation with Congress over the administrative presidency in 1973, but the Watergate crisis intervened. The changes that he had made so quickly were rescinded quietly as the president began to seek political support in Congress to save his presidency. One cannot predict whether the administrative presidency would have survived, but it seems unlikely that Congress would have permitted it to have done so in contravention of Congress's own constitutional responsibility to oversee all the departments. Nixon's impatience to control domestic policy, as he controlled foreign policy, got the better of him. Because his strategic impulses overwhelmed his tactical knowledge, he foolishly attempted to replace accepted processes of political accommodation. Nixon's intolerance for political bargaining and accommodation led him astray in his domestic-policy actions.

Had he not resigned from office in August 1974, Richard Nixon almost certainly would have been impeached by the House and convicted by the Senate of the impeachment charges that were voted against him in the House Judiciary Committee. His efforts to conceal the extent of White House involvement in a series of illegal wiretappings, burglaries, and other crimes represented the worst aspects of his political character. The illegal actions that were urged by the president were exaggerated and highly insecure responses to domestic challenges to his continuation of the war in Vietnam. He developed an obsession with secrets and security that caused him to lose his sense of political reality.[83] These transgressions were extreme manifestations of the intolerance for democratic politics and lack of respect for political opponents that had characterized Nixon's entire career. The psychological pressures of office, and the great self-discipline and control that were required to achieve his foreign-policy objectives, appeared in some way to have caused him to equate political

opposition with challenges to his own inner equilibrium. Nixon was not sufficiently sure of himself to be a strong president in the long run. As Elliott
Richardson, one of his cabinet officers, later put it: "He was never able to accept the fact that he was President of the United States."[84]

Nixon's tragedy, and the actions he took that destroyed him, ultimately
sprang from weakness rather than strength. Nixon could have been a brilliant
president of consolidation in both foreign and domestic policy and unified the
nation behind his policies of adaptation to the conflicts that had arisen from the
Vietnam War and Great Society programs. But, like Lyndon Johnson, he
ultimately and fatally lost his sense of political reality.

Presentation of Self.   Nixon had a great capacity for emotion-laden oratory
that personalized issues and created both strong partisan support and intense
opposition. Whether he intended it or not, his speeches drew more attention to
himself as a figure of controversy than they did to his subject.

Nixon's most famous speech as president was a televised talk in April 1970
in which he announced that U.S. and South Vietnamese troops had invaded
Cambodia in search of the supposed North Vietnamese command post. The action stimulated great popular opposition, particularly on college campuses.
Nixon described the incursion not only as crucial to the American role in Vietnam, but as important for the protection of freedom:

> Whether I may be a one-term President is insignificant compared to whether by our
> failure to act in this crisis the United States proves itself to be unworthy to lead the
> forces of freedom in this critical period in world history. I would rather be a one
> term President and do what I believe is right than to be a two term President at the
> cost of seeing America become a second rate power and to see this nation accept the
> first defeat in its proud 190-year history.[85]

Nixon's rhetoric released aggression and self-pity, often in highly personal
ways. He used the emotional language that was most appropriate for the particular issue without thought for future implications. Each major speech was a
"crisis" in which he would use his rhetorical gifts to demolish critics, disarm the
press, and score a "victory." He prepared for his speeches with infinite care,
often staying up all night to write the major addresses himself. His memoir
Six Crises describes the need for emotional intensity in the preparation of a
speech and the importance of guarding against emotional letdown after it is
over.[86] The night after his speech on Cambodia, he drove around Washington
in his car, visiting the Lincoln Memorial and the Capitol, finally eating
breakfast in a hotel. The need for emotional release was so great that he could
not sleep.

Nixon's 1969 inaugural address had emphasized the theme "bring us
together." This theme and many of his subsequent policy decisions were appropriate for a president of consolidation. But Nixon was not psychologically
constituted to play such a role comfortably.

Tactics.   Nixon, like Eisenhower, faced a Congress that was controlled by the opposition party and was determined to protect the social programs of the preceding president of achievement. However, there was support for improving programmatic organization and efficiency and for sorting out a better division of labor among federal, state, and local governments for implementation. Nixon made several attempts to build a coalition of Republican and Democratic centrists around his "New Federalism" proposals to give greater discretion for the administration of social programs to the states. But the results in Congress were mixed, and, as a result, Nixon alternated conciliation with periods of confrontation. He began his second term with an effort to establish his domestic program independently of Congress through the promulgation of administrative regulations. This effort was never carried out because of the revelations in the spring of 1973 about abuses of power in the administration.[87] As with Eisenhower, Nixon's policies were clearly centrist, but unlike Eisenhower, his tactics were too often confrontational.

Authority.   A president of consolidation must establish a general sense of confidence that public programs are being administered effectively. Nixon never was able to create this general reputation. His successes in foreign policy, the opening of China and the negotiation of détente with the Soviet Union, were achieved through highly personal diplomacy conducted by the president and Henry Kissinger, with limited participation by the Departments of State and Defense.[88] The initial departures may have required closely held secret negotiations, but the long-term implementation of policy required the participation of these departments. Nixon tacitly acknowledged this by appointing Kissinger secretary of state in 1973. It had become apparent that the Watergate scandal had so discredited the role of presidential staff assistants that foreign policy no longer could be conducted from the White House.[89] However, the change was reluctant and forced by events.

In the administrative leadership of domestic policy, Nixon lacked a consistent theory of action. Upon entering office, he proclaimed that he would delegate administration to the cabinet departments. This did not last long after the president and his aides detected the development of centrifugal forces throughout the government. Crucial matters then were pulled into the White House for the rest of the first term. However, the president and his aides recognized the overload and incapacity that subsequently resulted. At the start of the second term they attempted to establish a system of direct White House control of departments through the short-lived "Administrative Presidency." Nixon's shifting administrative strategies revealed his inability to come to terms with the routines and resources of the executive bureaucracy. This is something that an effective president of consolidation must do.

Nonetheless, a politics and policy of consolidation emerged from Nixon's presidency. Political divisions that had arisen from Great Society social programs and the cold war were resolved to a great extent. In this sense we can say that Richard Nixon was a president of consolidation.

CONTEMPORARY PRESIDENTS

Our placement of Jimmy Carter and Ronald Reagan in the typology of presidencies is necessarily tentative because of our lack of historical perspective. Only the passage of time can confirm our belief that a fourth three-stage cycle of policy and politics has begun but in a conservative direction.

Jimmy Carter

Strategy.   Jimmy Carter was a president of preparation who tried to alert the nation and his own party to new problems for which traditional Democratic solutions seemed inappropriate. In particular he believed that chronic inflation, the decline in industrial productivity, and the consequent reductions in national income called for new policies to foster the creation of wealth rather than its redistribution. But as a Democratic leader he sought to combine his fiscal conservatism with more efficient and effective methods of delivering human services. Carter was searching for a new synthesis of liberalism and conservatism in both policy and politics. He hoped to broaden the Democratic coalition through new policies without losing the old collection of groups that originally had been brought together by the New Deal. Unfortunately, Carter and his party were not moving in the same direction. Most of the party was not interested in centrist appeals. Such themes became popular only after the Reagan victory and, indeed, were invoked by most of the candidates for the 1984 Democratic presidential nomination.

Carter's greatest domestic problem was with his party's interest groups. As a fiscal conservative, he was determined to reduce federal spending and, therefore, could not satisfy all the demands of labor, farmers, and welfare groups for either spending on social programs or subsidies to their groups. These Washington-based groups were well organized and could weaken a Democratic president with the public by their attacks on him. Thus, Carter was caught between the intense demands of groups in his party's coalition and the diffuse, latent political support he hoped to win for his conservative liberalism. He sought to achieve "public goods" that would benefit all people; but citizens are organized not as "the public," but in groups. He would alienate the AFL-CIO by giving it a smaller increase in the minimum wage than it demanded but found no organized constituency to which to appeal for support on such an issue. Women's groups were uniformly critical of his restrained support for their causes.

Carter was not wholly unsuccessful. Although black leaders criticized his limited urban development programs, he kept the support of black voters and increased the funding of job training and compensatory education programs. Environmentalists were pacified by the Alaskan lands bill, which set aside great wilderness areas. The National Education Association received a new Department of Education. The governors and mayors worked well with the White House to develop urban programs and coordinate their implementation through a White House liaison staff. Still, Carter's insistence on curbing federal deficits to fight inflation was not popular with any of these groups or with congressional Democratic leaders.

Carter's foreign policies also were caught in a no man's land between past and future in which it was difficult to arouse political support. His forceful drive for passage of the extremely unpopular Panama Canal treaties revealed great foresight on his part, for had no treaty been achieved, the subsequent eruption of civil war in several Central American countries might have involved the United States in military actions to protect the canal. His resourceful achievement of an agreement on peace between the leaders of Egypt and Israel by sheer personal tenacity won the Nobel prize for the two leaders but little enduring domestic political credit for Carter. This was, after all, not an American question for most people. Carter might have been able to persuade the Senate to ratify the SALT II treaty in 1979 had it not been for the Soviet invasion of Afghanistan. But this contradiction between Soviet aggression and his desire to reduce tensions with the USSR weakened popular understanding of his foreign-policy objectives, especially when his own advisers appeared to be divided deeply. Finally, the seizure of hostages in the U.S. embassy in Iran, their imprisonment for over a year, and Carter's inability to do anything about it gradually established a picture of his administration as weak.[90]

Carter went against the grain of the Democratic coalition without mobilizing new constituencies. His hope was that the general public would reward him politically in 1980 on the basis of his total record.[91] Carter's image of himself was as a problem solver who would take on a whole host of challenges simultaneously and resolve them through intelligence and tenacity. In retrospect, most senior officials of the Carter administration felt that he tried to do too much too quickly. Thus, in his first few months as president he sent too many important bills to the House Ways and Means Committee, including energy, welfare reform, tax reform, and Social Security financing, with the expectation that the committee would deal with them all in one year. This was naïve, but Carter was very firm in his intention to be an "activist" president who would move on all fronts at once.[92] Congress did not act as he wished, and he was forced to set priorities in subsequent years. Carter began in foreign affairs with a similar burst of initiatives: the Panama Canal treaty, SALT talks, Middle Eastern peace talks, and campaigns to promote human rights in all nations and to reduce the sale of nuclear materials by the industrial nations to other countries. His national security adviser records that these policies were developed from a coherent set of foreign-policy objectives but that the problem was one of attempting to do too much at once. As with domestic policy, priorities had to be set.[93] For example, Carter had to learn that he could not preach to the Soviets about their poor record on human rights and expect to win their support for arms-control agreements.

It was not Carter's nature to pursue his goals strategically in terms of priorities and calculations of political support. He attempted to be a president of achievement when the historical situation was more appropriate for a president of preparation who would select a few crucial goals, nurture political support for them, and tie their enactment to a clear sense of policy direction. Although Carter had a sense of direction, he failed to make it clear because he did not discriminate among his objectives.

Carter had a more difficult task as a president of preparation than Kennedy, who was leading a rising tide in his party as well as in the country. Carter was swimming against the tide in his party, which was itself out of touch with the country.

Presentation of Self.   Carter resisted making rhetorical appeals to the general public. His speech writers remember that he would not meet with them as a group or even indicate the themes he would like to see in particular speeches. He would ask them to write a speech draft, then send it back with comments for another try. They complained that his idea of a good speech was a recital of the initiatives and accomplishments of the administration without any central theme.[94] Carter was not going to give a State of the Union message in January 1978, his first opportunity to do so, but simply wished to send a written copy to Congress. His aides dissuaded him but remembered his reply that, if he had to talk, he would just list all the things he was trying to do.[95]

Carter knew that he was poor at delivering written speeches, in person or on television, and, therefore, preferred not to do it. The strong and close contact that he had had with voters during his campaign for his party's presidential nomination had been primarily informal. He based his appeals on his personal honesty and integrity and on the need for new approaches to government. The same highly personal themes characterized the occasional "town meetings" he held in small towns around the country.[96] Yet Carter also was at his best before audiences that were brought to the White House for briefings from administration leaders on important legislative initiatives, such as the Panama Canal and SALT treaties. In talks before newspaper editors or business leaders in the East Room, Carter could demonstrate his knowledge of issues. He took pride in his ability to do this and did not like to be outshone by the secretary of state or other speakers.[97]

This change in Carter's style of presentation reflected his feeling that, once he was elected president, his job was simply to make the "right" decisions and explain them. Campaigning was left behind. His adviser on public opinion, Patrick Caddell, wanted Carter to pursue the symbolic themes of the primaries and the early presidency, seen in his walk down Pennsylvania Avenue after his inauguration, in order to strengthen the popular support that had formed for him in the campaign.[98] But such symbolic appeals were issueless and could not be tied to policy appeals, or at least Carter did not seek to do so. He made little attempt at the strategic education of public opinion. Carter believed that his plans and proposals would speak for themselves.

Tactics.   Carter did not think in terms of appealing to the political incentives of other power holders. He was surprised to discover that a Democratic Congress would not pass automatically the measures proposed by a Democratic president.[99] Eventually, the Carter White House developed an effective program of legislative relations. In particular, a staff headed by Anne Wexler took the lead in mobilizing groups in the country in behalf of Carter legislation. The president gave a great deal of time and attention to meeting with such groups and with members of Congress. His strategies of persuasion were based on rational argument. He gave little indication in his legislative leadership that he knew how to put together coalitions through political soundings and bargaining as a way of smoothing the passage of bills. For example, Carter encouraged extensive and intensive planning of a welfare reform measure and sent a most complex plan to Congress without discovering in advance, as he could have done through personal conversations, that the chances for passage of any kind of bill were limited.[100] It was not so much that Carter was politically naïve or inexperienced, but rather that he did not believe in developing measures on the strengths of bargains. Such an approach to policy formation always struck Carter as one that required premature concessions to interest groups, whose strength he deplored.[101] His belief was that intelligently designed programs would win assent for themselves, and his appeal was to "public goods" that transcended group interests. Carter was not insensitive to the importance of politics in winning legislative support. He simply practiced a different kind of politics from that of most congressional politicians. After Carter left the presidency, he told a group of political scientists that he had caused uneasiness and uncertainty among Washington elites, including members of Congress, because he had a different way of governing than his predecessors.[102] As an engineer and former governor, he said, he wished to move more rapidly than people with legislative minds.[103]

These personal qualities worked most effectively when there were relatively few people to persuade. The outstanding example was his negotiation of an accord between Prime Minister Menachim Begin of Israel and President Anwar Sadat of Egypt at Camp David in the summer of 1978. His tenacity and capacity for learning all the details of a problem worked for him brilliantly. They were less effective with a large and highly diverse Congress.

Authority.   Carter had two approaches to administrative leadership. He chose a few matters on which he personally would take the lead and learned all the details he could on the theory that he could not persuade anyone to support his position if he did not thoroughly understand the issues.[104] Carter's national security adviser records a successful demonstration of that theory when Carter met with Andrei Gromyko and other Soviet officials and impressed them with his mastery of the intricate substantive questions of the SALT talks.[105] His second approach to administrative leadership was to delegate the development of most other policies to cabinet officers and other subordinates.[106]

The strength and weaknesses of the first approach already have been assessed. It valued political knowledge too little and technical understanding too much. But it did give the president an impressive resource for persuasion. The second approach was standard for presidents, but Carter delegated responsibility in a particularly unstructured way that caused him trouble. He gave little guidance, presumably on the assumption that proposals were to be developed by experts. One result was that conflicts developed among his advisers that could not be resolved without being brought back to him. Carter would neither supply authoritative guidance nor empower assistants to arbitrate in his behalf. There were continual complaints throughout his administration that everyone seemed to be in business for himself.[107]

Conclusion.   Carter was judged by journalists and Washington professionals during his presidency by standards appropriate for presidents of achievement. His deficiencies as a leader of public opinion and legislative tactician were particularly emphasized. Yet the times were not appropriate for such leadership. It was difficult to take the Democratic coalition in directions it did not wish to go. It always will be an open question whether Carter could have disciplined his coalition and his administration more effectively if he had been more of a strategic president who sought to lead in terms of a few clear objectives that he tied to teaching about historical necessities. What is clear is that, in the absence of such coherent leadership, there was considerable disorientation and lack of discipline within American government. Carter presented himself as a president of achievement, and the style of leadership he consequently developed contributed to his problems.

Ronald Reagan

Strategy.   Jimmy Carter was the leader of a Democratic constituency that did not wish to hear that flagging economies in all the Western nations had made it more difficult to sustain or increase the commitments of government either to broadly shared entitlement programs like Social Security and medical care for the elderly or to welfare programs for the poor. The fiscal conservatism that seemed to be required by declining economic growth clashed with his party's commitments to social welfare. By the same token, the capacity of Keynesian economics to calibrate policy so that inflation could be curbed by tighter fiscal controls without risking recession and unacceptably high unemployment appeared to be increasingly limited as the Carter administration veered back and forth between budgets to fight inflation and recession. The term "stagflation" was coined to describe the unprecedented phenomenon of simultaneous rises in the rates of inflation and unemployment for which Keynesian theory had no remedy.[108]

Reagan was elected president in 1980 because many voters were seeking a fresh approach to government. He interpreted his victory as a conservative mandate that empowered him to address the new set of problems facing government in terms of his ideology. Reagan presented a theory to break out of the new economic problems and achieve renewed growth without inflation. The initial promises of "Reaganomics" were that massive tax cuts over a three-year period, joined to a policy of tight control of the money supply by the Federal Reserve Board and deep cuts in the domestic federal budget, would simultaneously revive the economy and reduce inflation. This was less a respectable economic theory than it was a skillful political strategy to achieve a number of long-standing Reagan goals. He strongly believed that government was the chief cause of the faltering economy. Domestic spending fed inflation, and excessive federal regulation deterred productivity. Therefore, Reagan iniitiated a strong campaign in Congress to cut the 20 percent of the federal budget that could be cut without touching defense or the various entitlement programs. The working poor and the dependent poor were the chief losers in this exercise. By reducing the budget for such programs and seeking to devolve responsibility for their administration to the states, Reagan was trying to eliminate the programmatic base for the Democratic coalition. At the same time, he was appealing to the middle and working classes by arguing that inflation could be cut without recession and growth could be induced through tax cuts. The amalgam presented logical difficulties, but it was political magic. Early surveys showed that even though citizens doubted specific claims in the Reagan economic program, they responded positively because it was a bold new strategy to pull the nation out of its economic malaise.[109]

Reagan's policies did not achieve all their goals in the short term. Because the budget cuts did not match the size of the tax cuts, federal deficits grew alarmingly. Increased expenditures for defense added to this problem. The Federal Reserve Board responded with a policy of tight money, which brought about the inevitable recession and the highest rates of unemployment since the Great Depression of the 1930s. Although a number of Reagan's advisers were prepared at several points to modify parts of his program by rescinding projected tax cuts and cutting projected defense spending, the president was undaunted.[110] Reagan believed that the credibility of the Carter administration had been undermined by its frequent, seemingly erratic changes in policy. He had created a belief in the public mind that root and branch solutions for the nation's economic problem were in the works and thereby had succeeded in seizing the political initiative away from the Democratic party, an initiative he was not about to yield. The results of the congressional vote at midterm in 1982, which increased the number of Democrats in the House, was interpreted by both parties as a message to Reagan to adjust but not fundamentally change his course.[111]

Reagan was attempting to prove an axiom of political leadership that had been validated by Franklin Roosevelt. The public does not expect the president to solve problems perfectly, but they do expect conditions to improve. As indicators of economic recovery began to grow stronger in 1983, the president held firmly to his strategy, banking on recovery not only to revive the economy without restoring inflation, but also to strengthen him politically. Reagan appeared to have persuaded large numbers of Americans that the severe recession and the cuts in social programs were worth the cost if fundamental problems in the working of the economy were being addressed so that, in the long run, economic recovery would take place without inflation. Thus, he established the central question that would be tested in the 1984 election. To that extent, Reagan's bold political strategy worked.

Presentation of Self.   Reagan saw himself from the start as a president of achievement in the Rooseveltian mold. He compared himself to Roosevelt in his acceptance of the Republican nomination. Like Roosevelt, Reagan wished to bring a "new deal" to the nation that would form the basis for a new political era, a Republican one. He has all the rhetorical skills required of a president of achievement and is particularly good at using language to serve his strategic goals. He has spent all his adult life as a public speaker, first as an actor, next as a lecturer for the General Electric Company, and then as governor and president. His delivery of set speeches, especially on television, reflects years of experience at clarifying complex questions through a simple, straightforward, smoothly delivered message. From the start, Reagan regarded this skill as the chief instrument for presidential leadership.[112] He consciously used televised appeals to the nation to persuade wavering members of Congress to support administration measures, and the correlation of favorable public response to his first-year talks on economic policy with support from many Democratic members of Congress suggests that the appeals were effective.[113]

Reagan is able to get his facts wrong both in spontaneous and prepared remarks without noticeable public criticism. He is far more interested in a general rhetorical appeal than in making accurate statements. For example, during the 1980 general election campaign he charged, in off-the-cuff talks that were made without any factual basis whatever, that trees and the eruption of the Mount St. Helens volcano caused more air pollution than cars and industrial sources.[114] This very casualness may explain why people are willing to overlook his lack of preparation. Reagan's relaxed manner carries with it hope, optimism, and resiliency that others find contagious. He exudes confidence that his initiatives will work and that problems can be solved. He does not complain about the difficulty of solving problems but, if anything, oversimplifies the difficulties. People know this, yet they respond to the positive message. Thus, polls sometimes find disapproval of Reagan's policies joined to approval of the president himself.[115] This suggests a connection between Reagan's public appeal and his strategic ability to structure the central issues.

Tactics.   The principal feature of Reagan's style of tactical leadership is to take a strong public position on an issue and then hold out for it, making compromises only when forced to by lack of support. He delegates negotiation for such matters to his lieutenants but sets the terms for eventual agreement. He is skilled at persuasion in face-to-face encounters and, as president, has been willing to call members of Congress to his office to ask them to support his legislative program. Reagan evidently handles such sessions with low-keyed good humor, charm rather than pressure, and appears to have the same contagious effect on individuals that he can have on the public.[116]

Reagan's principal style of legislative leadership is to press for the whole loaf but settle for half if that is all he can get. Sometimes this tactic is deliberate. He yielded, for example, to the urgings of Republican congressional leaders and supported increases in excise taxes in 1982 despite having made tax reduction the central theme of his economic policy. He did the same with the MX missile and Social Security, assigning the task of developing acceptable compromises to bipartisan presidential commissions after administration plans had been rejected by Congress.

Another aspect to this style, however, is Reagan's unwillingness to come to terms with unpleasant facts. Reagan entered office with a number of strong beliefs that have not stood the test of political or even factual reality. For example, his hostility to environmental regulation caused him to appoint people to run the Environmental Protection Agency whom he eventually fired and replaced with new leaders with strong environmental credentials. At times he gives the impression in his public statements that he believes the Soviet Union is the incarnation of evil in the world. Yet he supported two successive secretaries of state who were in favor of negotiation with the Soviets on a broad range of issues. Somehow Reagan finds ways to reconcile his beliefs with reality by making concessions to the facts. His detachment from issues and preference for broad strategic and ideological thinking is thus both a strength and a weakness. He seldom is committed to specifics and can be flexible if he wishes. But this can take time and usually happens only in the face of impending defeat or dramatic events.

Authority.   Reagan's management of his lieutenants most fully reveals the strengths and weaknesses of his style of leadership. The journalist who knows him best refers to it as "the Delegated Presidency."[117] The central principle is Reagan's belief that he should hold himself in reserve for public leadership on crucial questions. Therefore, he does not involve himself greatly in policy development or master the details of issues. This can cause him to resist new information and make his assistants reluctant to attempt to change his mind. Often he does not know the limits of his own knowledge.[118]

As a result of his detachment, Reagan often finds himself buffeted by competing sets of advisers with strongly contrasting policy views. For example, there has been a continuous and growing tension between the White House advisers who are responsible for working with Congress and his secretary of defense over the degree to which the president should compromise with congressional efforts to reduce defense increases. Reagan's pragmatism clashes with his ideology in such encounters. He deals with such disagreement and eventually works out a satisfactory integration of politics and principle for himself. But recurring and chronic disagreements of this kind are not his cup of tea. Reagan prefers orderly government and, despite his penchant for ideological rhetoric, appears to prefer practical people as his personal advisers.

Conclusion.   The same duality can be found in all four aspects of Reagan's skill. He is a highly intuitive leader who brings a temperament of hope and resilience to the presidency and who, although strongly ideological, is not politically rigid. But his very reliance on his intuition and temperament continually puts him in danger of being removed from the realities of politics and policy.

Reagan's greatest accomplishment was to alter the terms of political debate and thereby put enough of his imprint on public policy to justify the conclusion that he is a conservative president of achievement.

CONCLUSION

Political scientists have analyzed presidential leadership primarily in terms of the ability to acquire and use "power." The traditional variation of this theme has attached great importance to the exercise of constitutional powers, such as the veto and the prerogative to act in emergencies.[119] A more behavioral approach, articulated by Richard Neustadt, asks about the capacity of the president to use his limited powers to meet the political incentives of others in order that bargains may be made and coalitions built.[120]

This chapter and those that precede it have incorporated both these approaches in a larger perspective. To be sure, presidential understanding of how to use the formal and informal resources of the office to influence others is important. Johnson's ability to adapt legislative proposals to the political contours of Congress was far superior to Carter's, for example. Skill makes a difference. But the exercise of skill in tactical situations or even in the development of broad strategies of persuasion is only the necessary first step in understanding the wellsprings of presidential power.

We have set aside one cluster of skills as more important than all the rest and have called it strategic. The essence of strategic leadership is the president's capacity to define the nature of a historical situation and to persuade others to support the courses of action he develops to deal with policy problems. Presidents must understand their times. Such leadership is best understood less as the acquiring of power than as an activity of clarifying ambiguous situations for people who would like a sense of direction. The acquisition of power serves the larger vision, and the larger vision becomes the chief resource for the acquisition of power.[121]

NOTES

1. *Webster's New World Dictionary of the American Language* (Cleveland, Ohio: Williams Collins, 1979), pp. 133–34.
2. James H. Rowe, Jr., "Presidents I Have Known," in *Portraits of American Presidents*, Vol. I, *The Roosevelt Presidency: Four Intimate Perspectives of FDR*, ed. Kenneth W. Thompson (Washington, D.C.: University Press of America, 1982), p. 5.
3. James MacGregor Burns, *Roosevelt, the Lion and the Fox, 1882*–1940 (New York: Harcourt Brace Jovanovich, 1956), ch. 18.
4. John Gunther, *Roosevelt in Retrospect* (New York: Harper & Row, 1950), p. 4.
5. Arthur M. Schlesinger, Jr., *The Coming of the New Deal* (Boston: Houghton Mifflin, 1959), p. 573.
6. Frances Perkins, *The Roosevelt I Knew* (New York: Viking, 1946), p. 72.
7. Erwin C. Hargrove, *Presidential Leadership, Personality and Political Style* (New York: Macmillan, 1966), p. 64.
8. Burns, *Roosevelt*, p. 348.
9. *Ibid.*, ch. 9.
10. *Ibid.*, p. 174.
11. Schlesinger, *Coming of the New Deal*, p. 544.
12. *Ibid.*, pp. 535–36.
13. *Ibid.*, pp. 538–39.
14. *Ibid.*, p. 551.
15. *Ibid.*, pp. 522–27.
16. James MacGregor Burns, *Leadership* (New York: Harper & Row, 1978), pp. 392–94.

17. Charles C. Alexander, *Holding the Line: The Eisenhower Era* (Bloomington: University of Indiana Press, 1975), *passim*.
18. Fred I. Greenstein, *The Hidden-Hand Presidency, Eisenhower as Leader* (New York: Basic Books, 1982), p. 50.
19. Robert A. Devine, *Eisenhower and the Cold War* (New York: Oxford University Press, 1980), *passim*.
20. Herbert S. Parmet, *Eisenhower and the American Crusades* (New York: Macmillan, 1972), p. 573.
21. Hargrove, *Presidential Leadership*, p. 126.
22. Devine, *Eisenhower*, p. 11.
23. Greenstein, *Hidden-Hand Presidency*, p. 37.
24. *Ibid.*, p. 101.
25. *Ibid.*, p. 25.
26. Devine, *Eisenhower*, p. 20.
27. Alexander, *Holding the Line*, p. 289.
28. Raymond Saulnier, Oral History Interview, Institute for Public Policy Studies, Vanderbilt University, Nashville, Tenn., November 11, 1977.
29. John E. Mueller, "Presidential Popularity from Truman to Johnson," *American Political Science Review*, 64 (March 1970), pp. 31–32.
30. Greenstein, *Hidden-Hand Presidency*, pp. 230–31.
31. Richard E. Neustadt, *Presidential Power, the Politics of Leadership from FDR to Carter* (New York: Wiley, 1980), pp. 49–54, 80–91.
32. *Ibid.*, p. 22.
33. Greenstein, *Hidden-Hand Presidency*, pp. 20–24.
34. Alexander, *Holding the Line*, p. 289.
35. Alan Shank, *Presidential Policy Leadership: Kennedy and Social Welfare* (Washington, D.C.: University Press of America, 1980), pp. 227–50.
36. Walter Heller, Oral History Interview, Institute for Public Policy Studies, Vanderbilt University, Nashville, Tenn., December 14, 1977.
37. *Ibid.*
38. *Ibid.*
39. *Ibid.*
40. *Ibid.*
41. *Ibid.*
42. Richard J. Walton, *Cold War and Counter-revolution, the Foreign Policy of John F. Kennedy* (Baltimore, Md.: Penguin, 1972), ch. 9.
43. Bradley Greenberg and Edwin B. Parker, eds., *The Kennedy Assassination and the American Public: Social Communication in Crisis* (Stanford, Calif.: Stanford University Press, 1965), *passim*.
44. Rowe, "Presidents I Have Known," p. 8.
45. Wilbur J. Cohen, Oral History, John F. Kennedy Library, March 2, 1969, p. 25.
46. Shank, *Presidential Policy*, pp. 246, 250.
47. *Ibid.*, pp. 247–48.
48. *Ibid.*, pp. 65–66, ch. 2, *passim*.
49. *Ibid.*, ch. 5, *passim*.
50. Heller, Oral History Interview.
51. Wilbur J. Cohen, Oral History, John F. Kennedy Library, March 24, 1971, p. 66.
52. *Ibid.*, p. 67.
53. Garry Wills, *The Kennedy Imprisonment, a Meditation on Power* (Boston: Little, Brown, 1981), chs. 18 and 19.
54. Doris Kearns, *Lyndon Johnson and the American Dream* (New York: Harper & Row, 1976), pp. 216–17.
55. *Ibid.*, pp. 217–18, 291–92.
56. *Ibid.*, pp. 255–56.
57. Robert J. Donovan, *Tumultuous Years, the Presidency of Harry S. Truman, 1949–1953* (New York: Norton, 1982), *passim*.

58. Leslie H. Gelb with Richard Betts, *The Irony of Vietnam: The System Worked* (Washington, D.C.: The Brookings Institution, 1979), pp. 109, 127, 132, 284.
59. Kearns, *Lyndon Johnson*, pp. 251–52.
60. *Ibid.*, pp. 297–98, 300–2; Gardner Ackley and Arthur Okun, Oral History Interviews, Institute for Public Policy Studies, Vanderbilt University, Nashville, Tenn., February 3, 1978, and February 24, 1978.
61. Neustadt, *Presidential Power*, pp. 186–87, 191–93.
62. Gelb, *Irony of Vietnam*, pp. 172–73; Kearns, *Lyndon Johnson*, pp. 336–77.
63. Kearns, *Lyndon Johnson*, ch. 1.
64. *Ibid.*, p. 119.
65. *Ibid.*, p. 139.
66. Arthur Okun, Oral History Interview.
67. Kearns, *Lyndon Johnson*, pp. 187–89.
68. Francis Keppel, Oral History Interview, Lyndon B. Johnson Library, April 21, 1969, p. 8.
69. Kearns, *Lyndon Johnson*, pp. 190–93.
70. Rowland Evans and Robert D. Novak, *Lyndon B. Johnson: The Exercise of Power* (New York: Signet, 1968), ch. 23.
71. Kearns, *Lyndon Johnson*, pp. 336–37.
72. Gelb, *Irony of Vietnam*, pp. 102–4.
73. Joseph A. Califano and Wilbur J. Cohen, Oral History Interviews, Lyndon B. Johnson Library, June 11, 1973 (Califano); December 8, 1968, March 2, 1969, and May 10, 1967 (Cohen).
74. Ackley, Oral History Interviews.
75. Gelb, *Irony of Vietnam*, p. 157; Kearns, *Lyndon Johnson*, p. 319.
76. Kearns, *Lyndon Johnson*, p. 171.
77. A. James Reichley, *Conservatives in an Age of Change* (Washington, D.C.: The Brookings Institution, 1981), pp. 121–22.
78. *Ibid.*, pp. 115–16.
79. *Ibid.*, pp. 116–19.
80. *Ibid.*, p. 248.
81. Arthur M. Schlesinger, Jr., *The Imperial Presidency* (Boston: Houghton Mifflin, 1973), pp. 239–40.
82. Richard P. Nathan, *The Plot That Failed, Nixon and the Administrative Presidency* (New York: Wiley, 1975), ch. 4.
83. Theodore H. White, *Breach of Faith, the Fall of Richard Nixon* (New York: Atheneum, 1975), pp. 117–38.
84. *Ibid.*, p. 180.
85. Henry Kissinger, *White House Years* (Boston: Little, Brown, 1979), p. 504.
86. Richard M. Nixon, *Six Crises* (New York: Pocket Books, 1962), p. 103.
87. Reichley, *Conservatives*, pp. 96–97; Nathan, *Plot That Failed*, pp. 61–62.
88. Kissinger, *White House Years*, chs. 5 and 6.
89. Henry Kissinger, *Years of Upheaval* (Boston: Little, Brown, 1982), pp. 4, 6.
90. Jimmy Carter, *Keeping Faith, Memoirs of a President* (New York: Bantam, 1982), *passim*.
91. *Ibid.*, pp. 77–78, 84–90.
92. *Ibid.*, pp. 66, 87–88.
93. Zbigniew Brzezinski, *Power and Principle, Memoirs of the National Security Advisor, 1977–1981* (New York: Farrar, Straus & Giroux, 1983), pp. 53–57.
94. Interviews with Carter White House staff, Project on the Carter Presidency, Miller Center of Public Affairs, University of Virginia, Charlottesville, Va., December 1981.
95. Erwin C. Hargrove, conversation with former Carter administration official, Washington, D.C., April 1983.
96. Robert Shogan, *Promises to Keep* (New York: Crowell, 1977), p. 141.
97. Interviews with the Carter White House Staff, February 1982.
98. Interviews with the Carter White House Staff, April 1982

99. Carter, *Keeping Faith*, p. 80.
100. Laurence E. Lynn, Jr., and David de F. Whitmon, *The President as Policymaker, Jimmy Carter and Welfare Reforms* (Philadelphia: Temple University Press, 1981), *passim*.
101. Jimmy Carter, *Why Not the Best?* (New York: Bantam, 1975), p. 101.
102. Interview with Jimmy Carter, Project on the Carter Presidency, Miller Center of Public Affairs, University of Virginia, Charlottesville, Va., November 1982.
103. *Ibid.*
104. *Ibid.*
105. Brzezinski, *Power and Principle*, pp. 169–70.
106. Interview with Jimmy Carter.
107. Erwin C. Hargrove, interviews with former Carter advisers, Washington, D.C., spring and summer 1983.
108. Ben W. Heineman, Jr., and Curtis A. Hessler, *Memorandums for the President, a Strategic Approach to Domestic Affairs in the 1980s* (New York: Random House, 1980), pp. 252–66.
109. The Washington Post–ABC News Poll, *Washington Post* (February 24, 1981), pp. A1, A4.
110. Lou Cannon, *Reagan* (New York: Putnam's, 1982), p. 322; Steven R. Weisman, "Reaganomics and the President's Men," *The New York Times Magazine* (October 24, 1982), pp. 26–29, 82–89, 89–109.
111. "Message to the Captain of the Ship of State: Shift Your Direction," *Washington Post* (November 2, 1982), pp. A1, A10.
112. Cannon, *Reagan*, p. 371.
113. *Ibid.*, p. 333.
114. *Ibid.*, pp. 287–90.
115. "Voter Support for President Shows Sharp Increase," *Washington Post* (April 15, 1983), pp. A1, A9.
116. Martin Schram, "Reagan, the Tax Lobbyist: An Artist at Work," *Washington Post* (August 13, 1981), p. A3.
117. Cannon, *Reagan*, p. 371.
118. *Ibid.*, pp. 372–73.
119. Richard M. Pious, *The American Presidency* (New York: Basic Books, 1979), ch. 2.
120. Neustadt, *Presidential Power*, *passim*.
121. In the second edition of *Presidential Power* Richard Neustadt broadened his conception of power through an evaluation of John Kennedy. Neustadt argued that the first test of a president was whether his purposes ran with or against the "grain of history" (pp. 147–48). Robert Tucker has developed a definition of the essential function of leadership as teaching about the historical situation. See Robert C. Tucker, *Politics as Leadership* (Columbia: University of Missouri Press, 1981), pp. 15–30.

CHAPTER 5

Presidential Selection

Three basic components constitute our theory of presidential power. There are, first, the empowering elements: the constitutional nature of the office, which influences it in ways described in Chapter 2, and the environment, both cultural and political, in which the presidency functions (Chapter 3). In addition, there is the mix of individual presidential political skills, discussed in Chapter 4, that makes for leadership within the bounds set by Constitution, culture, and politics.

Of these three elements, the last is the most malleable. Changes in the constitutional nature of the office are both difficult *to* effect and somewhat unpredictable *in* effect. Only four amendments bearing on the presidency have been added to the Constitution, and their consequences rarely have been confined to those that were intended.[1] Political culture in a reasonably stable society is by nature slow to change. To be sure, different aspects of it can be stressed or reinterpreted in the service of new causes, as when Franklin Roosevelt defended his program for active federal involvement in the economy with the rhetoric of individual liberty. But invocations of culture such as this are at base creative acts of leadership, as are sensitive arousals of the public's political mood at different stages of the preparation-achievement-consolidation cycle. They are exceptions that demonstrate the rule—namely, that individual presidential leadership is the most variable ingredient of presidential power.

This draws our attention to presidential selection—the process through which individuals reach the presidency. The qualities that make for successful presidential leadership are such that a person must bring them to the presidency; presidents may "grow" while in office, but only on foundations that already are laid. These qualities are of two kinds: leadership *skills*, as described in Chapter 4; and leadership *suitability*, a mix of political ideas and purposes that is harmonious with public sentiment at each stage of the cycle. The body of this chapter describes the ways America has chosen its presidents in terms of which candidate qualities the selection process has tended to favor at various times.

But this "by-their-fruits-ye-shall-know-them" standard for evaluating presidential selection, as Austin Ranney calls it,[2] is not the only important standard inherent in American political culture. The selection process must have legitimacy as well. It "must be regarded by the public," writes James Ceaser, "as fair in its procedures and consonant with republican principles and basic democratic values."[3] To be sure, a selection method that produces skillful presidents whose purposes suit their times is more likely to enjoy public confidence than one that does not, but procedural legitimacy is nonetheless significant in its own right.

Historically, in fact, the quest for legitimacy has become more influential than the "good president" criterion in shaping the evolution of the presidential selection system. So, for that matter, has a third force, tangential at best to the quest for effective leadership: intraparty politics.

The first part of this chapter tells that history. It describes and analyzes the process by which the United States developed the selection system that now prevails. We then tell how — and to what ends — the present system works and analyze its effects on skill and suitability in the presidency. Finally, we assess the prospects for and importance of change in the process.

THE EVOLUTION OF THE PRESIDENTIAL SELECTION SYSTEM[4]

From Convention to Convention, 1787–1968

If ever there was a time when concern for candidate quality mattered to policy makers, it was at the Constitutional Convention of 1787. As we saw in Chapter 2, the framers' concern for presidential excellence was the source of the Constitution's age and reeligibility provisions, among others. But as great as was the framers' concern for effective presidential leadership, they had a narrow definition of it. Working in an age in which diplomacy was slow and the national government small, they cared less about getting presidents with the strategic, presentational, tactical, and authority-management skills necessary for reading the public mood and leading the government to appropriate action than they did about preserving the constitutional forms. As Ceaser points out, "Office holders, in their view, were to rest their claim to govern on the legally defined rights and prerogatives of their offices."[5] The electoral-college system of "peer review," the framers felt, would help the nation to choose presidents with a willingness to abide by such limits.

But, as John Roche has shown, the creation of the electoral college must be explained as much in terms of the political appeal (legitimacy) as quality. "To a body of working politicians," he writes,

> the merits of the plan were obvious: Everybody got a piece of the cake. First, the state legislatures had the right to determine the mode of selection of electors; second, the small states received a bonus in the form of a guaranteed minimum (3 votes) while the big states got acceptance of the principle of proportional power; third, if the state legislatures agreed (as six did in the first presidential election), the people could be directly involved in the choice of electors; and, finally, if no candidate received a majority, the right of decision passed to the national legislature with each state exercising equal strength.[6]

To the framers the presidential selection process was a seamless web. The electoral college not only was to *elect* the president but also to determine, within the bounds of constitutional *eligibility*, the pool of plausible candidates from which he would be drawn and narrow that down to a few final contenders. Indeed, given the framers' assumption that the House of Representatives often would have to make the final choice, the *winnowing* and *nominating* functions were the only ones the electoral college was expected to perform consistently.

The organization of American national politics into political parties took these expectations of how the four-stage selection process would work and stood them on their ear. Beginning in 1800, the year of the nation's first contested presidential election, the parties assumed the power to winnow and to nominate. The method by which they first did so was the congressional caucus, in which each party's members in Congress chose its candidate for president. The caucus is chiefly of historical interest except for one thing: it marked the introduction into the politics of the presidential selection process of intraparty politics as a third force, roughly equal in political importance to the concern for legitimacy and greater than that for candidate quality.

The caucus was developed when Alexander Hamilton came to the conclusion that the incumbent Federalist party president, John Adams, could not win reelection in 1800. Hamilton's hope was that if Federalist electors united behind Charles Cotesworth Pinckney, a popular South Carolinian, as well as Adams, Pinckney might draw enough additional votes from his Republican home state to squeak through. (At that time, members of the electoral college still voted for two men for president.) To get the word out to Federalists around the country, he persuaded party members in Congress to "caucus" and recommend both Adams and Pinckney.

The Jeffersonian Republicans of the day initially ridiculed the Federalist innovation, but quickly adopted it. The caucus preserved the peer-review principle; indeed, the honor roll of presidents it produced—Jefferson, James Madison, and James Monroe—has persuaded at least one political scientist to urge a modern-day return to the caucus.[7] But the caucus method had its flaws. For one thing it started a vicious cycle in Washington politics that sometimes made department heads as responsive to the Congress that could advance their own presidential ambitions as to the president who could not. Monroe, for example, spent much of his time as Madison's secretary of state currying favor on Capitol Hill. After the caucus made Monroe president, he, of course, was obliged to reward his leading supporters with cabinet posts. These new department heads soon began to conduct their own campaigns for president in Congress, turning their backs on Monroe in the process. Members of the cabinet also plotted against each other. William Crawford, secretary of the treasury, spread rumors that Secretary of State John Quincy Adams had appeared barefoot in church and forged changes in the original copy of the Constitution; Crawford, in turn, was accused of mental incompetence and of using his office to pry into the financial affairs of his cabinet colleagues.

Crawford's scheming won him his party's nomination in 1824, but little else: 150 of the 215 Republican congressmen boycotted the caucus, and Crawford ran a distant third in the fall election (fourth in the popular vote).

Voters clearly had had their fill of "King Caucus" and the petty intragovernmental bickering it seemed to encourage. The legitimacy of the caucus also was
undermined by its exclusion from the nominating process of voters who lived in
congressional constituencies represented by the other party.

After a brief period of confusion following the demise of the caucus (Andrew
Jackson, for example, received his first two nominations for president from the
Tennessee legislature and was elected in 1828), the national nominating convention came into being. New ideas of what was legitimate were part of the
reason. Westward expansion and the spread of the suffrage to the unpropertied
classes were giving American politics an electoral base that was broader and
more insistent on its right to have a say in the selection of its presidents. So was
intraparty politics. Searching for a way to unite geographically diffuse anti-
Jackson sentiment behind a single candidate in the 1832 election, the nascent
National Republican or Whig party decided to take a page from the book of the
small Anti-Masonic party, which had held a national nominating convention in
September 1831. (The practice already was widespread at the state level.) The
Whig convention met at Baltimore three months later and nominated Henry
Clay. Democrats, at the behest of President Jackson, followed suit in May 1832,
partly because Jackson was anxious to create a forum in which he could replace
Vice President John C. Calhoun on the ticket with Martin Van Buren.

The desire to select presidents who were qualified to meet the leadership
requirements of the office, although hardly foremost, was not absent in the
move to party conventions. But prevailing ideas of what those requirements
were began to be challenged. To be sure, Van Buren favored conventions
because he saw them as a way of shoring up the endangered principle of peer
review, the peers now being state party leaders instead of congressmen or electors. This, he felt, would keep the presidency secure from people who might
otherwise win an election with promises to the masses that, if fulfilled, would
widen the powers of the office beyond intended constitutional limits. Jackson,
however, more astutely realized that conventions, by taking selection one step
closer to the people, had made Van Buren's hopes futile. Convention-minded
presidents, he felt, not only would but should be "tribunes," listening to the
public and arousing it on behalf of shared causes.

Primaries did not develop until early in the twentieth century, when
leaders of the new, largely middle-class Progressive movement prevailed on
some states to allow voters a direct say in the selection process. Legitimacy in
the form of democracy again was the rallying cry. The Progressives complained
that under the existing system the selection of delegates to the presidential
nominating conventions was controlled entirely by state and local party professionals. Political "bosses" and their underlings, they charged, represented
themselves at the conventions, not their constituents, striking corrupt
patronage deals with each other in order to enhance their personal power and
wealth. Primaries, it was hoped, would break their monopoly on delegate
selection and thus make the conventions more responsive to the people.

The triumph of Jacksonian ideas about what constituted effective
presidential leadership went hand in hand with Progressive notions of
legitimacy in this period. "The general sense of the community may wait to be

aroused," argued Woodrow Wilson; "statesmen must formulate and make it explicit." Because presidents make up "that part of the government that is in most direct communication with the nation," they more than others are responsible to lead "not by reason of legal authority, but by reason of their contact and amenability to public opinion."[8] Primaries would encourage this symbiosis between president and public.

Again, however, intraparty politics underlay the alteration of nomination politics. The reason for the first state presidential primary to choose convention delegates, for example, was to help resolve a split among Wisconsin's Republicans that had caused both the Progressive supporters of Senator Robert La Follette and his "regular" Republican foes to send their own delegations to the Republican national convention and even to nominate their own slates of candidates for state office.

The primaries did not replace the convention in this period. They were a nuisance to party professionals, but a small one — "a series of guerrilla sorties, in which insurrectionaries attempted to harass the main forces that power brokers had already fielded for their candidates."[9] In 1912, for example, Theodore Roosevelt won ten of twelve primaries, but the Republican convention nominated William Howard Taft anyway. Democrats chose Adlai Stevenson as their nominee in 1952 even though Senator Estes Kefauver had won twelve of the thirteen primaries he entered. In 1960 Democratic pros conceded a use for primaries as a testing ground for candidates, much as the New Haven theater audience once served as a dry run for Broadway-bound shows. Still, however, the final decision rested with them and not the primary voters. In 1968, party professionals were able to nominate Hubert Humphrey, who had not won a single primary.

From Reform to Reform, 1969–1984

The 1968 Democratic convention was the last one at which party professionals could nominate a candidate on their own volition. The convention met in a setting of anti-Vietnam demonstrations and riots. Clearly, it seemed to many, something had gone wrong with a party system that offered a nation consumed by dissatisfaction with the war a choice between Humphrey and Richard Nixon. Clearly, too, the solution seemed to lie in somehow "opening up" the parties, making them more "responsive" to voters at the "grass roots" so that they could never get that far out of touch again. "Shamed, confused in the din of the floor," wrote Theodore White, "the regular delegates accepted a Minority Report on Rules that they did not understand. It demanded that all Democratic voters get 'full, meaningful and timely opportunity to participate in the selection of delegates' to the next convention and set up a commission to rewrite party rules."[10] The standard of democratic legitimacy towered above all others.

In practical terms, the situation that confronted the commission, which was headed by South Dakota Senator George McGovern and Congressman Donald Fraser of Minnesota, was as follows: about a third of the delegates to Democratic conventions were being chosen by the voters in primaries (37.5 percent in 1968); the rest according to state party procedures. Of this second group, about half were picked prior to the election year, often by unilateral appointment of the governor or party chairman. Others were chosen in caucuses at which rank-and-file party members were entitled to be present, but even then there was no assurance of openness. In Virginia, for example, the required local "mass meetings" to select delegates to the state convention often took place on the bus to Richmond. Unrepresentative (and thus illegitimate), it was charged, the nomination process was underrepresentative as well: only 5 percent of the delegates in 1968 were black; only 13 percent were women; only 4 percent under thirty.[11]

The commission spoke clearly on underrepresentation by establishing minimum delegate "quotas" for women, blacks, and youth commensurate with their share of the various state populations. But its answer to the misrepresentation issue was more equivocal. It gave the state parties a choice: either they could select their delegates in primaries, or they could select them in truly open caucuses, meetings in which any and all self-professed Democrats could participate equally. The commission apparently hoped that the states would select the latter course. But, writes Austin Ranney, a commission member, "we got a rude shock."[12] Six additional states instantly opted for a primary, raising the number of Democratic primary states to twenty-three in 1972.

Intraparty politics explains part of this. According to Ranney, rather than "radically revise their accustomed ways of conducting caucuses and conventions for other party matters," several state parties decided that "it would be better to split off the process for selecting national convention delegates and let it be conducted by a state-administered primary."[13] Of the state parties that went the less certain, open-caucus route, some soon regretted their decision. In 1972 supporters of McGovern's candidacy for president organized thoroughly, packed the state caucuses, and took them over from the surprised party regulars; even conservative Virginia found itself represented at the national convention by a pro-McGovern delegation. (He got 30 percent of the vote there in November.)

To avoid a second round of ideological takeovers, several more caucus states switched to primaries after the 1972 election, raising the total to thirty. Then another party rules commission, chaired by Barbara Mikulski, mandated that starting in 1976, a state's convention delegates must be allocated according to the principle of proportional representation. This time it was Jimmy Carter who figured out the new angle. Carter knew that if he entered all the primaries, he would win at least some delegates even when he finished second or third in the popular vote. By 1980 another five state parties had converted to primaries, bringing the total to thirty-five. At the same time, party rank-and-file seemed to have grown more accustomed to new-style caucuses, which meant that the similarities between caucuses and primaries—in openness to all interested voters and even in turnout—became perhaps more important than the differences. As a result, a few states changed from primaries to caucuses in 1984.

Concern for candidate quality came late to the post-1969 reform process. After the nominations of McGovern and Carter, some Democratic counter-reformationists argued that open delegate selection had banished peer review from the process almost entirely. In 1968, 68 percent of the party's senators, 39 percent of its members of the House of Representatives, and 83 percent of its governors were delegates or alternates to the convention; by 1980, their shares had dropped to 14 percent, 15 percent, and 75 percent, respectively—about 1 percent of all in attendance.[14] Another commission, which took its name from Governor James Hunt of North Carolina, was appointed in 1980 and propounded a rule for the 1984 Democratic convention requiring that 14 percent of its seats be reserved for specially selected party and elected officials, formally uncommitted to any candidate. The Hunt Commission also undid the proportional representation reform: as of 1984, a state party could adopt a "winner take all" or similar system that greatly rewards even a narrow primary victory. Finally, the commission sought to delay by one month the start of the delegate-selection season, which in recent years has begun with the Iowa caucuses in January.[15]

Although the Democrats took the lead in all this, the Republicans followed suit quite closely. Their "DO" commission (Committee on Delegates and Organization), also appointed in 1969, ushered in similar, if less explicit, rules with regard to open delegate selection. More important, perhaps, has been the Republicans' injunction to their state parties to follow state law, which in Democratic-controlled legislatures, often came to mean delegate selection by primary. Thus, Republican primaries increased in number from sixteen in 1968 to more than twice that number in 1980 and 1984.[16]

Conclusion

What the United States enjoys today is the culmination of two centuries of evolution in its presidential selection process. The engine driving historical change has been the desire to select candidates for president with requisite leadership qualities by a process that is considered legitimate by the American public, with intraparty politics a third and highly unpredictable force. Of these three the legitimacy criterion has been both consistent in direction (in its demand for ever-greater participatory democracy) and steadily more important in weight. The opposite is true of the concern for presidential quality, which has changed in its definition (from Madisonian to Wilsonian ideas)[17] and has shrunk in relative importance.

All this leaves us with a fundamental question: In a system in which concern for quality has been a junior partner for some years, what kinds of presidents have we been getting?

WHO BECOMES PRESIDENT?

The question of who becomes president in a given election year can be approached in the manner of Sherlock Holmes solving a crime. "Eliminate the impossible," Holmes always said, "and whatever is left, however improbable, is the answer." The process of eliminating "wrong" possibilities for president comes, as it always has, in four stages. First, constitutional and cultural standards of *eligibility* shape the pool of plausible presidential possibilities according to their legal qualifications, social backgrounds, and career experiences. Second, preelection-year *winnowing* sifts out from this pool a relatively small number of ambitious and "serious" candidates. The third, or *nominating*, stage is a continuation of the second: now the serious few become two, the nominees of the Republican and Democratic parties. Last is the fall campaign and *election*, from which the president-elect emerges.

Eligibility: Constitutional Criteria

The Constitution is expansive on the subject of who is not legally eligible to be president. Article I forbids the parliamentary practice of having a member of Congress serve simultaneously as chief executive. The Twenty-second Amendment disqualifies anyone who already has been elected president twice or who has served one term and more than half of another. Article II excludes all who are not "natural born citizen[s]" that have "been fourteen years a Resident within the United States" and "attained to the Age of thirty five Years." The Twelfth Amendment applies all these limits to the vice presidency as well.

The constitutional limits are broad, even if one assumes, as Edward S. Corwin somewhat dubiously did, that they have been added to by federal criminal laws that disqualify those convicted of violating them from "holding office under the United States."[18] The Constitutional Convention did not include property ownership or religious orthodoxy as qualifications, as most states then provided for their governors. It did not forbid senators and congressmen from running on a national ticket while in office, or even from running for both simultaneously (as John Nance Garner did in 1932 and Lyndon Johnson did in 1960). Custom has given a liberal definition to the other limiting provisions wherever there is room for interpretation. Although one could reasonably argue that the framers meant fourteen years *continuous* residency (they had in mind American Tories who had gone to England and Canada during the Revolution), Herbert Hoover's right to rule was not challenged in 1929, even though he had lived abroad for much of his recent life.[19] And although the issue never has been tested, it seems likely that a president-elect born of American parents on foreign soil would have no serious trouble assuming office.[20] So broad are the constitutional qualifications, in fact, that one could conservatively estimate that approximately 100 million Americans — more than half of the voting population — are legally eligible for the presidency.

Eligibility: Social Background Criteria

No one would pretend that constitutional eligibility makes one a plausible candidate for the presidency. The United States, which technically draws its presidents from an unusually large pool, actually draws it from a very small one.

How many are in this pool? Thomas Cronin estimates offhandedly that "there is an 'on-deck circle' of about fifty individuals in any given presidential year."[21] If the index for inclusion is one-time support from even 1 percent of an

Table 5.1   Size of the Pool of Candidates for President, 1936–1980

Year	5 Percent Support or More in Gallup Poll			1 Percent Support or More in Gallup Poll		
	Democrats	*Republicans*	*Total*	*Democrats*	*Republicans*	*Total*
1936	1	7	8	1	8	9
1940	2	7	9	7	14	21
1944	4	6	10	9	9	18
1948	6	8	14	16	12	28
1952	14	7	21	20	12	32
1956	5	1	6	13	6	19
1960	9	5	14	12	11	23
1964	2	8	10	7	11	18
1968	5	11	16	5	13	18
1972	9	3	12	17	3	20
1976	11	8	19	31	14	45
1980	6	5	11	9	17	26
Total	74	76	150	147	130	277
Average per election	6.2	6.4	12.5	12.3	10.9	23.1

individual's fellow partisans in Gallup polls on presidential nomination preference, then the number of plausible candidates has ranged from nine in 1936 to forty-five in 1976, with an average of 23.1 per election for the period 1936–80.[22] (A different index — mention of someone's name as a presidential prospect on a network evening news program — produces a similar figure: an average 27.7 per election from 1968 to 1980.)[23] If one raises the standard to 5 percent support in a Gallup poll — still low, considering that the lowest pre-convention poll showing for a major party nominee was 12 percent, for Adlai Stevenson in 1952 — the size of the pool shrinks by almost half, to 12.5 per election. (See Table 5.1.) And some of these were not aspiring to the presidency as much as waging campaigns in order to draw attention to their policy agendas. Governor George Wallace, for example, challenged President Johnson in several 1964 primaries to protest his party's pro–civil rights policies; Congressmen John Ashbrook and Paul McCloskey opposed President Nixon's renomination in 1972, attacking him for being too liberal or too conservative, respectively. Jesse Jackson's 1984 campaign in the Democratic primaries seemed more designed to advance the cause of blacks and other minorities than to win him the party's presidential nomination.

To state that the ranks of possible presidents in a given election are numbered in the low dozens is not very helpful unless we also know what kinds of people are in those ranks. One way of deducing who plausibly can become president is to look first at those who actually have been president. Table 5.2 lists the social background characteristics of all twentieth-century presidents. (A comparable table for defeated major party candidates would be very similar, as would be a table of nineteenth-century presidents.)[24] From this evidence, it seems that the system historically has eliminated the following kinds of people from the constitutionally eligible pool of millions: women, blacks and other racial minorities, non-Christians, and the never-married. To be sure, this list understates the exclusivity of the pool of plausible presidential candidates. There are other biases at play that, although less absolute, nonetheless have been confining. As Benjamin Page and Mark Petracca observe, presidents "usually have been white, well-to-do, Protestant males, of indistinct (or Anglo-Saxon) ethnic background; married, with a family; and in their middle fifties or older." Richard Watson and Norman Thomas add that presidential Protestantism has been "generally from a high-status denomination," and that presidents, "including those from modest backgrounds, have generally been well-educated at prestigious private institutions and have tended to practice law prior to their entry into public life."[25]

The roster of plausible candidates in recent elections has conformed to this racial, sexual, marital, and religious profile. This can be seen in Table 5.3, which groups together presidential possibilities who met one or another standard of "seriousness" in the 1972, 1976, or 1980 elections. Of the candidacies that attracted at least 5 percent support in even one Gallup poll in the four years preceding each election, one belonged to a black woman (Representative Shirley Chisholm), two to a bachelor (Governor Jerry Brown), and thirty-nine (92.9 percent) to white, male, married Christians. There is slightly more variety among those who crossed only the 1 percent barrier, but forty-five of fifty (90 percent) in this category filled the standard prescription entirely. The lowest threshold — mere mention on a television network's evening news program — is biased in favor of frivolous candidates who met the easy ballot requirements for the New Hampshire primary, such as comedian Pat Paulsen, community organizer Ed Coll (only thirty-two years old), and Harold Stassen. Even so, the overwhelming majority fit the mold.

Almost without exception, the plausible candidates for the 1984 presidential election fit it as well. Table 5.4 describes the social backgrounds of all Democrats and Republicans who met the 1 percent requirement in Gallup polls taken through the start of 1984.[26] (The Republican list includes not just Ronald Reagan, but those who were mentioned as presidential preferences in the event Reagan were to choose not to run for reelection.) Of the sixteen Democrats and nine Republicans who attracted at least 1 percent support for their party's nomination, all twenty-five were men, all were (or had been) married, all professed to be Christians, and all but one — Jesse Jackson — were white.

Still, changes in the list of social background criteria may occur. New standards may arise. Not every president has had a college degree, but everyone since 1933 has and the nation's ever-growing credentialist mores make it more likely that future presidency-seekers will have to as well. (All twenty-five of the 1984 "plausibles" were at least college educated.) Divorced or widowed single candidates may find it easier to be taken seriously (Reagan broke the remarriage barrier in 1980 with scarcely a mention), but aspirants who never have been married may find it harder. America's distaste for homosexuality and suspicion of bachelors seems to have caused one unmarried candidate in 1979 to publicize his friendship with a female celebrity just to prove his sexual bona fides.[27]

Table 5.2   Social Background Characteristics of Twentieth-Century Presidents

	Term	Father's Occupation and Social Class[1]	Age[2]
William McKinley	1897–1901	Ironmonger (middle)	54
Theodore Roosevelt	1901–1909	Businessman (upper)	42
William H. Taft	1909–1913	Lawyer (upper)	51
Woodrow Wilson	1913–1921	Minister (upper)	56
Warren Harding	1921–1923	Doctor (upper)	55
Calvin Coolidge	1923–1929	Storekeeper (middle)	51
Herbert Hoover	1929–1933	Blacksmith (working)	54
Franklin Roosevelt	1933–1945	Businessman (upper)	50
Harry Truman	1945–1953	Small landowner (middle)	61
Dwight Eisenhower	1953–1961	Mechanic (working)	62
John Kennedy	1961–1963	Businessman (upper)	43
Lyndon Johnson	1963–1969	Small landowner (middle)	55
Richard Nixon	1969–1974	Streetcar conductor, grocer (working)	55
Gerald Ford	1974–1977	Paint and lumber business (middle)	61
Jimmy Carter	1977–1981	Small landowner (middle)	52
Ronald Reagan	1981–	Shoe salesman (working)	69

[1]Classification drawn from Richard Watson and Norman Thomas, *The Politics of the Presidency* (New York: John Wiley, 1983), p. 110.
[2]At time of election.

It also is possible that some existing social criteria will disappear from the list, as others have in recent years. In 1960 Clinton Rossiter published a catalog of "oughts" and "almost certainly musts" for would-be presidents that included the following: "northerner or westerner" (southerners Lyndon Johnson and Jimmy Carter were elected in 1964 and 1976, respectively); "less than sixty-five years old" (Reagan turned sixty-nine in 1980); "more than forty-five years old," "Protestant," "a small-town boy," and "a self-made man" (forty-three-year-old John Kennedy, a rich urban Catholic, was elected the year Rossiter wrote); "a lawyer" (four of the five last elected presidents have not been); and so on.[28] The class origins of presidents also have broadened. Twentieth-century presidents from William McKinley to Franklin Roosevelt were, like their 19th-century counterparts, predominantly upper-class in social background. (See Table 5.5.) Yet of the eight presidents since 1945, only one (Kennedy) was born into an upper-class family; four have come from middle-class homes (Truman, Johnson, Carter, and Ford), and three from the working class (Eisenhower, Nixon, and Reagan.)[29]

Are public attitudes that still seem to exclude people from the presidency

Table 5.2   *(continued)*

Marital Status	Education	Religion	Home State[3]
Married	Law school	Methodist	Ohio
Married	College	Dutch Reformed	New York
Married	Law school	Unitarian	Ohio
Married	Ph.D.	Presbyterian	New Jersey
Married	Some college	Baptist	Ohio
Married	College	Congregational	Massachusetts
Married	College	Quaker	California
Married	Law school	Episcopal	New York
Married	Some law school	Baptist	Missouri
Married	College	Presbyterian	Kansas
Married	College	Catholic	Massachusetts
Married	College	Disciples	Texas
Married	Law school	Quaker	California
Married	Law school	Episcopal	Michigan
Married	College	Baptist	Georgia
Remarried (Divorced)	College	Disciples	California

[3]During most important adult years.

for reasons of race, religion, or other social background criteria likely to change in the near future? Public opinion surveys on voter prejudice seem encouraging, but perhaps less so than meets the eye. The Gallup poll reported in 1983 that, other things being equal, 88 percent of the electorate would be willing to vote for a Jewish candidate for president, up from 82 percent in 1978 and 62 percent in 1958. Seventy-seven percent say they could support a black candidate, the same proportion that was reported in 1978, but double the 38 percent who said they could in 1958.[30] In both cases, the figure is substantially higher than the 68 percent who said they could vote for a Catholic in 1959, a year before Kennedy's election. Kennedy's Catholicism, however, also won him many votes from among the quarter of the electorate who were Catholic — indeed, the net effect of religiously prejudiced voting in 1960 may have been favorable to Kennedy. In contrast, a Jewish candidate would have fewer co-religionists and a black fewer racial compatriots to draw upon for prejudiced support to outweigh the prejudiced opposition.

Women are in a more enviable position in this regard — not only has the electorate's tolerance for a female president risen from 52 percent in 1958 to 73 percent in 1978 and 80 percent in 1983, but women make up a majority of the electorate. Curiously, atheists are well-positioned, too. To be sure, voters' expressed will-

Table 5.3 Social Background Characteristics of "Plausible" Candidates for President: 1972, 1976, 1980

	Social Background				Candidates Who Met All Social Criteria (Percent)
	Racial Minorities	*Women*	*Non-Christians*	*Never Married*	
5 PERCENT SUPPORT OR MORE IN GALLUP POLL	Shirley Chisholm (1972)	Shirley Chisholm (1972)		Jerry Brown (1976, 1980)	92.9
1–4 PERCENT SUPPORT IN GALLUP POLL	Julian Bond (1976) Edward Brooke (1976)	Ella Grasso (1976)	Milton Shapp (1976)	Ralph Nader (1976)	90.0

Table 5.4   Social Background Characteristics of "Plausible" Candidates in 1984

	Age[1]	Marital Status	Education	Religion	Home State[2]
DEMOCRATS					
Reubin Askew	56	Married	Law school	Presbyterian	Florida
Bruce Babbitt	46	Married	Law school	Catholic	Arizona
Lloyd Bentsen	63	Married	Law school	Presbyterian	Texas
Bill Bradley	41	Married	M.A.	Protestant	New Jersey
John Y. Brown	51	Remarried (divorced)	Law school	Baptist	Kentucky
Dale Bumpers	59	Married	Law school	Methodist	Arkansas
Alan Cranston	70	Married	College	Protestant	California
John Glenn	63	Married	College	Presbyterian	Ohio
Gary Hart	47	Married	Law school	Presbyterian	Colorado
Ernest Hollings	62	Married	Law school	Lutheran	S. Carolina
Jesse Jackson	43	Married	College	Baptist	Illinois
Edward Kennedy	52	Divorced	Law school	Catholic	Massachusetts
George McGovern	62	Married	Ph.D.	Methodist	South Dakota
Walter Mondale	56	Married	Law school	Presbyterian	Minnesota
Daniel Moynihan	57	Married	Ph.D.	Catholic	New York
Jay Rockefeller	47	Married	College	Presbyterian	W. Virginia
REPUBLICANS					
John Anderson	62	Married	Law school	Evangelical	Illinois
Howard Baker	59	Married	Law school	Presbyterian	Tennessee
George Bush	60	Married	College	Episcopal	Texas
John Connolly	67	Married	Law school	Methodist	Texas
Robert Dole	61	Married	Law school	Methodist	Kansas
Jesse Helms	63	Married	Some college	Baptist	N. Carolina
Jack Kemp	49	Married	College	Presbyterian	New York
Charles Percy	65	Married	College	Christian Science	Illinois
Ronald Reagan	73	Remarried (divorced)	College	Disciples	California

[1]In 1984.
[2]During most important adult years.

ingness to consider electing an atheist as president still is quite low: 42 percent in 1983, up from 40 percent in 1978 and 18 percent in 1958. But unlike women, blacks, and Jews, atheists can profess to be something different from what they are, as some who are in Congress, for example, apparently do.[31]

For female, black, or Jewish candidates for the presidency to be taken seriously, of course, will require not only that the public be willing to consider them without prejudice, but that they be qualified in other ways as well. As we will see shortly, voters expect would-be presidents to be experienced in high office. In contrast to the public opinion surveys on voter tolerance, the data about minority officeholding seem discouraging on first inspection. The 98th Congress, for example, contained only 23 women, 21 blacks, 37 Jews, and two religious "unspecifieds." None of the blacks and only two of the women (both

Table 5.5:   Social Class Background of Presidents

	Pre-Twentieth Century		1900–1945		1945–	
	Number	*Percent*	*Number*	*Percent*	*Number*	*Percent*
UPPER-CLASS	13	56.5	5	62.5	1	12.5
MIDDLE-CLASS	3	13.0	2	25.0	4	50.0
LOWER-CLASS	7	30.4	1	12.5	3	37.5

Source: See note 29.

Republicans) were senators. The other 457 members, including 90 of 100 senators, were white male Christians. So were 49 of the 50 state governors.

Still, the ranks of black and female officeholders are rising rapidly at the state and local levels, which may precede greater breakthroughs in congressional and gubernatorial politics. In 1983 women occupied 13 percent of all state legislative seats, triple their share in 1969. Blacks occupied 4.5 percent, double their 1969 share.[32] In 1982 Los Angeles Mayor Tom Bradley won the first major party gubernatorial nomination by a black since Reconstruction; a year later, Martha Layne Collins of Kentucky became the second woman to be elected governor of any state in her own right. (Connecticut's Ella Grasso, elected in 1974 and reelected in 1978, was the first.) And on October 3, 1983 six of the candidates for the 1984 Democratic presidential nomination pledged to the annual conference of the National Organization for Women that they would seriously consider naming a female vice presidential running mate.[33]

It is, of course, one thing to observe that conditions are ripe for breaking down certain barriers of social background — that voters are more willing to accept the candidacies of minority persons who are qualified by virtue of their officeholding experience, and that more minority persons are acquiring such experience — and something else again to predict when that breaking down will occur. Recent history does suggest, however, that barriers to the presidency tend to fall in one of three ways: through a candidate's *facing the issue* during a campaign; through broaching it first in the *vice presidency;* or as an aftermath to an already broadened *social tolerance.*

Facing the issue.   No greater obstacle stood between John Kennedy and the presidency in 1960 than relatively widespread public fear of a Roman Catholic president. To blunt the issue's effect, Kennedy faced it squarely. In the midst of a crucial primary campaign, he told a television audience of West Virginians, 95 percent of them Protestant, that:

> When any man stands on the steps of the Capitol and takes the oath of office of President, he is swearing to support the separation of church and state; he puts one hand on the Bible and raises the other hand to God as he takes the oath. And if he breaks his oath, he is not only committing a crime against the Constitution, for which Congress can impeach him — and should impeach him — but he is committing a sin against God. A sin against God, for he has sworn on the Bible[34]

In September, after winning the nomination, Kennedy appeared before the

Greater Houston Ministerial Association and made an equally forthright statement.

In early 1980, Ronald Reagan faced a somewhat different issue—his age. Other nations, including most of the world powers, either ignore advanced age or reward it when selecting their leaders. That this has not been the case in the United States is evidenced by the fact that Reagan, who turned sixty-nine in 1980, was bidding to become the oldest candidate ever to be elected president. Reagan faced the issue less directly than Kennedy, seeking to render it trivial. He did so generally by trying to convey an image of physical vigor, and in particular by organizing his campaign appearances on February 6 into a series of public birthday celebrations in several New Hampshire locations.

Vice Presidency.   Historically, presidential candidates and their parties frequently have used the vice presidential nomination as a device to reach out to groups for which they have little appeal. This is a relatively safe strategy because vice presidential candidates seem less likely to activate hostile than sympathetic voter prejudices. Kennedy chose Lyndon Johnson, a southerner, in 1960 for this very reason, and did much better in the South than he otherwise might have. A 1983 Gallup poll suggests the strategy's further applicability to blacks: for the first time, a majority of people said they would be more likely to vote for a ticket if it included a black vice presidential candidate. A Harris survey, also taken in 1983, found almost three-to-one support for "having a woman run for vice president in 1984."[35]

Once in office, a vice president's race, religion, sex, or—in Johnson's case—regional background is less likely to remain frightening to previously prejudiced voters because his or her individual qualities will be more apparent. Familiarity seems to breed contentment in such cases; the share of voters willing to vote for a Catholic jumped from 68 percent to 82 percent right after Kennedy's election, and has been rising steadily to near-unanimity ever since. And however tragic the circumstances, should the vice president succeed to the presidency, as Johnson did after Kennedy's assassination in 1963, the waning of prejudice is likely to be quickened.

However probable are the good effects of a vice presidency on tolerance, the opposite also is possible. For example, if a member of a previously excluded group became vice president and behaved in a way that seemed to confirm people's fears, the effect might be to revive and intensify prejudices. (It was partly Johnson's awareness of this that led him to work so hard as president to promote the cause of civil rights.) Prejudices also might be reinforced if defeat at the polls were blamed—correctly or incorrectly—on the voters' response to the presence of such a person on the ticket. Kennedy, after all, was not the first Catholic to be nominated, only the first in thirty-two years after Governor Al Smith, also a Democratic Catholic, was trounced in the 1928 election.

Social Tolerance.   Like southernness and Catholicism, divorce long was considered a barrier to the presidency. Yet Reagan campaigned in 1976 and was elected in 1980 with scarcely a hint that his divorce from actress Jane Wyman should be held against him. The reason seems to be that society's tolerance for

Table 5.6   Career Background Characteristics of Twentieth-Century Presidents

			Federal			
	Vice President	*Cabinet*	*Other High Executive*	*Senate*	*House*	*Judge*
William McKinley 1897–1901					X	
Theodore Roosevelt 1901–1909	X[3]					
William H. Taft 1909–1913		X[2]	X			X
Woodrow Wilson 1913–1921						
Warren Harding 1921–1923				X[2]		
Calvin Coolidge 1923–1929	X[3]					
Herbert Hoover 1929–1933		X[2]	X[1]			
Franklin Roosevelt 1933–1945			X			
Harry Truman 1945–1953	X[3]			X[2]		
Dwight Eisenhower 1953–1961						
John Kennedy 1961–1963				X[2]	X[1]	
Lyndon Johnson 1963–1969	X[3]			X[2]	X	
Richard Nixon 1969–1974	X[2]			X	X[1]	
Gerald Ford 1974–1977	X[3]				X[1,2]	
Jimmy Carter 1977–1981						
Ronald Reagan 1981–						

[1]First government position.
[2]Last government position before election as president or vice president.
[3]Succeeded to the presidency on death or resignation of incumbent.

Table 5.6   *(continued)*

| Career Military | State | | | | | Private |
	Governor	Lieutenant Governor	Legislator	Judge	Local Office	
	X[2]				X[1]	Lawyer
	X[2]		X[1]			Lawyer, rancher
	X			X	X[1]	Lawyer
	X[1,2]					Scholar
		X	X[1]			Newspaper journalist
	X[2]	X	X	X	X[1]	Lawyer
						Engineer
	X[2]		X[1]			Lawyer
					X[1]	Small businessman
X[1,2]						University president
					X[1]	Teacher
						Lawyer
						Lawyer
	X[2]		X		X[1]	Farmer, small businessman
	X[1,2]					Actor

[1]First government position.
[2]Last government position before election as president or vice president.

divorce had grown so great during the 1960s that it was no longer a barrier when candidate Reagan encountered it.

Certainly the democratization of the nominating process will hasten the removal of the remaining religious, racial, and sexual barriers. In the past, the caution of old-style party professionals made them slow to recognize changes in popular prejudices until long after they had occurred. "He had to prove to them that he could win," said Theodore Sorensen of Kennedy's 1960 campaign for his party's nomination. "And to prove that to them, he'd have to fight hard to make them give it to him, he couldn't negotiate it. . . . So it evolved from the top down that you had to go into the primaries."[36] By their nature, primaries, which are far more important and pervasive now than they were in 1960, register changes in social tolerance almost directly.[37] They also provide a forum in which prejudices can be addressed openly.

Eligibility: Career Background Criteria

Although each of the social background criteria eliminates tens of millions of people from consideration for the presidency, an additional informal requirement — recent, prominent governmental experience — defines the pool of presidential possibilities most narrowly of all. A survey of the career backgrounds of all 20th-century presidents (Table 5.6) would seem to exclude from the pool all but present or recent vice presidents, governors, senators, members of the House of Representatives, cabinet secretaries, generals, judges, and the like. (Among defeated major party nominees, Wendell Willkie, the Republican candidate in 1940, is the sole exception.) So would a close look (Table 5.7) at the roster of people who drew at least 5 percent in the Gallup polls for 1972, 1976, and 1980 — 100.0 percent of whom met the career standard — or even of those who drew 1 percent (98.0 percent of whom met the standard).

Recent practice has given an increasingly narrow definition to suitable governmental experience. From 1892 to 1916, Robert Peabody and colleagues report, only 45.0 percent of the contenders for major-party presidential nominations were senators, governors, or vice presidents. That share grew steadily, to 60.9 percent in the years 1920 to 1944 and to 88.0 percent in the post–World War II period.[38] All but two of the fifteen people who have been

Table 5.7   Career Background Characteristics of "Plausible" Candidates for President: 1972, 1976, 1980

	Lacked Prominent Government Experience	Candidates Who Met All Career Criteria (Percent)
5 PERCENT SUPPORT OR MORE IN GALLUP POLL		100.0
1-4 PERCENT SUPPORT IN GALLUP POLL	Ralph Nader (1976)	98.0

elected president in this century last served in at least one of these three offices before being nominated, and all but one of the five vice presidents who succeeded to the presidency after a death or resignation were former governors or senators. (The three exceptions—Secretary of Commerce Herbert Hoover, General Eisenhower, and House Minority Leader Ford—were all leaders in the prominent governmental institutions in which they served.) Of the twenty-five "plausibles" for 1984, all of the Democrats except Jackson were present or former governors, senators, or vice presidents. So were seven of the nine Republicans, the exceptions being Representative Jack Kemp and former Representative John Anderson. (See Table 5.8.)

Success in the private sector has been less characteristic of American presidents. Carter, who built a prosperous business; Woodrow Wilson, the president of Princeton University; and Reagan, a successful movie actor, are among the few exceptions. It probably is not so much that the others could not have risen high in private life, but rather that they chose public careers instead. Had they devoted their thirties and forties to business or the professions, they might have found themselves in the position of many who have done exactly that: established in private life, inexperienced in elective politics, and unwilling, perhaps unable, to make the transition.

The explanation for the recent narrowing of the prominent governmental experience criteria to senator, governor, or vice president (the latter usually attained after service as a senator or governor) seems to lie partly in the democratization of the nominating system. When party leaders dominated the process, they were able to range somewhat widely in their choice of nominees. The rise of primaries and open caucuses placed cabinet members, members of the House of Representatives, and other potential candidates at a disadvantage. Unlike senators, governors, and vice presidents, they do not represent large electoral constituencies. Thus, they lack both the electoral base and, more important, the experience at campaigning on a grand scale that modern nominating politics rewards.[39]

Underlying the narrowing trend, however, is a broadening one that may turn out to be more significant. Fixed though the high elective office-holding standard may be, it has become steadily more easy in the last decade or so to attain such offices. Two closely related reasons account for this: the rapid loss of control by state party organizations of the candidate-selection and post-nomination campaign processes, and the simultaneous rise in the importance of individual entrepreneurial campaigning through the media. Celebrity status brings mass media exposure to a candidate automatically, which opens up the Senate and statehouse to famous astronauts (Senators John Glenn and Harrison Schmitt), athletes (Senator Bill Bradley), actors and television journalists (Governor Ronald Reagan, Senator Jesse Helms), and the like. Or money can buy such exposure in the form of paid advertising, a strategy that is especially suited to wealthy candidates because of the recent mix of campaign finance laws and court decisions that restricts the contributions one can receive from others but not those made to one's own campaign.[40] Several multimillionaires, including Lewis Lehrman of New York, Mark Dayton of Minnesota, and Frank Lautenberg of New Jersey, were able to win major party nominations for

Table 5.8   Career Background Characteristics of "Plausible" Candidates in 1984

	Federal					
	Vice President	Cabinet	Other High Executive	Senate	House	Career Military
DEMOCRATS						
Reubin Askew			X[2]			
Bruce Babbit						
Lloyd Bentsen				X[2]	X	
Bill Bradley				X[1,2]		
John Y. Brown						
Dale Bumpers				X[2]		
Alan Cranston				X[2]		
John Glenn				X[1,2]		X
Gary Hart				X[1,2]		
Ernest Hollings				X[2]		
Jesse Jackson						
Edward Kennedy				X[1,2]		
George McGovern			X	X[2]	X[1]	
Walter Mondale	X[2]			X		
Daniel Moynihan			X[1]	X[2]		
Jay Rockefeller						
REPUBLICANS						
John Anderson					X[1,2]	
Howard Baker				X[1,2]		
George Bush	X[2]		X		X[1]	
John Connolly		X[2]	X[1]			
Robert Dole				X[2]	X	
Jesse Helms				X[1,2]		
Jack Kemp					X[1,2]	
Charles Percy				X[1,2]		
Ronald Reagan						

[1]First political office.   [2]Most recent political office.

Table 5.8 *(continued)*

State						Private
Governor	High Executive	Lieutenant Governor	Legislator	Judge	Local Office	
X			X		X[1]	Lawyer
X[2]	X[1]					Lawyer
				X[1]		Lawyer
						Athlete
X[1,2]						Businessman
X[1]						Lawyer, businessman
		X[1]				Journalist, real estate
						Astronaut
						Lawyer
X		X	X[1]			Lawyer
						Minister
						Lawyer
						Scholar
	X[1]					Lawyer
						Scholar
X[2]	X		X[1]			
						Lawyer
						Lawyer
						Businessman
X						Lawyer
			X[1]		X	Lawyer
						Television executive
						Athlete
						Businessman
	X[1,2]					Actor

[1]First political office.   [2]Most recent political office.

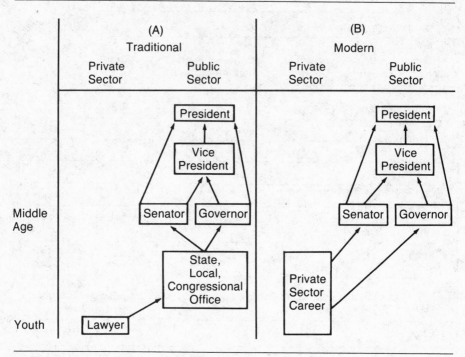

Figure 5.1   Career Paths to the Presidency

governor or senator in 1982 by spending millions of dollars from their own fortunes.

It already has been mentioned that few twentieth-century presidents have had noteworthy careers outside politics. As Watson and Thomas observe, "The career pattern of most American presidents has been to serve in elective public office from an early age until they are elected to the presidency."[41] Close reexamination of data that Joseph Schlesinger compiled in 1967 on 1,626 major-party senatorial and gubernatorial nominees—that is, those who form the pool from which presidents and vice presidents are drawn—reveals that 37.6 percent of them first attained public office during their twenties, and 61.4 percent before they reached age 35. The vast majority of the under-35 group—some 67.2 percent—were lawyers. (In contrast, only 32.2 percent of those who won their first office later in life were lawyers.)[42] The career path to the top of the political ladder, then, traditionally has looked something like Figure 5.1a.

It probably is no coincidence, however, that among the few exceptions to the lawyer-career politician rule are the two most recent presidents, farmer-businessman Carter and actor Reagan. Carter and Reagan-style exceptions well may become as much the rule as the career politician pattern, if the 1984 pool of contenders is any guide. Bradley, Glenn, Hart, Kennedy, Baker, Helms, Percy, Reagan, Brown, and Bumpers won their first political offices at the senatorial or gubernatorial level, and Kemp and Jackson hardly fit the careerist mode. (See Table 5.8.) The era of entrepreneurial media politics has so loosened the career background criteria that the life histories of an increasing number of future presidents are likely to include substantial time in the private sector. (See Figure 5.1b.)

Eligibility: Implications for Skill and Suitability

Eligibility that is based on race, religion, sex, age, marital status, nativity, or other social-background criteria arbitrarily reduces the size of the pool of presidential possibilities. As such, it impedes the search for presidents who have requisite leadership skills and are suitable to the requirements associated with their stage of the cycle of preparation, achievement, and consolidation. To this extent, at least, the democratization of the selection process has been useful: it has accelerated the breakdown of such prejudices.

Unlike the social-background barriers, however, which often are judged illegitimate on egalitarian as well as utilitarian grounds, attacks on the system's bias in favor of prominent government officials usually draw explicitly on the language of elitism. The title of a famous *Esquire* article by Steven V. Roberts expresses the sentiment: "Is It Too Late for a Man of Honesty, High Purpose, and Intelligence to Be Elected President of the United States?" Bemoaning the fact that "at a time when events seem to demand a different kind of alternative" the public is stuck with choosing from a "group of 'politicians,'" Roberts compiled a preferred list of university, corporation, and foundation presidents, cabinet secretaries, and a Supreme Court justice, none of whom were experienced in electoral politics.[43] This is not an isolated complaint. As Thomas Cronin summarizes the common lament: "Is this the best we can do? With our large and highly educated population, why can't we produce Washingtons, Jeffersons, Madisons, Franklins, and the like?"[44] Nor is it a new one. James Bryce entitled a chapter in his 1888 work *The American Commonwealth*, "Why Great Men Are Not Chosen President."[45]

To be sure, democratization has helped not only to buttress the system's informal career requirement for recent, prominent governmental experience, but also to define it to include only senators, governors, and vice presidents, that is, those who are experienced at large-scale campaigning. But as we have seen, this narrowing effect masks a deeper broadening one. The breakdown of party control over the nomination process at all levels of the federal system, along with recent changes in the rules that govern campaign finance and the rise of media campaigning, has made it possible for people who have spent most of their lives building reputations or fortunes in the private sector to mount serious campaigns for senator and governor without any prior experience in politics. If elected, they are in a position eventually to compete with career politicians for the presidency.

Both these conditions of modern presidential selection — the requirement for prominent governmental experience and the greater ease with which it can be acquired — further the goal of choosing politically skillful and suitable presidents. It would be dysfunctional to nominate, much less elect as president someone devoid of experience in high elective office. Skills of political rhetoric and bargaining seem to be developed best by running for office and serving in government for a period of several years. The same can be said of the subtle but vital capacity to sense the public's willingness to be led in different directions at different paces at different times. Success in the private sector alone speaks well of a person and usually requires some of these skills. But only politics requires all of them. Even management of authority is different in the public sector than in the corporate or academic world.

To say that political experience is essential to presidential success, however, is not to say that a lifetime of such experience is essential. It may not even be altogether desirable. One cannot be but humbled by the roster of Franklins, Jeffersons, and Washingtons that invariably is juxtaposed with subsequent generations of presidential contenders. Nor can one be but struck by a quality that distinguishes their careers: an ease of movement between the public and private spheres of life that allowed them to be seasoned by both and ignorant of neither. In this light, the trend toward easier lateral entry into political office at the congressional and gubernatorial levels for those whose lives have been spent primarily in private pursuits should be marked for its broadening effects on the pool of talent from which presidents are drawn.

In the final analysis, prominent governmental experience, lifelong or otherwise, carries no guarantee of successful leadership in the presidency. Politicians have different levels of rhetorical and tactical aptitude; only Lincoln and Franklin Roosevelt were outstanding presidents on both counts. And, of course, politicians vary in their sensitivity to the public mood.

What is virtually guaranteed by the eligibility criteria rooted in America's Constitution and culture, however, is that the relatively small pool from which the president realistically will be drawn will include people who have the capacity to serve in the office in response to the times, even if it includes other people as well. If obstacles of race, religion, sex, and the like were to fall, that pool would be even more comprehensive.

Winnowing and Nominating

In the second and third stages of the selection process, dozens become two, the nominees of the Republican and Democratic parties. Eligibility criteria have assured all through this century that they will be white, male, Christians; married or once-married; educated and experienced in political life at a high level. The winnowing and nominating processes help to determine what else they will be, and here we do see changes over time, both in the types of candidacies favored by the processes and in the processes themselves.

Candidacy Changes.   The most interesting set of candidacy changes has come in two shifts. From 1900 to 1944 five of the eight men who were elected president and five of the nine who were nominated but not elected were chosen by their parties from positions in state government, usually as governor. This was not only a twentieth-century pattern, but one that included the entire post–Civil War period. The 1948 election marked an abrupt shift, however. From then until 1972, all five elected presidents and four of the six defeated major-party nominees were drawn from the federal government. Indeed, every nominee in the final four elections of this period—Kennedy, Nixon, Johnson,

Table 5.9   **Major-Party Presidential Nominees, 1900–1972: Level of Government of Most Recent Office**

	Elected Presidents		Losing Major-Party Nominees (Incumbent Presidents Excluded)		
	State	*National*	*State*	*National*	*Other*
1900–1944	McKinley T. Roosevelt Wilson Coolidge F. Roosevelt	Harding Hoover Taft	Parker Cox Smith Landon Dewey	Bryan Hughes Davis	Willkie
1948–1972		Truman Eisenhower Kennedy Johnson Nixon	Dewey Stevenson	Nixon Goldwater Humphrey McGovern	

Goldwater, Humphrey, and McGovern—was either a senator or a vice president who had served most recently in the Senate. (See Table 5.9.) But no sooner had this pattern, its "consistency unmatched at any time in the history of the republic," taken root than a second shift appeared that seemingly undid it.[46] In 1976 and 1980 Jimmy Carter and Ronald Reagan, two ex-governors, were nominated and elected president.

The direction, as well as the abruptness, of the first shift (from state to national) can be accounted for easily. It reflected the seismic changes in American politics generated by the national welfare state that grew out of the depression and the "garrison state" of the post–World War II period. As Robert Peabody and Eve Lubalin described it at the time:

> Governors now appear to be isolated from national policy-making, and their immersion in parochial state concerns is considered more of a liability than an asset. Moreover, the purely administrative aspects of the president's job have contracted in comparison to presidential responsibility for formulating complex national economic and social policies, conducting American foreign affairs, and leading national public opinion. . . . Increasingly, because of the nationalization of American politics and disproportionate media coverage of the president and members of Congress, the latter political officials have become most familiar to the public and provide much of what national and partisan leadership of public opinion now exists.[47]

No such change in the locus of political power prefaced the post-1972 events. Nor, as we shall see, does the mere fact that both Carter and Reagan were governors capture the essence of what happened—it is more complicated than that. Whatever the essence, however, its explanation can be found in changes in the winnowing and nominating processes themselves.

Process Changes: Winnowing. Historically, the path from eligibility to plausibility was one that a candidate strolled rather than ran. As we saw earlier, if a prominent government official who met all the constitutional and cultural criteria for eligibility wished to be president, his only recourse was to impress party professionals, who presumably would wait until the last possible moment to commit themselves. To announce one's candidacy before the election year or to campaign in primaries was a strategy of desperation that betrayed weakness.

The recent history of presidential selection could not be more different. McGovern's successful candidacy for the 1972 Democratic nomination was announced in January 1971. Carter announced in December 1974 for the 1976 nomination. George Bush, a candidate for the Republican nomination in 1980, campaigned 329 days in 1979 at almost nine hundred political events. Walter Mondale, John Glenn, Alan Cranston, Gary Hart, Ernest Hollings, and Reubin Askew all began hard campaigning for 1984 almost as soon as the 1980 results were in. Jesse Jackson, the last candidate to enter the race, announced on November 3, 1983, several days earlier than the announcement of the first candidate to declare in 1968 (George Romney, on November 18, 1967) or in earlier elections. The ultimate purpose of this activity has not been to persuade ever less influential party professionals, but rather to win delegates directly in the primaries and caucuses.

Obviously, then, important things happen in the preprimary period. Candidates who do not raise sufficient money, develop appealing issues, devise shrewd campaign strategies, impress national political reporters, attract competent staff, and build active organizations well in advance of the election year have little or no chance of winning. This takes a great deal of time in the three preelection years. It also takes a particular kind of political personality. Woodrow Wilson looked in 1908 to a time when "we shall be obliged always to be picking our chief magistrates from among wise and prudent athletes";[48] had his foresight been sufficient, he might have written "marathon runners" instead. The new four-year campaign period and the "retail," or person-to-person, campaigning required for victory in the early caucuses and primaries place a premium on having an active political personality. The phrases Mondale used in withdrawing from the 1976 contest — "overwhelming desire to be president," "willing to go through fire," "sleeping in Holiday Inns," and the like — were backhanded definitions of what most candidates must be willing to undergo.

A significant part of the winnowing process, then, is internal: eligible candidates must choose to run. Considering the long odds against winning that most of them face, it seems reasonable to conclude that the ranks of serious presidential candidates will consist almost entirely of "risk takers," which John Aldrich defines as those "who [are] more likely than others to enter hazardous or uncertain situations." If in earlier stages of their careers candidates have shown a willingness to run for office when there was good reason to believe that they would lose, one may reasonably expect them to run for president at some point. The odds become especially high in elections in which the costs of losing a presidential bid are lower than usual. For example, a senator or governor may be more inclined to run for president in a year when he is not up for reelection to the Senate or a statehouse.[49]

One of the most important of the preprimary tasks for would-be presidents is to impress the few dozen journalists who work for news organizations that maintain constant coverage of national electoral politics: the television networks, news magazines, wire services and publishing chains, and a sprinkling of individual newspapers. "The early stages of the nominating process," writes Donald Matthews, "are so unstructured and ambiguous that the press then enjoys maximum discretion in defining the situation."[50] News organizations have limited resources. They rely on reporters to tell them which candidacies are "serious" enough to warrant coverage. David Broder notes *Boston Globe* reporter Martin Nolan's comparison of national political reporters to

> a band of traveling drama critics, covering the new political acts at their out-of-town openings in Sacramento or Lansing or Harrisburg. Their reports, like those in *Variety*, are frequently make-or-break. "No talent," they will say of one man, and his name is forgotten. "Promising," they'll say of another, and he is booked into the Gridiron Dinner or "Meet the Press."[51]

All this said, it is important to add that it is tendencies, not laws, that we have been describing. Reagan's slow-paced approach to the 1980 Republican nomination showed that a passive, television-centered campaign still can work, at least for someone with Reagan's media skills. And just as "traveling drama critics" are bound to some extent by the actual quality of the performances they review, so are national political reporters bound by events. A candidate who raises money and builds an organization sufficient to mount a serious campaign will be treated by reporters as serious regardless of their personal assessments. This helps to explain why some candidates try so hard to do well in preelection-year "straw polls" that are conducted at state party conventions or banquets. In October 1975, for example, Jimmy Carter's supporters packed a fund-raising dinner in Iowa for the sole purpose of winning the straw poll that was taken there. Cranston spent almost all of 1983 seeking similar endorsements. Both succeeded in attracting the serious attention of the national press, which they previously had lacked.

The importance of the winnowing stage, which is great, nonetheless can be overstated. For example, one author argues that the subsequent nominating stage is merely "a ritual encounter, a symbolic show whose results reinforce a victory already decided by events" prior to the election year in the "invisible primary."[52] Much of the evidence for this proposition comes from a 1973 study that found that in the major-party nomination contests that took place from 1936 to 1972, the "pre-primary [Gallup] poll leader became the nominee 85 per cent of the time," or seventeen times in twenty.[53] Such evidence is deceptive; eight of those twenty nominations were uncontested, and in another the actual preprimary poll leader was not counted by the author because he was not an "active" candidate (Nixon in 1964). More significant, since 1968 the success rate of the "invisible primary" winners in contested nominations has been only three in seven, or less than 43 percent.[54]

Process Changes: Nominating.   Formally, nominations are conferred at the national party conventions, held in July or August of the election year. The television networks, which give the conventions many hours of extensive live coverage and play up their intramural conflicts to sustain viewer interest, foster the idea that conventions are the real decision forums. At one time they were: between 1900 and 1952 one-third of the major-party conventions went more than one ballot, including one-half those in which no incumbent president was seeking renomination. But they tend not to be any longer — indeed, every convention from 1956 to 1980 chose its nominee on the first ballot in conformance with preconvention events. Ironically, television had much to do with this. As Nelson Polsby and Aaron Wildavsky observe:

> Nationwide television coverage of the primaries gives early-bird candidates a head start on the free publicity of the election year. . . . Thus the pressures upon state party leaders to decide what they want to do seem to be urging them to make decisions earlier in the election year.[55]

As a rule, then, the nomination decision is made sometimes in the preconvention election year. But when? Seldom, as may seem likely, on the first Tuesday in June, when the last round of primaries is held. In 1980 Edward Kennedy beat Jimmy Carter by 372 delegates to 323 in the primaries held on June 3. In 1976 Jerry Brown outscored Carter by 264 to 218 in this set of primaries, and Reagan bested Ford 180 to 151.[56] What distinguishes all three of these winners is that their opponents were nominated anyway on the basis of decisions that obviously had been made earlier in the process.

The exception in these elections was Reagan in 1980, who swept all the June primaries and went on to the nomination. But his victory illustrates another truth about the relative unimportance of the contest at this stage. Reagan was unopposed; each of the other active Republican candidates in 1980 had dropped out, just as most of Carter's original opponents had in 1976. Even if the final primaries had been decisive between the remaining candidates, the decision would have come from a range of choices severely limited by the time it was made. The ultimate irony in 1980 was that both Carter and Reagan sealed their nominations on the day of their chief opponent's greatest triumph. Carter's defeat on June 3 nonetheless gave him enough committed delegates to guarantee his majority at the convention. George Bush's landslide victory in the May 20 Michigan primary did the same for Reagan; Bush withdrew his candidacy just five days later.

Like the conventions that cast the actual votes to nominate and the late primaries that choose the last large bloc of delegates, the primaries and caucuses of the middle period (late March through May), in which the majority of delegates are selected, seem plausible claimants for recognition as the most important decision arena. But like them, too, they usually are less than that. As a rule, spring delegate selection is a time of what John Kessel describes as "Mist Clearing, . . . marked by a reduction of the uncertainty which has thus far attended the nomination process, and in this sense akin to the clearing of a mist that allows one to see the pine trees some distance across the woods."[57] The importance of the nomination contests at this stage is diminished by the amount of attention they tend to receive from both the media and the candidates. Michael Robinson found that in 1976, no primary in the middle period received more than half the total television coverage, or one-seventh the coverage per delegate chosen, of the New Hampshire primary.[58] Federal Election Commission data for 1980 showed candidates spending $13.89 per vote cast in the January Iowa caucus and $8.90 in the February New Hampshire primary, as compared to $2.21 in Florida (March), $1.36 in Wisconsin (April), and $0.45 in Nebraska (May). "A candidate who waits till mid-campaign," writes Rhodes Cook, "finds it virtually impossible to develop any [resources]."[59]

By now it should be evident that the train of events that leads to a nomination for president leaves the station early in the election year. "The consequences of the media infatuation with the New Hampshire primary are obvious," writes Matthews. "'Winners' of that contest receive far more favorable publicity and a far greater boost toward the Presidency than the 'winners' of other primaries."[60] Thomas Patterson's study of newspaper, magazine, and television coverage of the seven 1976 Democratic candidates in the two months after Carter's victory in the New Hampshire primary — fully half of which went to Carter alone — led him to describe the phenomenon as "winner-take-all" journalism.[61] Victory in New Hampshire brought Carter other resources as well: campaign contributions, higher poll standings, and political talent among them.[62] Eventually, all this led to his nomination.

In 1980 Iowa's January caucus, now the first arena for delegate selection, stood side by side with New Hampshire in the media spotlight. What this meant was that the most influential, if not the decisive, role in the process by which the American political system reduces to a few the number of people who realistically can be president was being played by two states that share the following characteristics: neither has a city of even 200,000 population; neither has a black population higher than 1 percent; each voted Republican in every presidential election from 1968 to 1980; and each has a "moralistic" political culture.[63] What's more, "winning" the Iowa caucus and New Hampshire primary is not always the same as winning in the usual sense — that is, getting more votes than any opponent. In the 1968 and 1972 New Hampshire primaries and the 1976 Iowa caucus, Eugene McCarthy, McGovern, and Carter, respectively, each "won" in the eyes of the media even though they got fewer votes than other delegate slates. The reason was that each did much better than had been expected. Even more perversely, George Bush "lost" by winning the 1980 Iowa caucus. His surprising victory there meant he then had to win in New Hampshire; the second-place finish Bush originally had been hoping for there (and got) no longer would do.[64]

Learning the early-decision lesson, many states began in 1984 to advance the dates of their primaries and caucuses. Twenty-four states and territories decided to select delegates during the week between the second and third Tuesdays in March, many of them by some variant of "winner-take-all." The New Hampshire primary was scheduled for the last Tuesday in February and the Iowa caucus for eight days earlier. This new calendar raised several possibilities for future nominating contests. One was that nomination contests increasingly would be shaped not in two states, but one, since the outcome in New Hampshire seems more likely to be affected by what happens in Iowa than in

1980, when five weeks separated them. (In 1980 Bush went from a 19-percentage-point deficit in New Hampshire in a poll taken just before the Iowa caucus to a 13-point lead a week after it. After another month of campaigning, Reagan won by 50 to 23 percent).[65] Another possibility was that the South would dominate the contest since almost half the first one thousand delegates to be selected would be from southern states. Less likely, but always possible, would be an early deadlock among two or three candidates that would not be resolved until later in the delegate-selection process or even at the convention. (The number of candidates at that stage seems unlikely to be higher than three because candidates who cannot win 10 percent of the vote in either of two consecutive primaries lose the federal campaign funds that make their candidacies possible.)

Regardless of which of these possibilities comes to pass, one effect of the 1984 changes is to make the preelection-year campaign more important. Candidates have no choice but to start their campaigns earlier than ever. Organizations must be built, issues developed, and campaign treasuries filled to overflowing well before January 1 because there are no breathing spells once the year begins. Further, because of the new emphasis on preelection-year campaigning, there has developed a corresponding emphasis on preelection-year events, such as straw polls and "cattle shows" at which all the candidates speak or debate. As for party leaders, who now are guaranteed 14 percent of the convention seats, they seem to have learned quickly that if they stay uncommitted until the convention, as they are supposed to, they may lose their best chance to throw their weight behind candidates early in exchange for access and influence.

Winnowing and Nominating: Implications for Skill and Suitability

What are the consequences for the presidency of a nomination process whose decisions are shaped or made in a few early and unrepresentative states? Among other things, the new, post-1968 way of choosing major-party presidential nominees favors certain candidacy qualities that previously had not been advantageous.

Underemployment.   The experiences of 1976, when former Governor Carter won the Democratic nomination, and 1980, when former Governor Reagan beat out former Ambassador Bush for the Republican nomination, have suggested to some that unemployment is a new prerequisite for the presidency. "Those of us who are already in government and public life don't have the time and the resources to run soon enough and early enough to succeed," said Senate Republican leader Howard Baker when he abandoned his own campaign in 1980.[66] Baker even retired from the Senate in 1984 so that he would be free to campaign for the 1988 nomination.

In truth, underemployment seems to do just as well. All that is needed is time to campaign steadily during the interelection years and constantly starting with the Iowa caucus and New Hampshire primary. Former governors have that time; incumbent ones may not. Neither do conscientious members of Congress who are intent on the business of Congress. But other senators do, which is why the Senate continues to be the main source of candidates for nomination in both parties.

Washington "Outsider" Status.   Candidates without Washington experience or support won in 1976 and 1980 because they articulated the anti-Washington mood of the country, not because of the new rules. What the rules did, however, was to make Carter's and Reagan's candidacies plausible in the first place, even though they had little support in the national party organizations or, like McGovern in 1972, little public recognition. As Ceaser points out:

> Under any system, of course, a person who has support from these quarters is better off, but with the sequential arrangements these advantages can be more easily overcome. . . . [In Iowa and New Hampshire] an outsider can concentrate an immense amount of his time—which, if he is nowhere else employed, he may have in abundance—and almost all the resources he can muster.[67]

Moralism.   Both Iowa and New Hampshire have political cultures that are primarily "moralistic"—that is, concerned with morally purposeful politics, local government, and nonpartisanship. This sets them off from about three-fourths of the nation's population. The South, newly influential in 1984 because of its early concentration of primaries and caucuses, is largely "traditionalistic" in culture.[68] Not surprisingly, then, their influence in the new system generally is exerted on behalf of candidates who "preach" traditional virtues.

A Simple Talent for Getting Nominated.   The new rules are extraordinarily complex, both on their face and in their deeper strategic and tactical implications. Those implications can be nothing less than Orwellian: victories easily translate into defeats, and defeats into victories. As we saw, both Muskie in 1972 and Bush in 1980 won battles that cost them the war. Conversely, Carter lost many middle and late primaries both times he ran but won in the end because he accumulated delegates in those defeats. The examples are endless, their meaning clear: presidential candidates now are nominated not just on the basis of their entire careers in public life, but also according to their ability to play the election game successfully. What's more, the game's rules tend to change every four years.

Thus, eligibility criteria that sift out women, blacks, non-Christians, bachelors, and nonpoliticians are refined further by new systems of winnowing and nominating that favor the candidacies of state or national officeholders who are underemployed but prominent; moralistic in their public appeals; and skilled at playing the system's new and ever-changing angles.

These changes are both obvious and important in their effects on presidential *candidacies*. But we would argue that their implications for the selection of presidential *candidates* endowed with necessary leadership skill and suitability to the times is probably insignificant but, if anything, functional. The kind of underemployment that frees one for campaigning is something that almost any candidate can arrange. Senator Cranston, for example, simultaneously served

as Senate Democratic Whip and one of the most active campaigners for his party's 1984 nomination. Former Vice President Mondale forswore a Senate campaign in 1982 so that he could be completely free to prepare for the presidency
and run for president. As for the addition of Washington outsiders to the pool
of plausible contenders, that merely restores the traditional status of governors
as contenders for the presidency without eliminating senators and vice
presidents. As chief executives of their states, governors may be presumed to
have certain authority management skills that senators may not. "Moralism"
means nothing more than a candidate's ability to invoke cultural ideals in the
service of rhetoric, another skill that is important to presidents. A tactical
talent for getting nominated by figuring out the complex and subtle biases in
the fragmented selection process is as necessary for presidents who will face an
equally complex and fragmented government as a talent for dealing with old-
style power brokers is not. Finally, the endless campaign, if it does nothing else,
probably sensitizes voters and candidates to each other in a way that should
facilitate the choice of a president in harmony with the mood of his times.

Winnowing and Nominating: Implications for Legitimacy

Ironic though it may be, democratic legitimacy, the paramount value sought
by post-1968 reformers, has been undermined by the new nominating process.
Almost everyone, including journalists themselves, deplores the responsibility
that the hybrid nature of the system places on the media to interpret who is
winning and even which candidacies will be taken seriously. Few think it proper that voters in the late-primary states have their choices circumscribed by
the decisions of voters in the early primaries. "There's a very real sense in which
this system violates the one man, one vote principle," says Ranney. "Somebody
who participated in those [1980] Iowa caucuses, or who voted in that New
Hampshire primary, counts for 10 or 15 times as much in determining the outcome as the people who voted in California, Ohio, and New Jersey."[69]

The characteristic of the present nominating process that is most corrosive
of democratic legitimacy is its sheer complexity. As Henry Mayo notes in his *Introduction to Democratic Theory*:

> If the purpose of the election is to be carried out — to enable the voter to share in
> political power — the voter's job must not be made more difficult and confusing for
> him. It ought on the contrary, to be made as simple as the electoral machinery can
> be devised to make it.[70]

Yet nothing could be less descriptive of the way we choose presidential candidates. Delegate selection is scattered haphazardly across space (fifty states,
several territories), time (late winter to early summer), and the procedural
spectrum (open primaries, closed primaries, primaries in which candidates
have to petition to get on — or off — the ballot, delegate selection by district
caucuses, delegate selection at state conventions, and so on). "No school, no textbook, no course of instruction," writes Theodore White, "could tell young
Americans how their system worked."[71] Or, as Richard Stearns, chief

delegate hunter for McGovern in 1972 and Kennedy in 1980, puts it: "I am fully confident that there aren't more than 100 people in the country who fully understand the rules."[72]

Electing

Perhaps the most noteworthy aspect of the electing stage of the presidential selection process is the narrowness of the remaining choice. We have discussed the winnowing and nominating stages of the process purely in terms of Republicans and Democrats because only Republican and Democratic candidates have any chance of being elected. Compelled to seek the broad middle of the electorate necessary for a majority, each becomes at this stage more like his opponent than different. In terms of the Sherlock Holmes analogy, it is the elimination of alternatives that narrows the choice to two that matters most, not the ultimate "solution" from which a single choice emerges.

Why is it that voters limit the choices to only the two major-party candidates? At one level the answer is simple: they fulfill their own prophecies. Even those who are strongly attracted to a "serious" third candidate, such as George Wallace in 1968 or John Anderson in 1980, are likely to back off eventually for fear of "throwing away their vote" on someone who cannot win. Judging from experience that either the Republican or Democrat will be elected, and disliking one more than the other, voters pick the "lesser of two evils." Thus, Wallace dropped from a peak of 21 percent in the Gallup poll to 13 percent on Election Day. Anderson declined even more precipitous, from 24 percent to 7 percent.[73]

At a deeper level, though, the election choice is limited to two because the two-party system is so deeply ingrained in our laws and Constitution. From the beginning American elections have been winner-take-all; minor parties that thrive in proportional representation systems in which their 10 percent of the vote will get them 10 percent of the seats die on the vine in the United States, where anything short of a plurality wins nothing. The electoral college reinforces this tendency by requiring an absolute majority for victory. So did the late nineteenth-century adoption of the Australian, or state-printed, ballot. Prior to the creation of official ballots, ballot access was not an issue. But Republican and Democratic leaders soon saw to it in many states that third-party candidates would have a very hard time getting the state to print their names on the ballot alongside those of the major-party nominees.

In recent years legislative and administrative actions have buttressed further the Republican and Democratic parties. American third parties have tended to be one-election affairs, led by a prominent political figure who articulates a popular cause that the major-party candidates seem to be ignoring. The Federal Election Campaign Act of 1974 requires that the treasury finance the fall campaigns of both major-party nominees for president; such third-party candidates have to raise their own money in small increments in the hope that they will receive 5 percent of the popular vote and be reimbursed after the election.[74] If they do, their parties are guaranteed federal funding for the next presidential election. The anomalous result is that the treasury funds third parties not when they are popular, but four years later, when they are likely to be politically irrelevant. Also, starting in 1976, a new Federal Communications Commission interpretation of Section 315 of the Federal Communications Act (the "equal time for all candidates" provision) has prevailed, which means that televised debates can be limited to the Republican and Democratic nominees.

The laws and Constitution that sustain two-party competition may themselves reflect some deeper cause; a historically rooted political culture of dualism within consensus, perhaps.[75] But whatever the ultimate explanation, the effect is the same: to limit the election choice to two candidates, each winnowed to reflect one set of qualities, each nominated by a process that favors still other qualities.

THE FUTURE OF PRESIDENTIAL SELECTION

Prescription

For the most part the presidential selection process has worked consistently over time. Criteria for constitutional eligibility have changed not at all, and social and career criteria not much. The last stages of the winnowing process now are performed more by national political reporters than by party professionals, but the pools of contenders that each group has produced have been more alike than different.[76] The modern fall campaign, although more active and media-centered than in the past, still is a two-party affair in which the candidate who appeals most successfully to the nonideological center of the electorate becomes president. Only the nominating process recently has seen great changes. Sensibly, then, those who are dissatisfied with the selection process look to the nominating stage when they think about reform.

Dissatisfaction with new-style nominating politics is especially great among those who regard the presidency as too weak. Their argument is that the presidency as an institution has been severely undermined by the democratizing effects of post-1968 party reforms that, in their view, shunted aside professional politicians and caused the decline of parties as electoral coalitions.[77] The reforms, critics contend, established a vicious cycle: presidential candidates increasingly run for office on their own, without benefit of party help, and have little incentive to try to develop a party coalition as a basis of governing; by the same token the parties, even in their weakened state, feel little loyalty to their own presidents. As single-interest groups of all persuasions develop to fill the void left by the weakening of parties, they seriously restrict the ability of presidents to construct governing coalitions of any kind.

Critics of the reformist trends argue that the presidency cannot be strong again until the trends are reversed. Not surprisingly, then, to most of these professional political analysts — scholars, journalists, and politicians alike — the old, pre-1969 nomination system looks ever more appealing. "In the old way," says David Broder, "whoever wanted to run for president of the United States took a couple months off from public office in the year of the presidential election and presented his credentials to the leaders of his party, who were elected officials, party officials, leaders of allied interest groups, and bosses in some cases. These people had known the candidate over a period of time and had carefully examined his work."[78] As it happened, the qualities those political peers were looking for were, according to Jeane J. Kirkpatrick, the very qualities that made for good presidents: "the ability to deal with diverse groups, ability to work out compromises, and the ability to impress people who have watched a candidate over many years."[79] And when they finally decided on someone, Ranney writes, "the delegates would follow their lead and choose him. The coalition of leaders also would see to it that the party's platform would help to unite the party and put it in the best possible position to win the election."[80]

But, to a very large extent, this is less history than nostalgia: the sepia tone that overlays memories of what Ranney calls the "good old days" obscures the warts.[81] When Kirkpatrick laments "the principal disadvantage of the present system — that the skills required to be successful in the nominating process are almost entirely irrelevant to, perhaps even negatively correlated with, the skills required to be successful at governing,"[82] she is vastly overestimating what we have shown to be the minimal and, in some ways, beneficial effects the post-1968 reforms have had on presidential skill. She also is echoing the century-old explanation by James Bryce, written at the absolute heyday of party strength, of why presidents tend not to be great:

> The merits of a President are one thing and those of a candidate another thing. . . . Now to a party it is more important that its nominee should be a good candidate than that he should turn out to be a good president.[83]

Soft-hued memories aside, one cannot look at the progression of twentieth-century policy cycles through the 1960s that was described in Chapter 3 without being impressed by how well the old nominating system produced presidents suitable to their times. Not surprisingly, then, when today's political doctors prescribe alterations in the process by which presidents are nominated, a common theme is "bring the good old days back." If implemented, for example, Ceaser's proposals to "reduce" and "devalue" the primaries, "allow ex officio delegates," and permit again the "untimely selection of delegates . . . before the election year" virtually would restore the status quo circa 1968.[84] So would Ranney's plan, which, though presented as a vision of the future, is in truth a clinically accurate description of the past: "Perhaps we ought to establish a system in which the elected and party officials would constitute, say, two-thirds of the delegates, and the remaining one-third would be elected by primaries."[85]

Even counterreformationist ideas that seem to be new and varied turn out to be roughly the same old thing. Kirkpatrick wants national legislation that would abolish all primaries and force the choice of presidential candidates onto conventions of each party's "elected public officials and party leaders."[86] Thomas E. Mann urges Everett Carll Ladd's plan for conventions consisting of one-third such officials and two-thirds delegates chosen in a national primary and allocated among the candidates by proportional representation.[87] This

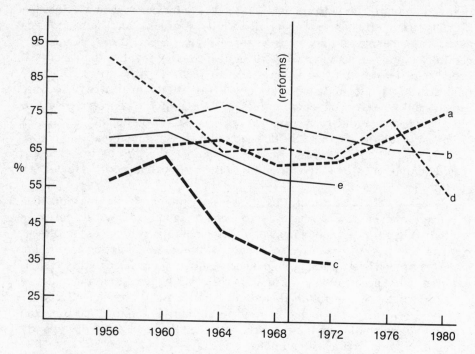

a. Party unity voting in Congress (Source: *Congressional Quarterly Almanac*, 1956, 1960, 1964, 1968, 1972, 1976, 1980 [Washington: Congressional Quarterly Press]).
b. Self-identified partisans (Source: Peter Eisinger *et al., American Politics*, 2nd ed. [Boston: Little, Brown, 1982], p. 341).
c. Straight-ticket voters (Source: Norman Nie *et al., The Changing American Voter* [Cambridge, Mass.: Harvard University Press, 1976], p. 53).
d. Citizens "highly favorable" to at least one major-party candidate (Source: Austin Ranney, ed., *The American Elections of 1980* [Washington, D. C.: American Enterprise Institute, 1981], p. 306).
e. Citizens offering positive evaluations of at least one major party (Source: Nie, *Changing*, p. 58).

Figure 5.2   Indices of Party Strength, 1956–1980

sounds like something new until Mann explains that what he really wants and believes his idea will achieve in practice is a Kirkpatrick-Ranney-Ceaser-like system of convention nominations by party elites, who, he guesses, would hold the balance of power there. Mann just feels that the bluntness of Kirkpatrick's proposal makes it "so inimical to the American political culture that it's an academic exercise to be talking about."[88]

One analytic flaw in all such proposals is their assumption that the foundation of strong political parties that supported the old system still is there if only one could clear away the reforms that presently obscure it. In truth political parties in modern America have been disintegrating for a long time. The 1969 reforms may have accelerated this process, but for the most part they just reflected it. Thus, as a close look at Figure 5.2 shows, although part of the decline in party identification and straight-ticket voting among citizens has occurred since 1969, the process had begun well before then. Party voting in Congress also was on its way down prior to 1969, as was party organizational vitality at the state and local level. The implications for counterreformation are, as Howard Penniman observes, fatal:

> Almost everyone in the Congress got there . . . by a process very similar to the one by which presidents now win primaries, are nominated, and are elected. Now we're going to tell them, and other people who are largely independent and powerless, like the national committeemen and state committeemen, that they are the heart of the party, and they are going to choose the presidential candidate. None of those proposals can resurrect the kind of people who went to conventions in the 1880s or 1920s or 1950s.[89]

The causes of the decline of old-style parties run deeper than procedural tinkering, to a changed society in which most citizens are more prosperous and better informed about national politics than in the past and no longer feel the need to rely on parties either for patronage jobs or advice on whom to vote for (and in which the remaining poor get their Thanksgiving dinners from food stamps, not precinct captains). Civil service reform, social services and income maintenance programs, and television have all contributed to the new voter independence, but nothing more than education. The ratio of college- to elementary school-educated voters in 1952 was 15 to 40; by 1976 it was 34 to 17.[90]

The other fundamentally flawed assumption in much current political analysis is that the public's concern about the legitimacy of the presidential nominating process can be satisfied by less democratic procedures. Actually, citizen discontent centers not on the excesses of democracy in the current process, but the impediments to it, especially the effective disfranchisement that accompanies residence in a state that does not choose its delegates at a strategic moment in the election year. More democracy is what voters seem to want. Almost all the evidence available — poll data showing consistently high support for direct election of the president, a direct national presidential primary, a proposed constitutional amendment to allow national initiatives,[91] and so on — indicates this, nothing more convincingly than the extent to which citizens have accelerated their use of state initiatives, the best behavioral indicator of the desire for direct democracy available in modern American politics. Initiative use has more than doubled since the 1960s; the rate of passage, historically about one-third, has jumped to almost one-half.[92]

Prediction

Even the counterreformationists, when they turn from prescription to prediction, seem to realize that history is against them. Intraparty politics again has much to do with it. Ranney's "guess as to what is likely to happen in the near future is that . . . [at] some point — probably before this century is out — Congress will adopt some form of a national primary."[93] Mann predicts that as states try to increase their influence by moving up their primary and caucus dates, "in effect, we would have a national primary in 15 or 20 days."[94] Patrick Caddell suggests (as does David Broder) that the collapsing of a majority of delegate selection in 1984 into March means that we have a de facto national primary already.[95]

The direct-national-primary idea is not new. Since 1911 and shortly after, when Representative Richmond Hobson of Alabama introduced the first piece of national primary legislation and Woodrow Wilson endorsed the concept, some 125 such bills have been offered in Congress. Most have been close kin to the one introduced in 1980 by Republican senator Lowell Weicker, which would work like this: Each major party's supporters, along with interested independents, would choose their nominee for president directly with their votes. To get on the primary ballot, a candidate would have until June 30 of the election year to round up valid signatures equal in number to 1 percent of the turnout in the most recent presidential election (around 865,000 in 1984) — a high enough standard to screen out frivolous candidacies. Ballots would be cast on the first Tuesday in August. If no candidate in a party got 50 percent, there would be a runoff between the top two finishers three weeks later.[96]

What would be the effects of a national primary on legitimacy and candidate skill and suitability, the main two criteria for judging a presidential nominating system? Legitimacy seems likely to be enhanced. Voters have expressed consistent and overwhelming support for a direct national primary in every Gallup poll on the issue since 1952; the 1980 survey found 66 percent in favor and 24 percent opposed.[97] The direct primary is the process by which they nominate virtually all other elected officials at all other levels of government in all states and localities in the country. It offers the kind of clear, direct connection between popular vote and outcome that research indicates produces larger and more representative turnouts.[98] By definition, it eliminates the corrosive effects of a protracted sequence of primaries — specifically, all the candidates are on the ballots of all the voters, and no candidate can be prematurely declared the winner. It is possible that a candidate with intense but narrow support could win a national primary, but state and local governments have not found this to be a serious problem, and most of them do not provide for a primary runoff.

The effects a national primary would have on candidate quality are not as obvious. Presidents who won their party nominations in a national primary would have to have demonstrated two requisites of successful leadership: a strategic sense of the public mood and rhetorical skill. Bargaining or tactical skill is not so clearly linked to the national primary. Still, by eliminating the opportunity outsider candidates have under the present system to lock up their parties' nominations with victories in small early states, the national primary would work to favor nominees with extensive governmental experience.[99]

Traditionally, opposition to the national primary has come from those who feel that it "would be the final nail in the coffin of the party system."[100] But it is by no means clear that a national primary would destroy the parties. As Richard Scammon points out, "Many of the strongest party machines in the country thrived in primary systems — Boss Crump in Memphis, Harry Byrd in Virginia, and Dick Daley in Chicago, among others."[101]

Would national party conventions become extinct if candidates for president were not chosen there? Not necessarily. There still would be the need to nominate vice-presidential candidates, make party rules, and, potentially most important, write the platforms. F. Christopher Arterton suggests that these latter activities, so central to the health of the party as an enduring organization, are submerged in the nomination politics of present-day "candidate-centered conventions."[102] Divorcing conventions from the nominating process may well free them to become idea and theme-setting forums.

At root, though, even the most serious efforts at institutional tinkering may be largely beside the point, not only with regard to presidential skill and suitability to the times, but in more fundamental respects as well. The forging of new institutional links to facilitate collective action in party and government — the stated goal of most reform and counterreform proposals — most likely will follow the development and articulation of collective purpose in the political system rather than cause it. Presidents will have their way in Congress only when they present policy ideas that the country will support.

As we argued in Chapter 3, President Reagan pointed his presidency and party in the right direction by his effort to create a new majority based on new theories and programs addressed to the new problems of the day. There was from the start the possibility that Reagan might fail in this effort, but policy is the proper path for restoration of strength and governing capacity to the presidency. It is also the right way to go about restoring unity and discipline to the political parties as instruments of governance and to create policy majorities within Congress. Politicians would link their fortunes to new policy programs and thereby create electoral and governing coalitions that would place some restraints on the claims of interest groups and provide greater capacities for government to act. A presidency that can create a new electoral policy coalition can also bring discipline and integration within electoral and congressional parties. The reforms often suggested for reducing the importance of primaries and restoring the influence of politicians and conventions in the nominating process will not provide the ideas that must form the necessary base of a new governing coalition. So we return to the theme of Chapter 3: ideas are crucial to the successful conduct of politics and government.

NOTES

1. See Chapter 2.
2. Quoted in John Charles Daly, *et al.*, *Choosing Presidential Candidates: How Good Is the New Way?* (Washington, D.C.: American Enterprise Institute, 1980), p. 5.
3. James W. Ceaser, *Reforming the Reforms: A Critical Analysis of the Presidential Selection Process* (Cambridge, Mass.: Ballinger, 1982), p. 81.
4. The summary history that follows draws heavily from the following works: Ceaser, *Reforming*; Ceaser, "Presidential Selection," in Joseph M. Bessette and Jeffrey Tulis, eds., *The Presidency in the Constitutional Order* (Baton Rouge: Louisiana State University Press, 1981), pp. 234–282; Austin Ranney, *Curing the Mischiefs of Faction* (Berkeley: University of California Press, 1974); William J. Crotty, *Political Reform and the American Experiment* (New York: Thomas Y. Crowell, 1977); James Sterling Young, *The Washington Community, 1800–1828* (New York: Harcourt, Brace and World, 1966); James W. Davis, *Presidential Primaries* (New York: Thomas Y. Crowell, 1967); Arthur M. Schlesinger, Jr., ed., *The Coming to Power* (New York: Chelsea House, 1972); and Richard P. McCormick, *The Presidential Game* (New York: Oxford University Press, 1982).

5. Ceaser, "Presidential Selection," p. 244.
6. John P. Roche, "The Electoral College: A Note on American Political Mythology," *Dissent* (Spring 1961), p. 198.
7. Michael Robinson, "The Presidential Nominating Caucus," *Congressional Record* (June 19, 1975), p. E3336.
8. Quoted in Ceaser, "Presidential Selection," pp. 263–64.
9. Theodore H. White, *America in Search of Itself: The Making of the President, 1956–1980* (New York: Harper & Row, 1982), p. 74.
10. Theodore H. White, "The Making of a President Ain't What It Used to Be," *Life* (February 1980), p. 71.
11. Robert J. Huckshorn, *Political Parties in America* (North Scituate, Mass.: Duxbury, 1980), p. 128.
12. Austin Ranney, "Changing the Rules of the Game," in James David Barber, ed., *Choosing the President* (Englewood Cliffs, N.J.: Prentice-Hall, 1974), p. 73.
13. *Ibid.*, pp. 73–74. See also Jeane Jordan Kirkpatrick, *Dismantling the Parties* (Washington, D.C.: American Enterprise Institute, 1978), pp. 7–8.
14. Data for 1968 and 1976 are from Ceaser, *Reforming*, p. 53. Data for 1980 are from Rhodes Cook, "New Democratic Rules Panel," *Congressional Quarterly Weekly Report* (December 26, 1981), p. 2565.
15. Rhodes Cook, "'Superdelegates' May Pick Next Democratic Nominee," *Congressional Quarterly Weekly Report* (January 23, 1982), pp. 127–28; Lanny J. Davis, "Reforming the Reforms," *The New Republic* (February 17, 1982), pp. 8–12.
16. Some differences between the two parties remain. See Ceaser, *Reforming*, pp. 38–39.
17. Jeffrey Tulis, "The Two Constitutional Presidencies," in Michael Nelson, ed., *The Presidency and the Political System* (Washington: Congressional Quarterly Press, 1984), pp. 59–86.
18. Edward S. Corwin, *The President: Office and Powers*, 4th ed. (New York: New York University Press, 1957), pp. 33–34.
19. Joseph E. Kallenbach, *The American Chief Executive* (New York: Harper & Row, 1966), pp. 158–61.
20. Charles Gordon, "Who Can Be President of the United States," *Maryland Law Review* (Winter 1968), pp. 1–32.
21. Thomas E. Cronin, *The State of the Presidency*, 2nd ed. (Boston: Little, Brown, 1980), p. 28.
22. William R. Keech and Donald R. Matthews, *The Party's Choice* (Washington: The Brookings Institution, 1975). Our own reading of the Gallup record for 1944, 1956, and 1964 led us to revise their figures upward. Polls have been compiled in George H. Gallup, *The Gallup Poll, 1935–1971*, 3 vols. (New York: Random House, 1972); *The Gallup Poll, 1972–1977*, 2 vols. (Wilmington, Del.: Scholarly Resources, 1978); and *The Gallup Poll* annuals (Wilmington, Del.: Scholarly Resources, 1979–   ).
23. Compiled from Vanderbilt Television News Archive, *Television News Index and Abstracts*, a monthly publication of the Vanderbilt University Library (November 1968–August 1980).
24. Of the twenty-five eighteenth- and nineteenth-century presidents only James Buchanan, a bachelor, was an exception in even one way. Among twentieth-century defeated major-party nominees the few exceptions for the most part support the rule. All were white male Christians. All but Adlai Stevenson were married, and his divorce seems to have cost him at the polls.
25. Benjamin I. Page and Mark P. Petracca, *The American Presidency* (New York: McGraw-Hill, 1983), p. 90; Richard Watson and Norman Thomas, *The Politics of the Presidency* (New York: John Wiley, 1983), pp. 115–16. Another possibility for such a list is a small-state residence. The three biggest electoral losers of the century were small-staters—Alfred Landon (1936), Barry Goldwater (1964), and George McGovern (1972). Still no known prejudice against small-state politicians exists (certainly none that is not outweighed by the favored place of Vermonters, Kansans,

and the like in popular culture), and the recent nationalization of American politics and media makes the need for a large-state electoral base less compelling than it used to be. Unitarians are included as Christians.

26. *The Gallup Poll* (September 1982), p. 12; (February 1983), p. 23; (June 1983), p. 18; (August 1983), p. 20.
27. Governor Jerry Brown and singer Linda Ronstadt earned the cover of *Newsweek*. See "Ballad of Jerry and Linda" (April 23, 1979), p. 26. A 1983 Gallup poll discovered that by a margin of 64 percent to 29 percent, Americans would not consider voting for a homosexual for president. "Prejudice in Politics," *The Gallup Report* (September 1983), pp. 9–14.
28. Clinton Rossiter, *The American Presidency*, rev. ed. (New York: New American Library, 1960), pp. 193–94.
29. Watson and Thomas, *Politics of Presidency*, p. 110.
30. Gallup data in this paragraph and the next are reported in "Prejudice in Politics."
31. A confidential random survey of 80 representatives and senators found that 95 percent believed in God (however defined) and 71 percent believed in the divinity of Jesus Christ. Peter L. Benson, "Religion on Capitol Hill," *Psychology Today* (December 1981), pp. 47–57.
32. George B. Merry, "Changing Makeup of State Legislatures, " *Christian Science Monitor* (November 17, 1982), p. 12.
33. Fay S. Joyce, "Democratic Contenders Appeal for Support by NOW," *New York Times* (October 3, 1983), p. 14.
34. Quoted in Theodore H. White, *The Making of a President 1960* (New York: Pocket Books, 1961), pp. 128–29.
35. *The Gallup Report* (May 1983), p. 19; Barry Sussman, "A Black or a Woman Does Better Today than a Catholic in '60," *Washington Post National Weekly Edition* (November 21, 1983), p. 42.
36. White, *Making of a President 1960*, p. 65.
37. Public opinion surveys on candidate preference also aid in this process, according to Keech and Matthews, *Party's Choice*, pp. 7–9.
38. Robert L. Peabody, Norman J. Ornstein, and David W. Rohde, "The United States Senate as a Presidential Incubator," *Political Science Quarterly* (Summer 1976), pp. 242–43. They define a "contender" as one who receives 10 percent or more of the votes on any national nominating convention ballot.
39. A fuller discussion of these issues can be found in Keech and Matthews, *Party's Choice*, ch. 1.
40. The federal election law of 1974 limited an individual's contributions to any candidate to $1,000. In the 1976 case of *Buckley* v. *Valeo*, the Supreme Court removed the limit on contributions to one's own campaign.
41. Watson and Thomas, *Politics of Presidency*, p. 103.
42. Joseph A. Schlesinger, *Ambition and Politics* (Chicago: Rand McNally, 1966), p. 178.
43. Steven V. Roberts, "Is It Too Late for a Man of Honesty, High Purpose and Intelligence to Be Elected President of the United States?" *Esquire* (October 1967), pp. 89 ff.
44. Cronin, *State*, p. 28.
45. James Bryce, *The American Commonwealth* (1888; repr. New York: Putnam's, 1959).
46. Robert Peabody and Eve Lubalin, "The Making of Presidential Candidates," in Charles W. Dunn, *The Future of the American Presidency* (Morristown, N.J.: General Learning Press, 1975), p. 27.
47. *Ibid.*, pp. 46–47.
48. Woodrow Wilson, *Constitutional Government in the United States* (New York: Columbia University Press, 1908), pp. 79–80.
49. John H. Aldrich, *Before the Convention* (Chicago: University of Chicago Press, 1980), ch. 2.

50. Donald R. Matthews, "Winnowing: The News Media and the 1976 Presidential Nominations," in James David Barber, *Race for the Presidency* (Englewood Cliffs, N.J.: Prentice-Hall, 1978), p. 56.
51. David S. Broder, "Political Reporters in Presidential Politics," in Charles Peters and James Fallows, eds., *Inside the System*, 3rd ed. (New York: Praeger, 1976), p. 216.
52. Arthur T. Hadley, *The Invisible Primary* (Englewood Cliffs, N.J.: Prentice-Hall, 1976), p. 2.
53. William H. Lucy, "Polls, Primaries, and Presidential Nominations," *Journal of Politics* (November 1973), p. 843.
54. The exceptions: Hubert Humphrey (1968), Richard Nixon (1968), George McGovern (1972), and Jimmy Carter (1976).
55. Nelson W. Polsby and Aaron Wildavsky, *Presidential Elections*, 5th ed. (New York: Scribner's, 1980), p. 148.
56. The Brown total assumes the support of sixty formally uncommitted New Jersey delegates, the number who said three days after the primary that they intended to vote for him. "Uncommitted Jersey Bloc Bars Byrne as Leader at Convention," *The New York Times* (June 15, 1976).
57. John Kessel, *Presidential Campaign Politics* (Homewood, Ill.: Dorsey, 1980), p. 8.
58. Cited in Matthews, "Winnowing," p. 65.
59. Cook, "New Panel," p. 2566.
60. Matthews, "Winnowing," p. 65.
61. Thomas Patterson, "Press Coverage and Candidate Success in Presidential Primaries: The 1976 Democratic Race," paper presented to the American Political Science Association annual meeting (September 1–4, 1977).
62. John H. Aldrich, *et al.*, "'To the Victor Belong the Spoils': Momentum in the 1976 Nomination Campaigns," unpublished paper, 1978; White, *America*, pp. 289–90.
63. U.S. Department of Commerce, *Statistical Abstract*, pp. 18–20, 30, 480; Daniel J. Elazar, *American Federalism*, 2nd ed. (New York: Thomas Y. Crowell, 1972), ch. 4.
64. Adam Clymer, "Primary Vote Will at Least Decide Party Strategies," *The New York Times* (June 8, 1980); Jack W. Germond and Jules Witcover, *Blue Smoke and Mirrors* (New York: Viking, 1981), ch. 6.
65. Germond and Witcover, *Blue Smoke*, p. 120.
66. Quoted in James Doyle, "Is There a Better Way?" *Newsweek* (June 16, 1980), p. 24.
67. Ceaser, *Reforming*, p. 56.
68. Elazar, *Federalism*, ch. 4.
69. Quoted in "Primaries '80: Once Again the System Worked, Sort of," *The New York Times* (June 8, 1980).
70. Henry Mayo, *Introduction to Democratic Theory* (New York: Oxford University Press, 1960), p. 73.
71. White, *America*, p. 289.
72. Quoted in "Is There a Better Method of Picking Presidential Candidates?" *The New York Times* (December 2, 1979).
73. *Gallup Opinion Index* (December, 1980), pp. 20, 13.
74. Yet if they do receive 5 percent, their party is guaranteed funding in the next election.
75. Frank J. Sorauf, *Party Politics in America* (Boston: Little, Brown, 1968), pp. 36, 39.
76. Peabody *et al.*, "The United States Senate as a Presidential Incubator," pp. 240–45.
77. Michael Nelson, "Sentimental Science: Recent Essays on the Politics of Presidential Selection," *Congress and the Presidency* (Autumn 1982), pp. 100–6; Clifton Mc-Cleskey, "The De-Institutionalization of Electoral Politics," in Ellis Sandoz and Cecil V. Crabb, Jr., eds., *A Tide of Discontent* (Washington: Congressional Quarterly Press, 1981), pp. 113–38.
78. Daly, *Choosing*, pp. 2–3.
79. Quoted in Allan J. Mayer, "Is This Any Way to Pick a President?" *Newsweek* (October 15, 1979), p. 69.

80. Austin Ranney, *The Federalization of Presidential Primaries* (Washington, D.C.: American Enterprise Institute, 1978), p. 34.
81. Quoted in "Primaries '80."
82. Quoted in Austin Ranney et al., *The Presidential Nominating Process: Can It Be Improved?* (Washington, D.C.: American Enterprise Institute, 1980), p. 11.
83. Bryce, *American Commonwealth*, p. 29.
84. Ceaser, *Reforming*, pp. 149–50.
85. Ranney, *Nominating*, p. 18.
86. *Ibid.*, pp. 16–17.
87. *Ibid.*, pp. 15–16; Everett Carll Ladd, "A Better Way to Pick Our Presidents," *Fortune* (May 5, 1980), pp. 132 ff.
88. *Ibid.*, pp. 25, 16.
89. *Ibid.*, p. 19.
90. Jack Walker, "Reforming the Reforms," *The Wilson Quarterly* (Autumn 1981), p. 90.
91. Gallup polls from 1948 to 1980 about the electoral college are reported in the *Gallup Opinion Index* (December 1980), p. 59; about the national primary (1952–1980) in the *Gallup Opinion Index* (January 1980), pp. 19–20; and the national initiative in the *Gallup Opinion Index* (October 1978), p. 24.
92. Michael Nelson, "Power to the People: The Crusade for Direct Democracy," *Saturday Review* (November 24, 1979), pp. 12–17.
93. Ranney, *Nominating*, p. 26.
94. Quoted in Cook, "Superdelegates," p. 127.
95. Elizabeth Drew, "A Political Journal," *The New Yorker* (March 28, 1983), p. 66. David Broder, "Democrats' New Calendar, Rules May Produce an Early Winner," *The Washington Post* (August 22, 1983), p. A2.
96. Other recent versions of the national primary proposal, such as those offered by Senators Mike Mansfield and George Aiken in 1972 and by Representative Albert Quie in 1977 differed from Weicker's in that they would not have allowed independent voters to participate. The Mansfield-Aiken bill also would have defined 40 percent as sufficient for victory in the first primary.
97. See note 91.
98. Michael Nelson, "The Presidential Nominating System: Problems and Prescriptions," in Richard Zeckhauser and Derek Leebaert, eds., *What Role for Government: Lessons from Policy Research* (Durham, N.C.: Duke University Press, 1983), pp. 34–51.
99. Also, local publicity in key early states can be obtained as a reward for campaigning in the preelection year; publicity in the national media, the most valuable kind for a national primary, would not be so easy to obtain that far ahead of the election.
100. Austin Ranney, in an interview with Michael Nelson (March 7, 1980).
101. Richard Scammon, in an interview with Michael Nelson (March 6, 1980).
102. F. Christopher Arterton, "Strategies and Tactics of Candidate Organizations," *Political Science Quarterly* (Winter 1977–1978), p. 671.

PART TWO

Presidents and the Policy Process

What is it that a nominating convention wants in the man it is to present to the country for its suffrages? A man who will be and who will seeem to the country in some sort an embodiment of the character and purpose it wishes its government to have.

—Woodrow Wilson, *Constitutional Government in the United States*

CHAPTER 6

Presidential Management of Policy Formation

Of the three main elements that constitute presidential power — the Constitution; culture and politics as manifested in the cycle of preparation, achievement, and consolidation; and the leadership skills of individual presidents — the Constitution is least important in the realm of presidential policy formation. Indeed, there is no constitutional requirement in regard to the organization of the presidency. The cabinet is not mentioned in the Constitution. The president is authorized to "require the Opinion, in writing" of department heads, but this is discretionary authority.

Still, before 1939 presidents had very little choice. They had only a personal secretary and a small, mostly clerical staff for processing routine business. Of necessity, they looked to their cabinet officers, informal advisers, and Congress for ideas about policy development. Franklin Roosevelt forced the question of institutional reform by appointing a number of his policy advisers to subordinate position in the departments and then assigning them to duty in the White House. It became increasingly clear during his presidency that such improvisation should give way to a more stable pattern.

The "institutional presidency" was created in 1939, when Congress enacted into law the recommendations to President Roosevelt of the Brownlow committee, which had prefaced its report with the dramatic plea that "the President needs help" and offered "salvation by staff" as its solution.[1] The practical effect of the reforms was to plant the seeds of the institutional presidency by creating the White House office and the executive office of the president (EOP) and moving the Bureau of the Budget (BOB), which had been in the Treasury Department, to the EOP, thus making it a direct instrument of presidential authority over the departments. The White House office was given six presidential assistants, who were personal advisers to particular presidents. The EOP, which consisted at the time primarily of the BOB, was created to serve successive presidents and provide the institution with continuity.

After World War II the institutional presidency increased in size and scope through the creation of new advisory units: the Council of Economic Advisers (1946); the National Security Council (1947); the congressional liaison staff, which was created informally in the White House office in the 1950s; the president's science adviser and professional staff (1958); and newly created inde-

175

pendent agencies that were placed under the presidential umbrella, including the CIA (1947), the Office of Economic Opportunity (1964), the Environmental Protection Agency (1970), and a host of smaller EOP units such as the Council on Environmental Quality (1970). In 1970 the Bureau of the Budget became the Office of Management and Budget, and a Domestic Council was created in the EOP in which a professional staff that was directed by an assistant to the president coordinated policy development for and among the departments. The Domestic Council per se did not survive the Nixon-Ford administrations, but a domestic-policy staff has continued to exist.

The linear growth of advisory units within the institutional presidency signifies that all modern presidents have found it necessary and valuable to seek help from staffs that are directly responsible to them for the conduct of government. But it would be misleading to imply that the institutional presidency has grown to the detriment of the departments. In fact, there have been variations and discontinuities in the relation of strictly presidential institutions to the departments of the executive branch. Presidents of preparation, achievement, and consolidation face separate tasks of strategic leadership with varying political demands and constraints that require different strategies for policy formation. Each type of presidency implies a different organization of the office in response to the political demands and constraints of the period. Presidents also have fashioned the White House office and EOP according to their varying personal preferences and skills at the management of authority, thus taking advantage of an inherent institutional plasticity that was assumed from the beginning to be crucial to the presidency.

In this chapter we describe first how presidents since Franklin Roosevelt have organized the executive for purposes of domestic, economic, and national security policy formation. We then offer some deductions from the theory of cycles about what styles of organization one would expect to find in presidencies at each stage, and conclude by comparing theory and historical reality.

DOMESTIC POLICY MAKING

As we saw in Chapter 3, Harry Truman attempted to be a president of achievement in domestic policy. The politics of the time did not permit this, but in making the effort Truman took steps toward the development of a White House staff for policy formation that were implemented fully by his ideological successors, Kennedy and Johnson.

Franklin Roosevelt had directed the Bureau of the Budget to inform him about the compatibility of departmental legislative proposals with his budget and policy goals. Truman went beyond this practice by using the legislative clearance process to draw up a list of presidential legislative priorities at the beginning of each year for the annual State of the Union message. Proposals from the departments and agencies were submitted before Christmas each year, then analyzed by BOB and White House staff members for possible inclusion in the president's message. The clearance process, which Roosevelt had created to stop agency initiatives that were not compatible with the president's objectives, was transformed into a device for developing the president's program.[2]

There were no White House staff members in 1946 who could be called domestic-policy advisers. The handful of presidential aides looked after the president's more immediate business of appointments, press relations, and speeches. Presidents always have turned to many and diverse associates, both official and informal, for policy initiatives. But the usual pattern prior to 1946 was to turn to the departments for the main building blocks of the president's program. Truman's decision to use the clearance process instead placed whomever he charged with pulling together the recommendations into a critical new White House role. The assignment fell to Clark M. Clifford, a young lawyer who had joined the staff as a naval aide and who in 1946 became special counsel to the president. Clifford's first task was to prepare the 1947 State of the Union message. He was looking for ideas rather than developed proposals. They would come later and would be done in the departments. Truman decided what to put in the message on the basis of a draft speech prepared by Clifford.[3]

Clifford and Truman together were creating a new institutional role in the White House — that of domestic-policy adviser — although neither would have recognized it at the time. The adviser's responsibility was to prepare a synthesis of proposals and choices for the president across the broad range of policy. Clifford's activities were not confined to domestic affairs, but, in time, other specialized roles emerged for advice on economic and foreign policy.

Aside from compiling the legislative program, Clifford was an independent initiator of policy ideas for the president. He belonged to a small group of administration "liberals" who met each week in an apartment at the Wardman Park Hotel in Washington to discuss the Democratic domestic-policy agenda. Ideas that later were to emerge as legislative proposals for national health insurance, civil rights, and other social policies were proposed and discussed in this group. Clifford found the group valuable because he could discuss with it the policy problems that were facing the president and bring back fresh ideas for Truman's consideration.[4] The Fair Deal developed partly out of these discussions, as did Clifford's famous memorandum to Truman that suggested themes for the 1948 presidential campaign.[5]

Clifford preferred to work with only one assistant. But his successor as counsel, Charles Murphy, had five people on his staff. James Webb, the director of the Bureau of the Budget, sent Murphy several bright young BOB program analysts to work for the White House staff on program development.[6] This action signified the difference between legislative clearance, the task of the bureau, and policy development, now clearly understood to be a White House responsibility. BOB staff members continued to assist the White House in developing policy through budgetary and program analysis. But the differentiation of roles was apparent by the late 1940s.

Eisenhower had a special counsel, but the counsel's work was legal. There was no domestic-policy adviser as such. Streams of advice came from department heads, White House staff members, and the president's brother, Milton, who was president of The Johns Hopkins University but spent weekends at the White House.[7] Sherman Adams was an all-purpose assistant to the president whose responsibilities in regard to domestic-policy development appear to have been occasionally to draw together ideas from the departments. But because the administration did not have an extensive domestic legislative program, it was possible for the president to work with individual department heads on major proposals. It was the Eisenhower rule that, with the exception of Adams, White House staff members should see themselves as junior to cabinet officers. The regular processes of legislative clearance through BOB continued as they had in the Roosevelt and Truman presidencies.

John F. Kennedy became president in 1961 with the conviction that he needed a system of policy development that was sufficiently quick and innovative to develop programs "to get the country moving again," his perennial campaign theme. He asked his principal assistant, Theodore Sorensen, to create a number of policy task forces both during the campaign and after the election in order to be ready with a program in January.[8] To some extent this was a campaign gesture because it was not repeated during his presidency. But it was indicative of his attitude. Kennedy made clear to the White House staff and cabinet early in his term that Sorensen was responsible for the compilation of the president's legislative program. Like Clifford, Sorensen worked in all policy areas, but he was the major assistant for domestic policy.[9] Sorensen and his two aides, Myer Feldman and Lee White, worked much as Clifford and Murphy had to develop ideas for the State of the Union message from which Kennedy could choose. The actual programs then were developed by the departments under Sorensen's direction. But there was a subtle change from the Truman period. Sorensen was given implicit authority by the president to be his agent for policy development to an extent not shared by Clifford and Murphy.[10]

An operation as small as Truman's, Kennedy's, and that which was to follow in the Johnson administration had to meet three conditions in order to serve the president well. First, the assistant to the president had to be able to take ideas from diverse sources, analyze and reconcile differences, and present a coherent whole to the president. Second, he needed the confidence of the president, and this had to be widely known. Clifford and Sorensen possessed both intellectual ability and presidential confidence. But they also understood that they could not analyze all proposals by themselves. Thus, the third condition for success was a willingness to rely upon BOB staff for help in analyzing department recommendations. Kennedy at first did not understand the need for such staffing and, in his impatience for action, tried to settle questions with cabinet officers directly. But BOB director David Bell, acting in concert with Sorensen, educated the new president on the need for thorough staffing of proposals to protect presidential interests against departmental claims.[11]

Lyndon Johnson was determined to be the greatest president since Roosevelt, his idol, and to him this meant passing a creative legislative program of social reform. He was very skeptical of the capacity of the permanent government to produce new, fresh ideas for presidential programs. Several of his aides suggested to him in 1964 that task forces consisting of experts outside government should be created to develop ideas. This was done under the supervision of Bill Moyers, a member of the White House staff who, after the task forces reported in November 1964, convened ad hoc groups to hammer ideas into concrete proposals.[12] In July 1965 Moyers became press secretary and Joseph A. Califano became the assistant to the president who was charged to develop legislative proposals and coordinate domestic programs and related economic policy.[13] His immediate task was to keep the momentum going in the development of Great Society programs. Califano convened a number of interagency task forces and a smaller group of outside committees. The emphasis on intragovernmental groups reflected Califano's judgment that the 1964 task-force reports had required a great deal of subsequent work within government to make them administratively feasible. He also saw a need to force an exchange of views among departments and agencies.[14]

Califano's normal way of operating was to canvas ideas from task forces and visits to universities, develop a general policy direction, and discuss it with the cabinet and subcabinet officials who also had served on the task forces. He then would present a list of programmatic ideas to the president, often at Johnson's Texas ranch over the Christmas holidays. This was done in graphic form, with charts depicting estimated program structures, costs, and benefits. If Johnson approved an idea, Califano returned to the cabinet officers with a request that legislation be drafted.

Califano built on the practices of Clifford and Sorensen but strengthened the role of the assistant, in part by using task forces to break down parochial forces within departments. This was a stronger role than that of compiling department requests and presenting them to the president, with advice, as originally was played by Clifford. And it was more authoritative than the strong coordinating hand supplied by Sorensen. But, more important, Califano was given greater authority as an arbiter and agent for the president than any staff aide ever had. He was empowered to settle disagreements among cabinet officers and to tell a department head that his pet proposal was not going to go to the president. There was always the right of appeal, but Johnson did not care to spend much time discussing policy ideas with his cabinet officers. That was Califano's job.[15]

Califano's greater authority reflected the different styles of Kennedy and Johnson. Kennedy took a keen interest in the substance of policy and liked to discuss the analytical foundations for alternative courses of action. Johnson had strong beliefs about the directions in which he wished to proceed, such as equal educational opportunity and improved health care, but he only wanted to know enough about a particular idea to satisfy himself that it suited his broad goals. It was Califano's responsibility to present such ideas. Johnson saw his own task as then testing their political feasibility, directing politically necessary changes, and selling them. Califano remembered the Johnson approach:

> On the education bill he might say, "Look, I want you to go talk to [Democratic senator] Wayne Morse about that. See whether he thinks it's a good idea because if he doesn't like it, it's never going to see the light of day, it will never get out of subcommittee, and you might as well forget it." Something would tick in his memory.

He might have run into a problem with Morse in 1958 on this type of bill or something. You'd go up and see Morse. Even if you didn't understand exactly why he wanted you to see him, at the time you saw him you understood.[16]

Skepticism about the bureaucracy was much stronger in the Kennedy and Johnson administrations than had been the case with Truman and Eisenhower. This was probably a by-product of the later presidents' desires to invent new programs, but it became an increasingly strong refrain among subsequent presidents who tried to free themselves from the bureaucratic commitments of Great Society programs. Thus, for both policy invention and devolution the bureaucracy came to be seen in the White House as an obstacle. Califano expressed this frustration, with a particular concern about leaks;

> The tremendous conscious or unconscious intransigence on the part of bureaucracies . . . inability to think big . . . couldn't quite see that Johnson had a picture of educating the world, the whole country. And . . . premature leaks if they didn't like the program. Before you had a shot to really explain the program to them, before they really had a grasp of it, if instinctively they didn't like it, they thought it would hurt their empire or do this or that, leak, and you're cut up. . . . The problem was the premature triggering of interest groups who in turn would trigger the Hill.[17]

Fear of leaks meant that the work of Califano's task forces had to be secret. The somewhat strange result was that presidential appointees in the departments were working on their own, to some extent, without the help of the career officials who usually reported to them. Even though Califano wished program proposals to be administratively feasible, it was difficult to achieve this goal by denying the civil servants who would administer the programs an opportunity to contribute to their design. In fact the greatest single criticism of the Great Society programs was that considerations of program implementation in a complex federal system were given minimal attention during the policy development phase.

Many observers concluded during the latter part of the Johnson presidency that although the White House staff could develop policy ideas with the help of task forces, the price was a lack of thoroughness and a failure to tap institutional knowledge in the government. William Carey, a high BOB official during the Johnson years, comments on the adequacy of the process:

> What Johnson had to rely upon for digestion of task force studies and the development of a policy strategy based on them was the small group of White House staff generalists headed by Joseph Califano, together with the resources of the Bureau of the Budget. In marathon meetings held in Califano's office, interrupted by irascible jinglings of the telephone, task force proposals were combed and debated under conditions of pressure and human exhaustion hardly conducive to sensible outcome. The results were then worked over for review by the President on a highly summarized flip-chart basis which left little room to expose and discuss alternatives, much less minority opinion.[18]

These critics saw a need for a balance between the traditional approach of relying upon departments for ideas and the Johnson-style use of White House staff and ad hoc task forces. A Bureau of the Budget self-study was undertaken in 1967 because of BOB distress about the weaknesses of the policy development process. The study concluded that the bureau itself had contributed to the problem by playing only its traditional budgetary role, an essentially negative and critical function. It recommended that a new division for policy development be created in the BOB to be headed by a presidentially appointed assistant director. Such a unit could both respond to the president and tap institutional knowledge throughout the government. However, there was no enthusiasm for the recommendation in the White House. Presidential staff members are not likely to think that civil servants will be sufficiently responsive to the president's needs. And some veteran BOB officials felt that such a body would be too responsive and, therefore, would politicize the agency.[19]

The Nixon administration developed an altogether different approach that was intended to institutionalize both policy development and program management. The Ash Council, an advisory group on government organization, recommended to the president in 1970 that the model of the National Security Council be followed in domestic policy with the creation of a Domestic Council. The council would consist of the relevant department heads, who would be served by a professional staff under the direction of an assistant to the president. The one-person role that had begun with Clifford in 1946 was to be given institutional breadth. Clifford's successor (several times removed) would be able to develop policy ideas in response to the president and yet work constructively with departments and their staffs.[20]

An assumption underlay this reform, which was approved by Congress. It was that the Domestic Council staff would be able to balance fresh ideas with the institutional memory and administrative insights of the departments. The assumption passed only a partial test. The Domestic Council as a cabinet body never amounted to much. What did develop was a large staff led by John Ehrlichman. It proceeded to formulate programs for the president in much the same manner that Califano's operation did, but, because the Nixon White House staff component was much larger (perhaps thirty professionals compared to five), the departments were consulted less.

In actual operation the Domestic Council became a vehicle for Ehrlichman to gain control over policy formation on behalf of President Nixon. A number of broad criteria to guide domestic policy, such as the devolution of federal social programs to the states, were set down early. Task forces that were chaired by assistant directors of the council staff and composed of departmental officials met to develop choices for the president and plan programs. Cabinet officers, however, often were by-passed. Ehrlichman and his staff developed relationships with departmental officials as if the president were their direct boss. This approach suited Nixon's style of authority. He was remote and preferred to make decisions on the basis of memoranda. He did not like to hear and resolve disputes among cabinet members and left such arbitration to Ehrlichman.[21] So when Ehrlichman required cabinet officers to make their arguments to the president through his own assistant directors, it did not sit well with them, but Nixon backed him.

Nixon's system was highly efficient. It also enabled the president to develop policies that bargaining with and among his cabinet officers could not have produced, such as proposals for reorganization of the departments and special revenue sharing with the states. But the Domestic Council structure did not achieve the Ash Council objective of joining the initiatives of presidential government with the institutional competence of the permanent government. The Ehrlichman operation was strong on the first but weak on the second.

The Watergate scandals of 1973 and 1974 so weakened the Nixon White House that domestic policy formation faltered. The vacuum was filled by the Office of Management and Budget (OMB) in a way that would not have been predicted by the Ash Council. In response to an Ash recommendation Congress had authorized in 1970 the creation of four presidentially appointed associate directors in OMB who were to be the chief links between the White House, the OMB director, and the OMB program-examining staffs. Each had a broad area to oversee, such as national security or human resources. This new structure provided stability and continuity for the late Nixon and early Ford administrations. The associate directors worked with cabinet and subcabinet officers to keep departmental activities in line with administration objectives. Responsibility to initiate new legislative ideas returned to the departments. However, the informal transition committee of close advisers that was appointed by Gerald Ford when he became president advised him to reduce the influence of OMB, arguing that it had become a surrogate White House.[22]

The Domestic Council and its staff operations were continued by President Ford, who gave Vice President Rockefeller nominal responsibility for domestic policy formation, working through the council. However, neither the council nor its staff was important in the Ford administration. The president did not support new domestic legislation and gave most of his attention to foreign affairs and economic policy. There were tensions between Rockefeller's staff and various staffs and principals in the White House. A new Economic Policy Board, which will be described in the next section, took over some of the work of the Domestic Council. The departments were more assertive after the dominance of the Nixon White House had passed, and this was very congenial to Ford. He sincerely wished to have an open, collegial administration and genuinely enjoyed and valued meetings of his main advisers in which policy ideas were freely discussed. Ford was the product of many years of listening and negotiating in Congress and liked to work in groups.[23]

Jimmy Carter campaigned against the excessive centralization of the White House staff under Nixon and promised to restore "cabinet government." In the process he ignored the fact that Ford had achieved much that he was advocating. Of course, the phrase "cabinet government" is misleading if it is taken to mean frequent discussions of policy by the entire cabinet. This has never worked, and presidents who attempt it quickly give it up. The secretary of state has little interest in off-shore leasing or welfare reform, nor does he think his colleagues are capable of telling him much about the Middle East. Carter actually meant that his cabinet officers would be his principal policy advisers and that White House staff members would not come between cabinet officers and himself. Not only did this structure reflect Carter's reaction against Nixon's practices but, probably more importantly, it was a manifestation of the way he liked to work. He was a glutton for work, with great confidence in his own intelligence, and believed that his chief responsibility as president was to make decisions based on the best available knowledge. Carter was confident that he could cope with the streams of memoranda that would come to him through a loosely joined process of policy development. White House assistants were not to have strong initiating or coordinating roles, but simply were to advise Carter. In the aftermath of Watergate it would have been politically difficult for a president to have another Califano or Ehrlichman, but Carter's style precluded it as well.[24]

Both Carter and his designated assistant for domestic policy, Stuart Eizenstat, thought it was important to retain a domestic-policy staff but saw little value in the Domestic Council. It was, therefore, abolished and replaced by a staff of twenty-five professionals, most of them experienced Washingtonians whom Eizenstat recruited from congressional staffs and public interest groups. Their job was to help Eizenstat to advise the president on proposals that were developed in the departments.

Carter's model of policy development was to charge a specific cabinet officer with the responsibility to develop an idea, bringing other departments along as required. Thus, he asked Joseph Califano, the secretary of health, education, and welfare, to take the lead in developing a welfare reform proposal and Patricia Harris, the secretary of housing and urban development (HUD), to convene and chair an interagency task force to develop a set of urban policies.[25] But Carter's experience with these two proposals and many others revealed in the first year that "cabinet government" would not serve the interests of the president. Califano was unable to develop a welfare reform proposal that would be supported by F. Ray Marshall, the secretary of labor, yet both departments necessarily were involved in a program that was to involve both the nationalization of welfare and the provision of public service jobs to welfare recipients. A large, complex, jerry-built proposal eventually was developed through a process of discussion with the president and vice president, but it was not the kind of proposal that Califano would have developed when he was working for Lyndon Johnson. Hard choices and simplifications were avoided in the effort to obtain agreement. The final plan, which was sent to Congress, actually was forced out of the two departments by Eizenstat's deputy, who acted unofficially with threats that lack of agreement would not sit well with Carter.[26] An even clearer case was seen in the effort by HUD to develop an urban package, which required the cooperation of several departments. Secretary Harris could not obtain genuine cooperation among departments that simply wished to add their favorite programs to the package. She finally turned to Eizenstat for help, and he became the coordinator for development of the urban package.[27]

The president's response to these experiences was to charge Eizenstat with the coordination of domestic and economic policy proposals throughout the administration. Cabinet officers still might have the lead, but Eizenstat and his staff were authorized to set timetables, call for studies, and write the final option papers that would go to the president. However, Carter stopped short of giving Eizenstat the authority to arbitrate disputes and develop authoritative proposals that Johnson had given Califano. This was due in part to Carter's preference for receiving multiple options. It also was politically intelligent because the Carter administration was more ideologically divided than the Johnson administration. Carter was a fiscal conservative: he supported liberal social programs but thought primarily in terms of rationalizing them through improved organization and reduced costs. He felt at odds with the organized Democratic constituencies, such as labor, the environmentalists, women's groups, even the farmers. A great many policy decisions required Carter to face the conflict between his own prudential approach and the intense demands of these interest groups, which were influential in Washington. His own administration represented these tensions. OMB and the treasury secretary tended to speak for the fiscal conservatives, and Eizenstat, Vice President Mondale, and Califano for the liberal groups, although Eizenstat was very careful to keep his personal advice to the president separate from the option papers developed by his staff. In any event, although the administration's loose structure caused a lot of wear and tear on the president and his aides, it was not a bad way to encompass the political conflicts that existed within the Democratic coalition and resolve them as best as could be done.

Ronald Reagan entered the presidency intending to manage it much as he had the governorship of California, through close consultation with cabinet members under the supervision of a central staff. With the guidance of Edwin Meese, counselor to the president and his former chief of staff as governor, Reagan created five cabinet councils in addition to the National Security Council: Economic Affairs, Human Services, Commerce and Trade, Food and Agriculture, and Natural Resources and Environment. Each is chaired by a cabinet member, and all, except NSC, are staffed by professionals from the Office of Policy Development, the successor to Eizenstat's Domestic Policy staff. The purpose of the councils, each of which is composed of several cabinet members, is to discuss policy proposals and make recommendations to the president. Reagan sits with each of the councils when the time arrives for presidential decisions. He is comfortable with this mode of operation and prefers listening over reading as a way of informing himself. The work of the councils appears to have sorted itself out over time into two levels of decisions—those that the president must make and those that can be settled without him and only referred to him for approval. Reagan increasingly made the former type of decision in discussion with a small legislative strategy group consisting of James Baker, his chief of staff, Meese, and other generalists on the Baker and Meese staffs who saw their role to be resolving questions that had been discussed in the councils in ways that would be most politically profitable for the president.[28]

The Office of Policy Development (OPD) initially was weak because the director was a policy advocate who had no interest in directing strong staff analyses of the costs and benefits of policy options. His successor, who had worked on the Domestic Council under Ehrlichman and at OMB, sought not only to provide analytic staff support for the work of the cabinet councils, but

to launch staff studies on nondepartmental questions. As in previous administrations, both OMB and the departments are called upon by OPD to help provide the analyses the councils need.

Reagan's objective of binding cabinet officers closely to himself so that
they are not coopted by their departments appears to have been achieved. Cabinet officers are not cut off from direct access to Reagan on questions that are
important to them. Also, their recommendations are moderated to some extent
by policy analyses that are carried out by OPD staff. However, the Legislative
Strategy Group increasingly has become the forum within which the most important presidential decisions are made. Major budgetary strategies are
developed there, as well as the principal foreign and defense policy decisions.[29]
The Reagan team believed that the collegiality of cabinet government could be
achieved only if tightly monitored from the center.

ECONOMIC POLICY MAKING

The American people hold the president accountable for the health of the
economy and punish presidents at the polls when their economic policies do not
appear to be succeeding. Much domestic policy can be delegated by presidents,
but the large questions of macroeconomics — employment, inflation, economic
growth, participation in the international economy, and the relation of fiscal
and monetary policies — are squarely on the president's shoulders.

The Employment Act of 1946 charges the president to foster the achievement of both "maximum employment, production, and purchasing power" and
"free competitive enterprise." A tension between government intervention and
reliance on free markets thereby was articulated.[30] The tension reflects long-
standing disagreements within American political culture. As we saw in
Chapter 3, Americans are devoted to individual liberty and spontaneous social
activity, including the maintenance of free markets, and are ambivalent about
government authority. However, Americans also are pragmatic "operational
liberals" whose searing experience in the Great Depression of the 1930s underlies their belief that government must not permit the private economy to bring
misery into people's lives again.

Thus, in addition to the New Deal stabilizers against hard times that were
added by law, such as unemployment compensation and social security, there
was general agreement among national leaders at the end of World War II that
the national government, and particularly the presidency, should be formally
charged to maintain the health of the economy. However, the word "full" was
struck from the language of the (Full) Employment Act of 1946 because of continuing disagreement about the proper scope of government responsibility.
There was to be no central planning. Since 1946 liberals have been comfortable
with the idea of selective government interventions in economic markets, and
conservatives, while not rejecting that responsibility, have been more disposed
to leave things alone in the belief that government intervention leads to market
inefficiency, budget deficits, and inflation. Those same tensions between intervention and caution exist within the discipline of economics. They

are manifested in the councils of government through the Treasury Department, the Council of Economic Advisers, and other agencies so that the larger external political debate about the role of government in the economy is reproduced in intragovernmental discussions.

The chief action of the Employment Act of 1946 was to create the Council of Economic Advisers as a new unit in the executive office of the president. The council consists of three economists, one of whom is chairman, and is served by a staff of approximately fifteen professional economists. It has not changed in structure, composition, or size since 1946.

Continuity and Change

Harry Truman did not ask Congress to give him a Council of Economic Advisers (CEA), but it did so anyway. The congressional view was that the president's economic advisers should be accountable to both him and Congress for their advice, in contrast to the loose collection of Roosevelt "brain trust" counselors. The first CEA chairman attempted to advise Truman from a lofty nonpartisan "scientific" stance and hoped to stay on to serve President Thomas Dewey after the 1948 election. He was asked to leave after Truman won the election, thus establishing the principle that the CEA and its staff are useful to a president only if they serve his policy objectives.[31] There never again was confusion about who the CEA worked for.

President Eisenhower asked Arthur Burns, his first CEA chairman, to create an advisory board on economic growth and stability (ABEGS). It consisted of Burns, as chairman, the undersecretaries of treasury, agriculture, commerce, and labor, the director of the BOB, the head of the Federal Reserve Board, and a member of the White House staff.[32] This was a first effort to create a formal collegial structure through which choices might be sifted and sorted for the president's attention. Burns was clearly the president's preeminent economist, but Eisenhower also listened to two strong secretaries of the treasury. In the second term Burns's successor, Raymond Saulnier, worked in an even more structured collegial fashion with the secretary of the treasury, the director of the Bureau of the Budget, and the head of the Federal Reserve Board when discussing the state of the economy and possible policy actions.[33]

The Kennedy-Johnson years were characterized by the formalization of a "troika" consisting of the secretary of the treasury, the CEA head, the director of OMB, and their respective staffs. Because a broad division of labor among the troika members was established, one could say that economic advice to the president was "institutionalized."[34] The secretary of the treasury became the chief spokesman for the president on economic policy. The CEA chairman became the president's personal adviser on economic policy. He is entitled to see the president alone at regular intervals in a sort of student-professor relationship, although it can be argued that the chairman teaches the president about economics and the president teaches the professor about politics. The director of BOB (later OMB) was the president's chief adviser on the size and structure of the annual federal budget and on the effectiveness of programs. These three roles were and still are complementary, with each bringing its particular institutional perspective to meetings with the president. The treasury secretary and his staff understand the structures of the financial world, both domestic and international, and usually are a primary link between the president and the business community. The CEA chairman brings the discipline of economics to bear on economic events and trends, including its way of thinking about trade-offs among difficult choices. The director of OMB is the guardian of the president's interests against the departments, which would spend money without limit for new or old programs. In most administrations, the bias of these three positions generally is conservative, with the CEA chairman sometimes the odd man out because the terms of the Employment Act commit that agency to advise the president on how to promote employment.

The "institutionalization" of the troika during the Kennedy and Johnson administrations also was seen in the layering of working groups beneath the three principals in which analysis and evidence were developed to achieve as much agreement as possible. The idea was to keep the number of presidential decisions small enough and their character broad enough for presidents to make competent decisions. Thus, for each annual budget cycle the treasury staff would estimate the revenues the federal government would receive in the coming fiscal year. The CEA would estimate how the private economy would function, and the Budget Bureau would anticipate the probable level of federal expenditures. This deliberate effort to reduce unknowns, assess probabilities, and minimize disagreement served presidents well because the remaining issues and uncertainties then could be discussed with the troika in a coherent way. The chairman of the Federal Reserve Board, an independent agency that regulates the supply of money, also would attend some meetings with the president to make a "quadriad."

There were two features of the Kennedy-Johnson troika arrangement that differentiate it from what came before and after. First, the CEA, through its chairman, provided the principal ideas for innovative administration policies, the most dramatic being the tax cut of 1964 and the economic analysis that led to the war on poverty.[35] Second, each of the troika institutions was acting as a presidential staff on important questions of macroeconomic policy. By general agreement they did not want the other departments of government to be at the policy-making table. Departments such as Labor, Commerce, and Agriculture were seen as serving the claims of their interest-group constituencies rather than the purposes of the president. They were not seen as having any particular competence in macroeconomic policy questions.[36] Indeed, even on matters of microeconomic policy, such as the minimum wage, subsidies for farmers, tariffs, and government regulation, the CEA, with help from the Bureau of the Budget, screened and analyzed proposals to the president from the departments in order to protect presidential purposes from undue claims.[37] This separation of the troika from the rest of the government particularly suited Kennedy and Johnson because of their concern for policy innovation and their skepticism about the departments' ability to provide ideas that would meet presidential standards.

The Nixon administration made an initial weak effort at collegiality by superimposing a cabinet Committee on Economic Policy over the troika in order to join the consideration of macroeconomic and microeconomic issues in one forum and bring the constituency departments to the main table. But the group was large and unwieldy, and the president, who usually was bored with economic policy issues, found it tiresome to sit and listen to disagreements within his administration.[38] The troika system, therefore, continued until Nixon dramatically intervened in 1971, using presidential emergency powers to impose wage and price controls on the economy. This was the kind of dramatic action Nixon liked in preference to, as he put it, the Woody Hayes theory of football: "Four yards and a cloud of dust."[39] Nixon's intervention reflected the promptings of the new secretary of the treasury, John Connally, who thought drastic action to be politically necessary. For the rest of his administration Nixon virtually delegated the management of economic policy to Connally and his successor, George Shultz. They did not make important decisions without the president's approval, but it was they who managed debate and disagreements and brought recommendations to Nixon.

Connally, an ex-Democrat, is reported to have dominated policy councils, but Shultz worked in a collegial manner to take broad soundings.[40] This appears to have been congenial to his fellow Republicans in the administration, many of whom were comfortable with collegial decision processes from corporate life. The same advisers continued into the Ford administration and, with the encouragement of the president, created the Economic Policy Board (EPB), an institution that superseded the troika and embodied Nixon's initial search for a way to integrate macroeconomic and microeconomic policy.[41]

The EPB was not a return to the drawing board, but to the loose collegiality of the 1950s. Its membership consisted of the secretary of the treasury, as chairman, the chairman of the CEA, the director of OMB, the secretary of state and other cabinet officers who were concerned with economic policy, the chairman of the Federal Reserve Board (informally), the vice president, and other economic policy officials who would attend from time to time, depending upon the issue under discussion. The EPB was served by a small staff headed by an executive secretary who also was assistant to the president for economic affairs. It was his responsibility to develop an agenda and oversee the preparation of the staff papers that framed policy options for the president.

The creation of the EPB was an organizational accommodation to the nation's changing problems of economic policy. During the heyday of the troika it was possible to separate macroeconomic and microeconomic policy to a great extent. But by 1970 the nature of the economic problems confronting the nation had changed so perceptibly that it became increasingly difficult to separate domestic and international economic policy and to tell macro from micro policy. The OPEC oil boycott in 1973 introduced a new generation of problems in which all of these dimensions of policy were inextricably intertwined. The high price of energy promotes inflation, a macro problem with both domestic and international origins, but the solutions to a great extent are to be found in micro policies—the incentives provided to domestic suppliers of oil, gas, coal, and solar power; deregulation and increased competition in industry to promote greater efficiency and productivity; and so on. Policy becomes a seamless web. Yet according to the testimony of the chairman of Ford's Council of

Economic Advisers, although the EPB settled a number of secondary questions in an efficient manner, it was too large and cumbersome to deal with major policy issues. For these matters an informal troika continued to operate.[42]

The Carter administration created an Economic Policy Group (EPG) to replace the EPB. It was chaired by the secretary of the treasury, and its staff reported to him. In practice the EPG did not function as a unit to any extent but rather worked as a small executive committee that included the troika, the vice president, the president's assistant for domestic policy, the head of the Council on Wage and Price Stability, and individuals such as the special trade representative on an ad hoc basis. This group regularly discussed important macroeconomic issues; micro policy questions were handled in a piecemeal manner by the CEA and OMB staffs, as in previous Democratic administrations.[43] The urge for collegiality and integration that had characterized the Ford administration simply receded. This was not because Carter was particularly innovative in economic policy, but rather that, as a conservative president of preparation, he was going against the grain of accepted economic policy in the departments. This argued for a centralized operation.

The Reagan administration formed a Cabinet Council on Economic Affairs chaired by the secretary of the treasury. This is not unlike the Carter EPG except that microeconomic issues are handled by other cabinet councils. There is, therefore, a much higher degree of integration in the management of economic policy formation in the Reagan administration than under Carter. The form is different from those used by Ford and Nixon but the spirit is the same. However, the Reagan administration's greater policy innovativeness is manifested in the high degree of central control of this collegial apparatus. This has led to strong disputes at the very top about the proper course of economic policy. There is neither the looseness of a traditional Democratic administration nor the cohesive unity of a traditional Republican government.[44]

Politics and Organization

The politics of macro and micro policy historically have been separable, and even manageable, for presidents, but recent history has complicated the economy in such a way that conflicts have been intensified and reinforced. Macroeconomic choices have been made within a context of macro politics — that is, a concern on the part of presidents about how their decisions will affect rates of inflation, interest, growth, and unemployment with obvious consequences for their own political fortunes. These decisions have become more difficult in recent years as it has become apparent that the chief cure for high inflation is a severe recession, and that economic recovery brings in its wake the threat of unacceptably high interest rates. The choices are much starker than they were in the 1960s, when it seemed possible to have economic expansion without bad side effects.

Microeconomic policy choices are conditioned by an increasingly volatile and intense kind of micro politics that is now so much a part of macroeconomic choices that presidents face both kinds of politics at once. The Carter administration provides many rich illustrations. President Carter and his economic advisers knew that fiscal restraint to limit the growth of the federal budget, and, therefore, limit the annual deficit, would be a strong antidote to inflation. Yet Carter, as a Democratic president, was presumed to be friendly by organized labor, farmers, and a large number of federal social programs advocates, all of whom placed intense pressures on the administration to spend money on programs that benefited their groups. Time and time again, the fiscally conservative Carter was forced to compromise with Democratic interest groups on the level of the new minimum wage, on the size of agricultural subsidies, on federal expenditures for public service employment, on any number of matters. None of these seemed crucial by themselves, but taken together they contributed to an increasingly unacceptable rate of inflation.[45] President Carter eventually was damaged by both macroeconomic politics and microeconomic politics in the 1980 election. Not only was there general unhappiness about a 10-percent rate of inflation and a 20-percent interest rate, but the Democratic groups were unhappy that they had not gotten all that they had asked for.

The politics of macro and micro policy, therefore, have overlapped, as have the problems and policy responses. This helps explain the push to integrate all economic policy making into one body such as Ford's Economic Policy Board. But this is easier for some administrations to do than for others. It is easier for a president of consolidation to integrate policy development because there is greater unity on goals than in other kinds of presidencies. It is more difficult for presidents of preparation or achievement because innovation brings diversity and disagreement in its wake. President Reagan has tried to have it both ways. Because politics shapes presidential organization, dislocations and discontinuities in economic problems have destabilized both the politics of economic policy and presidential organization for formulating that policy.

NATIONAL SECURITY POLICY MAKING

To whom does the president turn for information and advice on national security? In November 1979, when a skeleton staff in the United States embassy in Iran was seized by militants and held prisoner, President Carter relied on the same advisers with whom he had been discussing alternative responses to the revolution in Iran that had taken place earlier that year. This also was the group with which he had discussed Arab-Israeli conflicts, relations with the Soviet Union and China, and a host of other major foreign-policy questions. During the Carter administration this group met every Friday morning for breakfast with the president in the cabinet room of the White House. Other presidents have convened their principal foreign-policy advisers in similar fashion. The regular members of the group have varied little from one president to another: the vice president, the secretaries of state and defense, the assistant to the president for national security, and one or more senior White House aides such as the chief of staff and the counselor to the president. Sometimes the director of the CIA or the chairman of the Joint Chiefs of Staff attends if a special intelligence briefing is required or if military action is being considered. The president spends hours each week talking, in person and on the telephone, with this small group of advisers, reading, and responding to their views. The conversations shift continually from one subject to another, but in the process of coping with a variety of complex problems presidents must transform a group of individuals, who have never worked together or perhaps known each other before, into an effective team. Even the president may not have known all of these people before he appointed them, and he certainly could not know in advance how they would get along with each other.

The president comes to know his advisers well and to understand how they think about the world. He must balance their diverse views so that his own knowledge and understanding are enlarged. He must achieve unity without conformity. Yet if the chemistry of the group is not right, he must make a change. If one individual continually disagrees with the others, the president may wish to remove him. No one can do these things for the president.

Beyond this highly subtle task of personal leadership is an even more complex one. All of the president's advisers represent institutions on which they, and the president, are dependent for information and for the implementation of decisions. Thus, the simple management of interpersonal relations among a small group of advisers is not enough. Organizational strategies must be developed as well.

To say that the advisory system must be designed to provide accurate information and generate policy ideas that will help reduce the difficult problems the nation faces in world politics is to state objectives that can be approximated rather than achieved. No generation fully understands the world in which it lives, and the knowledge that forms the basis for action, therefore, is always incomplete. The problems of American foreign policy are not soluble in any final sense. But it is possible to devise effective policies for coping with them. For example, the postwar policies of the Truman and Eisenhower administrations succeeded in reviving western Europe economically and in creating a strong Western alliance as a counterbalance to Soviet power in Europe. Both understanding and creativity were at work. When these ingredients are missing, policy can fail badly, as in the case of America's military intervention in a Vietnamese civil war of long standing.

A policy-making system that will infallibly prevent errors of great magnitude cannot be designed because no set of institutional and formal procedures can replace the world views that policy makers bring to office with them. These world views are widely shared in the society. Five successive presidents believed it was important to prevent a communist victory in Vietnam. The historical record reveals that most of the searching and agonizing debate within American government on this question was over how to prevent such a takeover—the implicit goal seldom was challenged. Still, on a great many lesser matters and in debates that are appropriately about means on the great questions, the character of the policy-making system can contribute to more or less "rational" decisions, judged by whether the means chosen are appropriate to the ends sought.

Since the end of World War II the presidency has been affected by a continuing development of executive institutions for national security policy making.

The Department of Defense was created to coordinate military strategies and procedures. The position of secretary of defense periodically has been strengthened to that end. The National Security Council was established as a result of the National Security Act of 1947. It was to be a committee composed of the secretaries of state and defense and the three military-service secretaries. President Truman regarded the NSC proposal as a potential threat to presidential authority but accepted it as part of a compromise to win navy support for military unification.[46]

NSC advocates within the Pentagon saw the council as a unit to coordinate military questions that would be dominated by the Department of Defense. But the Bureau of the Budget, acting in the president's interest, insisted that the NSC existed to serve the president alone. Not only was it important that the NSC include the State Department and that it meet in the Executive Office Building rather than at the Pentagon, but the BOB argued strongly that the executive secretary of the NSC should be designated as an assistant to the president. Eisenhower formally implemented the last suggestion, but Truman understood the point and the NSC executive secretary worked for him, not the secretary of defense.[47] The historical irony is that a council that was created to foster collegiality among departments and to assure departmental representation to the president has been used by Truman and his successors as a lever against the departments. The NSC itself has become less important, and the NSC staff as a White House institution has become more important.[48]

Under Truman, the substantive work of the NSC was done in the departments. The NSC executive secretary was a neutral coordinator of departmental position papers, and his staff worked as a secretariat. The NSC was dominated by the State Department, which at that time had an influential policy planning staff that was led by George Kennan, the architect of the U.S. policy of "containment" of the Soviet Union.[49] The burst of foreign-policy creativity that led to the Truman Doctrine for the defense of Greece and Turkey, the Marshall Plan for the economic recovery of western Europe, and the North Atlantic Treaty Organization came from the State Department. In 1950 Truman began to develop a senior NSC staff composed of civil servants on temporary duty, but foreign policy was firmly in the hands of the president and secretary of state. The NSC and its staff existed to advise the president on how best to coordinate the implementation of policy decisions.[50]

Eisenhower was a product of the military staff system and revised the NSC structure accordingly. The executive secretary became an assistant to the president but remained a coordinator. The senior staff was enlarged and charged to coordinate the work of a new NSC Planning Board, in which position papers written by the departments were discussed, and a new Operations Coordination Board, which was responsible for seeing that the agencies implemented presidential decisions.[51] Eisenhower used these NSC bodies for long-range planning on particular issues and for coordinating policy and administrative questions among departments. The most important policy decisions were discussed in small ad hoc groups of presidential advisers, but the general-turned-president thought it very important that such questions be fully staffed through a comprehensive process in which all institutional viewpoints were explored. The NSC's coordinating role, which was implemented by a self-effacing assistant to the president, fitted well with Eisenhower's strong secretary of state because the president ensured that the assistant was the custodian of a process and not a substantive expert in foreign policy or an advocate.[52]

Eisenhower administration officials themselves were increasingly critical of the NSC procedures toward the end of the second term. Their concern was that there was too much paper, too many meetings, and too much building of bland interdepartmental compromises before the president got a crack at issues. President Kennedy actually abolished the planning and implementation bodies. He was influenced by a report of the Senate Government Operations Committee, which, after holding long, comprehensive hearings, criticized the Eisenhower NSC structure as too bureaucratic and recommended that it be dismantled in favor of a less formal NSC.[53] Political scientist Richard Neustadt also advised the president-elect not to be burdened by elaborate staff structures that might foreclose his options through bureaucratic collusion. In hindsight it appears that the Senate committee and Kennedy failed to understand that Eisenhower had used the NSC system primarily for planning and implementation and that actual decisions were taken in informal forums.[54] The consequence of Kennedy's decision was to place a heavy burden on the president and his principal advisers to scrutinize proposals that came from the agencies. They failed their first test by not challenging the CIA on its defective plans for the Bay of Pigs invasion. An Eisenhower-like staffing process, in which the departments were required to comment, might have exposed the plan's weaknesses.

Kennedy initially looked to the secretary of state to "take charge" of foreign policy. But this did not happen, to the president's disappointment. Neither the secretary nor his department saw itself as having authority over other departments. They stuck close to the historic mission of the department—conducting diplomacy. On military questions they deferred to the Pentagon. In addition, the department had little capacity to deal with international economic questions and its policy planning staff had lost its inventiveness. Thus, Kennedy strengthened the position of the assistant for national security affairs. McGeorge Bundy, with a small staff, began to fill the vacuum left by the State Department. Bundy and his assistants, who were drawn from academic life, sought out issues for the president to address, challenged departmental opinions, and established presidential control over information by creating the White House Situation Room, in which the White House received cables to and from the State and Defense Departments and the Central Intelligence Agency. Bundy and his staff met the president's desire for central coordination and for the impressing of a presidential perspective on the departments.[55] The role of the assistant under Bundy no longer was that of a custodian; it became an active policy-making role. There was no elaborate NSC process to coordinate. The emphasis was on ad hoc decision groups and staffing arrangements. The question is whether the capacity to examine choices carefully in advance of decisions was lost. The Eisenhower and Kennedy systems each had the defect of their virtues.

Lyndon Johnson also tried to prod the State Department. Because he wanted it to lead a system of interdepartmental committees, he used the

NSC structure very little. However, the department did not provide decisive leadership for him any more than it did for Kennedy. It settled for a system of consensus opinions. Johnson initially gave Bundy's successor, Walt Rostow, little authority and limited responsibility, but over time, through the default of State, Rostow and his small staff began to manage the flow of decision papers to the president, challenge departmental positions, and monitor operations because there was no one else to do these things.[56] Major foreign-policy decisions in the Johnson administration increasingly were made in small, informal, closely held groups consisting of the president and a few advisers. The best known of these gatherings was the "Tuesday lunch," the setting in which most of the decisions for the conduct of the Vietnam War were made. It consisted of Johnson, the secretaries of state and defense, the director of the CIA, and Rostow. No assistants were present, and decisions were not recorded. This sometimes led to a certain confusion about what had been decided, but it met the president's demand for secrecy and dispatch.

Each president tries to avoid what he sees as the deficiencies of his predecessor, and Nixon was no exception. He did not wish to return to the inflexible Eisenhower system, having seen it firsthand, but he believed that Kennedy's freewheeling style worked at the expense of a concern about how specific policies fit an overall pattern. Johnson really had not improved upon the Kennedy system because most policies had developed by default in the face of the Vietnam War and his crisis style of decision making. Nixon was determined to impose a new set of priorities on American foreign policy.

The main achievement of Henry Kissinger's White House national security staff was to impose an analytic responsibility on the departments. Kissinger directed the preparation of policy analyses in State, Defense, and other departments that would explicate problems of policy more than once, through rewriting. Members of his staff usually would rework those papers and add analyses of their own. The purpose was to permit Kissinger to go to the president with the widest possible range of options for decision. This fit Nixon's preference for working with documents rather than people and for dealing with others through one intermediary. But the primary purpose in designing the system as he did was to avoid both the uncritical collation of fixed bureaucratic positions that characterized the Eisenhower system and the loose ad hoc procedures of the Kennedy period. In the latter case it was felt that coherence and even careful analysis sometimes were lost in the emotionally charged crisis atmosphere.

The Kissinger apparatus concentrated mainly on the major issues such as Vietnam, arms control, and relations with China and the USSR. Even so, there were some conspicuous omissions, including the Arab-Israeli conflict, international economics, and weapons strategy and development. Weaponry was handled in the Pentagon, and international economic questions, about which Kissinger was not expert, were dealt with by a number of White House and Treasury Department groups.[57]

The State Department role in policy formation was confined to the NSC arena. But the main reasons that Kissinger became the second man in the government on foreign policy, thus leaving the secretary of state in an embarrassing limbo, were Nixon's preferred style of operating, Kissinger's strength of mind and personality, and the secret nature of the negotiations for a Vietnam peace settlement, the overture to China, and the SALT arms-control talks.

Nixon and Kissinger initially tried to restore the distinction between decision and operations that Kennedy had erased. They concentrated their efforts on a few overriding policy choices, hoping to give the government direction by imposing a new intellectual framework. Before long, however, Kissinger saw that the separation of decision and implementation was artificial, and the NSC staff began to work on policy implementation as well as analysis. At this point the fundamental institutional weaknesses in the model became apparent. Kissinger really was trying to play two roles, those of policy adviser to the president and policy leader throughout the government, and the two proved to be incompatible for a staff person in the White House. But he always sacrificed the second role for the first when he had to. Closeness to the president and the immediate meeting of Nixon's demands were the foundations of Kissinger's influence. Often there was neither time nor energy to do anything else.[58] A related problem was that most policy matters that were not covered by the NSC system led to decision by default at lower levels in the departments in the process of day-to-day execution.[59]

After having served as secretary of state from 1973 to 1977 Kissinger concluded that, as a general rule, it was a mistake for foreign policy to be formulated in the White House without the participation of the State Department.[60] During the Ford administration he attempted to have the best of both worlds by retaining the position of assistant to the president while also serving as secretary of state. Eventually Ford separated the posts, but Kissinger was the dominant foreign-policy maker under an inexperienced president. There was a general consensus that a new balance should be secured between the White House NSC operation and the departments that reduced the role of the assistant, but the search for a formula to achieve this purpose was left to President Carter.

Carter explicitly sought a division of labor in which the NSC staff would supply innovative ideas and the State Department would both provide institutional memory against which to test such ideas and be the implementer of policy. He valued the assistant for national security, Zbigniew Brzezinski, as an idea man and gave less attention to the traditional coordination role. Brzezinski accordingly recruited an expert staff that could generate ideas. Carter looked to Cyrus Vance, the secretary of state, to be the public spokesman on foreign policy and to advise him as well as oversee policy implementation. He felt that the balance of ideas and institutional knowledge between the NSC staff and State served him well in his need to clarify choices and never changed that opinion during his tenure.[61] Hamilton Jordan, a senior Carter aide, felt that the Brzezinski-Vance duality reflected the activist and conservative strains in Carter's own personality.[62] However, there were two difficulties. Vance was reluctant to be a public spokesman because it was not a congenial role for him. Carter, therefore, turned to Brzezinski, who was more than eager to give speeches and appear on television. The visibility of the NSC assistant inevitably stimulated press stories about tension between Brzezinski and Vance and, since it was clear that the two men had different policy views, caused commentators to wonder to whom the president was listening. Critics charged that the administration's foreign policy lacked a clear, coherent pattern. There also was considerable criticism of Brzezinski for acting as a policy advocate rather than as a custodian, and his hard-line view of relations with the USSR inevitably was contrasted with Vance's faith in détente.[63] The problem for the president was less in the reality, for he felt capable of handling both Brzezinski and Vance, than in the image of uncertainty given to the world. If Brzezinski had been more of a custodian and less of an advocate, especially in public, the problems would have been reduced. But Carter liked having an idea man nearby, and he was skeptical that any fresh ideas would come from the State Department.

Ronald Reagan's determination to downgrade the assistant for national security reflected his collegial approach to government. The NSC assistant initially was placed under Edwin Meese, the counselor to the president. There were periodic complaints from within the administration that many options were going to the president without careful analysis because the NSC staff had been curbed so effectively. A more serious problem was the absence of a coordinating process to contain the conflicts that developed between the strong-minded secretaries of state and defense, Alexander Haig and Caspar Weinberger. The NSC system was too weak to contain their frequent public disagreements. The senior White House staff was increasingly unhappy because the central principle of the Reagan style is collegial harmony.[64] Haig resigned in 1982, less over issues than because of his temperamental incompatibility with the Reagan collegial system. George Shultz, an experienced Nixon administration hand who had headed OMB and had been secretary of labor and the treasury, succeeded him, but the structurally rooted problems reappeared after a time.

TYPES OF PRESIDENCIES AND ORGANIZATIONAL STRATEGIES

Presidents of preparation, achievement, and consolidation each have different policy purposes, and, therefore, one would expect them to organize the development of policy differently.

Presidents of Preparation

The policy task of a president of preparation is to generate, distill, and present new ideas. The political situation calls on him to attempt to build a rising tide of support for such ideas. The organizational implication is that the initiative for policy development will come from the White House, but in balanced tension with the departments. In part this reflects the president's likely reaction against the close integration of the institutional presidency and the permanent government that existed in the previous presidency of consolidation.

Kennedy and Carter, as presidents of preparation, both sought fresh ideas with which to broaden their political constituencies. Kennedy had the easier task because he was the beneficiary of ideas that had been incubating in Democratic circles in the 1950s. Carter attempted to begin the incubation process virtually through the presidency itself. That process has continued in the

Democratic party since his administration left office. Both presidents believed that good new ideas were most likely to emerge if there were a balanced tension between their own staffs and those of the departments.

The same pattern held for Kennedy and Carter in foreign-policy formation. They wanted action and innovation and, therefore, were willing to use the national security adviser's staff to prod the established departments. But, again, they valued the multiple perspectives that derived from tension.

This strategy of policy formation has strengths and corresponding weaknesses. Ideally, new concepts are balanced by the departments' institutional memory about feasibility and realism. But balance is difficult to maintain in the rush to develop new ideas. The use of the presidential staff to create policy alternatives in a free-form, catalytic way encourages people to advance fresh thoughts. But the very freewheelingness of the structure, with ideas coming from a variety of sources, makes it hard to integrate the final choices coherently. Because his staff does not have the authority to overrule cabinet officers, the president often is confronted with incommensurate options, some of which may not have been studied thoroughly. A great deal hinges upon his capacity to analyze competing arguments and integrate diverse claims into coherent positions.

Presidents of Achievement

The policy task of a president of achievement is to get an ambitious legislative program passed. His political situation is one of strong but temporary empowerment, and the president must seize the day by mobilizing the public in favor of action. The clear implication for the organization of policy development in such a presidency is White House dominance over the permanent government. Speed in pursuit of the presidential agenda is the chief necessity.

Roosevelt achieved his domestic program before there was an institutional presidency, but there are strong parallels between his presidency and Johnson's. Both men pulled responsibility for domestic-policy formation into the White House through the use of informal advisers in Roosevelt's case and through a domestic-policy staff for Johnson. At the same time both presidents were responding to a variety of group demands for legislative appeals. In comparison to presidents of preparation, not only was there a greater volume of policy, but considerably more bargaining and compromise was required in constructing the legislative program. This task also was highly centralized.

In foreign affairs Roosevelt and Johnson themselves were the initiators and arbiters of policy choices. They used a number of different administrative devices to dominate policy; indeed, the very determination to dominate was incompatible with a visible, set administrative system.

Ronald Reagan centralized policy formation in the White House Legislative Strategy Group and the Office of Management and Budget leadership when developing his legislative program. However, as a conservative, he bears a closer resemblance in his ideological preferences to previous presidents of consolidation than to Roosevelt and Johnson. Not surprisingly, then, he accords more value to having cabinet officers and department administrators involved in policy formation because he has the conservative's concern for the feasibility of program implementation. Similarly, Reagan has used the National Security Council staff less to analyze options than to ensure departmental implementation of presidential policy. But policy itself seems to have been made in closely held discussions at the top of government, much as with other presidents of achievement.

These strategies of policy development have both strengths and weaknesses. Their very haste is politically necessary when empowerment is temporary. But presidents may place such a premium upon invention, action, and legislative achievement that they shunt aside efforts to assess the feasibility of implementing programs not only as something they do not want to hear about, but as a possible lodestone in the legislative process. A price later is paid, because implementation problems, both in domestic and foreign policy, eventually emerge as paramount political problems.

Presidents of Consolidation

Consolidating presidents have the task of rationalizing existing programs. They need to foster a bipartisan coalition: previous proponents of the programs must agree to their alteration and previous opponents to their survival. The logical organizational pattern for policy formation is one of closeness between the institutional presidency and the department so that presidential purposes may be implemented efficiently.

Eisenhower was the classic president of consolidation for both domestic- and foreign-policy formation. The changes in programs that he proposed were incremental. Domestic-policy initiatives were drawn from the departments with the White House staff playing a facilitating role. The administrative feasibility of policy was a salient question at the presidential table, and the departments always had their say. Potential interdepartmental conflict was subdued by the president's efforts to foster cabinet collegiality. Cabinet officers were not turned loose on their own but were carefully socialized into a tightly integrated system in which Eisenhower aides were the conveners and coordinators. This was more apparent in domestic than foreign policy, where Eisenhower usually worked with his secretary of state alone. (Eisenhower, because of his unique experience, was his own secretary of defense.)

An effective presidency of consolidation is not one in which the departments are given free rein, but is instead an exercise in tightly held collegiality. There is a limited premium on new ideas in such a system, and considerable attention is given to asking what actually will work at the implementation stage. The dangers are that conventional wisdom will preclude fresh insights and that collegiality will induce conformity. Bureaucratic collusion may even limit the choices that are presented to the president. Thus, there is the added risk of failing to recognize emerging problems. Still, there also may be fewer overreactions to problems and less inclination to invent symbolic and superficial solutions that serve the president's political needs without meeting the nation's policy requirements.

The Nixon administration exhibited a great many impulses toward consolidation. The creation of the Domestic Council was designed to overcome the disorganized manner in which the Johnson White House staff had worked with the departments. Cabinet officers were to sit as members of the Domestic Council and work closely with a White House staff directed by John Ehrlichman, an assistant to the president. Most of the domestic-policy themes that emerged from this system were consolidating—they attempted to retain the purposes of the Great Society but in more efficient organizational form. However, Nixon's distrust of the civil servants in the departments led him to disdain his own cabinet officers as well and encouraged Ehrlichman to build a highly centralized system in the White House.

One study suggests that such suspicions were justified—the president and most civil servants were divided ideologically during the early Nixon administration.[65] In part, however, this was because too many Nixon appointees in the departments failed to learn how to work with civil servants and never overcame the mistrust that they themselves generated. Elliott Richardson at Health, Education, and Welfare and George Shultz at Labor, on the other hand, demonstrated that skillful administrators could win the support of civil servants for consolidating program adaptations.[66] After Ehrlichman left the White House in the spring of 1973, his successor, Melvin Laird, an experienced Washington hand, secured the passage of the Comprehensive Employment and Training Act, which embodied administration policy objectives of decentralization and simplification of the federal role in program implementation. Laird did this in full cooperation with the secretary of labor and with agency-level appointees in the department, who in turn worked closely with Congress. A subsequent study of the Nixon bureaucracy revealed that the beliefs of Nixon and the civil service converged over time. The president promoted a number of Republicans to high civil-service positions, and increasing numbers of senior bureaucrats began to identify with administration programs.[67]

The Nixon system of developing national security policy clearly was not what one would expect of a president of consolidation. It is a matter of historical judgment whether Nixon's bolder initiatives, particularly the overture to China, required the secretive, centralized methods used by the president and Henry Kissinger. The negotiations with North Vietnam for ending the war had to be closely held, but there is no obvious reason why they could not have been conducted by the State Department; the same is true of the real negotiations of the SALT treaty, which were carried out by Kissinger through a back channel. But this was not Nixon's personal style.

EVALUATION OF PRESIDENTIAL ORGANIZATION

Much criticism of presidents, by scholars and journalists, invokes absolute standards about how presidents should organize their administrations. Presidents who do not practice the prevailing conventional wisdom are chastised. Sometimes the standards are those of "establishments," such as the foreign-policy elites who support the secretary of state and deplore the rise of the assistant for national security to power. Or a criticism may be made for partisan purposes, such as the claim that Eisenhower was detached from his own government by his elaborate staff system. At other times the advantages and disadvantages of alternative organizational arrangements are debated in the sincere hope that one best system can be discovered. Some scholars argue, for example, that the presidency is underinstitutionalized for the needs of the president. Common criticisms include the lack of professionalism in the domestic-policy staff, the great strain on a small Council of Economic Advisers, weak links between domestic and international economic policy, inadequate attention to implementation questions in policy development, and amateurism and lack of institutional memory among presidential aides. These problems pose difficulties for all three types of presidencies.

Beyond this, however, we contend that presidents will organize their administrations according to their own purposes and not by external criteria. Presidents of preparation wish to distill new ideas and put them in programmatic form. Presidents of achievement want to translate ideas into law and settled policy. Presidents of consolidation seek to be effective in improving the organization of programs and government for policy implementation. The appropriate standard of judgment is to ask if each model of organization served the president's purpose.

NOTES

1. *Administration Management in the Government of the United States* (Washington, D.C.: Superintendent of Documents, 1937).
2. Richard E. Neustadt, "The Presidency and Legislation: Planning the President's Program," *The American Political Science Review*, 49, no. 4 (December 1955), pp. 980–1021.
3. Clark M. Clifford, Oral History Interview, The Harry S. Truman Library, Independence, Mo., March 16, 1972, pp. 349–50.
4. *Ibid.*, May 10, 1971, pp. 186–90.
5. *Ibid.*, p. 214.
6. Charles S. Murphy, Oral History Interview, The Harry S. Truman Library, Independence, Mo., July 25, 1969, p. 442.
7. Fred Greenstein, *The Hidden Hand Presidency, Eisenhower as Leader* (New York: Basic Books, 1982), pp. 138–49.
8. Lester M. Salamon, "The Presidency and Domestic Policy Formulation," in Hugh Heco and Lester M. Salamon, eds., *The Illusion of Presidential Government* (Boulder, Col.: Westview Press, 1981), p. 181.
9. Communication of Walter Heller to author, July 1980.
10. Elmer Staats, Oral History Interview, John Fitzgerald Kennedy Library, Boston, Mass., July 13, 1964, pp. 23–25. Staats, an experienced BOB official who worked closely with Sorensen, described his role:

    We had many meetings in which Sorensen would meet with key people in the Executive Office and the agencies concerned to hammer out issues involved in legislative programs. Everyone understood that he was doing this as a result of the President's request, with the President's knowledge and that 9 chances out of 10 whatever we came out with would be Presidential policy. Here around this small conference table would be Cabinet officers, Dave Bell [director of BOB] almost without exception, Walter Heller [CEA chairman], in most cases if the issue involved anything in the domestic area, Larry O'Brien or one of his staff [congressional liaison] and, of course, Ted Sorensen's own immediate staff [Feldman and White].

But the thing that needs to be understood about these meetings is that it was always clearly fixed as to who had the follow-up, who would prepare the next draft. Sorensen always kept notes. He would always summarize, go down through his notes before we were finished so that there could be no misunderstanding on conclusions or next steps. If so, he could raise the issue at that point.

But Sorensen did not overstep the staff role, as an additional comment by the same person makes clear:

I think in more cases than not if we talked to Sorensen on some matter we could predict what the President's thinking was likely to be, but Sorensen never attempted in any sense of the word to try to set himself up as a person who could speak for the President. . . . If there was any question he would say he would check with the President or say "Why don't you go check with the President?" . . . I don't recall that he ever attempted to fix his role as being the intermediary.

11. David Bell, Oral History Interview, John Fitzgerald Kennedy Library, Boston, Mass., July 11, 1964, p. 9.
12. Salamon, "Presidency and Domestic Policy Formulation," pp. 181–82.
13. Joseph A. Califano, Jr., *A Presidential Nation* (New York: Norton, 1975), p. 39.
14. Emmette S. Redford, "The Development of the Legislative Program" (January 1982), ch. 5 from a forthcoming volume on policy development in the Johnson administration. This book is one of several studies of the Johnson presidency at the Lyndon Baines Johnson School of Public Affairs, Austin, Texas.
15. Joseph A. Califano, Jr., Oral History Interview, Lyndon Baines Johnson Library, Austin, Texas, June 11, 1973, *passim*.
16. *Ibid.*, p. 25.
17. *Ibid.*, p. 35.
18. William D. Carey, "Presidential Staffing in the Sixties and Seventies," *Public Administration Review*, 29 (September–October 1969), pp. 450–58.
19. Larry Berman, *The Office of Management and Budget and the Presidency 1921–1979* (Princeton, N.J.: Princeton University Press, 1979), pp. 88–89.
20. For a description of the Ash Council plan, see U.S. Congress, House Committee on Government Affairs, *Hearings on Reorganization Plan No. 2 of 1970*, 91st Congress, 2d Session, 1 (April–May 1970), p. 11; and Memorandums to the President of the United States from the Advisory Council on Executive Organization, October 17, 1969.
21. Stephen J. Wayne, *The Legislative Presidency* (New York: Harper & Row, 1978), pp. 45–51.
22. Erwin C. Hargrove, interview with assistants to President Ford, Washington, D.C., October–November 1975.
23. *Ibid.*; Wayne, pp. 52–54, 122–28.
24. Interviews with the Carter White House staff, Project on the Carter Presidency, Miller Center of Public Affairs, University of Virginia, Charlottesville, Va., January 8–9, 1982.
25. Interviews with the Carter White House staff, January 29–30, 1982.
26. Lawrence E. Lynn, Jr., and David de F. Whitman, *The President as Policymaker, Jimmy Carter and Welfare Reform* (Philadelphia: Temple University Press, 1981), p. 192.
27. *Ibid.*
28. Lou Cannon and Lee Lessage, "Cabinet vs. White House Staff: Seeking a Workable Process," *The Washington Post* (May 27, 1981); Dick Kirschten, "Decision Making in the White House: How Well Does It Serve the President?" *The National Journal* (April 3, 1982), pp. 584–89.
29. Dick Kirschten, "Reagan's Cabinet Councils May Have Less Influence Than Meets the Eye," *The National Journal* (July 11, 1981), pp. 1242–47.
30. Stephen K. Bailey, *Congress Makes a Law* (New York: Vintage, 1964), pp. 17–18.
31. Leon Keyserling, Oral History Interview, Institute for Public Policy Studies, Vanderbilt University, Nashville, Tenn., October 14, 1977.

32. Arthur Burns, Oral History Interview, Institute for Public Policy Studies, Vanderbilt University, Nashville, Tenn., July 16, 1980.
33. Raymond Saulnier, Oral History Interview, Institute for Public Policy Studies, Vanderbilt University, Nashville, Tenn., March 11, 1977.
34. Walter Heller, Oral History Interview, Institute for Public Policy Studies, Vanderbilt University, Nashville, Tenn., December 14, 1977.
35. *Ibid*.
36. *Ibid*.
37. Gardner Ackley, Oral History Interview, Institute for Public Policy Studies, Vanderbilt University, Nashville, Tenn., February 3, 1978.
38. Paul McCracken, Oral History Interview, Institute for Public Policy Studies, Vanderbilt University, Nashville, Tenn., March 31, 1978.
39. *Ibid*. Woody Hayes was a long-time football coach at Ohio State.
40. Herbert Stein, Oral History Interview, Institute for Public Policy Studies, Vanderbilt University, Nashville, Tenn., April 27, 1978.
41. Roger B. Porter, *Presidential Decision Making, the Economic Policy Board* (New York: Cambridge University Press, 1980), *passim*.
42. Alan Greenspan, Oral History Interview, Institute for Public Policy Studies, Vanderbilt University, Nashville, Tenn., May 26, 1978.
43. Charles Schultze, Oral History Interview, Institute for Public Policy Studies, Vanderbilt University, Nashville, Tenn., July 6, 1982.
44. Steven R. Weisman, "Reaganomics and the President's Men," *The New York Times Magazine*, (October 24, 1982), p. 26.
45. Ben W. Heineman, Jr., and Curtis A. Hessler, *Memorandum for the President: A Strategic Approach to Domestic Affairs in the 1980s* (New York: Random House, 1980), pp. 252–66.
46. Anna Kasten Nelson, "National Security I: Inventing a Process (1945–1960)," in Hugh Heclo and Lester M. Salamon, eds., *The Illusion of Presidential Government* (Boulder, Col.: Westview Press, 1981), p. 231.
47. *Ibid*., p. 234.
48. *Ibid*., pp. 236–37.
49. *Ibid*., pp. 241–45.
50. *Ibid*., pp. 246–47.
51. *Ibid*., pp. 249–50.
52. *Ibid*., pp. 253–57.
53. I. M. Destler, "National Security Advice to U.S. Presidents: Some Lessons from Thirty Years," *World Politics*, 29, no. 2 (January 1977), pp. 156–57.
54. Nelson, "National Security," pp. 255–58.
55. Destler, "National Security Advice," p. 157.
56. *Ibid*., pp. 157–58.
57. I. M. Destler, *Presidents, Bureaucrats, and Foreign Policy* (Princeton, N.J.: Princeton University Press, 1972), pp. 149–50.
58. *Ibid*., p. 147.
59. *Ibid*., p. 148.
60. Henry Kissinger, *White House Years* (Boston, Mass.: Little, Brown, 1979), p. 30.
61. Jimmy Carter, *Keeping Faith, Memoirs of a President* (New York: Bantam, 1982), p. 53.
62. Hamilton Jordan, *Crisis, the Last Year of the Carter Presidency* (New York: Putnam's, 1982), p. 47.
63. I. M. Destler, "National Security II: The Rise of the Assistant," in Heclo and Salamon, *Illusion*, p. 273.
64. Lou Cannon, *Reagan* (New York: Putnam's, 1982), p. 273.
65. Joel D. Aberbach and Bert A. Rockman, "Changing Beliefs Within the Executive Branch: The Nixon Administration Bureaucracy," *American Political Science Review*, 70, no. 2 (June 1976), pp. 456–68.
66. Erwin C. Hargrove, interviews in the Department of Labor, 1973–1975; see

Lawrence E. Lynn, Jr., guest ed., "Special Issue on the HEW Mega-Proposal," *Policy Analysis*, 1, no. 2 (Spring 1975), for a description of Elliott Richardson's effectiveness as an administrative leader, pp. 232–73.

67. Richard L. Cole and David A. Caputo, "Presidential Control of the Senior Civil Service: Assessing the Strategies of the Nixon Years," *American Political Science Review*, 73, no. 2 (June 1979), pp. 408–12.

CHAPTER 7

Presidential Leadership of Congress

Presidential power is the product of a blend of the presidency's "genetic code" (the Constitution), its enduring cultural and more fluctuating political environment, and the leadership skills that individual presidents bring to the office. Nowhere is this blend better illustrated than in the presidency's relationship with Congress.

The president-Congress relationship contains some elements of stability. These "constants," which developed during the century and a half that preceded the inauguration of Franklin Roosevelt in 1933, were chronicled at length in Chapter 2. But much of the contemporary relationship between the two branches remains variable, including those aspects of it that are of greatest topical interest at any moment. The relationship varies over time, depending mostly on the public's disposition for achievement, consolidation, or preparation for another round of achievement. It also varies from policy to policy, in part according to biases inherent in the nation's Constitution and culture that either favor or impede presidential ascendancy; and from president to president, according to the nature and extent of each one's political skills. This is all very complex but, fortunately, not infinitely so. Sorting out the ways in which the constitutional, cultural, political, and skill elements in our model of presidential power affect the relationship between president and Congress is the task of this chapter.

CONSTITUTION

In a review of recent presidential scholarship, political scientists Joseph M. Bessette and Jeffrey Tulis note that their colleagues "tend not to attach much explanatory weight to the Constitution in their accounts of American politics—either because they believe that 190 years of social, economic, and technological change have rendered the original arrangements obsolete or because in their view constitutional forms never have much more than a tenuous relationship to practice."[1] Bessette and Tulis go on to argue, first, that this is a plausible contention and, second, that it is wrong. Careful consideration of the relationship between president and Congress demonstrates that they are correct on both counts.

Certainly the Constitution seems generally irrelevant. Articles I and II and Amendments Twelve, Twenty, and Twenty-five go on at great length about various aspects of the relationship, including impeachment, the Senate's role in ratifying treaties, the responsibility of the House to choose a president in the event of an electoral-college deadlock, and so on. Yet of the hundreds of words in the Constitution that treat the president-Congress relationship, only fifteen are devoted to the aspect of it that is now most prominent: legislative guidance by the president. And few would argue that "He shall . . . recommend to their Consideration such Measures as he shall judge necessary and expedient" tells very much about how that role is performed.

A true measure of the Constitution's influence on president and Congress, however, will show that it is both pervasive and great. It is pervasive to the point that one cannot usefully talk about other influences on the relationship—culture, politics, or skill—without talking about the Constitution as well. American political culture includes a variety of ideas about how the president and Congress are supposed to work with each other, but it is partly the Constitution's electoral arrangements through which these ideas are channeled into influence. Similarly, presidents need a host of political skills to lead Congress successfully, but the Constitution helps to determine what those skills are. This will become apparent in the remaining sections of this chapter.

The Constitution's influence is great as well as pervasive. The basic characteristics of the president's relationship with Congress in the modern era are exactly those that were established by the Constitution two centuries ago: in foreign policy, presidential primacy; in domestic affairs, the veto, the right of appointment and removal, and legislatively, the system of separated institutions sharing powers. These characteristics will be considered in turn.

Foreign Policy

As we saw in Chapter 2, although the language of those provisions of the Constitution that bear explicitly on foreign affairs is ambiguous on the issue of whether Congress or the president, if either, is in charge, the meaning is not and seldom has been. Presidential ascendancy flowed from the Constitutional Convention's decisions to make the executive, in striking contrast to the legislature, a unitary office chosen independently by a national constituency.

The first 150 years of American history under the Constitution bore this out: even as presidents struggled to invigorate the enumerated powers of their office in domestic policy, they usually were able to get their way when deciding how the United States ought to deal with other countries. Sometimes this came about through explicit congressional assent, as with the 674 of 786, or 85.8 percent, of presidentially submitted treaties that the Senate ratified through 1928.[2] But more often, presidents succeeded by *faits accomplis*—Washington's neutrality proclamation, Monroe's doctrine, and Wilson's Fourteen Points, all unilaterally proclaimed; Polk's secret negotiations for the annexation of Texas and his sending of troops into disputed territory, which provoked the war with

Mexico; the dispatch of American forces into foreign countries without congressional consultation by McKinley, Taft, Wilson, and Coolidge; uncontested presidential decisions from Washington's administration forward about which foreign governments to recognize; and so on. Indeed treaties themselves gave way to executive agreements based solely on presidential authority as the chief form of contract between American and foreign governments. Even before 1900 executive agreements not only had begun to overwhelm treaties in number, but often in importance as well. Then-Senator Walter Mondale noted in 1975 that while the Senate was ratifying treaties to preserve archaeological artifacts in Mexico, the president was making commitments to defend pro-American regimes in Southeast Asia through executive agreements.[3]

When criticized for their assertiveness, presidents invariably invoked the number and selection-based strengths of their constitutional office: energy, unity, secrecy, and dispatch. James Sundquist summarizes the standard (and highly persuasive) presidential litany of response:

- that American lives, property, and interests were at stake and quick decision was imperative;
- that the Congress was not in session to be consulted, or in any case the decision could not be subjected to the delays of congressional deliberation;
- that the moves had to be made, or negotiations conducted, in secret, and only the executive branch could maintain confidentiality;
- that only the president has the essential information;
- that effective intercourse with other nations requires the United States to speak with a single voice, which can only be the president's.[4]

Arguments such as these came to seem especially compelling in the post–World War II era. World War II itself was like other wars in that the president's temporary powers were vast. What made it different was what happened afterward. Instead of lapsing back into relative isolation from world political affairs, the United States entered into a "cold war" with the Soviet Union. Complicating matters further were new technologies of atomic weapons and intercontinental delivery systems that raised the specter of virtually instant total war. All this combined to make the executive's constitutional qualities seem more important even than in past conventional wars. Increased reliance not only on executive agreements instead of treaties but on secrecy in all diplomacy made the conduct of foreign policy a shared power with Congress in only the most nominal sense. The Republican Eightieth Congress of 1947–1949, angrily partisan on domestic political issues, readily assented to such far-reaching Truman administration initiatives in foreign policy as the Marshall Plan, the North Atlantic Alliance, and Point Four. Congress supported the American role in the Korean War, which it never had been asked to declare, with annual military appropriations, as it did the war in Vietnam in the 1960s and early 1970s. In the intervening years it wrote virtual blank checks in advance support of whatever actions Presidents Eisenhower and Kennedy might decide to take in the Middle East, Berlin, Cuba, and elsewhere.

Much has been made in the post-Vietnam era of Congress's supposed resurgence in foreign-policy making. But although the last decade or so has been an exceptional period of congressional assertiveness, the exception has been of a kind that demonstrates the rule of presidential dominance. When Congress has tried to seize the reins, it generally has done so in ways that are either negative (short-term prohibitions on trade or military assistance to the Soviet Union, Vietnam, Turkey, and a few other countries) or ineffective, as with the War Powers Resolution of 1973. The latter is an especially telling example because it was so ambitious in purpose.

The War Powers Resolution recognizes the power of the president to single-handedly commit American troops to combat (itself no small concession), but demands that Congress be consulted prior to such a decision and that afterward it approve the action formally within sixty days, lest it be terminated. Yet in only one of the seven cases that arose under the act through the start of 1984 (Reagan's commitment of marines to Lebanon) did presidents consult with Congress: at most, they generally notified a few members of what they intended to do. And although none of these six instances (four in Southeast Asia in 1975, the Iranian hostage rescue mission in 1980, and the 1983 invasion of Grenada) tested the sixty-day limit, the likely outcome of most such events is that forecast by Senator Frank Church in 1977: "I cannot imagine a situation in which the President would take us into a foreign war of major proportions under circumstances that would not cause both the public and the Congress to rally around the flag, at least for 60 days."[5]

Part of the explanation for Congress's weakness in foreign policy making is inherent in its character as an institution: large, diverse, unwieldy, and slow. Part, too, can be traced to public expectations of the institution: constituents want their representatives and senators to concern themselves more with local than national interests, which leaves out most foreign policies.[6] Not surprisingly, perhaps, both Senate Foreign Relations Committee Chairman J. William Fulbright and his successor, Senator Church, were defeated in reelection bids by opponents who charged that they cared more about world politics than about their constituents.

Still, although Congress's institutional nature is not likely to change, the political environment may. Historically, Congress has been most vigorous on the minority of foreign-policy issues that have a clear domestic-politics coloration: the legislative requirement that at least half of foreign-aid cargo be carried in American ships, support for nations such as Israel and Greece that have vocal and well-organized ethnic lobbies in this country, and the like. (As one representative put it, "There are more Greek restaurants in my district than there are Turkish baths.") The growing internationalization of the economy, evidenced most prominently by American competition with foreign auto makers, steel manufacturers, and others for the domestic market, may make "intermestic" issues that blur traditional foreign- and domestic-policy boundaries so prominent that members of Congress will have to expand their concern for international politics just to fulfill their function of representing local interests.

The Veto

The president's constitutional right to veto a bill or joint resolution passed by Congress — either by returning it to the house in which it originated within ten days, Sundays excepted, of its passage (a "regular" veto) or, if Congress has adjourned in that period, exercising a "pocket" veto by simply not signing it—is an oft-underestimated power. Richard Neustadt, for example, characterizes it as a strategy of desperation:

> The less his demonstrated power at the Capitol, the more he is confined, downtown, to realms where sheer command proves workable. The weaker his apparent popular support, the more his cause in Congress may depend on negatives at his disposal, like the veto.[7]

In truth the veto is a strong power of the presidency. Pocket vetoes, which made up 42.3 percent of all vetoes cast through 1981, are unchallengeable, and regular vetoes can be overridden only by a two-thirds vote of each house of Congress. (This has happened only 6.8 percent of the time.)[8] More important, the veto is a central presidential power. It was thought of as such at the start: the framers included the veto in all their drafts of the Constitution, even the Virginia Plan, which enumerated no other specific powers. And it generally remains central to at least two kinds of modern presidents: first, those who are more conservative than Congress and thus less interested in seeing new programs begun or old ones expanded by legislation; and second, those who, regardless of ideology, are likely to be in conflict with Congress because they are of a different political party.[9]

Until recently, it was thought unlikely that either of these two conditions would obtain very often, which is why it was easy to underestimate the veto as an element of presidential power. Straight-ticket voting by citizens seemed a near-guarantee of interbranch party control, and for a long time it was. From 1900 to 1948 the average share of House districts that were carried by a presidential candidate of one party and a congressional candidate of another was only 12.0 percent per election.[10] The consequence for presidents from William McKinley through Harry Truman was that the president's party controlled both houses of Congress 84.6 percent of the time (forty years out of forty-eight), and at least one house 92.3 percent of the time (all but four years).[11] In addition the contrasting ideological biases of large, liberal, industrial-state–oriented presidential politics and a seniority system in Congress that tended to favor conservatives of both parties seemed to assure that presidents as a rule would be more liberal than Congress.[12]

In recent years, however, the conservative influence of the seniority system has been undermined, and, conversely, presidential campaigning has been weighted as much to conservative big states in the expanding sunbelt as to more liberal ones in the industrial Northeast. Straight-ticket voting has declined: from 1952 to 1980 the average share of divided districts has been 30.8 percent. During the presidencies of Eisenhower, Kennedy, Johnson, Nixon, Ford, Carter, and Reagan (1953–1985) both houses of Congress were controlled by the president's party only 43.8 percent of the time (56.3 percent if one adds the years when party control of the House and Senate was divided).[13] The norm in the post-1953 period has been a Republican president and a Democratic Congress, with the former decidedly more conservative than the latter. And, as one can

Table 7.1 Presidential Vetoes of Public Bills, 1953–1983

	Years	Vetoes	Vetoes/Year
Republican presidents/Democratic Congresses	14.0	162	11.6
1955–1961: Eisenhower/84th, 85th, 86th Congresses	6.0	61	10.2
1969–1974: Nixon/91st, 92d, 93d Congresses	5.6	40	7.1
1974–1977: Ford/93d, 94th Congresses	2.4	61	25.4
Republican presidents/Republican Congresses	2.0	18	9.0
1953–1955: Eisenhower/83d Congress	2.0	18	9.0
Republican presidents/divided Congress	2.0	15	7.5
1981–1983: Reagan/97th Congress	2.0	15	7.5
Democratic presidents/Democratic Congresses	12.0	52	4.3
1961–1963: Kennedy/87th, 88th Congresses	2.8	9	3.2
1963–1969: Johnson/89th, 90th, 91st Congresses	5.2	14	2.7
1977–1981: Carter/95th, 96th Congresses	4.0	29	7.3

Sources: Presidential Vetoes, 1789.1976 (Washington: Government Printing Office, 1978); various issues of *CQ Weekly Report* (1977–83).

see in Table 7.1, the tendency of conservative Republican presidents such as these to veto public bills is pronounced. They use the veto almost three times as often against Democratic Congresses as Democratic presidents and about twice as often even when the Republicans control one or both houses of Congress.

The presidency of Gerald Ford illustrates the veto's potential as a source of presidential power. Ford's political position was unusual. He was the nation's first wholly unelected president: he came to the vice presidency by appointment after Spiro Agnew resigned in October 1973, and to the presidency by succession when Nixon left ten months later. He served at a time when presidential power was in great disfavor and Democrats controlled Congress by almost a 2-to-1 margin. Yet Ford managed to keep a fair amount of control in his relationship with Congress by wielding the veto freely. Eighty percent of his sixty-one vetoes of public bills were sustained, and the twelve overrides were more than outnumbered by the twenty to thirty measures that William Timmons, Ford's chief congressional liaison, estimates were "cleaned up sufficiently" by Congress for Ford to sign them after threatening to veto.[14]

This "clean-up" function of veto threats may be more useful to presidents than the veto itself. In December 1982, for example, both the House and the Senate passed appropriations bills containing jobs programs that President Reagan vigorously opposed. The programs differed in size, which meant a conference committee had to compromise the differences. The "compromise," however, turned out to be no jobs programs at all. As Republican Congressman

Silvio Conte put the matter to fellow conference committee member Jamie Whitten, a Democratic congressman, "Why make us go through this? We'll just get a veto and be right back here."[15]

The Appointment Power

The clause in Article II, Section 2, of the Constitution that deals with appointments is exercised some 50,000 to 70,000 times per year: "He shall nominate and by and with the advice and consent of the Senate, shall appoint Ambassadors, other public Ministers and Consuls, Judges of the Supreme Court, and all other officers of the United States, whose appointments are not herein otherwise provided for, and which shall be established by law." As a measure of presidential power, this figure is both less and more impressive than it may seem. More than 90 percent of a president's nominations are technical appointments — military officers, foreign-service officers, Public Health Service officials, and others. Of the remaining 10 percent, some, notably local United States attorneys and federal district court judges, are covered by the tradition of "senatorial courtesy." If a senator from the president's party objects to a presidential nominee for a federal office in his state, the Senate as a body ordinarily will refuse to confirm the nomination. What this often means in practice is that individual senators share with presidents the privilege of filling these offices as patronage positions.

That still leaves two very important arenas for appointment in which the Senate almost always defers to the president's leadership: Supreme Court and Courts of Appeals appointments (though particularly influential senators of the president's party sometimes have a say in the latter); and high-level positions in the executive branch. Instances in which the Senate has refused approval to presidential nominations to the top two levels of the three-tier federal court system can be found, but they are rare. Since 1945 only three Supreme Court nominations of twenty-two went unconfirmed (one each in the politically charged years of 1968, 1969, and 1970) and none of the more than two hundred Court of Appeals selections. Senate deference is even greater when presidents are seeking to fill the several hundred executive-branch positions in the Executive Office of the President, the departments and independent agencies, and the regulatory commissions. The importance of the executive appointments is evidenced in this assessment by Hugh Heclo: "In affecting the everyday work of the government, these hundreds of personnel selections add up to a cumulative act of choice that may be at least as important as the electorate's single act of choice for president every four years."[16]

To be sure, a few rejections can go a long way. G. Calvin Mackenzie, who found only thirty-nine instances of Senate rejections — scarcely more than two per year — in the period 1961–1977, nonetheless concluded: "The deterring power of defeated nominations is far more salient and pervasive than the numbers would indicate" because "implicitly a rejection says, 'These are our standards; keep them in mind in making future nominations.'"[17] Most of the Senate's influence over appointments is exerted in even more subtle ways. As many as 10 percent of its committee and subcommittee meetings are confirmation hearings. These almost always are used by senators to alert presidential nominees to their policy concerns, and sometimes to secure specific promises. Walter Hickel, whom Nixon nominated as secretary of interior but who as governor of Alaska had complained about Interior Department restrictions on Alaskan land use, was forced to pledge that he would not lift these restrictions. In a more spectacular case, Attorney General-designate Elliot Richardson not only pledged to the Senate the independence of the Watergate special prosecutor as a condition of his appointment in 1973, but resigned in the famed "Saturday Night Massacre" when Nixon ordered him to violate that pledge several months later.

Realistically, however, the greatest limits to the presidency's powers of appointment are self-imposed, especially when it comes to executive appointments. Most presidents do not use their powers to maximum effectiveness, which would mean getting people who are both competent to run their agencies and loyal to the president so that they will run them in pursuit of his policies. In the rush of the transition from election to inauguration that precedes their first terms, basking in the glow of general good will that marks the honeymoon period, presidents generally stress the competence criterion and assume that loyalty will not be a problem. Eventually they find that many of their appointees (who, once in office, spend almost all of their time immersed in the life of their agencies) have adopted a bureaucratic perspective, coming to see their role as their agency's advocate with the president, not the other way around. "We only see them at the annual White House Christmas party," said Nixon aide John Ehrlichman. "They go off and marry the natives."[18] Frustrated, presidents tend to "clean house" around the middle of their terms for the sake of obtaining more loyal appointees. (The average tenure of both secretaries and assistant secretaries is just over two years.)[19] The usual consequence is that they then get people who, although dedicated to the president's interests, are not talented or experienced enough to do much to advance them.

Nonetheless, the presidency's constitutional power of appointment is potentially great for presidents who use it carefully. The Reagan administration, for example, seemed to learn from the common errors of its predecessors in staffing the executive branch. It took a great deal of time to weigh appointment possibilities in its first year, leaving "acting" appointees from the Carter administration or the career civil service in positions for several months. In the long run this meant that Reagan got generally competent people into office who shared his goals. And the short-run costs were not great: acting holdovers seem to have done their best to show the new administration just how loyal they could be.

Separated Institutions Sharing Powers

As a rule, presidents can conduct foreign policy, thwart legislative assertiveness, and fill most nonelective, high-level government positions with great leeway. But when it comes to directing the role of the federal government in American society, there is hardly a presidentially desired activity that can be undertaken without the consent of Congress, which shares this power with the executive in practice as well as in theory.

As we saw in Chapter 2, no constitutionally explicit power of the presidency was slower to develop than its share of the legislative power. Lincoln showed that exceptional times allowed for exceptional behavior. But not until the turn of this century, with its simultaneous rise in both popular demands for action by the federal government and admiration for executive leadership of all kinds, was the stage set for a president of unusual political skill to break precedent and, without need of invoking crisis, recommend legislation to Congress as a matter of course. Theodore Roosevelt and Wilson played that role so successfully that their less skillful and more Whiggish successors of the 1920s and early 1930s found that they now had to play it to some extent whether they wanted to or not.

The chief characteristic of the modern era is the meaning that "share" has taken on in the shared legislative power relationship. Again and again since 1932 Congress has shifted to the presidency most of the obligation to initiate: that is the executive share.[20] Congress has reserved the power to modify or reject: realistically, that is most of its share. The axiom "president proposes, Congress disposes" is hardly the whole truth, but it has become a large part of it.

This began to be true with the Great Depression. The public's political demands had changed quite a bit since the depression year of 1820: in 1932 it gave President Hoover not a Monroe-style near-unanimous reelection victory, but a landslide defeat. Congress, reflecting public opinion, in turn gave Franklin Roosevelt a virtual blank check to deal with the depression as he saw fit. In the fabled first hundred days, it passed more than a dozen major pieces of Roosevelt-spawned legislation, often virtually without debate and sometimes before the bills actually were written. As the decade wore on, Congress authorized a number of actions that allowed the presidency to institutionalize its role as policy initiator. The Bureau of the Budget was transferred from the Treasury Department to a newly created Executive Office of the President and was empowered to screen all departmental proposals for legislation before Congress could see them. The president was authorized to hire a personal political staff, largely for the purpose of developing and selling legislation. He also was given general, if limited, authority to reorganize the executive branch.

In succeeding administrations, both these trends — the explicit assignment of initiating responsibility to the president and the development of support institutions within the White House — continued. The Employment Act of 1946 charged the president (with the aid of a new Council of Economic Advisers) to monitor the economy and recommend corrective legislation in times of economic distress. Similar congressional calls for presidential initiative in domestic and economic policy were included in the Manpower Development and Training Act of 1962, the Housing and Urban Development Act of 1968, and the National Environmental Policy Act of 1969, among others. The theory was that the complexity of new-style policies required more planning and that the hierarchical structure and ready access to abundant information of the executive made it better suited to this task. Remarkably, in 1971, when Congress wanted to express its deep dissatisfaction with President Nixon's economic policies, it did so by passing a law that forced on him the power to impose at his discretion wage and price controls on the entire economy. Meanwhile, Presidents Truman, Eisenhower, and Kennedy were developing and expanding a specialized White House staff for legislative liaison; and Nixon won authorization to create a Domestic Council and expand the national security adviser's staff for policy development within the White House. These innovations survived their creators and became part of the institutional presidency.

Much of the explanation for this shifting of initiating responsibility to the presidency can be found in the mix of constitutional, environmental, and personal factors in Congress. Congress, like the presidency, operates in a post-1932 cultural and political setting in which demands for action by the federal government have become great. To take the lead consistently in meeting such demands through policy innovation requires an institutional capacity to speak with one voice. But Congress is by constitutional nature a multimember, bicameral branch that contains many voices, all of them independent. In theory its members could subordinate their individual wills to a party leader or caucus, but, as later will become clear, to do so would violate the expectations of the voters that selected them and thus jeopardize their hopes of winning reelection. Congress has handed over much of the responsibility to initiate to the presidency because to do so has suited its members' needs.

But responsibility, even when coupled with support institutions such as the Executive Office, does not always equal power. Indeed, the very characteristics of Congress that have caused it to insist that the president lead also make it less than inevitable that he will be followed. Congress's internal fragmentation of power provides many roadblocks to action: one subcommittee in one house may be all it takes to thwart presidential leadership on an issue. And the unwillingness of members to subordinate their wills to each other often applies to the president as well.

Conclusion

Sweeping generalizations about the presidency's strength or weakness in relation to Congress are at best incomplete. The Constitution's direct influence on presidential leadership of Congress is great and pervasive, but hardly unidirectional. As Figure 7.1 indicates, the Constitution extends great latitude to some presidents at certain stages of the domestic-policy cycle (see Chapter 3), and to all presidents when they are exercising certain kinds of powers. A condition of relatively low presidential dependence exists when the president's policy agenda does not require a high degree of programmatic support from Congress, as shown in the bottom half of the figure. The dependence on Congress of a would-be president of consolidation is relatively low regardless of his support there because his concerns are primarily with moderating the growth of the domestic federal sector. (This is true even when he is out of touch with the public mood, like Taft.) Similarly, almost all presidents have a comparatively free rein when dealing with most foreign-policy issues, staffing the upper levels of the executive and judicial branches, and vetoing legislation.

Politics as well as the Constitution can minimize presidential dependence. When elections produce a large majority for the president in Congress, his dependence on it will be relatively low even if he wishes to propose an ambitious legislative agenda. Such is the case in presidencies of achievement, which occupy the upper left-hand quadrant, if only for relatively brief periods

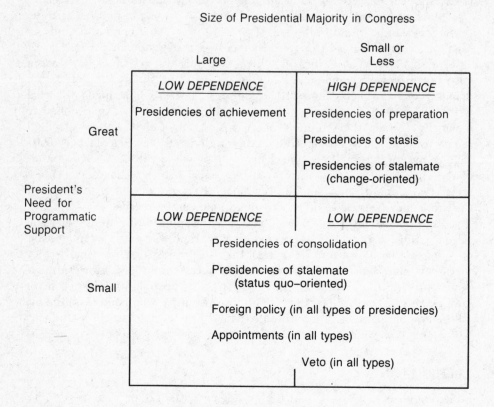

Size of Presidential Majority in Congress

	Large	Small or Less
Great	*LOW DEPENDENCE* Presidencies of achievement	*HIGH DEPENDENCE* Presidencies of preparation Presidencies of stasis Presidencies of stalemate (change-oriented)
Small	*LOW DEPENDENCE* Presidencies of consolidation Presidencies of stalemate (status quo–oriented) Foreign policy (in all types of presidencies) Appointments (in all types) Veto (in all types)	*LOW DEPENDENCE*

President's Need for Programmatic Support

Figure 7.1   Presidential Dependence on Congress

of the term. What we refer to in the figure as the "presidential majority in Congress" may be greater or less than his party's majority. In the Ninety-seventh Congress, for example, Reagan's majority included several dozen "Boll Weevil" Democrats as well as nearly all Republicans. In general, House Democrats have supported Republican presidents on foreign-policy issues more reliably than have House Republicans.[21]

To be sure, the three low-dependence quadrants in Figure 7.1 represent tendencies, not rigid laws or categories. As we saw in Chapter 3, presidents of consolidation are not spared all concern with legislation: if nothing else, Congress must approve their budgets and major reorganization efforts, such as those that dominated Nixon's consolidating agenda. This chapter has shown that congressional intervention in foreign policy and the appointment process and congressional willingness to override presidential vetoes, although not the rule, are nonetheless not infrequent exceptions. Later in the chapter, the need

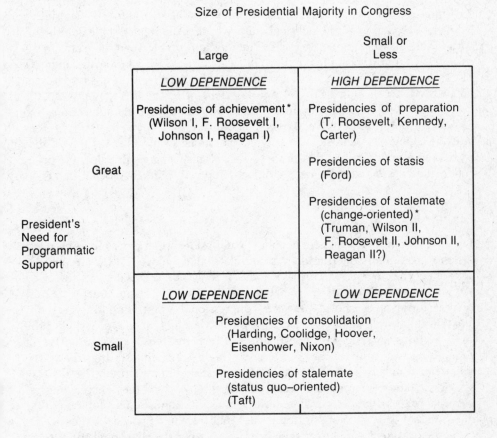

Size of Presidential Majority in Congress

		Large	Small or Less
President's Need for Programmatic Support	Great	*LOW DEPENDENCE* **Presidencies of achievement*** (Wilson I, F. Roosevelt I, Johnson I, Reagan I)	*HIGH DEPENDENCE* Presidencies of preparation (T. Roosevelt, Kennedy, Carter) Presidencies of stasis (Ford) Presidencies of stalemate (change-oriented)* (Truman, Wilson II, F. Roosevelt II, Johnson II, Reagan II?)
	Small	*LOW DEPENDENCE* Presidencies of consolidation (Harding, Coolidge, Hoover, Eisenhower, Nixon) Presidencies of stalemate (status quo–oriented) (Taft)	*LOW DEPENDENCE*

*The Roman numeral refers to the first or second part of the president's term.

Figure 7.2   Twentieth-Century Presidents' Dependence on Congress, Domestic Policy

for even presidents of achievement to work skillfully and resolutely for congressional support will become apparent.

In sum, all presidents some of the time find themselves somewhere in the upper right-hand quadrant of Figure 7.1, needing programmatic support from Congress but lacking the large majority there that would make such support relatively easy to come by. So do most presidents much of the time when it comes to domestic policy. The "great need–small or less majority" category includes presidents of preparation, presidents of stasis, and change-oriented presidents of stalemate — that is, those who seek major legislative achievements at a time when the public is seeking consolidation. Included in this last category are presidents of achievement during the latter parts of their terms, among others. Omitting foreign policy, appointment, and veto powers, Figure 7.2 places twentieth-century presidents into the classifications of Figure 7.1.

CULTURE

The influence of two cultures is felt in presidential efforts to give legislative leadership to Congress: the political culture of the American people and the institutional culture of Congress itself. The relationship between these cultures is complex. In many ways the popular political culture is the source of Congress's institutional culture, which is not surprising: Congress is, after all, a representative body. But a powerful "refracting" element in the linkage between the people and their Congress — namely, the constitutional system of elections — so distorts the connection that congressional culture turns out to be very different in its behavioral consequences from what the public would like. Because of that refraction, a voting public that on the whole wants Congress to follow the president's lead ends up encouraging legislators to do very different sorts of things.

Popular Political Culture

The proposition that, particular policy issues aside, Americans generally want Congress to support the president is not self-evident; indeed, it flies in the face of much of the current scholarly wisdom. Hazel Erskine, for example, reviewed a wide variety of poll data from the period 1936–1973 and concluded that "whenever given a choice between congressional vs. presidential decision-making, the people tend to trust Congress over the chief executive. Whether the issue pertains to specific domestic or military matters, or to authority in general, seems immaterial."[22] Donald Devine agreed, stating that "the American people believe . . . that the Congress should be supreme" and citing as evidence the 61 percent to 17 percent margin by which they chose Congress in response to a 1958 Survey Research Center question: "Some people say that the president is in the best position to see what the country needs. Other people think the president may have good ideas about what the country needs but it is up to Congress to decide what ought to be done. How do you feel about it?"[23] A 1979 Gallup poll question that asked whether Congress or the president "ought to have major responsibility" in three policy areas found Congress preferred for energy and the economy and the president only for foreign policy.[24]

The near–half century of data such as these that scholars have accumulated certainly supports the idea that Americans are "philosophical congressionalists." But all this means is that the public tends to side with Congress against the president when abstract questions of a theoretical nature are put to them by pollsters. (It is hard to imagine that such questions come up very often in ordinary discussion.)[25] When one looks at evidence about political attitudes and emotions that bear more directly on political behavior, the balance shifts.

One finds, first, that Americans are "operational presidentialists." Whatever they may say about proper institutional roles in theory, the presidents they like are the ones who take the lead, and the Congresses they like are the ones that follow. Stephen Wayne provides evidence for the first half of this proposition in his report on a 1979 survey that asked people what qualities they liked best about their favorite president. "Strong" led the list by far; "forceful," "ability to get things done," and "decisive" ranked third, fifth, and seventh, respectively.[26] As for Congress, the only years in which a majority of respondents have rated its performance as either "excellent" or "pretty good" in two decades of Harris surveys were 1964 and 1965.[27] Not coincidentally, those were the two years in which Congress was most responsive to presidential leadership.

Americans also can be said to be "emotional presidentialists," propresidency at the level of feelings. The evidence is "soft" but compelling. For a brief time, at least, every president enjoys the warm public feelings that characterize the honeymoon period; Congress does not. The mass grief that presidential deaths evoke bespeaks deep layers of emotion that have no equivalent in popular feelings about Congress. America's political heroes from the past are mostly presidents;[28] Congress (the only "distinctly native American criminal class," in Mark Twain's gibe) serves in political folklore as the butt of jokes. When candidates run for president, they promise to be like the best of their predecessors. Congressional aspirants, however, commonly attack Congress and promise not to be typical of its members. Or as Richard Fenno puts it, "Members run *for* Congress by running *against* Congress."[29]

Constitutional Refraction

Physicists define refraction as the change in direction of a ray of light as it passes through some distorting medium. In similar fashion the constitutional system of congressional elections and apportionment distorts the translation into influence of the public's widely felt desires concerning Congress and, in particular, its relationship with the presidency.

As a general rule, the public wants the president to lead and Congress to follow. Its basic channel for expressing these wants is the electoral process, through which it chooses the officials who constitute the presidency and Congress. But in the case of Congress, that channel is severely limited by the constitutional system of geographical apportionment — by state in the Senate and by district in the House. Voters in, say, Nashville may have a low regard for how Congress is performing, but their leverage on the institution is, by constitutional design, insignificant. In a given biennial election they will be able to influence the selection of 1 representative of 435 and, in most but not all election years, 1 senator of 100. Such a system provides little incentive for voters to transform a congressional election into a referendum on Congress.

Not surprisingly, the use to which most voters do put congressional elections is as a device for assessing how well their own legislators are doing at advancing local interests. In a 1977 survey conducted for the House Commission on Administrative Review, Harris found that when asked if "you think your congressman should be primarily concerned with looking after the needs and interests of his own district or . . . of the nation as a whole?" people chose "own district" by a margin of 57 percent to 34 percent. Asked "What kinds of jobs, duties, or functions do you expect a good congressman to perform?" they mentioned the following more frequently than any others:

- Work to solve problems in his district, help people, needs of our area
- To represent the people of his district, vote according to the wishes of his district

- Keep in touch; contact with people; visit district; hold meetings; know constituents
- Find out what people think, need, want; send out polls, questionnaires[30]

The relevance of such attitudes to voting was demonstrated in a 1978 CBS-*New York Times* Election Day poll that asked which of three factors — "what you think he can do for this community," "his stand on national issues," or "you respect him as a person" — had influenced voters most in House elections. Forty-seven percent said "community," 36 percent "national," and 17 percent "respect."[31]

Just how members of Congress respond to these desires awaits discussion below, but clearly they respond successfully. In a series of polls taken between 1978 and 1982, Harris found that the same public that gave Congress an average approval rating of 29 percent approved their own legislator's performance by 52 percent.[32] In actual elections, when they are comparing their representative or senator to a flesh-and-blood opponent rather than to some ideal standard, voters have been even more generous. From 1946 to 1982 they returned to office 90.6 percent of all representatives who offered themselves for re-election, 68.1 percent of them by a vote of 60 percent or more. (Even in the worst year for incumbents, 1948, 79.2 percent were reelected.) The share of senators seeking reelection who were successful has been more variable, ranging as high as 96.6 percent in 1960 and as low as 55.2 percent in 1980 (then back up to 93.3 percent in 1982). But the average senatorial success rate in this period has been 78.8 percent.[33]

Thus, the American voting public, which generally disapproves of Congress because it does not follow the president's lead, keeps sending back to Washington the very individuals who collectively provoke this disapproval. Given the choices offered to voters, this is reasonable behavior on their part. But the refraction of their desires that is caused by the constitutional system of elections results in an undesired, even perverse, effect on presidential leadership of Congress. For although most presidents legitimately can go to Congress with the claim that they alone have been elected by the entire nation and that the public expects them to lead and Congress to follow, members of Congress who outran the president in their states and districts can reply with equal certainty that their constituents expect them to look out after local interests and that, furthermore, those same constituents gave them a stronger mandate in the last election than they gave to the president. Evidently some do reply that way: the more poorly a president runs in a district, the less support he is likely to receive from that district's representative.[34] And, as Table 7.2 demonstrates, anywhere from 60.3 to 93.8 percent of the representatives who served in the Congresses that met after the 1972, 1976, and 1980 elections got a higher share of the vote in their districts than the president. Only after the 1972 election could less than a majority of newly elected senators have made that claim; after 1976 and 1980, 97.0 percent and 72.2 percent, respectively, could. Available data suggest that similar results probably have obtained since at least 1960.[35]

In sum, voters seem to want Congress to follow the president's lead for the most part. But with their individual points of leverage over Congress as an in-

Table 7.2 Presidential Vote in Congressional Districts and States, 1972–1980

	1972		1976		1980	
	Number	Percentage	Number	Percentage	Number	Percentage
House of Representatives						
Districts in which the winning presidential candidate's percentage of the vote exceeded the winning congressional candidate's percentage of the vote	171	39.3	27	6.2	66	15.2
Districts in which the winning congressional candidate's percentage of the vote exceeded the winning presidential candidate's percentage of the vote	264	60.7	408	93.8	369	84.8
Total	435	100.0	435	100.0	435	100.0
Senate						
States in which the winning presidential candidate's percentage of the vote exceeded the winning senatorial candidate's percentage of the vote	24	72.7	1	3.0	10	27.8
States in which the winning senatorial candidate's percentage of the vote exceeded the winning presidential candidate's percentage of the vote	9	27.3	32	97.0	26	72.2
Total	33	100.0	33	100.0	36	100.0

stitution constitutionally limited in a typical election year to one-four hundred thirty-fifth of the House and two-thirds of 1 percent of the Senate, they naturally do not use their votes just to promote that purpose. Instead, they assess congressional candidates in large part according to how well they think local interests will be served. In most cases their judgments are overwhelmingly supportive of incumbents.

Thus, Congress, a national policy-making institution whose cooperation a programmatically minded president must have, is in truth a collection of locally oriented politicians whose elections empower them primarily for purposes other than national policy making. One can make too much of this: as we will see, members of Congress are quite sensitive to constituency opinion on policy issues. But it remains no less the case that because of constitutional refraction, a president must deal with a Congress whose perspective on matters of shared responsibility is structurally different from his own.

The Institutional Culture of Congress

That the overwhelming majority of Congressional incumbents earn reelection when they seek it is an important consequence of constitutional refraction. That the overwhelming majority seek reelection in the first place is equally important. The strong desire for reelection on the part of representatives and senators powerfully affects their behavior in office in ways that, aggregated at the institutional level, help to create a culture of Congress that contributes to the relationship between it and the presidency.

The importance of reelection to members of Congress seems clear enough: from 1946 to 1982 an average of 91.6 percent of all representatives sought reelection, as did 83.7 percent of all senators.[36] Their motives doubtless have been mixed: some have been driven by a personal desire for "status, excitement, and power," others by more altruistic goals such as "good public policy."[37] But as Fenno, among others, has pointed out, whether animated by the urge to do well for themselves or to do good for others, "For most members of Congress most of the time, [the] electoral goal is primary. It is the prerequisite for a congressional career and, hence, for the pursuit of other member goals." And, Fenno found in his own research, the electoral goal is as fretful to incumbents as it is important: even members of Congress with long histories of landslide victories "see electoral uncertainty where outsiders would fail to unearth a single objective indicator of it."[38]

Not surprisingly, the combination of strong ambition and obsessive worry affects how legislators behave in office. Most channel their energy and resources into activities that translate readily into votes. Many such activities are nonlegislative, primarily "pork barreling" and casework.[39] Pork barreling means getting federal money into their home states and districts, whether for traditional rivers and harbors projects, highway construction, and defense contracts, or for new-style grants for law enforcement, mass transit, sewage treatment, and a whole host of health, education, and social services. Casework involves handling particular constituents' complaints about their personal experiences with the federal bureaucracy. (David Stockman, when he was a freshman representative from Michigan, said he learned quickly that the people he helped through personal interventions in the bureaucracy "will probably vote for me forever, regardless of my position on the B-1 bomber or the cruise missile.") David Mayhew adds "advertising" to the list of leading congressional activities: newsletters or questionnaires mailed home, personal visits, and similar efforts to "disseminate one's name among constituents in such a fashion as to create a favorable image but in messages having little or no issue content."[40] Any number of data could be marshaled to illustrate the increasing resort to all these activities: the near-tripling in the size of home-based House and Senate staffs from 1972 to 1981; the half-billion and more pieces of franked mail sent annually from legislators to citizens, which always is substantially higher in election years; the average thirty-five annual visits home by representatives (not counting recesses); and so on.[41]

Reelection-oriented legislative activity comes in two primary forms. First, members introduce legislation pleasing to their voters on any and all subjects: in Congresses from the Eightieth (1947–1949) to the Ninety-sixth (1979–1981), the average representative introduced 34.1 bills and resolutions and the average senator 41.7 (not counting the numerous cosponsorships of bills already introduced by others).[42] This takes little effort but enables them both to gain publicity in local media and to answer any constituent's inquiry about policy or legislation with "I introduced (or cosponsored) a bill on that very subject." At the same time, it commits them to none of the difficult, time-consuming" and largely invisible activities needed to get legislation over the hurdles of subcommittee, committee, and floor passage in each house.

Certain areas of legislative concern — namely, those that are of particular interest to one's constituency — require more than "position taking," however. A legislator from a farm constituency can be certain that his effectiveness, not just his rhetoric, on agricultural issues will be monitored closely by national interest groups and by opinion leaders at home. This requires, first, a suitable committee assignment, for it is as true today as when Woodrow Wilson wrote it a century ago that "Congress in session is Congress on public exhibition, whilst Congress in its committee-rooms is Congress at work."[43] In most cases a desirable assignment can be obtained from party leaders anxious to help their copartisans. Fenno found that 81 percent of the House members he interviewed served on committees they had sought to be on.[44] This explains why the Agriculture committees in both houses are dominated by farm-state members, the House Interior and Senate Environmental and Public Works committees by westerners, the House Merchant Marine and Fisheries committee by coastal-state representatives, the committees in each house that deal with education, labor, urban affairs, and banking by urbanites, and so on.[45] Once on these committees, members may enter into mutually beneficial exchange relationships with the interest groups and executive agencies in their policy areas that enable all three parties in each "triple alliance," or subgovernment, to maximize their influence. With interest groups, legislators exchange support of programs the groups favor for campaign contributions and other electoral benefits; from agencies, they receive special consideration for their constituents and influence over the distribution of patronage and contracts in return for generous appropriations and loose statutory reins.

Constitutionally, the primary task of Congress is to legislate in the national interest. The institutional culture of Congress, which reflects the cumulative (and nonconflicting) reelection ambitions of its members, discourages the fulfillment of this task. Legislation is not the major activity of Congress — casework, pork barreling, and advertising are. And such legislative interest as there is tends to be directed to particularistic rather than national concerns. Structure reflects culture in this system. Power is widely decentralized in Congress: toward the bottom (in the Ninety-seventh Congress the average representative had 16.5 staff members and the average senator 36.3);[46] toward the middle, among some 310 committees and subcommittees; and away from the top, where party leaders such as the speaker of the House and the minority and majority party leaders in each house are expected to serve members' reelection needs, not direct or discipline them.

For presidents who have an extensive legislative agenda, this is discouraging. To move bills through a constitutionally bicameral legislature is difficult enough by nature. Congress's culture of constituency service makes the task even more difficult: first, by encouraging the proliferation of subcommittees, each of them potential veto points, and then by distracting members away from serious legislative activity into more electorally rewarding ones. Successful presidential leadership also requires that representatives and senators direct their attention to national concerns. But congressional culture is such that local issues, or the local effects of national issues, come first. Members care most about how proposed legislation will affect their own geographical constituencies or the national interest groups that are powerful in those constituencies. Finally, most presidential initiatives call for legislative alterations of the status quo. These often conflict with the general satisfaction that each component of the various subgovernments in each policy area, including the congressional committees and subcommittees, have in existing arrangements.

All in all, the cultural element in the president-Congress relationship is a highly perverse one from the standpoint of presidents. The public generally wants the president to lead and Congress to follow. But the combination of constitutional refraction through the election system and a congressional culture that reflects the reelection ambitions of legislators can cause things to turn out very differently.

POLITICS

The Constitution adequately empowers all presidents some of the time and some presidents, notably those of consolidation, almost all of the time. In combination with American political culture, however, it also charges most presidents most of the time with responsibility but not power to enact domestic legislative policy — indeed, sometimes with formidable obstacles to power. Can the political environment provide resources to overcome these obstacles?

Elections

Historically, elections have been the engine that drives the policy cycle from consolidation to preparation and, most significantly, to achievement. Growing and, at the achievement stage, very large working majorities for the president in Congress are basic to successful legislative leadership by presidents. Until recently, congressional elections tended to produce party majorities, at least in presidential election years. Randall Calvert and John Ferejohn found that in the period 1868–1896 the degree of correspondence between the congressional vote and the presidential vote was .95; as late as 1932–1944, it still was .81. But by 1948–1964 the strength of the relationship had declined severely, to .37, and by 1968–1976 to .19.[47] As we saw earlier, the average share of congressional districts that are carried by a presidential candidate and a congressional candidate of the same party also declined dramatically after the 1940s, from around nine-tenths to around two-thirds. Nor can the president count any longer on his party controlling Congress: since 1952 that has been the exceptional condition, not the normal one. The consistency of such data is obvious and striking: congressional elections since around 1950 clearly have become less responsive to presidential coattails than they used to be. So is the apparent implication of the data — namely, that congressional elections are less useful to presidents as sources of influence in Congress.[48]

There may be less here than meets the eye. Two of the century's four presidents of achievement, Lyndon Johnson and Ronald Reagan, have served in the recent period, and each managed to push a change-oriented legislative program through Congress. For both Johnson and Reagan it was the gains for their parties in Congress that accompanied their own landslide elections that made these legislative achievements possible. These gains were not as large as those that attended the elections of Woodrow Wilson in 1912 and Franklin Roosevelt in 1932 (see Table 3.1). In fact they were about half the size. But politically, they were every bit as impressive to the representatives and senators of their day.

The explanation for this lies in the realm of political perception. As we saw in Chapter 3, the reason why it is large gains for the president's congressional party in an election that makes achievement possible (rather than the size of his party's congressional majority) is that such an election strikes representatives and senators as an unusual one whose implication is that the only safe political course is to support the president whenever possible. In the Wilson and Roosevelt eras, when presidential coattails were longer in all elections, it took gains of sixty-three and ninety-seven seats, respectively, to create this impression among legislators. But for the same reason that on a flat landscape a hill looks like a mountain, in the modern period Johnson and Reagan-style gains of thirty to forty seats have the same effect. In addition, modern representatives and senators seem more politically impressionable: the same congressional preoccupation with reelection that has led members to try to insulate their relationship with their voters from national political forces through pork barreling, constituency service, and the like also has made them extremely sensitive to any national force that may cost them votes, including a popular president.

Midterm congressional elections have undergone a similar transformation, but one that carries opposite political implications for the presidency-Congress relationship. Accurately or not, midterm elections tend to be perceived as referenda on the president's performance. (In truth, the effect of presidential popularity seems to be less on voter choices than on the decisions of potential contributors and politically attractive candidates to get involved in the election or not.)[49] From 1902 to 1946 the average midterm loss of House seats by the president's party was 41.2; since the 1940s it has been 27.5.[50] Thus, much to the chagrin of modern presidents, it takes a smaller loss of seats for them to be perceived the loser. Reagan, for example, argued that his party's twenty-six-seat loss in 1982 should be declared a victory, since it was considerably below the century-long average. He got a less-than-sympathetic hearing from most political analysts, who confined their comparison to more recent elections and judged 1982 a defeat.

Postelection Presidential Popularity

The obsession with reelection that governs legislators' reaction to election results causes them to respond in a similar manner to indices of interelection presidential popularity. As Roger Davidson and Richard Fenno, among others, have pointed out, reelection-oriented members of Congress "are hypersensitive to anticipated constituent reaction" to their actions.[51] This is not a groundless apprehension: constituents do, in fact, expect their representatives to reflect public opinion. What Richard Neustadt wrote of Washingtonians in general, then, is of greatest applicability to members of Congress in particular:

> Dependent men must take account of popular reaction to their actions. What their publics may think of them becomes a factor, therefore, in deciding how to deal with the desires of a President. His prestige enters into that decision; their publics are a part of his. Their view from inside Washington of how outsiders view him thus affects his influence with them.[52]

Or, as an aide to President Carter put it, "When you go up to the Hill and the latest polls show Carter isn't doing well, then there isn't much reason for a member to go along with him."

This aide's reference to polls was more than illustrative. George Edwards and Harvey Zeidenstein have found in separate studies that, as a general rule, the higher a president's approval rating in the national Gallup poll, the greater the support Congress gives to his legislative agenda.[53] To be sure, this is not because representatives and senators care mainly about national public opinion. Their primary concern is with sentiment in their individual districts and states, and when they have a strong sense of constituency opinion about the president or one of his legislative proposals, they will respond to that. Indeed, as we saw earlier, "constitutional refraction" can defeat presidents in Congress even when national public opinion is on their side. But on many issues, legislators lack reliable information about local preferences; "grave difficulties in discovering what are the preferences of their constituents" are chronic on Capitol Hill.[54] In such cases the president's popularity as measured in the Gallup poll provides members of Congress with at least a rough index of the public's views.

Is this linkage of popularity to legislative success a cause for rejoicing or despair among presidents? Most political scientists would say the latter. A strong consensus exists among presidency scholars that the president's approval rating is all but destined to go steadily downward during the course of his term, even as they disagree about why. Some say the president's loss of approval is, literally, a matter of time: time in which each decision that a president must make inevitably will alienate one or another group no matter how he makes it,[55] or time in which people become disillusioned with the president because they are measuring him against some unrealistically high ideal.[56] Others explain the president's public-approval rating in terms of actual events — peace or war, high or low inflation, "good" or "bad" news — or the public's perception of how well he is handling those events.[57] But even in these seemingly less fatalistic theories there is the implication that eventually the president must lose, either because public political behavior is more influenced by negative than positive opinions[58] or because citizens' expectations of the president are contradictory and thus, in the long run, unsatiable.[59]

It may be that joining the quarrel over *why* presidential approval must decline is a less important task than reopening the question of *whether* it must decline, at least to a point where a president's effectiveness is ruined. Among modern presidents, Roosevelt, Eisenhower, Kennedy, and, after a second year slump, Reagan maintained their initial popularity through all their years in office, Johnson and Nixon kept theirs for the first two years, and even Carter held his ground in the polls for at least the first year. (The bottom fell out from Ford's rating when he pardoned Nixon but stayed fairly steady after that.) Of the elected presidents all but Johnson were able to revive their initial popularity, at least for short periods. And Johnson and Reagan held on long enough to get their substantial legislative programs through Congress virtually intact.

Many scholars have pointed out that presidential approval ratings are down in general; both the peaks and valleys in presidential "fever charts" are lower in the 1970s and 1980s than they used to be.[60] But as with presidential coattails, hills now are as impressive to Congress as mountains once were. Reagan's highest approval rating barely exceeded Kennedy's lowest, but members of Congress were more impressed by Reagan's popularity, which contrasted so favorably with his predecessors', than by Kennedy's, which seemed typical after Eisenhower.

SKILL

An empowering presidential election victory — one that convinces members of Congress that their own reelection may be jeopardized if they fail to support the president — creates a setting in which legislative leadership can take place. So does a president's continuing popularity in office. Presidents can best capitalize on such conditions through the successful use of political leadership skills.

Modern presidential scholarship has tended to describe tactical skills of bargaining and persuasion as the essence of presidential leadership of Congress. "Presidential power is the power to persuade" and "the power to persuade is the power to bargain," according to Richard Neustadt. "The essence of a president's persuasive task is to convince [members of Congress] that what the White House wants of them is what they ought to do for their own sake."[61] This skill can be exercised in varied form. It can involve bargaining in the narrow sense: specific rewards in exchange for specific votes on legislation. For example, when Senator Robert Kerr's response to President Kennedy's case for an investment tax credit bill was to ask why the administration was opposing his Arkansas River project, Kennedy wryly replied, "You know, Bob, I never really understood that Arkansas River project before today."[62] But a president's legislative agenda is too extensive and representatives and senators too numerous for him to make such offers or even hold personal meetings very often, lest members of Congress come to expect them as a matter of course. Bargaining in the broader sense of rewarding a president's friends in Congress and not his opponents over the long run — what Neustadt calls "professional reputation" — is a more effective exercise of this skill. "I think they knew that we would try our best to help them on all kinds of requests if they supported the president," said William Timmons, Nixon's chief legislative aide, "and we did."[63] "Help on all kinds of things" includes personal amenities, campaign assistance, and the like. President Johnson once used sixty-nine pens and took twenty minutes to write his name at a bill-signing ceremony, all so that he could give a pen to — and publicly share credit for the bill's enactment with — sixty-nine grateful congressmen. President Reagan implicitly offered not to campaign against Democrats who supported his economic policies in 1981.

Tactical skill, as we defined it in Chapter 4, includes capacities other than bargaining. The timing with which legislative proposals are sent to Congress can affect their chances of passage. As a rule, Johnson sent bills to Capitol Hill one at a time, usually when the agendas of the committees that would have to consider them were clear. In 1965 he pushed Medicare and aid to education before sending bills for housing and home rule for the District of Columbia because he sensed that the latter would be more controversial and might bog Congress down. Jimmy Carter, on the other hand, placed his income tax, welfare, hospital cost control, and energy tax proposals before the House Ways and Means Committee simultaneously, to the detriment of them all. Presidents also benefit or suffer according to how forthrightly they stand behind their legislative proposals. Johnson left no uncertainty in anyone's mind about the steadfastness of his commitment to the proposed Civil Rights Act of 1964. In contrast President Eisenhower said in consecutive press conferences that he did not completely understand his own 1957 civil rights bill and did not agree with all of it. The long-run effects of presidential vacillation are more telling than the immediate ones: members of Congress will be less willing to go out on a limb for a president if they cannot count on his staying out there with them. Finally, the efforts of presidents and their staffs to woo interest-group support are important in convincing legislators that their support for the president may make a difference when they seek group endorsements or campaign contributions.[64]

Chapter 4 identified other leadership skills that are particularly relevant to a president's success in the role of chief legislator. A strategic sense of what is politically possible at his stage of the cycle is vital. The management of authority for policy formation is another useful skill: a capacity to develop specific legislative proposals that resonate with the political culture, crystallize the public mood, and impress politicians, policy analysts, and the press as workable. Franklin Roosevelt developed the Social Security Act so that it could be sold as a system of insurance rather than welfare in times of old age, unemployment, and disability — "operational liberalism" in the artful guise of "ideological conservatism." (Socialist Norman Thomas complained that even TVA, Roosevelt's most explicit commitment to public ownership, was rationalized in terms of the inspiration it would give to private enterprise.)[65] Reagan's success at persuading Congress to pass his massive budget reductions in domestic social programs, after Ford and Carter had failed to win smaller ones, illustrates a different aspect of this skill. What Reagan realized was that although defenders of the targeted programs would mobilize in opposition to any cuts at all, members of the general public would become active supporters of the president's proposal only if the cuts seemed sufficiently large to affect them personally through reduced taxes or the like.

Skills of self-presentation — the ability to dramatize oneself and one's causes to audiences of mass opinion — also can be useful to presidents in their dealings with Congress. The dramatization of self often is achieved most effectively through symbolic actions. Nixon's donning of a hard hat at a construction site in 1970 helped link him to the "silent majority" of mostly Democratic blue-collar workers by expressing their shared resentment of the student radicals who disdained them both. Pollster Patrick Caddell found that although Carter's election in 1976 did not win him the "automatic grant" of public confidence that presidents-elect usually enjoy, his Inauguration Day walk down Pennsylvania Avenue from the Capitol to the White House did.[66] All presidents do their best to "appear presidential" by, for example, greeting foreign heads of state in dignified White House ceremonies.

Rhetorical speechmaking skill is especially valuable to presidents who are trying to move the public to action on behalf of specific policies. President Truman's March 21, 1947 "Truman Doctrine" speech in defense of aid to Greece and Turkey not only won public support for that bill, but laid the foundation for acceptance of the Marshall Plan that followed.[67] According to Louis Harris's study of the effects of televised presidential addresses by Kennedy, Johnson, and Nixon on behalf of specific policies, public opinion responded in every case.[68] Carter quickly dissipated the effects of his July 1979 "crisis of confidence" speech, but the effects he dissipated were great: gains of 20-30 percentage points in the public's assessment of his handling of some issues, 75-80 per cent support for his energy proposals, and an 11-point increase in his Gallup approval rating.[69] Reagan's speeches in support of his tax and budget cuts in 1981 and the invasion of Grenada in 1983 roused exactly the response he requested from viewers: many thousands of calls, telegrams, and letters to congressmen saying, "Support the president." But as with personal bargaining, rhetoric is a strategy with limits. Contradictory metaphors aside,

Nixon was right in saying both that televised speeches are a potent resource "to build a fire under Congress" and that "you can go to the well too often."[70]

The importance to presidential success of all of these leadership skills — bargaining and other tactical skills, management of authority for legislative policy formation, and symbolic and rhetorical skills involving the presentation of self — varies at different stages of the domestic policy cycle. In dealing with Congress, presidents of consolidation can rely extensively on their constitutional powers. Legislative leadership skills are not irrelevant to such presidents: if nothing else, they have annual budgets to pass. But such skills are not central; nor are the occasional demands for them as rigorous for presidents of consolidation because they are not trying to alter the status quo.

Presidents of preparation need rhetorical and other presentational skills more than they need any others. Public uncertainty and congressional resistance define their stage of the cycle. In such a setting, tactical legislative skills are of secondary importance because the political foundation has not yet been laid: the task is to move new issues to the top of the public agenda and build popular support for the president's policy solutions. Managing authority to develop those policies is also important to presidents of preparation, but since serious congressional consideration is still some time away, they have room for trial and error. As we saw in Chapter 3, Roosevelt, who acted as his own president of preparation in foreign affairs, made several false starts in his effort to move the public in an internationalist direction before he hit on a policy (lend-lease) and a moralistic rationale for it that worked. Similarly, Kennedy learned that modest initiatives pleased neither civil rights advocates nor opponents. In June 1963 he introduced a bold piece of civil rights legislation, presented it in a televised address as "a moral issue . . . as old as the Scriptures and as clear as the American Constitution," and reaped the harvest of supportive public opinion.

A president of achievement inherits the benefits of his immediate predecessor's efforts, but rhetoric and management of authority for policy formation remain the primary skill requirements for his stage of the cycle as well. Since the president of achievement is favored by a groundswell of public opinion in support of substantial legislative change, his main task is to rouse citizens to actively pressure their representatives and senators (who already are impressed by the election results that inaugurate a presidency of achievement) to enact the legislative proposals he has developed or chosen. Even then, constitutional refraction means that congressional acquiescence is less than automatic. Tactical skills must be exercised adroitly. As Neustadt argues:

> Even when most players of the governmental game see policy objectives much alike, [the president] cannot rely on logic (or on charm) to get him what he wants. . . . Even then most outcomes turn on bargaining. The reason for this is a simple one: most men who share in governing have interests of their own beyond the realm of policy *objectives*. The sponsorship of policy, the form it takes, the conduct of it, and the credit for it separate their interest from the president's despite agreement on the end in view.[71]

Perceptive as Neustadt's insights into bargaining and persuasion are, it still is the case that such tactical skills are not the main ingredient of presidential leadership of Congress and probably never have been. Such skills really come into play in presidencies of achievement, and even then they are not of central importance. Tactics had little to do with Wilson's first-term legislative achievements or with Franklin Roosevelt's first hundred days. (They were of considerable value to Roosevelt in passing the Second New Deal but could not sustain his period of achievement beyond that.) George Edwards has shown that it was Johnson's post-assassination honeymoon, landslide election, and temporary popularity that account most for the Great Society; his "mastery of the legislative process seems to have had considerably less significance than conventional wisdom indicates."[72] Similarly, notes Samuel Kernell about Reagan's 1981 victories, although "'savvy' members of the press for whom the 'wheeling and dealing' of pluralist politics had made good copy over the years busied themselves sniffing out bargains to explain the president's success, . . . [f]ew deals were discovered because few were transacted. President Reagan did not simply fail to bargain, he openly disdained it."[73]

As hard as it is to credit the legislative success of these presidents of achievement to tactical skill, it is harder still to attribute the legislative failures of their later terms or of presidents of preparation to the absence of such skills. More adroit bargaining could not have transformed the presidencies of Theodore Roosevelt, Kennedy, or Carter because public support for their policy initiatives was so fragile and precarious. And as limited as the value of tactical skills is to both types of change-oriented presidents, that is how irrelevant they are to presidents of consolidation. Neustadt's criticism of Eisenhower for being a "Roosevelt in reverse" who lacked Roosevelt's "sense of power and his taste for it" may or may not be accurate in the narrow sense, but it certainly is beside the point.[74] To be a Roosevelt in reverse was the essence of Eisenhower's contract with the voters of his time.

The reason tactical skills never have been as important as Neustadt thought is implicit in his own analysis. He is right in arguing that most members of Congress most of the time will support a president's legislative proposals only when they feel it will serve their personal reelection interest to do so. But to argue that a president's persuasive powers, however great, will figure foremost in the process by which representatives and senators assess their own interests is only reasonable if one assumes that members of Congress do not make those calculations themselves. Surely, though, they do, or else how did they succeed in politics in the first place? And they are unlikely to think that a president's reading of opinion in their individual constituencies is either better or less biased than their own. If presidents had a large supply of tangible goods to trade for legislative support, members of Congress might be willing to buck their districts in the short run in exchange for favors they later could translate into votes. But presidents lack such a supply: patronage is limited by the civil service merit system, and the pork barrels mostly are filled in Congress anyway.

SUMMARY

The Constitution gives presidents extensive power over Congress in most nonlegislative matters—namely, appointments and foreign policy, and, through the veto, for legislative issues on which Congress has taken initiatives the president opposes. For the most part, this is empowerment enough for presidents of consolidation. But when it comes to the central presidential role with regard to Congress for presidents of preparation and achievement, that of "chief legislator," the Constitution is less helpful and the cultural and political environment is variable. Essentially, presidents can get Congress to pass their programs only when representatives and senators are convinced that it is in their individual political interests to do so. Constitutional refraction and the institutional culture of Congress make this a difficult task: presidents are forced to sell change-oriented national policies to locally oriented legislators whose disposition, however subliminal it may be, is likely to be to the status quo in which they have prospered politically. A landslide presidential election victory can help to overcome these obstacles if it was prompted by campaign promises for dramatic change and accompanied by substantial gains for the president's party in Congress. So can relatively high presidential popularity in office. But even when conditions are favorable, success is not automatic. Presidents must be able to make general support specific through the exercise of political skill. This means strategically assessing the political possibilities, managing authority for policy formation, then selling the proposals with adroit tactics and, in particular, compelling rhetoric.

NOTES

1. Joseph M. Bessette and Jeffrey Tulis, *The Presidency in the Constitutional Order* (Baton Rouge: Louisiana State University Press, 1981), p. 8.
2. Royden J. Dangerfield, *In Defense of the Senate: A Study in Treaty Making* (Norman, Okla.: University of Oklahoma Press, 1933).
3. Treaties outnumbered executive agreements in the period 1789–1889 by 275 to 265. From 1889 to 1939, executive agreements predominated over treaties by 917 to 524. In the period 1940–1979 this predominance became overwhelming (8,628 to 466). James MacGregor Burns, Jack Peltason, and Thomas E. Cronin, *Government by the People*, 11th ed. (Englewood Cliffs, N.J.: Prentice-Hall, 1981), p. 362. The Mondale quote is from Walter F. Mondale, *The Accountability of Power* (New York: McKay, 1975), pp. 114–15.
4. James L. Sundquist, *The Decline and Resurgence of Congress* (Washington: The Brookings Institution, 1981), p. 42.
5. *Ibid.*, p. 267.
6. See Chapter 3, note 13.
7. Richard Neustadt, *Presidential Power*, 3rd ed. (New York: Wiley, 1980), p. 67.
8. Calculated from data presented in Roger H. Davidson and Walter J. Oleszek, *Congress and Its Members* (Washington: Congressional Quarterly Press, 1981), p. 296.
9. Truman cast 15.2 vetoes per year when the Republican party controlled Congress, compared to 7.8 per year when his own party was in control. Eisenhower cast 10.2 per year against Democratic Congresses, 9.0 against Republican Congresses. Calculated from information presented in *Presidential Vetoes, 1789–1976* (Washington: Government Printing Office, 1978).
10. Calculated from data presented in Norman J. Ornstein *et al.*, *Vital Statistics on Congress, 1982* (Washington: American Enterprise Institute, 1982), p. 53.
11. The exceptions: 1919–1921 and 1947–1949, when Democrats were in the White

House but Republicans controlled both houses of Congress; and 1911–1913 and 1931–1933, when Republican presidents confronted a Democratically controlled House of Representatives.

12. James MacGregor Burns, *The Deadlock of Democracy* (Englewood Cliffs, N.J.: Prentice-Hall, 1963).

13. From 1955 to 1961 and 1969 to 1977 Republican presidents faced Democratic Congresses.

14. Stephen J. Wayne, *The Legislative Presidency* (New York: St. Martin's, 1978), p. 159.

15. Walter Isaacson, "'Not Our Finest Hour,'" *Time* (January 3, 1983), p. 43.

16. Hugh Heclo, *A Government of Strangers* (Washington: The Brookings Institution, 1977), p. 88.

17. G. Calvin Mackenzie, *The Politics of Presidential Appointments* (New York: Free Press, 1981), pp. 177, 181.

18. Richard Nathan, *The Administrative Presidency* (New York: Wiley, 1983), p. 30.

19. Mackenzie, *Presidential Appointments*, pp. 7–9.

20. Congress sometimes takes the initiative to fill "policy gaps." See David K. Price, *Who Makes the Laws? Creativity and Power in Senate Committees* (Cambridge, Mass.: Schenkman, 1972).

21. George Edwards, *Presidential Influence in Congress* (San Francisco: W. H. Freeman, 1980), p. 60.

22. Hazel Erskine, "The Polls: Presidential Power," *Public Opinion Quarterly* (Fall 1973), p. 488.

23. Donald Devine, *The Political Culture of the United States* (Boston: Little, Brown, 1972), p. 158.

24. Thomas E. Cronin, "A Resurgent Congress and the Imperial Presidency," *Political Science Quarterly* (Summer 1980), p. 211.

25. Richard F. Fenno found that "most citizens find it hard or impossible to think about Congress as an institution. They answer questions about it; but they cannot conceptualize it as a collectivity." *Home Style: House Members in Their Districts* (Boston: Little, Brown, 1978), p. 245.

26. Stephen J. Wayne, "Great Expectations: What People Want from Presidents," in Thomas E. Cronin, ed., *Rethinking the Presidency* (Boston: Little, Brown, 1982), pp. 192–95.

27. Davidson and Oleszek, *Congress*, p. 152.

28. Devine, *Political Culture*, p. 128.

29. Fenno, *Home Style*, p. 168.

30. Morris P. Fiorina, "Congressmen and Their Constituents: 1958 and 1978," in Dennis Hale, ed., *The United States Congress* (Chestnut Hill, Mass.: Boston College, 1982), p. 39.

31. "What Moved the Voters?" *Public Opinion* (November–December 1978), p. 22.

32. "The Harris Survey," various eds. (1981–82).

33. Calculated from data presented in Davidson and Oleszek, *Congress*, p. 70; *CQ Weekly Report* (November 6, 1982); and Ornstein, *Vital Statistics*, pp. 50–51. The 60-percent-margin data is only for the period 1956–82.

34. Edwards, *Presidential Influence*, pp. 100–8.

35. Ornstein, *Vital Statistics*, p. 54.

36. *Ibid.* pp. 46–48.

37. Richard F. Fenno, *Congressmen in Committees* (Boston: Little, Brown, 1973), p. 2.

38. Fenno, *Home Style*, pp. 31, 10–11.

39. Morris P. Fiorina, *Congress: Keystone of the Washington Establishment* (New Haven: Yale University Press, 1977), pp. 41–49.

40. David Mayhew, *Congress: The Electoral Connection* (New Haven: Yale University Press, 1974), p. 49.

41. Ornstein, *Vital Statistics*, pp. 112, 140; Fenno, *Home Style*, p. 32.

42. Ornstein, *Vital Statistics*, pp. 130–33.

43. Woodrow Wilson, *Congressional Government* (New York: Meridian Books, 1956), p. 69.
44. Fenno, *Congressmen in Committees*, p. 2.
45. Kenneth A. Shepsle, *The Giant Jigsaw Puzzle: Democratic Committee Assignments in the Modern House* (Chicago: University of Chicago Press, 1978).
46. Ornstein, *Vital Statistics*, p. 110.
47. Randall Calvert and John Ferejohn, "Presidential Coattails in Historical Perspective," *American Journal of Political Science*, forthcoming. The degree of correspondence is measured in regression coefficients.
48. Morris P. Fiorina, "The Presidency and the Electoral System," in Michael Nelson, ed., *The Presidency and the Political System* (Washington: Congressional Quarterly Press, 1984), pp. 204–26.
49. Gary C. Jacobson and Samuel Kernell, *Strategy and Choice in Congressional Elections* (New Haven: Yale University Press, 1978).
50. Ornstein, *Vital Statistics*, p. 41.
51. Roger H. Davidson, *The Role of the Congressman* (New York: Pegasus, 1968), p. 121; Richard Fenno, "U.S. House Members in Their Constituencies: An Exploration," *American Political Science Review* (September 1977), pp. 886–87.
52. Neustadt, *Presidential Power*, p. 64.
53. Edwards, *Presidential Influence*, ch. 4; Harvey G. Zeidenstein, "Presidential Popularity and Presidential Support in Congress: Eisenhower to Carter," *Presidential Studies Quarterly* (Spring 1980), pp. 224–33.
54. Leroy Rieselbach, *Congressional Politics* (New York: McGraw-Hill, 1973), p. 218.
55. John E. Mueller, *War, Presidents, and Public Opinion* (New York: Wiley, 1970), pp. 205–6.
56. James A. Stimson, "Public Support for American Presidents: A Cyclical Model," *Public Opinion Quarterly* (Spring 1976), pp. 1–21.
57. See, for example, Samuel Kernell, "Explaining Presidential Popularity," *American Political Science Review* (June 1978), pp. 506–22; Henry Kenski, "Inflation and Presidential Popularity," *Public Opinion Quarterly* (Summer 1979), pp. 86–90; George Edwards, *The Public Presidency* (New York: St. Martin's, 1983), ch. 6; and Richard A. Brody and Benjamin I. Page, "The Impact of Events on Presidential Popularity," in Aaron Wildavsky, ed., *Perspectives on the Presidency* (Boston: Little, Brown, 1975), pp. 136–48.
58. Samuel Kernell, "Presidential Popularity and Negative Voting," *American Political Science Review* (March 1977), pp. 44–66.
59. Edwards, *Public Presidency*, pp. 195–98.
60. *Ibid.*, pp. 221–22.
61. Neustadt, *Presidential Power*, pp. 10, 28, 27.
62. Edwards, *Presidential Influence*, p. 129.
63. *Ibid.*, p. 133.
64. Martha Kumar and Michael Grossman, "The Presidency and Interest Groups," in Michael Nelson, ed., *The Presidency and the Political System* (Washington: Congressional Quarterly Press, 1984), pp. 282–312.
65. Louis Hartz, *The Liberal Tradition in America* (New York: Harcourt, Brace and World, 1955), p. 267.
66. Jack Germond and Jules Witcover, *Blue Smoke and Mirrors* (New York: Viking, 1981), p. 23.
67. Samuel Kernell, "The Truman Doctrine Speech: A Case Study in the Dynamics of Opinion Leadership," *Social Science History* (Fall 1976), pp. 20–45.
68. Robert O. Blanchard, ed., *Congress and the News Media* (New York: Hastings House, 1974), pp. 106–13.
69. Germond and Witcover, *Blue Smoke*, p. 37.
70. Quoted in Samuel Kernell, *The Paradox of the Modern Presidency*, forthcoming.
71. Neustadt, *Presidential Power*, p. 36.
72. Edwards, *Presidential Influence*, p. 200.
73. Kernell, *Paradox*.
74. Neustadt, *Presidential Power*, p. 120.

CHAPTER 8

Presidential Management of Policy Implementation

Presidents are institutional leaders rather than administrators. Institutional leadership requires the articulation of the purposes of the organization for its members and constituents and the relating of organizational programs and technologies to those purposes.[1] The leader is responsible for seeing that means and ends are joined in a constructive manner, but he leaves administration— the task of fashioning those links—to others. Administration, in this sense, is the day-to-day coping with problems of budgeting, personnel, rule making, field work, and the evaluation of results.

The president can assess the state of administration in the myriad parts of the federal government, but he cannot administer that government. For one thing, the structure and composition of the institutional presidency are not well suited for centralized administration of the executive bureaucracy. The president is surrounded and assisted by political advisers and staff experts whose basic orientation, as we saw in Chapter 6, is toward the development of policy rather than its implementation. A president's closest advisers handle his personal political business, such as dealing with interest groups, the media, and Congress. Professional staffs in the Executive Office of the President are accomplished at analyzing policy alternatives through the lenses of political, economic, and budgetary analysis, but their skills are not administrative.

If small units in the White House or EOP become overextended by riding herd on the departments on administrative questions, they cease to do what the president expects of them, which is to advise on policy choices. Even the Office of Management and Budget, which ostensibly is charged not only to prepare the president's budget but to guide the departments on administrative questions, has not proved to be an effective instrument for administration. The strength of OMB lies in the knowledge of its program examiners about how well programs are working. Such information is crucial for the intelligent preparation of the budget. It is also extremely useful as a goad, in behalf of the president, from high levels of OMB to the departments, to manage their business better. But experience has shown that devices installed in OMB to permit its staff to oversee departmental administration have had limited results because the OMB professionals lack administrative leverage over departmental staffs.[2]

A president's cabinet secretaries, who serve as department heads, are more directly responsible for the implementation of presidential programs. But policy implementation problems are no more tractable from their perspective than from the White House. The conventional wisdom holds that presidents and department heads often are at odds because the departments are so involved in servicing their constituencies, whether it be the Department of Agriculture and farmers or Labor and workers. Department heads are said to lose sight of presidential objectives in their efforts to create alliances with constituency groups in order to work effectively with Congress. There is something to this analysis, at least in the sense that a department head who was at odds with the constituencies served by his department would be ineffective. But beyond that, it is not so simple. Most departments serve many constituencies, and it is not possible to keep them all happy. Liberal and conservative presidents, therefore, are likely to ask their department heads to pursue different policy balances. Recent presidents also have paid less attention to choosing department heads who represent constituencies than was once the case; they are more interested in appointing people who will adhere to a few central presidential objectives. This became possible, in part, because the great multiplication of federal programs during the 1960s created new, conflicting constituencies for most departments, giving presidents greater latitude in appointing people to head them.

However, it still is true that department heads necessarily spend the bulk of their time in external political relations, as do presidents. They testify before Congress, give speeches, and attend numerous meetings within the presidential family to discuss policy development and coordination. This leaves little time for administration, and, in fact, departments mostly are administered by undersecretaries, assistant secretaries, and the civil servants of the permanent government. Presidents are thus dependent for the implementation of programs on subpresidential appointees whom they hardly know.

Many federal domestic-policy programs are administered by state and local governments, further limiting presidential control. Before the early 1960s only a few, well-accepted federal "grant-in-aid" programs linked the federal and state governments. In programs such as the U.S. Employment Service and its forty-eight state agencies, the Interstate Highway Program, and the National Defense Education Act, the federal government supplied the money, general guidelines, and some technical assistance, but the goals were believed to be clear and within the capacity of state governments to administer with a minimum of federal oversight. The New Frontier and Great Society and the great spurt of regulatory legislation that was enacted by Congress during the Nixon administration changed that stable equilibrium radically by creating programs that state and local governments were to administer under tight federal supervision.

The proliferation of federal programs and the increase of federal authority created a number of problems for which presidents are held responsible but about which they can do little. The problems of presidential control of federal agencies pale in comparison with the effort required to exercise authority over multitudes of state and local organizations charged with carrying out federal programs. In addition, many of these are controversial programs in which human services are delivered or businesses are regulated. Their administration can become a matter of national politics in which the authority of presidents to implement programs is challenged by interest groups that have influence in Congress and the implementing bureaucracies.

The implementation of foreign and defense policies also poses problems of intergovernmental relations but among, rather than within, nations. Presidential objectives often depend upon the concurrence of foreign governments for their implementation. Economic and military agreements with allies are reciprocal matters that can be achieved only through bargaining. Ignorance is in all cases a barrier to intelligent action, but the picture is murkiest in foreign policy. It is very difficult for presidents and their advisers to understand enough about foreign countries to act intelligently toward them. For example, the U.S. response to the Iranian revolution of 1979 was to try to establish amicable relations with the new government of Iran. This strengthened the hand of the fanatic anti-Western religious leaders in Iran and contributed to the takeover by the Ayatollah Khomeini.[3]

Presidential policy making for national security consists of choices that of necessity are implemented elsewhere. For example, the State Department is responsible for carrying out American foreign policy. But that department has its own view of things. Presidents often find that they must push and prod to get their directives carried out. Often the letter of a command is implemented rather than its spirit. President Kennedy was determined that U.S. ambassadors be held responsible for all the activities of the American government that were carried out within their embassies, including the Central Intelligence Agency, the Agency for International Development, and the military attachés. The response of most ambassadors was perfunctory at best. Their incentives were served better by deference to the separate missions of the CIA, AID, and the military services, which defer in turn to the autonomy of State for the diplomatic role that ambassadors care about. Kennedy's directive could not change those realities.

In crucial foreign-policy matters, presidents often take things into their own hands. The conduct of diplomacy with powerful nations or the supervision of major military operations is handled from the White House. But these important areas are usually also highly sensitive political questions. For example, the conduct of arms reductions talks with the Soviets is carried out according to the constraints that presidents feel are imposed by domestic politics. Problems of implementation are first political and then administrative questions.

Historically, the political incentives of presidents have not encouraged a concern for questions of policy implementation of any kind, either at the time policy is initiated or afterward in its administration. Both Congress and the president have sought short-term political rewards from the public and from interest groups that approved the objectives of the new programs, their general principles, and their policy innovations. This concern for the short term is predictable in a political system with frequent elections. A second reason for the lack of presidential concern for how programs will be implemented after enactment is that the political task of winning agreement for legislation usually requires compromises that may break apart any carefully defined program design. A third reason is that the people who know about the actual implementation of programs are out in the field, in the states and localities or abroad, not in the White House. Even higher civil servants and OMB program examiners are inclined to see complex programs in the "code" of statistics, economic costs, and evaluation studies. Their personal knowledge of the actual administration of programs often is limited. Program designers at the presidential level, therefore, draw more on aspirations than experience.

For all of these reasons—the institutional capacities of the White House, the distracting demands on department heads, the fragmented nature of domestic- and foreign-policy implementation, and the political incentives of presidents—the nature of the relationship between the president and the bureaucracy in the realm of policy implementation is determined more by the bureaucracy than by the president. We would expect to find some variation of management styles among presidents of achievement, consolidation, and preparation, but not as much as in policy formation.

This chapter begins with an extended discussion of the "constants" in the presidency-bureaucracy relationship. We then describe chronologically how individual presidents since Franklin Roosevelt have attempted to manage policy implementation, and conclude by offering some insights from the theory of cycles.

PRESIDENTS AND BUREAUCRATS

In Chapter 6 we described three presidential advisory systems—domestic, economic, and national security. The bureaucracy was not described in detail because the task of policy formation, from the president's perspective, is to organize the institutional presidency in relation to the departments so that choices come to him clearly structured and as free as possible of organizational bias. The president sees little of what goes on in the departments in the process of policy formation. He cares about the results; indeed, he would be neglecting his job if he became preoccupied with questions of departmental governance.

The implementation of presidential policy is a different story. The influence of the White House and EOP down into the many layers of implementation is limited. Implementation invokes the entire range of departmental cultures and bureaucratic routines. Therefore, if one is to understand the strategic choices that are presented to presidents in the oversight of policy implementation, it is necessary to look more carefully at what goes on inside departments than was the case for policy formation. For this purpose we will collapse the three categories of policy used in Chapter 6 into two: domestic, including social and economic policy, and national security, including both diplomatic and military policy.

The Domestic Bureaucracies and Policy Implementation

Cabinet officers are the official administrators of federal laws. They receive this authority directly from Congress. But to think of implementing policy simply as a matter of administering statutes is naïve in the extreme. The task is one of organizational leadership.

A high-ranking official who was learning the ropes at the Department of Health, Education, and Welfare (HEW) in 1969 was heard to utter: "The place is unbelievable. It appears to run by itself."[4] HEW represented an extreme both in its size and in the degree to which it was a holding company of disparate agencies, but all of the "outer," or constituency-based, cabinet departments share its internal diversity of mission. Congress prefers it that way and habitually has written the fragmentation into law so that it can watch over the individual parts and thereby limit the power of a secretary over his own domain. For the same reason, Congress has favored categorical legislation that gives specific grants of authority and money to particular agencies to perform certain functions so that the specialized congressional committees can oversee their bailiwicks closely and limit secretarial authority to reshuffle programs and funds. This means that departments get locked into responses to past problems and may lack the flexibility to move on their own to meet new ones.

Other constraints operate on a department head. Because of the fixed structure of most departments, as set by Congress, he often has very limited authority to transfer funds from one program to another or to reorganize bureaus without congressional approval. Because programs and bureaus are insulated from his control in this respect, he usually must persuade his subordinates to support him in terms of their own perspectives and incentives. The independence of bureaus brings about a split between policy and operations, with the latter assuming more importance. A secretary can develop a policy and get a new program and budget, but there is no guarantee that anything will be done.

A department head also has to worry about constraints set by the White House and OMB. Without presidential support for his legislative initiatives and OMB endorsement of his budgets, a secretary is helpless. At the same time, he must respond to constellations of interest-group, agency, and congressional pressures that often run counter to presidential demands. Finally, there are the seemingly insuperable problems posed by the ambiguous and often conflicting nature of departmental goals and the great difficulties of estimating program effectiveness. It is virtually impossible for a multipurpose department like HUD or Interior to have a coherent set of policy goals. Either the goals are different in kind, or they conflict directly. Coordination thus becomes a hopeless task.

These many forces make it hard for a secretary to build stable coalitions of support for policies across his many constituencies. He cannot run a department in terms of a hierarchy of goals, even if he has such a vision. Rather, he must pick a few issues carefully and seek to build supporting coalitions for his positions. The temptation is great to concentrate on the passage of new presidential programs and pay less heed to the administration of existing ones.

These obstacles and temptations notwithstanding, secretaries have tried a variety of devices to assert control over their departments.[5] Two such methods that usually are paired are the extensive use of analytic staff and a system of program evaluation.

A number of the domestic departments now have assistant secretaries for policy analysis and evaluation. The titles vary, as do the institutional strengths of the offices. For example, some are responsible for budget preparation, which strengthens their position vis-à-vis the bureaus. Each assistant secretary has a staff of analysts who work on policy development and program evaluations and, to a lesser extent, do research on problems. These are domestic department variations on the original McNamara unit of "whiz kids" in the Pentagon and the Kissinger White House staff.[6] A department head can use analysts to sharpen debate, challenge poor programs, widen his own choices, improve the evidence available for decision, and permit the actual evaluation of existing programs. Still, analysts and evaluation systems do not overcome the most important constraints upon a secretary in administering a department as he wishes: conflicting and ambiguous goals, external constraints from Congress and the White House, interdepartmental conflicts, the difficulty of getting direct control over bureau operations, the lack of continuity among fellow political executives in his own department, and their uneven experience and ability both in the subject matter at hand and in guiding large organizations.[7]

Therefore, a secretary, like the president, must find help by enlisting the support of career civil servants throughout his department. This is institutional leadership: the imparting of shared purposes to those within an institution. There is a great deal of slack energy and desire to serve in the civil service, and an executive with a gift for moral leadership can tap this resource.

Such leadership ultimately is the key to presidential control of bureaucracy as well, especially in regard to the administration of programs. A president must be able to count on descending chains of like-minded associates who will do his business throughout the government. These chains of presidential associates not only must administer policy, but must build conditions of political support for it as well. A president needs department heads and others in each department to work with Congress, interest groups, the press, and the agencies to develop support for ideas. Institutional leadership in government is thus inherently political, and to be effective it may have to run counter to many of the canons of rational organization, planning, and analysis. In the final analysis presidents and their associates have to live with inadequate organizations and work through them. But skillful institutional leadership can break down many barriers and create alliances for action.[8]

The range of policy implementation responsibilities that are faced by the several domestic departments cannot be characterized easily or illustrated in a few pages. But a simple typology of domestic issues that are shared by the departments will permit us to describe how implementation problems present themselves to presidents. It also will set the stage for a subsequent analysis of alternative strategies of presidential leadership for policy implementation. As will be seen later in the chapter, such strategies vary according to the type of presidency.

Distributive Policy

A colloquial and somewhat unkind term for distributive policies is "pork barrel." This is not altogether fair because many such policies convey benefits to the entire population. Is the system of interstate highways a "pork barrel" or a public good from which all citizens benefit? The answer is in the eye of the beholder. In any event, distributive policies are those programs that are widely dispersed throughout the country in behalf of general goals and to everyone's apparent benefit.[9]

Congress loves distributive programs because no one seems to lose. The lack of conflict that characterizes the congressional process of passing such legislation carries over into implementation. Not only are the benefits widely spread, but the federal government asks little of the state and local governments that actually administer the programs. Each level of the implementing bureaucracy shares the goals of that above it. Since the intention is to spend funds for agreed purposes, little attention is given to evaluating the usefulness of the effort. It is assumed that public expenditures will have the desired result.[10]

Presidents usually do not initiate distributive programs, although Eisenhower's Highway Act is an exception. Such programs are integral to the politics of congressional reelection and have their origins there. A number of problems with distributive programs can be pointed out to presidents, particularly by OMB. Funds may be spread so thinly across political constituencies that the purpose is negated. Because results seldom are evaluated, considerable money may be wasted. But it is rare for a president to challenge a distributive program. Jimmy Carter's 1977 effort to eliminate a number of congressionally sponsored water development projects from the budget was an unusual action for a president to take.

When presidents do move against distributive programs, it is at the level of policy rather than implementation. These programs pose few implementation problems as such. Challenges to such programs usually center on budgetary questions. But even on this level, most presidents are loath to challenge a well-entrenched congressional system for the distribution of tangible benefits throughout the nation.

Regulatory Policy

Regulatory policies take the form of statutes in which the government specifies rules of conduct for individuals and institutions, with sanctions for failure to comply. There are many different kinds of regulatory programs, including those that seek public goods such as the Clean Air Act and those that protect specific populations such as the Civil Rights Act of 1964.[11]

Regulatory programs are characterized by active support from organized groups, such as environmentalists for the Clean Air Act; wide support from the general public; and opposition of varying degrees and intensity from the regulated. Often the regulated come to terms with stable regulation to the extent that they resist its removal as only creating new problems for them. Legislators are far more inclined to support regulation in principle than in practice. Symbolic support for occupational safety and health is one thing, but the imposition of a regulation on a textile factory in a congressman's district is quite another matter. For the implementation of regulatory measures to be effective over time depends upon continuing strong support for them from the public. For example, high levels of public support for environmental regulation persist despite the economic costs. To the degree that such support falters, regulatory agencies have less authority over the regulated and must bargain with them to achieve compliance with the law, perhaps compromising goals.[12]

Presidents almost always enter into regulatory controversies at the stage of policy formation, but our interest here is in what they do about implementation. When a new president enters office, he is confronted with an array of regulatory programs in many institutions, not all of which he wishes to address. He and his associates decide what is important to them and act accordingly. The instruments for presidential action in the implementation of regulatory policies are several.

First, the president has the legal authority to appoint the heads of regulatory agencies. These are of two kinds: the long-standing independent agencies such as the Interstate Commerce Commission and the Federal Communications Commission, which legally are the creatures of the Congress; and the regulatory bodies that have been placed by law within departments, such as the Occupational Safety and Health Administration (OSHA) in the Department of Labor and the Environmental Protection Agency, which stands within the Executive Office of the President itself. He also appoints the members of the independent agencies, but only when the term of a sitting member expires.

Second, allocations of money for both types of regulatory agencies are in the annual budgets that are sent to Congress by the president. Congress may not comply, but the threat alone is clearly a way to influence the work of an agency. President Reagan sharply reduced EPA budgets at the outset of his term.

Third, presidents may encourage agencies to interpret regulations in accordance with administration priorities. This is not easily done to the independent agencies, which can be influenced only indirectly. But an agency like EPA, the Office of Civil Rights, or even the Bureau of Land Management in the Department of the Interior has the latitude to interpret and reinterpret broad legislative language to meet administration policies. For example, the number of inspections of factories under OSHA or the requirements about safeguards on machinery lie within the discretion of agency directors.

Fourth, presidents may deploy the Department of Justice as a friend of the court in important regulatory test cases. For example, if a president favors the strong implementation of affirmative-action regulations for minority hiring under the Civil Rights Act, he may send the solicitor general to court to argue against a challenge to such regulations in a specific case. Or he may use legal resources to attempt to diminish the force of regulatory legislation.

Fifth, presidents must decide where and when to put their weight behind concerted administrative action in behalf of regulatory laws. They will leave the majority of such statutes alone because they cannot get in too many fights at the same time. But some policies may be so important to their objectives that they require special attention. John Kennedy compensated for his failure to introduce civil rights legislation with a firm stand on the racial integration of southern universities, even to the extent of sending a small army of U.S. marshals to Oxford, Mississippi, in order that one black student might matriculate. Ronald Reagan initially placed the Environmental Protection Agency in the hands of presidential appointees who so reduced its regulatory role, angered

EPA adherents in Congress, and created the appearance of collusion with industry that he was required to do an about-face, remove them, and appoint as agency head the environmentalist who had been the agency's first director.

Finally, presidents may pursue regulatory reform through legislative action: an entirely new approach to the implementation of regulation may be attempted. The deregulation of the airline, trucking, and banking industries at the initiative of the Carter administration are cases in point.

All of these kinds of choices by presidents are policy decisions about how much they want to lean into the law to support it or lean away to dilute it. Most regulatory statutes do not receive much attention from presidents because the consequent controversy is too high a price to pay for the incremental gains that can be achieved through changes in regulatory strategy. But when controversies arise that presidents must address, such as the government's commitment to environmental protection, it is a sign that an implementation question has stimulated unresolved policy disagreements. Presidents must be ready to respond when this happens.

Redistributive Policy

Redistributive policies generally are understood as the allocation of resources to some social groups at the expense of others. They arise from divisive politics. Many such policies redirect resources to the wealthy in the form of subsidies or tax breaks, but these usually are "self-implementing." Thus, we will confine our discussion to programs that are intended to help the disadvantaged.[13]

Redistributive programs may have a greater or lesser distributive component. To the extent they are distributive, they will broaden the group of beneficiaries and perhaps reduce the regulations that accompany implementation. Pure redistributive programs, on the other hand, are governed by specific rules about who may and may not benefit. Social Security and Medicare are redistributive programs with a broad distributive element. Aid to families with dependent children and Medicaid are pure redistributive programs.

Redistributive programs with a high distributive component have greater political support than pure redistributive programs. They not only have more people behind them, but lack the taint of "welfare." However, a mix of redistributive and distributive elements can create an ambiguity about the goals of a program. For example, the Elementary and Secondary Education Act of 1965 calls for federal funds to be targeted to school districts with disadvantaged children in order to provide such children with compensatory services. However, school administrators throughout the country have sought to persuade Congress to write the funding formulas so that the largest possible number of districts would receive funds, thus serving the distributive principle of general aid. Because such ambiguities are fought out as political questions during the implementation of a program, presidents must take stands through their department heads. If such issues can be resolved politically, the implementation problems are not out of the ordinary.

Pure redistributive programs are more difficult to implement because more rules are attached. Although rising Medicare costs are a problem, the actual administration of services is not. But Medicaid, a program for the poor, poses all of the problems that are associated with testing for eligibility, weeding out people who receive services without entitlement, and working with a diversity of fifty state programs (in contrast to the universal Medicare system) — all of this colored by the persistent theme in American welfare policies of disdain for the weak and the search for "fraud" and "cheaters." The administrative tasks of implementation for the federal departments are much greater for such programs than for the universal measures.

There are a number of programs that combine redistributive goals with regulatory structures. The civil rights laws fall into this category, along with programs that deliver complex human services to a specific population such as handicapped children in the public schools. The federal government must ensure that lower levels of government comply with the law; it also is responsible for learning whether the services being delivered are meeting the needs of those being served. This causes great frustration because, in the implementation of affirmative-action laws or services to the handicapped, technical compliance with a federal law is not equivalent to enforcement of its spirit.[14]

Presidents face two broad types of implementation problems in regard to redistributive programs. First, they often are confronted with unresolved disputes about how much the redistributive principle should be emphasized in writing departmental regulations. Title I of the Elementary and Secondary Education Act (ESEA) is a case in point. A Democratic president, Lyndon Johnson, could embrace the ambiguity of purpose at the time of ESEA's passage because it was assumed that plenty of money would be available to meet both distributive and redistributive goals. Implementation problems seem less important when policy is expansionary. His successors have had to confront the question of how increasingly scarce resources are to be allocated. The Reagan administration supports block grants of such funds to the states in order to eliminate the issue from the federal political agenda.

The second problem that presidents face on redistributive issues is that of enforcement. Secretaries of health and human services are endlessly devising ways to control Medicare and Medicaid costs and reduce fraud and waste. Regulations for the distribution of food stamps, for serving handicapped schoolchildren, and for the application of affirmative-action laws constantly cause political problems. Presidents worry about the politics of these implementation problems and charge their department heads to cope with them administratively. But the actual delivery of service or application of a federal rule is so far away from the White House that it is very difficult for presidents, or their department heads, to keep much control. One scheme of command and control succeeds another as administrations succeed each other in office. Presidents can deal with the politics of implementation as they present themselves in Washington far more easily than they can cope with or even address hard questions of program administration throughout the country. These problems are left to presidential appointees in the departments in the hope that presidents will not have to be bothered with them.

The National Security Bureaucracies and Policy Implementation

Before examining implementation from a presidential perspective, we must know something of the bureaucratic cultures of the two departments that carry out national security policies, State and Defense.

The State Department. Franklin Roosevelt loved to joke that a Foreign Service officer could get to be an ambassador if he met three requirements: he was loyal to the service; he did nothing to offend people; and he never became intoxicated at public functions. Presidents perhaps always have had a certain disdain for the diplomat. In the immediate postwar period, however, the State Department was creative because of a conjunction of talented leaders and extraordinary problems. The department's policy-planning staff invented the Marshall Plan for economic aid to Europe, devised the Truman Doctrine of aid to Greece and Turkey, and laid the intellectual basis for the containment policy toward the Soviet Union and for the development of collective security systems around the world. The times required such creative responses, and the cluster of personalities was able to meet the challenge. Harry Truman was very open to advice from his principal cabinet officers, whom he respected. Secretary of State George Marshall was a strong manager of the department who charged the policy-planning staff to develop ideas, then used them. George Kennan, director of that staff, was a brilliant and articulate expert on Soviet affairs.

The next two secretaries of state, Dean Acheson and John Foster Dulles, were lawyers who were used to dealing with issues and individuals, but not managing organizations. This limitation was accompanied by a hardening of policy positions in an intensified cold war so that policy planning diminished in importance. Policy responses increasingly became products of bureaucratic routine. Secretaries of state advised presidents and coordinated high diplomacy in relative disengagement from their own department. External harassment of the State Department by anticommunist demagogues (especially Senator Joseph McCarthy) contributed to the department's decline.

The triumph of routine and rigidity was not solely the result of external causes. The Foreign Service Officer Corps and the State Department as an institution had developed habits of thinking and working that were uncongenial to policy innovation. Foreign Service officers have a strong sense of collective identity and common style that is protective of their traditional responsibilities but precludes their taking on new ones.[15] They see themselves as diplomats who are skilled in political negotiation and reporting, but place secondary emphasis on economic matters. This leads to a general world view that may be called "classical realism," which is perhaps characteristic of the foreign-office elites of other nations. The world is seen as relatively unchanging, despite surface manifestations of change. Thus, there is doubt about the efficacy of any effort to transform the world, whether it be through foreign aid or counterinsurgency warfare. In short, there is a skepticism about activist foreign policies that go against fundamental realities of power politics.

This mode of thought probably corresponds to reality more closely than most world views. Nonetheless, it left its adherents at a disadvantage in a series of activist administrations, beginning with that of John Kennedy, that wanted new ideas and innovations. Much of the thinking in State had become hardened around official positions of the past.

The "living system" of the State Department as an organization reinforces these predispositions.[16] One important dimension of the department's status system is that Foreign Service officers want to be ambassadors. As in the military, they subordinate themselves to the requirements of rising in an organizational hierarchy. This means being circumspect, not provoking conflicts, pleasing superiors, and compiling a good record of evaluations. The emphasis is on safety and conformity—to get ahead, go along. This norm is strengthened by the mystique of diplomacy as a special elite skill. The dominant pattern is one of playing it safe and withdrawing from potential conflict before it occurs. This is "groupthink" on an organizational scale, and it is the basic cause of the frustration presidents feel toward the State Department. To them, State seems to exist in a world of its own, and, to a large extent, they are right.

In recent years, State has not been even potentially effective as an instrument for either policy analysis or implementation. The secretary of state has had no special office to provide analyses, but rather a policy-planning staff that works in a vacuum divorced from current policy. This has put the secretary at the mercy of his bureaus, each with special interests to protect. The insularity of the Foreign Service officer's definition of his role has prevented any serious effort to make State the chief implementer and coordinator of presidential policy. Such authority has not even been exercised within State's official domain in foreign aid, education and information, and international economic matters.

The State Department's greatest deficiency is in military matters. Bureaucracies do not always seek to expand and often prefer a safe, limited role if it protects their prerogatives. In the years after World War II, State worked out an implicit jurisdictional agreement with the Pentagon: it would not meddle in military matters if Defense would leave diplomacy to State. This was seen in the relationship of Rusk and McNamara. Because Rusk regarded Vietnam as a military matter, McNamara became, by default and his own energy, the chief foreign-policy adviser to the president. Because of State's restraint and because of the tendency of presidents and their associates to see foreign-policy crises as military problems, the Pentagon has had far more influence over foreign policy than it might have had if State had been vigorous. The line between diplomacy and the use of military force is an unclear one, but the Pentagon crossed it by default on the part of State.

In sum, presidents seldom have been able to call on State for a fresh "political" perspective on national security matters. Nor have the diplomats in State been interested in riding herd on policy execution across the range of national security agencies.

The Department of Defense and the Military.   The relation of the White House to the Pentagon presents serious difficulties for presidential authority because of the special problem of civilian control of the military. This problem takes a number of different forms. Civilians must find ways to direct weapons development to serve long-term strategy in the face of efforts by each service to secure hardware of its own. They must be able to assert political perspectives over the military impulse to perceive many foreign-policy problems as susceptible to military resolution. The military machine must not be permitted to set its own strategies even in time of war since their strategies may contradict political objectives. These problems are partly organizational. They will be considered in turn.

A legally strong secretary of defense was created in 1958 by amendments to the National Security Act of 1947, which originally had set up the Defense Department as a holding company for the three services — army, navy, and air force. In 1958 continuing interservice competition for the development and control of strategic weapons led President Eisenhower to ask Congress for a strengthening of the role of secretary of defense. The three service secretaries were removed from the chain of command and replaced by unified multiservice commands that were responsible to the secretary of defense. The secretary's office also was strengthened by an increase in assistant secretaries and staff.

The secretary who profited from these changes was Robert McNamara, for it was too late for the Eisenhower administration to change its style. Eisenhower had relied on his own military knowledge and prestige to control the Pentagon. He chose secretaries of defense who saw themselves as economic managers of a defense establishment rather than as strategists or policy makers. However, Eisenhower's secretaries lacked the analytic staff to link a coherent defense strategy to budgets and service programs.[17] They merely set upper budgetary limits and relative service allocations and then allowed each service to set its own means toward strategic goals. Toward the end of his tenure, Eisenhower became worried about unceasing service pressure for the development of new weapons, pressure that was backed by pork-barrel impulses in Congress and industry, and warned of a "military-industrial complex" in his farewell address.

McNamara's influence on the organization of the federal government was original and creative. He was instructed by President Kennedy to strengthen and diversify American military strategy so that a "flexible response" would be possible.[18] But because the cost of maintaining multiple strategic options was high, McNamara designed a system to relate alternative strategies to budgets. Through systems analysis his talented staff of civilians, who had come from backgrounds in economics, statistics, and operations research, was able to decide which new weapons would achieve specified goals at the least possible cost. A second innovation was program budgeting, in which strategic programs were organized across service lines. Nuclear strike capability, conventional forces, home defense, and alternative weapons systems within each category were compared for cost and effectiveness.

McNamara used analytic methods in a completely new way to sort out the claims of the services. Such analysis inevitably strengthens the hand of the central decision maker, and the services strongly resisted his innovations. Ironically, the real effect of his system was to strengthen the military's influence in both the Kennedy and Johnson administrations. McNamara made military policy making so centralized and efficient that the influence of the Pentagon — now speaking with one voice for the first time — was enhanced. The military-industrial complex also thrived as the variety of weapons systems increased.

These political effects aside, it would be a mistake to claim too much for systems analysis and program budgeting. Although analytic procedures were brought to bear on the selection of specific weapons systems under McNamara, some of the decisions that were guided by analysis turned out to be blunders. The F-111 fighter plane, which was to be used jointly by the air force and navy in preference to separate service planes, was selected because of the smaller cost of having one plane, but it has never flown successfully. Effectiveness may have been sacrificed to cost. Still, one could find many opposite examples of particular services continuing for years with unscrutinized weapons that never become effective regardless of their great cost, such as army efforts to develop tanks that are so mechanically and electronically sophisticated that they continually break down.[19] Analytic planning heightens the intellectual quality of decisions, but it will not show policy makers what decisions to make. Policy makers must pick their way among competing claims and cope with unknowns. For this reason interservice competition can be useful. It produces conflicting sets of facts and arguments for decision makers — a sort of competitive market system within the Department of Defense. Without such conflict, there would be less information for decision making.

It should not be assumed that policy analysis at the decision-making level guarantees responsiveness to presidential or secretarial directions. For example, despite the considerable talk in the Kennedy administration about the need to develop a new capability for counterinsurgency warfare, none of the services was ready to fight such a war in Vietnam. The army massed troops in large formations, as in Korea and World War II. The air force simply bombed, as it had in World War II, ignoring all the lessons of strategic-bombing studies about the limitations of saturation bombing. The navy was not prepared for river patrols, but for deep-water work, and simply bombarded the shore from the rivers as if there were ships in the jungles. The consequence of all of this was that the massive power of the American military was no match for the small detachments of highly mobile Vietcong and North Vietnamese, who could outmaneuver American forces at will. Presidents cannot force the military to change its strategies and tactics because it has a monopoly over the means of implementing policy. A president cannot replace large sections of the military that refuse to adapt to new situations or orders. The same kind of conformity to received doctrine, smothering of dissent, and pursuit of advancement by catering to superiors that occurs in the State Department is also endemic in the military officer corps.[20]

Implementing Foreign and Defense Policies

The tasks and problems of presidential management of national security policy are similar to domestic responsibilities. Indeed, it could be argued that they are more difficult because policies must be implemented not just within one federal system, but around the world. Also, although the perspectives of presidents are necessarily global and strategic, the Departments of State, Defense, Treasury, and others that carry out particular policies are not required to take such a broad view. One thus finds a permanent tension between the presidential imperative to think and act according to global designs and the preference of departments for jurisdictional interpretations of policy. Henry Kissinger tells the story of the conflict between the Nixon White House and the State Department when India and Pakistan went to war in 1971. Nixon and Kissinger sided with Pakistan because that country had been the broker when the president sought to have secret conversations with the Chinese government about a possible U.S.-Chinese rapprochement. In addition, China was allied with Pakistan. The State Department did not present its case for evenhandedness between India and Pakistan in terms of a grand presidential strategy for easing the cold war and obtaining a strategic ally against the Soviet Union. State had not participated in the opening to China and, therefore, found it difficult to implement a policy toward Pakistan that reflected a new conception of U.S.-Chinese relations.[21] So its career diplomats argued that there was no reason to alienate India by favoritism to Pakistan.

One could argue the correctness of policy from either position. But the purpose of the example is to illustrate the gap between presidential and departmental perspectives. Oftentimes presidents who are determined to put their stamp on the world conceive of international relations in superficial and ideological terms that could stand correcting from the perspective of the departments' historical memory, experience, and realism. And, just as often, departments fail to see a larger picture because of bureaucratic narrowness. What is certain in either case is that implementation of presidential policy suffers in the long run if the departments that must carry out policy do not understand it or are not involved in its formation.

Presidents often believe that they can shape foreign policy personally. The link between policy formation and implementation is less apparent to presidents in foreign than in domestic policy because the arena in which they work appears to include only a relatively small number of world leaders. Presidents realize that these leaders, including presidents themselves, are constrained in their actions by governmental and geopolitical factors. But the hope that personal intervention can produce a breakthrough is strong, and sometimes it happens, as it did for President Carter when he personally achieved a peace agreement between Egypt and Israel at Camp David in 1978. It is, therefore, all the more disturbing to presidents to discover that they depend upon bureaucracies to implement the actions that are required in the aftermath of such interventions. Successive presidents have learned to mistrust and despise the State Department because advice requested by the White House has been slow in coming or, upon arrival, has seemed to be biased by departmental positions. Presidents find the department too remote to be a partner in the kinds of personal interventions that they favor. The same kinds of frustrations apply to the implementation of policy. Presidential policy decisions usually are made in general terms without consideration for the details of implementation. But for this reason they rarely are self-executing. The process of implementing presidential directives starts with the cabinet officers who are responsible for execution. But then it goes to others, further down in the departments, who must find concrete ways to carry them out.

Again, one can impose two valid interpretations on the tension that occurs between presidents and bureaucrats over implementation. Presidential policy sometimes is distorted because officials in the departments resist doing what they have been ordered to do. They may do this because the president has challenged the standards and routines of bureaucracy by, for example, suggesting to the navy that aircraft carriers are obsolete. Often, departments think the president is mistaken and will delay acting on a request until an effort has been made to change his mind. For example, the State Department thought it would be a great mistake to give any assistance to the Biafran rebels in the Nigerian civil war of the 1970s because the long-term national interest of the United States favored the maintenance of one Nigerian nation. The president had great difficulty getting even shipments of food sent to Biafra. On the other hand, presidents often fail to communicate their objectives clearly to departments, and policy, therefore, is made by default as it is implemented. This is unavoidable when an issue is so torn with conflict that the only feasible policy is a vague one. The internal disagreements within an administration then are transferred downward and become fights about implementation. It also is the case that presidents cannot possibly give explicit guidance on every decision. There are too many decisions, and presidents feel they are too busy making them to spend scarce time and energy on implementation questions. The best that can be expected is for presidents to make their policies clear to their cabinet officers and for those persons, in turn, to act vigorously to ensure that presidential directives are carried out at lower levels. However, the simultaneous existence of clear presidential policy, a high degree of mutual understanding between presidents and cabinet officers, and a capacity for vigorous administrative leadership by those officers is a rarity. These relationships are very loosely joined, and much falls by the wayside as a result.

In response to these bureaucratic frustrations, and because they are so keen to place their personal stamp not only on policy but on its execution, presidents are tempted to pull responsibility for the implementation of foreign policy into the White House. As we have seen, this often takes the form of authorizing the special assistant to the president for national security to conduct diplomatic negotiations, sometimes without the knowledge of the rest of the government. The most extreme modern example of this approach has been the Nixon presidency. But the extreme case illustrates a general rule, namely that the exclusion of cabinet officers and their subordinates from decisions causes implementation to suffer. Henry Kissinger reflects in his memoir that he doubts whether the SALT or China initiatives could have been made through the departments.[22] However, he also concludes that a president should not institutionalize White House control of policy implementation because it cuts off his own cabinet officers and makes them less willing to advocate presidential policy in their own spheres of influence.[23]

Still, White House direction is essential. Even if Foreign Service officers were more managerial in their style, it would not follow that the State Department ever would be able to secure the authority and leverage to direct other departments in the implementation of presidential directives. In the executive bureaucracy only the authority of the president is superior to that of individual cabinet officers and departments. Thus, central direction and coordination is a presidential function that cannot be delegated. To be sure, presidentially appointed task forces on specific subjects that are chaired by the cabinet officer with central responsibility, such as the Treasury for international monetary questions, Defense for strategic deployments, and State for the conduct of negotiations, will work well if it is clear that they have the support of the president. But only so much of national security policy can be implemented through task forces. The great bulk of work is carried out routinely through regular departmental channels. Further, interdepartmental groups most often work through mutual accommodation rather than centralized leadership.

PRESIDENTIAL IMPLEMENTATION STRATEGIES

All presidents face the same strategic tasks in getting programs implemented according to their intent. They must appoint subordinates who share their views. Supportive coalitions must be fostered down the chain of command. Presidential priorities must be communicated clearly and ambiguities clarified. Bureaucratic obstacles must be overcome. Delegation to avoid overload at the top must be combined with oversight to permit assessment and evaluation of how things are working.

Presidents differ according to their purposes and their personal understanding of effective organizational leadership. One would expect presidents of preparation to devote most of their attention to policy development and to delegate implementation to the permanent government. Presidents of achievement would follow an initial push for new policies by giving great attention to the reorganization of government in order to carry out the new programs. Presidents of consolidation would seek to regularize the implementation of previously enacted programs by modifying and specifying responsibilities in the permanent government. Yet one also would expect individual presidents of each type to vary in their understanding of effective strategies of managerial leadership.

The brief history of presidential implementation strategies from Roosevelt to Reagan that follows will provide material for a concluding analysis of the relations between presidential purposes and skills and leadership for policy implementation.

Franklin D. Roosevelt

Roosevelt went through three stages in his approach to program implementation. The first stage was to get new programs on the books as fast as possible without thought of how they would be implemented. The second stage was to get action out of these programs either by placing them in new agencies that were free of the existing departments or by assigning responsibility for implementation to trusted presidential assistants. The third stage, which developed from the realization that such strategies of improvisation ultimately were ineffective, was a presidential call for government reorganization to permit more effective administration and institutionalization of new programs.

Roosevelt set up new agencies like the Works Progress Administration (WPA) and Public Works Administration (PWA), both of which were intended to provide jobs for the unemployed, and then let their administrators, Harry Hopkins and Harold Ickes, compete. He guided important parts of foreign policy through assistant secretaries of state like Raymond Moley and later the long-time undersecretary, Sumner Welles, without bothering to tell the secretary of state, Cordell Hull, whom he primarily valued for his good relations with Congress. He used the competitive principle throughout the first term in order to stay informed, keep assistants on their toes, and learn by experiment what worked best.[24]

As the term wore on, Roosevelt became aware that it was increasingly difficult to supervise an executive branch in which a multitude of agencies reported directly to him rather than to department secretaries. Before the 1936 election, he responded favorably to a paper written by Charles E. Merriam, a University of Chicago political scientist, about the need to integrate the New Deal agencies into the regular departments. The result was the appointment of the President's Committee on Administrative Management, which was chaired by Louis Brownlow, a prominent public administrator.[25] The contributions of the committee to the development of the institutionalized presidency were discussed in Chapter 6, but it often is forgotten that the primary emphasis of Brownlow and his colleagues was not solely on increasing presidential staff, which was the chief result, but on enhancing the president's capacity to oversee the executive branch, in part through reorganization. The committee's 1937 report recommended not only the creation of six assistants to the president in the White House office and the transfer of the Bureau of the Budget from the Treasury Department to a newly created Executive Office of the President, but the establishment of the National Resources Planning Board (NRPB) in EOP as a permanent planning agency to coordinate government programs. Congress approved these changes but later abolished the NRPB. It would not agree to the creation of two new executive departments for Public Works and Public Welfare, nor to a broadening of the mission of the Department of the Interior under the new name of a Conservation Department. The reasons were in part ideological, such as opposition to institutionalizing public works or welfare, which were thought to be temporary programs developed in response to the depression, and in part jurisdictional, such as whether the Forest Service should stay in Agriculture or go to a new Conservation Department and whether the U.S. Employment Service should stay in the Department of Labor or go to a new Department of Welfare. Western groups and labor interests had strong views on these questions and much influence in Congress.

The Brownlow committee also recommended that every executive agency be placed under the authority of one of the twelve departments, something that Roosevelt in some degree accomplished when Congress later gave him the authority to reorganize executive-branch agencies subject to congressional veto. He used his reorganization authority to create the Federal Security Agency (the precursor of the Department of Health, Education, and Welfare of 1953), a Federal Works Agency, and a Federal Loan Agency. He also established the Executive Office of the President. But, in the final analysis, the work of the Brownlow committee resulted in an increase of the presidency's capacity for policy formation rather than for management of the executive branch.

Harry S. Truman

Chapter 6 described how Truman promoted the development of the institutional presidency through his use of the CEA, NSC, and CIA. His advocacy of a unified Department of Defense reflected his strong belief in centralized departmental management, a principle he extended to the Department of Labor when he eventually was able to return the Employment Service to the department. Truman believed in orthodox public administration on the basis of his experience as a county executive in Missouri, his military experience in World War I, and his own self-image as one who could make decisions. He drew the inference that this capacity would be enhanced by orderly administrative arrangements.[26] In addition, Truman found the federal government, after the helter skelter of depression and war, to be organizationally chaotic and used the theme of reorganization to preserve public confidence in the New Deal agencies and to counteract growing popular fear of "big government."[27]

Truman's most effective efforts at reorganization came when Congress gave its assent to specific recommendations of the Commission on the Organization of the Executive Branch of Government, which was chaired by former President Herbert Hoover. Truman selectively presented those recommendations to Congress as they emerged through 1952. The president had his own appointees and allies on the commission, but his most important achievement was to persuade Hoover that the New Deal programs should not be rejected but improved in their administration. Truman's upset victory in the 1948 election may have eased the task of persuasion. In any event the Hoover commission provided the vehicle through which congressional opponents of the Brownlow committee, Roosevelt, and the New Deal could embrace the managerial presidency.[28]

Truman was able to persuade Congress to follow most Hoover commission recommendations to strengthen the controls of department secretaries over their departments. But exceptions arose, sometimes because the policies of a secretary were politically controversial, as with Secretary Charles Brannan of Agriculture, who was thought to be "radical." In addition, Truman never could get the Federal Security Agency elevated to department status because the American Medical Association argued that the new department would be the vehicle for national health insurance, the first step toward "socialized medicine."[29] Truman eventually became discouraged about reorganization as a tool of management because the fights to win approval were so time-consuming and costly politically and the actual reforms did not always achieve the goals intended.[30] After Truman the government was as "inherently unmanageable" as it ever had been, but it now was clearer than ever that politics permeated all administration and limited the control of presidents.[31]

Still, Truman's presidency saw the creation of a number of new institutions in response to problems of international politics. These institutions, in their first years, were innovative and responsive to the directions of presidential policy. The unified Department of Defense, the Central Intelligence Agency, the U.S. Information Agency, and the National Security Council were effective instruments of presidential action, especially when joined to a revitalized State Department, which supplied most of the leading ideas for the administration in foreign policy. One can perceive greater unity of purpose and action among these organizations than in subsequent periods, when the organizations no longer were new or their conceptions of the world universally shared. There had been insufficient time for bureaucratization to occur.[32] This is one reason why Truman was more willing to rely on the departments for both policy advice and implementation than subsequent presidents have been. However, there obviously were problems of coordination among so many different agencies. In 1950 a Bureau of the Budget study that was undertaken for the president pointed out the difficulties of policy implementation under an NSC structure in which cabinet officers participated in common discussions prior to presidential decisions but then took separate responsibility for implementing these decisions, with attendant consequences for the quality of coordination and cooperation. The report recommended the creation of a position for a special assistant to the president for national security who would oversee both policy development and implementation, a step Eisenhower later took.[33]

Dwight D. Eisenhower

Eisenhower had much in common with Truman as an administrator. He subscribed to the orthodoxies of centralized management and practiced them by using cabinet officers as his primary advisers and administrative aides.

Eisenhower used the regular meetings of the cabinet to discuss issues of general importance to the administration and communicate presidential decisions clearly. Most policy decisions were made in smaller forums, but Eisenhower strongly believed in using the cabinet to establish an atmosphere of collegiality.[34] He also used the cabinet secretariat to follow up presidential decisions. After every meeting the secretary of the cabinet would meet with the immediate subordinates of the department secretaries in the White House cabinet room to explain the president's decisions and the reasoning behind them. These officials were expected to return to their departments and relay what they had been told to any departmental officials who needed such information in order to implement actions.[35]

Eisenhower's system was more formal in national security policy. Chapter 6 described the manner in which NSC assistants to the president oversaw the development of policy through the preparation of agency papers and the coordination of views by the NSC planning board. The same method was applied to the implementation of policy when Eisenhower created the Operations Coordinating Board as the executive arm of the NSC. Its members were the second-ranking executives in each department or agency that was concerned with national security, and its responsibility, under the oversight of the presidential assistant for national security, was to carry out presidential decisions through thirty or forty standing interdepartmental task forces.[36] Most of the task forces were chaired by State Department officials. The system was simultaneously a test of the president's capacity to get decisions implemented through mechanisms that were responsible to the White House and of the ability of the State Department to provide leadership in a collegial system.

In the domestic sphere Eisenhower saw little need to innovate beyond the completion of goals that had been set by Truman, such as the creation of the Department of Health, Education, and Welfare in 1953, the strengthening of the powers of the secretary of agriculture (this time a Republican conservative), and, on his own initiative, the enhanced unification of the Department of Defense by downgrading the service secretaries in favor of the secretary of defense. Eisenhower used his great personal authority as former general to achieve this change.[37]

John F. Kennedy

Kennedy came to the presidency with a public commitment to "get the country moving again" after eight years of alleged quiescence under Eisenhower. To Kennedy this meant fresh, innovative policies. His conception of the role of the president accordingly was activist; the primary responsibility was to articulate the national agenda. Kennedy's specific ideas about presidential leadership were shaped by political scientist Richard Neustadt, who first published his classic book *Presidential Power* in 1960.[38] Neustadt, who advised Kennedy during the transition on how to staff the presidency, used his interpretation of Franklin Roosevelt's presidential style to support his argument that the president is the catalyst that causes things to happen. He was critical of what he perceived to be a bureaucratization of the Eisenhower presidency in which the elaborate staffing of issues through interdepartmental committees tended to filter out choices that a president who was more personally involved might make. Neustadt advised Kennedy to travel light by not encumbering himself with a large White House staff, and to avoid interdepartmental committees. Such advice appealed to Kennedy, whose personal style was to rely on individuals rather than committees or organization plans.

The manifestations of this energetic approach to government in regard to policy formation were described in Chapter 6. Kennedy used Theodore Sorensen, Walter Heller, and other senior staff assistants as catalysts to stir up and to extract fresh ideas from a wide range of presidential advisers in and out of government. McGeorge Bundy and a small national security staff functioned in the same manner for foreign policy. Kennedy also used his principal cabinet officers as advisers, particularly in foreign and economic policy, but he was skeptical of the bureaucracies beneath them. One Kennedy White House aide recalled that the president gradually lost confidence in the State Department "because the State Department advice wasn't the crisp, well-reasoned advice that he was accustomed to. It just kind of slid along. . . . It didn't have any bright, forward thinking."[39]

Kennedy paid considerably more attention to the development and enactment of policy than to its implementation. But he handled the management and implementation of his administration's policies and programs with the same style he applied to policy formation. Because Kennedy disliked interdepartmental committees, he abolished those that had been established under

Eisenhower and substituted ad hoc task forces to oversee the implementation of policies. Each task force was itself overseen by a member of his staff. He thus could monitor the bureaucracy's responsiveness to presidential goals.[40]

Kennedy's efforts to overcome the natural tendencies of bureaucracy may have gained him an increased capacity for action. They also may have forfeited opportunities to get the permanent government on board through means of regular, bureaucratic procedures. Kennedy would disregard formal jurisdictional lines at times and use personal assistants for missions that might otherwise have been given to the departments. For example, Arthur Schlesinger, Jr., was not only an adviser in the White House, but was used by Kennedy as an emissary to Latin America.[41] Myer Feldman of the White House staff, who had close ties to Israeli officials and was well versed in Middle East issues, was used by Kennedy as a liaison to Israel, along with State Department counterparts. At no time were regular State Department channels circumvented, but Feldman was able to give Kennedy a perspective on people and issues that was more personal and direct than that of the Department of State, which balanced advice to the president with its responsibility to reconcile a number of different viewpoints within the department and among the nations of the Middle East.[42]

The Kennedy administration showed early signs of what was to become increasing tension between the White House and the departments in the years that were to follow. But the Kennedy balance was to attempt to capture both the drive for innovation from the White House and the stability and institutional knowledge of the permanent government. The general pattern, both in aspiration and reality, was genuine cooperation between White House and departmental staffs, each of which needed the other to do its work. Sorensen and Bundy and their small staffs could not hope to influence the departments without the cooperation of allies in those departments. They made no attempts to override departments. Instead, the role of presidential staff was to make sure that the president had the widest range of advice possible prior to decisions and knew what was happening after decisions had been made.[43]

Lyndon B. Johnson

After his massive landslide victory in 1964, Johnson knew that he had only a limited time to win approval of the Great Society programs from Congress. He would tell his aides over and over that maximum pressure had to be applied quickly because Congress soon would rebel, which in fact it did after the 1966 elections. The result was that most of the social programs that constituted the Great Society were developed by Bill Moyers and his successor, Joseph Califano, on the basis of task-force reports and in hurried consultation with the BOB and departmental groups. As we saw in Chapter 4, Johnson concerned himself with the likely attitudes of congressional and interest-group leaders toward proposals, not with matters of implementation. When he raised questions about program design, it was to increase political appeal. In many cases this compounded future administrative problems. For example, the Model Cities program, which came to him in 1966 as a demonstration plan intended for two cities, was immediately expanded by Johnson to more than one hundred cities to increase its appeal in Congress. The president explained to his aides that a carefully designed demonstration program would mean nothing to members of Congress, who wished all social programs to embody the distributive principle of geographic dispersion.

One difficulty with the Great Society was that implementation too often was not considered carefully at the outset. Another was that there were so many programs. From 1965 to 1969 some five hundred new social programs became law that had not existed before.[44] There were two major consequences of this growth in government. First, the overlapping responsibilities of departments and agencies increased greatly, as did the need for cooperation and coordination between Washington and "the field." Second, the balance of authority among federal, state, and local governments was tipped drastically in the direction of the federal government. This was the intent, and there is considerable evidence that national objectives were approximated. But the Great Society programs generated puzzling administrative problems. It was difficult to enforce national standards on so many diverse jurisdictions. There was failure to comply with federal regulations through subtle indifference or institutional incapacity. Conflict among the different levels of the federal system was common. Questions of compliance with the letter of the law often became more important to federal officials than local implementation within the spirit of the law. By the late 1960s it was apparent that the great burst of federal activity had created unanticipated administrative problems that strained the managerial capacities of the federal government and, therefore, of the presidency.

Johnson learned about the implementation problems in many of his programs from politicians rather than through administrative channels, and, since he was not experienced in management, he initially was at a loss about what to do. His first response was to ask Califano and his small staff to ride herd on problems of coordination among departments and agencies. Califano remembers:

Beginning at the end of 1966, through the time Lyndon Johnson left office on January 20, 1969, the White House Domestic Affairs staff devoted less time to devising new programs and helping gain their enactment than to the problem of implementing and coordinating the cornucopia of Great Society legislation that had been and was still being enacted. . . .

Seemingly interminable meetings were held in my White House office. . . . Most of that time was spent . . . on such bureaucratically thorny issues as who would do what and who would have how much authority over which programs. Arguments at the highest levels of government can often be reduced to absurd bickering. . . .

As a president's frustration with operational fragmentation increases, he discovers with each missed objective that there is no one person in his government he can hold bureaucratically and politically responsible. . . . Whether Republican or Democratic, liberal or conservative, the presidential reaction will be instinctively identical: Get someone in the White House to handle it. So common is this reaction in national security matters that we hardly notice it. But the same orders are increasingly issued in domestic affairs.[45]

The reliance on White House staffers to do what someone else should be doing is ultimately self-defeating. A small staff cannot possibly cover such a wide territory. Presidential staff intervention in policy implementation is fire fighting rather than comprehensive oversight. Johnson finally concluded that the extensive reorganization of the executive branch was the ultimate solution to the administrative confusion that he faced on all fronts.[46] He had achieved some coherence with the creation of the Departments of Housing and Urban Development in 1965 and Transportation in 1966. But a more fundamental question was being asked throughout government, especially by governors and mayors who were discontented about the problems of administering federal grant-in-aid programs: Could there be an effective central guidance and coordination system for the implementation of the Great Society programs?[47] In response to these promptings Johnson appointed a task force of experienced government hands in September 1966 with Ben W. Heineman, a railroad executive from Chicago, as its chairman. Their key recommendation was that an Office of Program Coordination be created in the Executive Office of the President to monitor and settle jurisdictional disputes among departments in Washington and the field on behalf of the departments. They also recommended as a blueprint for the future that the existing departments be organized into superdepartments along such comprehensive themes as economic affairs, social services, and natural resources, all in order to permit department heads better to manage the government on behalf of the president.[48]

The task force sent many reports to the president, but its principal attention was given to the problems of organizing and managing the Great Society programs. In contrast to the Brownlow committee, the task force stressed words like "guidance," "influence," and "coordination" rather than "management." This reflected the belief that the presidency could not manage programs directly but should be able to guide their development with increased administrative help. The goal was to "presidentialize" departmental and agency structures so that they would be more responsive to the top. There also was a fresh emphasis on decentralization of field operations within this framework of accountability.[49]

There is no record of Johnson's view of the Heineman recommendations. His preoccupation with the Vietnam War precluded his giving them much attention. The task-force reports have not been published, and, indeed, Johnson ordered that they be sent to the Johnson Library and not shown to Nixon. But Heineman gave the papers to Roy Ash, the head of Nixon's reorganization effort, and they influenced the thinking and conclusions of the Ash Council.[50]

Johnson also sought stronger implementation authority in foreign policy by having the NSC publish National Security Action Memorandum 342 on March 4, 1966, in which the secretary of state specifically was authorized to exercise authority on behalf of the president and the NSC in the implementation of presidential policy. But military issues were not included in the grant of authority, and the lack of enthusiasm on the part of Rusk and his Foreign Service professionals was sufficient to nullify NSAM 342. A memorandum was not sufficient to alter the problem of creating presidential authority within bureaucracies that are remote from the president.[51] The Heineman committee later recommended a similar State-centered system, but by that time Johnson's mind was taken up with Vietnam and nothing was done.[52]

Johnson, like Roosevelt, created new programs that in time became institutionalized. But the logic of their purposes did not bring administrative coherence to government. They introduced centrifugal political and administrative forces that sustained action but not implementation. The kinds of political obstacles to the reorganizations of the executive branch that were proposed by the Brownlow committee would have reappeared in the Johnson administration had the Heineman recommendations been put to the test.

Richard M. Nixon

Nixon had little administrative experience when he became president. He appears to have accepted the conventional wisdom that the president should limit his attention to a few major policy questions and let cabinet officers manage the government. Management, in this view, was some mysterious skill practiced in business that could be transferred to government. He initially structured his administration to have a small White House staff and to permit no barriers between himself and his cabinet officers. This arrangement lasted only six months because it matched neither Nixon's administrative temperament nor his real feelings about government. Nixon preferred to work not through conversation or committees, but from paper. In addition, he and his aides saw confirmation of their worst fears about Republican cabinet officers being "captured" by the supposedly Democratic civil service. In response to these perceptions the president turned to top White House aides as his principal policy advisers.[53]

By the end of the first term Nixon and his principal advisers had concluded that it was impossible to run the government from the White House. A combination of overload and incapacity had resulted from trying to do so. As the Domestic Council amd OMB staffs took on more and more authority over the departments, White House clearance was required for a growing number of policy and administrative questions, and EOP staffs found themselves mired deeper and deeper in the details of departmental administration. Cabinet officers increasingly were cut off from the president and uninformed about the work of presidential staffs in their departments. The White House staff itself had grown so large that internal confusion prevailed. More importantly, less time was available for policy development, the initial intention, and more time was given to riding herd on details of departmental administration, a matter in which White House staffs had little competence or experience. It was these difficulties that convinced Nixon that the bureaucracy could not be controlled by a counterbureaucracy in the White House.[54] Thus, at the beginning of his second term in 1973 he attempted to carry out a revolution of three complementary parts.

The Ash Council had recommended the consolidation of several domestic departments into four superagencies to be called Human Resources, Community Development, Natural Resources, and Economic Affairs. Its debt to Heineman, and even to Brownlow, was obvious. Nixon presented this reorganization plan to Congress in 1971, and it was ignored for the reason that all comprehensive reorganization schemes are ignored—too many political relationships, both in and out of Congress, would be upset by such massive changes. But in late 1972 Nixon hit upon the idea of implementing the recommendations without legislation. He asked all of the members of his cabinet to resign and, although some were retained, he created a two-tier cabinet along the lines of the Ash model. Three secretaries were to be "counselors" to the president with offices in the old Executive Office Building next to the White House, and in that capacity they were to chair Domestic Council committees composed of subordinate secretaries. The secretary of agriculture was to oversee natural resources; the secretary of health, education and welfare, human resources; and the secretary of housing and urban development, community development. George Shultz, the secretary of the treasury, also would be an assistant to the president for economic affairs. These four broad groupings corresponded to the Ash recommendations for four superdepartments. At the same time, people without governmental experience were appointed to lesser cabinet positions, and large numbers of White House staff members were sent to the departments to fill undersecretary and assistant-secretary posts. The idea was that cabinet officers in the lesser departments would be virtually bypassed on important matters—the Nixon people in the departments would take their orders from the supersecretaries and OMB, a chain of command that would flow directly from the president.[55]

A second feature of the attempted revolution was the effort to implement central features of Nixon's program to consolidate grants-in-aid into special revenue-sharing block grants without congressional approval. Congress had rejected the special revenue-sharing proposals, but now the administration would implement them through departmental regulations. For example, manpower training grants had been divided among hundreds of private and public organizations under contracts from the regional offices of the Department of Labor. Gradually the department began to issue new regulations that would favor the sponsorship of training through state and local government organizations designated for that purpose. This was an attempt to make the delivery of manpower services more efficient and coherent.

A third part of the revolution was the war that Nixon declared on Congress in 1972 and 1973 when he impounded and refused to spend appropriated funds that in his judgment exceeded a reasonable budget size. Congress was not assuming its responsibilities to balance income and expenditures, Nixon argued, so it was his responsibility to do that for it through impoundment.

These three initiatives—reorganization and rule from the top, devolution of programs to the states and localities, and budget reduction—were parts of a coherent strategy to increase the president's command over the federal bureaucracy while reducing the importance of the federal government. The Watergate scandal intervened, and in the spring of 1973 both Haldeman and Ehrlichman left the White House, to be replaced by more seasoned professionals such as Melvin Laird, a former congressman, who promptly forced the cancellation of the supercabinet and initiated cooperation with Congress for the passage of compromise special revenue-sharing programs. Nixon also lost several cases in the courts on the impoundment question.[56]

When Gerald Ford succeeded to the presidency in 1974, he was advised by a special transition committee of prominent Republicans to reverse the Nixon policies of central administrative control, even to the extent of limiting OMB's efforts to improve administrative management in the departments. Ford, a legislative man, happily accepted this advice, and for two and a half years the White House and EOP staffs concerned themselves with policy formation and public relations, leaving implementation to the departments.[57]

Nixon attempted no comprehensive organizational reform for the implementation of national security policy, but the closely held White House system of policy formation that was described in Chapter 6 had consequences for policy implementation as well. In the process of strengthening the analytic role of the National Security Council staff, Nixon and Kissinger restored the distinction between policy and operations that Kennedy and Bundy had "rubbed out," in Bundy's words. Nixon and Kissinger originally intended policy decisions to be made in the White House and implemented by the State Department. Kissinger, therefore, directed the work of the NSC staff into the analysis of policy issues. He was slow to recognize that it seldom was enough to get a decision made; he and his staff then had to spend time getting it carried out.[58] The result was that there was increasing pressure on Kissinger from the president to play an operational role. For example, in 1970 the Washington Special Action Group was created to conduct detailed operational administration of crises, such as the Cambodian incursion, because Nixon did not believe that delegation of such matters to the departments would permit the necessary presidential control of operations. The problem, which Kissinger later acknowledged, was that to the extent the NSC staff is pulled into day-to-day bureaucratic combat on questions of implementation, it neglects its function as a staff for the analysis of policy choices.[59]

It was beyond the capacity of the Nixon-Kissinger structure to build centers of strength that were responsive to the president in other parts of the foreign-affairs government.[60] Kennedy and Johnson had used their White House staffs to try to build such support and had met with mixed success. But Nixon and Kissinger lacked even a strategy. The replacement of appointed department professionals that characterized the brief domestic "administrative presidency" was not possible with the Foreign Service Officer Corps or the professional military. Because he had built no supportive alliances among them, Nixon often encountered resistance to his policies in both the State Department and the military services. For example, the State Department dragged its heels on relief for Biafra in the Nigerian civil war. The military delayed the president's order to destroy stockpiles of biological weapons. The White House had great difficulty during the Nixon years applying policy analysis to defense budgets because it had not worked to develop analytic allies in the Defense Department who could work with the NSC staff.[61] On even more important issues, Kissinger learned that the highly personal foreign policy in which he and Nixon had engaged with the Soviet Union and China could not be continued during the second term:

If we had built well and true, the nation's foreign policy would have to be institutionalized. To leave a legacy rather than a tour de force we would have to entrust greater responsibility to the permanent officials of the Department of State and the Foreign Service.[62]

Kennedy and Johnson failed to get the secretary of state to build the positions of strength in the permanent government necessary to implement presidential policy. Nixon's experience made it clear that the assistant to the president for national security affairs also lacks the institutional strength to perform that function. The failure of both strategies illustrates the weakness of the presidency in regard to policy implementation.

Jimmy Carter

The Carter administration emphasized policy development rather than implementation because, like the Kennedy administration, it was seeking to establish a new policy agenda. Carter delegated policy implementation to cabinet officers and generally kept the White House staff out of administrative oversight. The one exception was the very effective intergovernmental relations staff that was developed by Jack Watson, who served as a point of contact with the cabinet officers and departments and the mayors and governors on both policy and implementation questions. Watson also was secretary of the cabinet. But, for the most part, Carter deliberately avoided any sign of the imperiousness that had characterized the Nixon White House. It was, however, assumed that the passage of welfare reform and, perhaps, of national health insurance would require sustained attention to administrative questions in a second term.[63]

Carter's fundamental approach to managerial questions may have been derived from his engineering cast of mind. He thought in terms of reorganizing structures as the way to make them work more efficiently. He regarded his primary achievement as governor of Georgia to have been consolidation into a few comprehensive departments of a large number of archaic agencies and independent boards that were closely tied to local courthouse politics.[64] After he became president, he created the Presidential Reorganization Project in OMB and looked to it to make continuous recommendations for the improvement of executive-branch organization. As could have been predicted, departmental reorganizations that were politically feasible were accomplished, but much else simply fell into a political vacuum. The Department of Energy was created in response to a widely perceived need to combine a loose collection of separate agencies. The Office of Education in the Department of Health, Education, and Welfare was transformed into a new Department of Education because of the political support of organized education groups. More complex plans for Departments of Urban Economic Development and Natural Resources never got off the drawing board because of political opposition.[65]

Yet Carter never paid much personal attention to reorganization. He approached it, much as he approached most policy issues, with the belief that through intelligent planning one could formulate proposals to which all right-minded people would give assent. He learned only gradually that there are no intellectually correct solutions to questions of either policy or organization.

People divide strongly on such questions because their values clash.[66]

Nor did Carter give much personal attention to building alliances within his own government for policy implementation. As a result, there was a real lack of unity in his administration. A number of his cabinet officers had prior experience in national government, so he permitted them to select their immediate associates in the departments. What pressure there was from the White House was to place representatives of the Democratic constituencies in sub-cabinet posts. The layer just beneath the top was filled, to a great extent, with representational appointments from the environmental and consumer movements, the women's movement, and minority groups. Not only was there a great gap in style and approach between top Carter appointees and their own subordinates in many cases, but the president found that many departmental administrators were primarily policy advocates rather than managers, and indeed were advocates of more liberal policies than he supported. It was difficult to assemble coherent management teams within the departments and even more difficult to do so for the administration as a whole.[67]

Carter's principal administrative initiative was the reform of the senior civil service that the director of the Civil Service Commission steered through Congress in 1978. The principal achievement of the Civil Service Reform Act was to create a Senior Executive Service that high-level civil servants might join if they wished. They would receive higher pay and bonuses for good performance but could be transferred to different positions by presidentially appointed executives. The purpose of the reform was to combine greater responsiveness from career officials to the president with increased incentives for superior performance. The reform is a modern response to the old tension between presidents and bureaucrats. It promises greater flexibility and responsiveness but also threatens to politicize the higher civil service. As senior career officials lose their independence, they may become more reluctant to give candid advice to their political superiors. Continuity and institutional memory may be weakened as career officials are shuffled, reshuffled, and retired by succeeding administrations.

Carter attempted no innovations in the implementation of national security policy. With one or two exceptions, the assistant for national security and his staff were not injected into operations, and the implementation of policy proceeded through departmental chains of command as in the Ford administration.

Ronald Reagan

Reagan simultaneously pursued both legislative and managerial strategies to enhance his control of the executive branch and the implementation of programs. Reduction in the growth of programs was one such strategy. In January 1981 Reagan proposed budget reductions in more than two hundred programs, amounting to $180 billion over a four-year period. Most of these cuts were approved by Congress, and the across-the-board rate of budgetary increase for fiscal 1982 was reduced to almost half the Carter administration proposal for the same period, down from 4.1 percent to 2.3 percent.[68] Another Reagan strategy was the successful consolidation of a number of specific programs into block grants to the states, which were given increased discretion about expenditures. This was a first step in Reagan's plan to devolve authority and responsibility onto state government and reduce the federal role.[69] It was followed in 1982 by a proposal to Congress and the states for an intergovernmental "swap" of responsibilities: the federal government was to assume financial and administrative responsibility for Medicaid in return for assumption by the states of responsibility for welfare programs. Most governors opposed the Reagan plans, which prevented a compromise solution from emerging.[70] That failure aside, however, Reagan was able to combine budgetary policy with program redesign in order to both reduce federal authority and increase presidential control.

Reagan also moved quickly to assert the authority of the presidency within the executive branch. Presidential appointments were used to put Reagan loyalists into the top positions of the departments and agencies. Being a Republican was not enough; one also had to share Reagan's conservative ideology and give evidence of personal support for the president before Inauguration Day. The intention was to compose an administration of such like-minded people that the managerial authority of the president would be exercised automatically. The creation of cabinet councils, each guided by White House aides, manifested the Reagan principle of collegiality through central oversight and control.[71] To be sure, it was easier to find people to serve in departments and agencies whose mission was compatible with Reagan's ideology, such as deregulation of business, than it was to fill positions in agencies whose purposes clashed with Reagan goals, such as the Environmental Protection Agency.[72] In some cases, posts were not filled for months, and when they were filled, conflict ensued between presidential and career appointees, usually in the form of press leaks. However, with a few exceptions, the administration established control over such agencies by moving aside unsympathetic members of the Senior Executive Service and replacing them with allies. Also, much more attention was paid to middle-level civil service appointments and promotions than in past administrations. Reagan showed that it is possible for a determined president to achieve bureaucratic compliance with administration policy through infiltration rather than hierarchical control.[73]

There were other manifestations of Reagan's intent to use the discretion of executive agencies to loosen federal controls over the society. Thus, Secretary of the Interior James Watt rewrote regulations to alter the balance against conservation of federal lands and in favor of oil and gas exploration. White House and Health and Human Services officials succeeded in removing the "working poor" from most welfare rolls in line with administration budgetary policy.[74]

Reagan's pattern of centralization, devolution, and reduction in the federal role is similar in some ways to Nixon's. But there is a significant difference. Nixon attempted to consolidate and rationalize federal programs. Reagan was determined to abolish a number of programs and to eliminate the federal role from others. He did not fully succeed, but the direction was clear.

The management of national security policy also revealed Reagan's centralizing predisposition but without the accompanying theme of devolution. His militant cold-war view of the world meant that he was not willing to set limits to U.S. intervention abroad, as Nixon had done in response to public reaction against the Vietnam War. Rather, intervention was the theme, as seen in Central America and the Middle East. By the same token Reagan's pattern of tight collegiality enforced from the top was even stronger in national security policy than in domestic policy. Reagan initially promised primacy to the State Department, pledging that his assistant for national security would be *only* an assistant. But early in the administration senior White House aides rejected a memorandum by Secretary of State Alexander Haig that would have enforced such primacy. Haig's action conflicted with the teamwork principle that was so strong in the new administration. Continuous clashes between Haig (and his successor, George Shultz) and Secretary of Defense Caspar Weinberger eventually had the effect of strengthening the hand of Reagan's second appointee as assistant for national security. William Clark, an old Reagan colleague from California, did not seek to be a policy rival to either secretary but increasingly felt that he had to assert the president's goals in foreign policy. This was managerial rather than policy action, but it illustrates again Reagan's principle of centralized collegiality.

TYPES OF PRESIDENTS AND IMPLEMENTATION STRATEGIES

All presidents face the same strategic problems of policy implementation. They must make their goals clear, place supporters in important positions, resolve managerial conflicts, and ensure that presidential policy is followed down the chain of command. These tasks must be carried out in a governmental structure in which presidential control is limited by constitutional and political constraints. The Constitution gives Congress considerable influence over bureaucratic organization and practice, which permits organized interests to build alliances between the bureaucracy and Congress that may undercut the president. The management of implementation is thus a political task.

There are maxims of management that all presidents can heed if they wish to implement their programs effectively. Presidential staffs can monitor programs but should not try to manage them. Presidents should bind cabinet officers closely to themselves and their objectives because the department secretaries are the chief engines for presidential management. Skillful use of the appointment power throughout the executive branch is the best means to ensure adherence to presidential programs.

But presidents with different policy purposes also will have different management strategies. Policy formation, which was described in Chapter 6, and policy implementation are two sides of the same coin. The president's styles of managing policy formation and policy implementation manifest a unified presidential style of authority.

Presidents of Preparation

Presidents of preparation care most about the development of new policies. Many of the policies are not enacted, which means that these presidents do not have to pay much attention to implementation questions. Still, such presidents have a certain restlessness about the "inertia" of the permanent government and are inclined to use the White House staff as a catalyst to stir things up both for policy development and implementation. Because Kennedy was skeptical of the capacities of bureaucratic committees and institutional structures to produce ideas or action, he looked to his own staff for oversight of policy implementation. But he did not attempt to run the government from the White House. Carter trusted less in persons and more in mechanisms and, therefore, looked to impersonal procedures such as zero-base budgeting and departmental reorganization. For the most part, however, the political forces that these presidents invoked were directed toward developing new policies rather than managing existing ones.

Presidents of Achievement

Policy development is carried to enactment by presidents of achievement. But the rush to push presidential programs into law is so great that little time or attention is given to the feasibility of implementing them. In fact the need for legislative acceptability may make for compromises on program structure that later make implementation problematic. Once the new programs are in place, however, presidents of achievement are forced to address problems of implementation because the interest groups for which the programs were enacted have shifted their attention to the implementation process.

Roosevelt and Johnson both dealt with the implementation challenge in stages. They first tried to rely on individuals within the presidential orbit to manage implementation on an ad hoc basis. When the limitations of this approach became apparent, they sought to reorganize the executive branch in ways that would both increase presidential authority and improve the capacities of agencies to administer programs. The objective, which in each case was to strengthen government, was a manifestation of the belief in the efficacy of government that had inspired the burst of new policies. However, progressive presidents of achievement, such as Roosevelt and Johnson, unleash political forces through their policy creativity that are not easily harnessed by organizational reform. The resort to reorganization ultimately is disappointing.

As a conservative president of achievement, Ronald Reagan reveals a different pattern. Legislative enactment was crucial to the success of his agenda, but the agenda itself was directed toward administrative change. Programs were to be reduced, and federal responsibilities devolved to the states. These goals permitted a strategy of tight presidential control of the departments and agencies from the outset, since management was the main objective. Such a strategy would not suit progressive presidents of achievement. The generation of ideas and mobilization of political forces for new programs that these presidents require is served by a loose, pluralistic management strategy that makes implementation more difficult in the long run. Reagan's achievement was in implementation itself.

Presidents of Consolidation

Presidents of consolidation direct policy development primarily to the modification and consolidation of existing programs. When they propose new policies, as Eisenhower did with federal aid for school construction, civil rights, and the interstate highway system, careful attention is paid at the outset to administrative feasibility. Nixon's introduction of comprehensive welfare reform was accompanied by months of careful planning for policy implementation by the HEW and Labor Department staffs. The logic of a presidency of consolidation requires that the president establish relationships of confidence, through delegation, between presidential and departmental staffs. This principle was much more apparent in the Eisenhower administration than in Nixon's government. Eisenhower was an army man who believed in careful staff analysis prior to decisions at the command level and subsequent delegation of administration to the field. Nixon lacked a consistent theory and moved impulsively from one strategy of management to another. He tried two different forms of hierarchy, the first through the use of personal assistants and the second through administrative control. Neither approach worked because neither was consistent with the pluralistic character of American government.

NOTES

1. Philip Selznick, *Leadership in Administration: A Sociological Interpretation* (New York: Harper & Row, 1957), *passim*.
2. Richard Rose, *Managing Presidential Objectives* (New York: The Free Press, 1976), *passim*.
3. Zbigniew Brzezinski, *Power and Principle* (New York: Farrar, Straus & Giroux, 1983), chs. 10 and 13.
4. George P. Greenberg, "Governing HEW: Problems of Management and Control at the Department of Health, Education and Welfare" (Ph.D. diss., Harvard University, 1972), p. 1.
5. *Ibid.*, ch. 4.
6. Alain C. Enthoven and K. Wayne Smith, *How Much Is Enough: Shaping the Defense Program, 1961–69* (New York: Harper & Row, 1971), *passim*.
7. Greenberg, "Governing HEW," pp. 169–72.
8. Selznick, *Leadership, passim*.
9. Theodore Lowi, "American Business, Public Policy, Case Studies and Political Theory," *World Politics*, 16 (July 1963), pp. 677–715. Lowi is the inventor of the typology of distributive, regulatory, and redistributive domestic policies.
10. Erwin C. Hargrove, "The Search for Implementation Theory," in Richard J. Zeckhauser and Derek Leebaert, eds., *What Role for Government? Lessons from Policy Research* (Durham, N.C.: Duke Press Policy Studies, 1983), pp. 285–86.
11. Lowi, "American Business," *passim*.
12. Hargrove, "Search," pp. 286–89.
13. Lowi, "American Business," *passim*.
14. Hargrove, "Search," pp. 289–93.
15. I. M. Destler, *Presidents, Bureaucrats and Foreign Policy: The Politics of Organizational Reform* (Princeton, N.J.: Princeton University Press, 1972), pp. 156–67; John E. Harr, *The Professional Diplomat* (Princeton, N.J.: Princeton University Press, 1969), *passim*.
16. Chris Argyris, "Some Causes of Organizational Ineffectiveness Within the Department of State," Center for International Systems Research, Occasional Paper Number 2 (January 1967).

17. Samuel P. Huntington, *The Common Defense: Strategic Programs in National Politics* (New York: Columbia University Press, 1961), *passim*.
18. Enthoven and Smith, *passim*.
19. James Fallows, *National Defense* (New York: Random House, 1981), *passim*.
20. Adam Yarmolinski, *The Military Establishment: Its Impact on American Society* (New York: Harper & Row, 1971), p. 391.
21. Henry Kissinger, *White House Years* (Boston: Little, Brown, 1979), pp. 897–98.
22. *Ibid.*, p. 822.
23. *Ibid.*
24. Arthur M. Schlesinger, Jr., *The Coming of the New Deal* (Boston: Houghton Mifflin, 1959), pt. VIII.
25. Richard Polenberg, *Reorganizing Roosevelt's Government: The Controversy over Executive Reorganization, 1936–1939* (Cambridge: Harvard University Press, 1966).
26. William E. Pemberton, *Bureaucratic Politics, Executive Reorganization During the Truman Administration* (Columbia: University of Missouri Press, 1979), pp. 2–27.
27. *Ibid.*, pp. 29–30.
28. *Ibid.*, pp. 91–95.
29. *Ibid.*, pp. 116–18.
30. *Ibid.*, pp. 174–75.
31. *Ibid.*, pp. 175–77.
32. John E. Harr, "Organizational Change in U.S. Foreign Affairs: 1945–1975," in *Commission on the Organization of the Government for the Conduct of Foreign Policy*, vol. 6 (Washington: U.S. Government Printing Office, 1975), p. 15.
33. Anna Kasten Nelson, "National Security I: Inventing a Process (1945–1960)," in Hugh Heclo and Lester Salamon, eds., *The Illusion of Presidential Government* (Boulder, Col.: Westview Press, 1981), pp. 243–44.
34. Fred I. Greenstein, *The Hidden Hand Presidency, Eisenhower as Leader* (New York: Basic Books, 1982), ch. 4.
35. Bradley H. Patterson, Jr., *The President's Cabinet: Issues and Questions* (American Society for Public Administration, May 1976), pp. 110–11.
36. Nelson, "National Security," pp. 246–48.
37. Harvey C. Mansfield, "Reorganizing the Federal Executive Branch: The Limits of Institutionalization," *Law and Contemporary Problems*, Duke University, vol. XXXV, no. 3 (Summer 1970), p. 486.
38. Richard E. Neustadt, *Presidential Power, the Politics of Leadership from FDR to Carter* (New York: Wiley, 1980).
39. Myer Feldman, Oral History Interview, The John F. Kennedy Library, Boston, Mass., July 29, 1967, vol. VII, p. 512.
40. Louis W. Koenig, "Kennedy's Personal Management," in Earl Latham, ed., *J. F. Kennedy and Presidential Power* (Lexington, Mass.: D. C. Heath, 1972), pp. 6–7.
41. *Ibid.*, pp. 8–9.
42. Feldman, Oral History Interview, August 20, 1966, vol. IX, pp. 409, 423–24, 433–34, 474–75.
43. Destler, *Presidents, Bureaucrats and Foreign Policy*, pp. 102–4.
44. Joseph A. Califano, Jr., *A Presidential Nation* (New York: Norton, 1975), pp. 14–16.
45. *Ibid.*, pp. 31–32, 34.
46. *Ibid.*, pp. 25–26.
47. Emmette S. Redford and Marlan Blissett, *Organizing the Executive Branch, the Johnson Presidency* (Chicago: University of Chicago Press, 1981), chs. 2 and 3.
48. *Ibid.*, pp. 199, 200, 204.
49. *Ibid.*, p. 208.
50. *Ibid.*, p. 214.
51. John E. Harr, "Lessons to Be Learned," *Commission*, p. 26.
52. Redford and Blissett, *Organizing*, pp. 205–6.
53. Richard E. Nathan, *The Plot That Failed, Nixon and the Administrative Presidency*

(New York: Wiley, 1975), pp. 40–43.

54. *Ibid.*, p. 61.
55. *Ibid.*, pp. 63–69.
56. *Ibid.*, pp. 70–76.
57. Erwin C. Hargrove, interviews with Richard Cheney and James Conner in the White House, October 1974.
58. Destler, *Presidents, Bureaucrats and Foreign Policy*, pp. 138–39.
59. *Ibid.*, p. 140.
60. *Ibid.*, p. 141.
61. *Ibid.*, p. 142.
62. Henry Kissinger, *Years of Upheaval* (Boston: Little, Brown, 1982), p. 6.
63. Erwin C. Hargrove, interview with Carter White House domestic policy adviser, April 1983.
64. Jimmy Carter, *Why Not the Best?* (New York: Bantam, 1975).
65. Harold Seidman, *Politics, Position and Power, the Dynamics of Federal Organization* (New York: Oxford University Press, 1980), p. 129.
66. Hargrove interview with Carter White House domestic policy adviser, August 1983.
67. James L. Sundquist, "Jimmy Carter as Public Administrator: An Appraisal at Mid-Term," *Public Administration Review* (January–February 1979), p. 6.
68. Richard E. Nathan, *The Administrative Presidency* (New York: Wiley, 1983), pp. 58–59.
69. *Ibid.*, p. 61.
70. *Ibid.*, pp. 65–67.
71. *Ibid.*, p. 69.
72. *Ibid.*, p. 75.
73. *Ibid.*, p. 76.
74. *Ibid.*, pp. 76–80.

CHAPTER 9

Reform the Presidency?

The literature of contemporary political science contains three main models of presidential reform, all of them empirically grounded. Each of these models was developed out of admiration for a particular presidency and in reaction against other presidencies. Each calls for only one of the three main types of presidencies — preparation, achievement, and consolidation — and is, therefore, in our view incomplete.

Admirers of Franklin Roosevelt would have all presidents be presidents of achievement and find no place in their pantheon for an Eisenhower style of presidency. Those who react against the excesses of some of Roosevelt's successors or who do not think it possible for many presidents to be innovative reformers take the Eisenhower presidency of consolidation as their ideal. A third view is derived mainly from the institutional and political weakness of the Kennedy and Carter presidencies of preparation. It calls for constitutional reform to strengthen the office.

THE POWER-MAXIMIZING PRESIDENT

The most persuasive advocate of the "power-maximizing president" model is Richard Neustadt, whose book *Presidential Power* argues that the latent powers of the presidency can and should be activated by presidents who know how to acquire power in the office.[1] A president has rewards to offer other power holders, particularly his support for ideas and proposals, and is able to punish others by denying them favors and opportunities or, perhaps more importantly, by leading them to believe that he will do so if they do not cooperate. Bargaining with other power holders in a government of "separated institutions sharing powers" is the path to presidential effectiveness. The presidential end of the bargain is enhanced to the degree that other power holders perceive that the public and important organized groups support a president. The converse also is true. A president can enhance his influence by teaching the public in conjunction with events.

According to this theory, the essential requirement for presidential power is the sensitive use of presidential resources and actions to affect the interests and incentives of others in directions favorable to the president. The essence of the model is tactical leadership. There is no explicit thesis of "empowerment" through politics or the Constitution.

268

In Neustadt's analysis Franklin Roosevelt was the president to be emulated and Dwight Eisenhower the example to be avoided. Roosevelt was sensitive to his power stakes, according to Neustadt, and Eisenhower was not. The experience of Johnson and Nixon caused Neustadt to modify his thesis to the extent that power maximizing was seen as potentially harmful to presidents and the presidency if not joined to broader purposes and personal integrity. But his comparative evaluation of Roosevelt and Eisenhower stands.[2]

Neustadt would have all chief magistrates seek to be presidents of achievement. Yet one cannot envision a succession of presidents as skillful as Roosevelt. Nor would this be politically possible. Such forcefulness of personality on a continuing basis eventually would create so much opposition in other quarters that the institutions of government would be cast in a stalemate unforeseen by advocates of the power-maximizing presidency.

LEADERSHIP OF RESTRAINT

The central argument of the "restrained presidency" school is that presidents should expect to accomplish a limited number of goals during their tenure. The worst thing a would-be president can do is to inflate public expectations about the supposed omnicompetence of the presidential office in the effort to get elected.

Fred Greenstein offers Eisenhower as a model of what presidents should be. The exemplary feature of Eisenhower's leadership style was that he carefully conserved his political resources as chief of state and dealt with divisive questions by a "hidden hand," through private, and often secret, negotiating processes.[3] Greenstein argues that the Rooseveltian president who deliberately and publicly takes on the hardest, most divisive issues may be appropriate for crisis times of depression and war, but not otherwise.[4] In fact, as succeeding presidents have sought to lead in the Rooseveltian style, their popular support predictably has fallen over time. The remedy for presidents is to conserve their resources—to do less, but also to do it well.

Greenstein admits that the Eisenhower strategy is not well suited for carrying out major change.[5] But he adds that other strategies have not proven to be particularly effective in noncrisis times either. In a careful analysis of Eisenhower's legacy to future presidents, Greenstein concludes that the primary lessons are Eisenhower's chief-of-state stance and the coherent manner in which he organized the presidential office for decision and implementation.[6] These are recommendations for a continuing presidency of consolidation.

CONSTITUTIONAL REFORM

The "constitutional reform" approach is both very old and quite new. The objective is to strengthen the capacity of the presidency for leadership, not through the selection of strong, skillful leaders, but through changes in the rules of government so that members of Congress will have greater incentives to cooperate with presidents. Its most recent manifestation is a reaction against the weakness of the Ford and Carter administrations. Lloyd Cutler, a Washington lawyer who was counsel to President Carter, is a recent advocate of constitutional reform.[7] But it is a long-standing position within political science. A previous formulation was offered during the Kennedy presidency by James MacGregor Burns in *The Deadlock of Democracy*, who returned to it two decades later, after Carter.[8] Many other reformers—most notably during the Truman presidency—have aspired to graft characteristics of the British parliamentary system onto the American system so that president and Congress would act in concert, usually through the linking capacity of majority political parties.[9]

The means by which such unity and coherence are to be achieved have varied in different schemes over the years, but Cutler's suggestions are typical. He would join the presidential, vice-presidential, and congressional candidates of each party so that voters would have to vote for all or none. Members of Congress thus would come to office as part of a presidential team. The president would be authorized to dissolve Congress and call for new congressional elections once in his term as a device for breaking executive-legislative deadlocks. Presidents would be permitted one six-year term so that they would be able to learn the job, carry through on their policies, and not adulterate governing with an extended campaign for reelection in their fourth year.

It is not coincidental that Cutler's proposals are reactions against the weaknesses of the Carter presidency. Such ideas usually are most fashionable during periods of preparation, stalemate, or stasis, when presidents are struggling without success to produce majorities. But reforms of this kind would not strengthen such presidents because they seek to substitute rules for politics, and this cannot be done effectively. Presidents of preparation are seeking to build a consensus in the nation. If they are successful, their programs will be passed and the power of their successors may be enhanced. But new rules will not cause legislators to follow presidents. They could just as easily hamstring presidential leadership in the name of party unity. Presidencies of stalemate and stasis would not be made any more unified or coherent by rules. Indeed, conflict may increase as the safety valves provided by institutional separation are closed.

A HISTORICAL PERSPECTIVE

The main flaw of the power-maximizing, restrained leadership and constitutional reform models is that they are ahistorical. Each presents one formulation as sufficient for all time, thus failing to capture the range of historical possibilities. None of the models looks to culture and politics as sources of presidential empowerment. Perhaps this is because all reflect the contemporary conventional wisdom that recent history has greatly, and perhaps permanently, weakened the presidency.[10] Congress, it is said, is beyond the control not only of presidents but of its own leadership; parties have disintegrated as electoral machines, group coalitions, and agencies of government; the proliferation of organized special interests has made it increasingly difficult to construct majority coalitions of any kind; and the fragmentation of bureaucracy in response to interest-group politics, congressional individualism, and the politics of federalism undercuts any authority that presidents may have over the executive branch. If one believes that these conditions are likely to prevail for the indefinite future, then it is logical to derive remedies for strengthening the presidency not from politics, but from the manipulation of the presidential office itself, either through skillful leadership or changes in the constitutional rules.

According to the theory of cycles that is presented in this book, "weaknesses" in the presidency are temporary phenomena. They seemed obvious and eternal when Kennedy was president but not under Johnson, just as they applied more to the Carter period than to the Reagan years. Indeed, there were clear signs as early as 1981 that the Democratic coalition was seeking to develop new intellectual capital, formulate political appeals that would reach beyond the organized groups within its constituency, and pull the disparate elements of the party together. These are exactly the kinds of things that the cycle theory predicts will happen after a period of political and intellectual exhaustion. The Republicans began this process of renewal before their competitors, and the Reagan presidency was the result.

The central point, which is not incorporated in any of the three prescriptive models of the presidency, is that presidential leadership and national politics are inextricably intertwined. Institutional reforms that are intended to enhance presidential capacities are most effective when they emerge as adaptations to enhance presidential policy. Certainly, they cannot be substituted for policy purpose and political empowerment as a means to strengthen the presidency.

Thus, although presidential scholars often turn to organizational reform, both in political parties and in the organization of the presidency, as a device for rejuvenating governance, we would do better to seek fresh ideas about policy for emerging problems. That is why this book has not addressed a number of current proposals for enhancing the capacities of the institutional presidency. For example, a panel of the National Academy of Public Administration has recommended that the professional capability of the White House staff should be improved and that domestic-, economic-, and foreign-policy staff units should be integrated to improve communication and cross-fertilization.[11] This and other recommendations in the report may be excellent, but we foresee their implementation occurring only when a president who is trying to achieve new policy goals feels that he needs that sort of institutional help. Reform does not come in response to the designs of experts. The Brownlow committee gave President Roosevelt tools that he had discovered he needed from experience. The institutional innovations of the Truman years came in response to new presidential responsibilities in economic and foreign policy. The Great Society and the period of regulatory reform that followed are what strengthened presidential capacities for the analysis of domestic and economic policy and for management. New institutional innovations await new policy challenges.

CONCLUSION

We do not offer the theory of cycles and the propositions derived from it as a normative view of American politics. But anyone who would make normative judgments about politics, policy, and the presidency should take account of the reality described. Although it may be appropriate to criticize the system for lacking radical politics, for exhibiting fragmented and incoherent government, or for a host of other faults, such criticisms carry no implications for the presidency per se. But if the historical framework of American politics is accepted as the reality within which presidential politics and policy likely will continue to be played out, it is appropriate to ask if the presidency is capable of coping with the problems of the society at home and abroad.

The presidency, in our view, is responsive to the pressures of domestic politics and can deal with domestic problems as they emerge. In a complex society this takes time. It is incredible that it occurs at all, considering the difficulties that other, less socially complex industrial democracies have in building coalitions for effective government. In the process of developing policy responses to new problems, politics and knowledge proceed on similar, though not always connected, paths. Ideas are a resource in seeking political support, and politics is the only means for the implementation of ideas. There often is a lag with one element ahead of the other, but in the long run reinforcement takes place.

The foreign-affairs presidency is strong, and for the most part Americans have been prepared to give presidents the authority to conduct foreign policy. There is no guarantee of "wise" action in this respect. No political system can guarantee that some "correct" balance of realism and idealism in foreign policy will be achieved. Such a balance is a cultural phenomenon beyond the reaches of politics.

The conduct of the presidency does depend to a great extent upon the mind and character of the president. It is an elective kingship in that sense. Some would see this as undue dependence. But the overall record of the presidential selection process reveals that successive presidents have understood their times and have sensed what could and could not be accomplished. Not all presidents have been political geniuses, but no political system could produce a succession of geniuses. Nor would this necessarily be desirable.

The institutions of American government are manifestations of the society and culture in which they are rooted. Institutions are not machines to be designed and redesigned according to the blueprints of planners or reformers. The American presidency is a manifestation of our history, culture, and politics. In studying the presidency we study ourselves. This explains the sharply varying assessments of the state of the presidency one finds in different historical periods. We recently have lived in a period of uncertainty and confusion about the directions and purposes of the society. If the past is any guide, those confusions will give way to new and effective articulations of the character of the national community, and what was once derogation of the presidential office will turn to praise.

NOTES

1. Richard E. Neustadt, *Presidential Power, the Politics of Leadership from FDR to Carter* (New York: Wiley, 1980), *passim*.
2. Neustadt's growing awareness of the limitation of tactical leadership has caused him to emphasize considerations that we have called "strategic." See his essay "Presidential Leadership: The Clerk Against the Preacher," in James Sterling Young, ed., *Problems and Prospects of Presidential Leadership*, vol. I (Washington, D.C.: University Press of America, 1982), pp. 1–36, a publication of the Miller Center of Public Affairs at the University of Virginia.
3. Fred I. Greenstein, *The Hidden Hand Presidency, Eisenhower as Leader* (New York: Basic Books, 1982), *passim*.
4. *Ibid.*, p. 229.
5. *Ibid.*, p. 230.
6. *Ibid.*, ch. 6. This chapter contains an acute analysis of the lessons for leadership to be derived from Eisenhower's example.
7. Lloyd Cutler, "To Form a Government," *Foreign Affairs* (Fall 1980), pp. 126–43.
8. James MacGregor Burns, *Deadlock of Democracy: Four Party Politics in America* (Englewood Cliffs, N.J.: Prentice-Hall, 1963); *The Power to Lead: The Crisis of the American Presidency* (New York: Simon & Schuster, 1984).
9. *Toward a More Responsible Two-Party System*, Report of the Committee on Political Parties of the American Political Science Association, *American Political Science Review* (September 1950, supplement).
10. For systematic statements of this institutional weakness see the introduction and conclusion to Hugh Heclo and Lester M. Salamon, eds., *The Illusion of Presidential Government* (Boulder, Col.: Westview Press, 1981).
11. *A Presidency for the 1980s*, Report on Presidential Management by a Panel of the National Academy of Public Administration (Washington, D.C., 1980).

APPENDIX

The Presidency and Vice Presidency in the Constitution

ARTICLE I

Section 1

6. The House of Representatives shall chuse their speaker and other Officers; and shall have the sole Power of Impeachment.

Section 3

4. The Vice President of the United States shall be President of the Senate, but shall have no Vote, unless they be equally divided.

5. The Senate shall chuse their other Officers, and also a President pro tempore, in the Absence of the Vice President, or when he shall exercise the Office of the President of the United States.

6. The Senate shall have the sole Power to try all Impeachments. When sitting for that Purpose, they shall be on Oath or Affirmation. When the President of the United States is tried, the Chief Justice shall preside: And no Person shall be convicted without the Concurrence of two thirds of the Members present.

7. Judgment in Cases of Impeachment shall not extend further than to removal from Office, and disqualification to hold and enjoy any Office of honor, Trust or Profit under the United States: but the Party convicted shall nevertheless be liable and subject to Indictment, Trial, Judgment and Punishment, according to law.

Section 6

2. No Senator or Representative shall, during the Time for which he was elected, be appointed to any civil Office under the Authority of the United States, which shall have been created, or the Emoluments whereof shall have been encreased during such time; and no Person holding any Office under the United States, shall be a Member of either House during his Continuance in Office.

274

Section 7

2. Every Bill which shall have passed the House of Representatives and the Senate, shall, before it become a Law, be presented to the President of the United States. If he approve he shall sign it, but if not he shall return it, with his Objections to that House in which it shall have originated, who shall enter the Objections at large on their Journal, and proceed to reconsider it. If after such Reconsideration two thirds of that House shall agree to pass the Bill, it shall be sent, together with the Objections, to the other House, by which it shall likewise be reconsidered, and if approved by two thirds of that House, it shall become a Law. But in all such Cases the Votes of both the Houses shall be determined by Yeas and Nays, and the Names of the Persons voting for and against the Bill shall be entered on the Journal of each House respectively. If any Bill shall not be returned by the President within the ten Days (Sunday excepted) after it shall have been presented to him, the Same shall be a Law, in like Manner as if he had signed it, unless the Congress by their Adjournment prevent its Return, in which Case it shall not be a Law.

3. Every Order, Resolution, or Vote to which the Concurrence of the Senate and House of Representatives may be necessary (except on a question of Adjournment) shall be presented to the President of the United States; and before the Same shall take Effect, shall be approved by him, or being disapproved by him, shall be repassed by two thirds of Senate and House of Representatives, according to the Rules and Limitations prescribed in the Case of a Bill.

ARTICLE II

Section 1

1. The executive Power shall be vested in a President of the United States of America. He shall hold his Office during the Term of four Years, and, together with the Vice President, chosen for the same term, be elected, as follows.

2. Each State shall appoint, in such Manner as the Legislature thereof may direct, a Number of Electors, Equal to the whole Number of Senators and Representatives to which the State may be entitled in the Congress: but no Senator or Representative, or Person holding an Office of Trust or Profit under the United States, shall be appointed an Elector.

3. [The Electors shall meet in their respective States, and vote by Ballot for two Persons, of whom one at least shall not be an Inhabitant of the same State with themselves. And they shall make a List of all the Persons voted for, and the Number of Votes for each; which List they shall sign and certify, and transmit sealed to the Seat of the Government of the United States, directed to the President of the Senate. The President of the Senate shall, in the Presence of the Senate and House of Representatives, open all the Certificates, and the Votes shall then be counted. The Person having the greatest Number of Votes shall be the President, if such Number be a Majority of the whole Number of Electors

appointed; and if there be more than one who have such Majority, and have an equal Number of Votes, then the House of Representatives shall immediately chuse by Ballot one of them for President: and if no Person have a Majority, then from the five highest on the List the said House shall in like Manner chuse the President. But in chusing the President, the Votes shall be taken by States, the Representation from each State having one Vote; A quorum for this purpose shall consist of a Member or Members from two thirds of the States, and a Majority of all the States shall be necessary to a Choice. In every Case, after the Choice of the President, the Person having the greatest Number of Votes of the Electors shall be the Vice President. But if there should remain two or more who have equal Votes, the Senate shall chuse from them by Ballot the Vice President.][1]

4. The congress may determine the Time of chusing the Electors and the Day on which they shall give their Votes; which Day shall be the same throughout the United States.

5. No person except a natural born Citizen, or a Citizen of the United States, at the time of the Adoption of this Constitution, shall be eligible to the Office of President; neither shall any Person be eligible to that Office who shall not have attained the Age of thirty five Years, and been fourteen Years a Resident within the United States.

6. [In Case of the Removal of the President from Office, or of his Death, Resignation, or Inability to discharge the Powers and Duties of the said Office, the Same shall devolve on the Vice President, and the Congress may by Law provide for the Case of Removal, Death, Resignation, or Inability, both of the President and Vice President, declaring what Officer shall then act as President, and such Officer shall act accordingly, until the Disability be removed, or a President shall be elected.][2]

7. The President shall, at stated Times, receive for his Services a Compensation, which shall neither be encreased nor diminished during the Period for which he shall have been elected, and he shall not receive within that Period any other Emolument from the United States, or any of them.

8. Before he enter on the Execution of his Office, he shall take the following Oath or Affirmation: —"I do solemnly swear (or affirm) that I will faithfully execute the Office of President of the United States, and will to the best of my Ability, preserve, protect and defend the Constitution of the United States."

Section 2

1. The President shall be Commander in Chief of the Army and Navy of the United States, and of the Militia of the several States, when called into the actual Service of the United States; he may require the Opinion, in writing, of the principal Officer in each of the executive Departments, upon any Subject relating to the Duties of their respective Offices, and he shall have power to grant Reprieves and Pardons for Offences against the United States, except in Cases of Impeachment.

[1] Superseded by the Twelfth Amendment.
[2] Modified by the Twentieth and Twenty-fifth Amendments.

2. He shall have Power, by and with the Advice and Consent of the Senate, to make Treaties, provided two thirds of the Senators present concur; and he shall nominate, and by and with the Advice and Consent of the Senate, shall appoint Ambassadors, other public Ministers and Consuls, Judges of the supreme Court, and all other Officers of the United States, whose Appointments are not herein otherwise provided for, and which shall be established by Law; but the Congress may by Law vest the Appointment of such inferior Officers, as they think proper, in the President alone, in the Courts of Law, or in the Heads of Departments.

3. The President shall have Power to fill up all Vacancies that may happen during the Recess of the Senate, by granting Commissions which shall expire at the End of their next Session.

Section 3

1. He shall from time to time give to the Congress Information of the State of the Union, and recommend to their Consideration such Measures as he shall judge necessary and expedient; he may, on extraordinary Occasions, convene both Houses, or either of them, and in Case of Disagreement between them, with Respect to the Time of Adjournment, he may adjourn them to such Time as he shall think proper; he shall take Care that the Laws be faithfully executed, and shall Commission all the Officers of the United States.

Section 4

1. The President, Vice President and all civil Officers of the United States, shall be removed from Office on Impeachment for, and Conviction of, Treason, Bribery, or other High Crimes and Misdemeanors.

AMENDMENT 12 (1804)

The Electors shall meet in their respective states and vote by ballot for President and Vice President, one of whom, at least, shall not be an inhabitant of the same state with themselves; they shall name in their ballots the person voted for as President, and in distinct ballots the person voted for as Vice President, and they shall make distinct lists of all persons voted for as President, and of all persons voted for as Vice President, and of the number of votes for each, which lists they shall sign and certify, and transmit sealed to the seat of the government of the United States, directed to the President of the Senate; — The President of the Senate shall, in the presence of the Senate and House of Representatives, open all the certificates and the votes shall then be counted; — The person having the greatest number of votes for President, shall be the President, if such number be a majority of the whole number of Electors appointed; and if no person have such majority, then from the persons having the highest numbers not exceeding three on the list of those voted for as President, the House of Representatives shall choose immediately, by ballot, the President. But in choosing the President, the votes shall be taken by states, the representation from each state having one vote; a quorum for this purpose shall consist of a member or members from two-thirds of the states, and a majority of all the states shall be necessary to a choice. [And if the House of Representatives shall not choose a President whenever the right of the choice shall devolve upon them, before the fourth day of March next following, then the Vice President shall act as President, as in the case of the death or other constitutional disability of the President].[3] The person having the greatest number of votes as Vice President, shall be the Vice President, if such number be a majority of the whole number of Electors appointed, and if no person have a majority, then from the two highest numbers on the list, the Senate shall choose the Vice President; a quorum for the purpose shall consist of two-thirds of the whole number of Senators, and a majority of the whole number shall be necessary to a choice. But no person constitutionally ineligible to the office of President shall be eligible to that of Vice President of the United States.

AMENDMENT 20 (1933)

Section 1

The terms of the President and Vice President shall end at noon on the 20th day of January, and the terms of Senators and Representatives at noon on the 3d day of January, of the years in which such terms would have ended if this article had not been ratified; and the terms of their successors shall then begin.

Section 3

If, at the time fixed for the beginning of the term of the President, the President elect shall have died, the Vice President elect shall become President. If a President shall not have been chosen before the time fixed for the beginning of his term, or if the President elect shall have failed to qualify, then the Vice President elect shall act as President until a President shall have qualified; and the Congress may by law provide for the case wherein neither a President elect nor a Vice President elect shall have qualified, declaring who shall then act as President, or the manner in which one who is to act shall be selected, and such person shall act accordingly until a President or Vice President shall have qualified.

Section 4

The Congress may by law provide for the case of death of any of the persons from whom the House of Representatives may choose a President

[3] Superseded by the Twentieth Amendment.

whenever the right of choice shall have devolved upon them, and for the case of the death of any of the persons from whom the Senate may choose a Vice President whenever the right of choice shall have devolved upon them.

AMENDMENT 22 (1951)

Section 1

No person shall be elected to the office of the President more than twice, and no person who has held the office of President, or acted as President for more than two years of a term to which some other person was elected President shall be elected to the office of the President more than once. But this Article shall not apply to any person holding the office of President when this Article was proposed by the Congress, and shall not prevent any person who may be holding the office of President, or acting as President, during the term within which this Article becomes operative from holding office of President, or acting as President, during the remainder of such term.

AMENDMENT 25 (1967)

Section 1

In case of the removal of the President from office or of his death or resignation, the Vice President shall become President.

Section 2

Whenever there is a vacancy in the office of the Vice President, the President shall nominate a Vice President who shall take office upon confirmation by a majority vote of both Houses of Congress.

Section 3

Whenever the President transmits to the President pro tempore of the Senate and the Speaker of the House of Representatives his written declaration that he is unable to discharge the powers and duties of his office, and until he transmits to them a written declaration to the contrary, such powers and duties shall be discharged by the Vice President as Acting President.

Section 4

Whenever the Vice President and a majority of either the principal officers of the executive departments or of such other body as Congress may by law provide, transmit to the President pro tempore of the Senate and the Speaker of the House of Representatives their written declaration that the President is unable to discharge the powers and duties of his office, the Vice President shall immediately assume the powers and duties of the office as Acting President.

Thereafter, when the President transmits to the President pro tempore of the Senate and the Speaker of the House of Representatives his written declaration that no inability exists, he shall resume the powers and duties of his office unless the Vice President and a majority of either the principal officers of the executive department or of such other body as Congress may by law provide, transmit within four days to the President pro tempore of the Senate and the Speaker of the House of Representatives their written declaration that the President is unable to discharge the powers and duties of his office. Thereupon Congress shall decide the issue, assembling within forty-eight hours for that purpose if not in session. If the Congress, within twenty-one days after receipt of the latter written declaration, or, if Congress is not in session, within twenty-one days after Congress is required to assemble, determines by two-thirds vote of both Houses that the President is unable to discharge the powers and duties of his office, the Vice President shall continue to discharge the same as Acting President; otherwise, the President shall resume the powers and duties of his office.

Index

ABOUT THE AUTHORS

ERWIN C. HARGROVE, who earned his B.A., M.A., and Ph.D. at Yale University, teaches political science at Vanderbilt University and is director of the Vanderbilt Institute for Public Policy Studies. He has contributed articles to numerous professional journals, including the *Midwest Journal of Political Science*, *Public Administration Review*, and *Comparative Politics*, and is the author of *Presidential Leadership, Personality, and Political Style* (1966), *Professional Roles in Society and Government: The English Case* (1972), *The Power of the Modern Presidency* (1974), *The Missing Link: The Study of the Implementation of Social Policy* (1975), and *TVA: Fifty Years of Grassroots Bureaucracy* (1984).

MICHAEL NELSON, who earned his B.A. at the College of William and Mary and his M.A. and Ph.D. at the Johns Hopkins University, teaches political science at Vanderbilt University. A former editor for *The Washington Monthly*, he also has written articles for the *Journal of Politics*, *The Public Interest*, the *Virginia Quarterly Review*, the *Harvard Business Review*, *Newsweek*, *The Nation*, *Saturday Review*, and *Congress and the Presidency*, among others. He has won awards for his essays on classical music and baseball, including the ASCAP-Deems Taylor Award for 1979, and has edited and coauthored two books: *The Culture of Bureaucracy* (1979) and *The Presidency and the Political System* (1984).

A NOTE ON THE TYPE

The text of this book was set on the Editwriter 7500 in a typeface called California. It belongs to the family of printing types called "modern face" by printers — a term used to mark the change in style of type letters that occurred about 1800. California borders on the general design of Scotch Modern but is more freely drawn.

Printed and bound by R. R. Donnelley & Sons Company, Harrisonburg, Virginia.